FANNY HILL in BOMBAY

FANNY HILL
in BOMBAY

The Making & Unmaking of John Cleland

Hal Gladfelder

The Johns Hopkins University Press
Baltimore

© 2012 The Johns Hopkins University Press
All rights reserved. Published 2012
Printed in the United States of America on acid-free paper
2 4 6 8 9 7 5 3 1

The Johns Hopkins University Press
2715 North Charles Street
Baltimore, Maryland 21218-4363
www.press.jhu.edu

Library of Congress Cataloging-in-Publication Data
Gladfelder, Hal.
Fanny Hill in Bombay : the making and unmaking of John Cleland / Hal Gladfelder.
p.   cm.
Includes bibliographical references and index.
ISBN-13: 978-1-4214-0490-5 (hdbk. : acid-free paper)
ISBN-10: 1-4214-0490-7 (hdbk. : acid-free paper)
1. Cleland, John, 1709–1789. I. Title.
PR3348.C65Z66 2012
828'.609—dc23
[B]   2011029770

A catalog record for this book is available from the British Library.

*Special discounts are available for bulk purchases of this book. For more information,
please contact Special Sales at 410-516-6936 or specialsales@press.jhu.edu.*

The Johns Hopkins University Press uses environmentally friendly
book materials, including recycled text paper that is composed of at least
30 percent post-consumer waste, whenever possible.

CONTENTS

ACKNOWLEDGMENTS

For help in locating archival and rare published materials, I would like to thank the librarians, archivists, and readers' assistants at the British Library (especially staff working with the India Office Collection in the Asian and African Studies reading room); the British National Archives, Kew; the Bodleian Library, Oxford; the Lambeth Palace Library, London; the John Rylands Library, Deansgate; and the John Rylands University Library at the University of Manchester. The staff and librarians at the Rush Rhees Library of the University of Rochester were also of great help in this project's early days. Some of my preliminary research was carried out during a period of sabbatical leave from the University of Rochester, and the manuscript was drafted and largely completed during a yearlong research leave jointly supported by the University of Manchester and an Arts and Humanities Research Council fellowship.

A portion of chapter 3 appeared in different form as "In Search of Lost Texts: Thomas Cannon's *Ancient and Modern Pederasty Investigated and Exemplify'd*," *Eighteenth-Century Life* 31:1 (2006): 22–43. I thank Duke University Press for permission to include a revised version here, and the journal's editor, Cedric D. Reverand II, for his exacting and astute close reading. Other portions of chapters 3 and 4 appeared in different form under the title "Plague Spots" in *Social Histories of Disability and Deformity*, edited by David M. Turner and Kevin Stagg (New York: Routledge, 2006), 56–78. Still other portions of chapter 4 formed part of the introduction to my edition of Cleland's *Memoirs of a Coxcomb* (Peterborough: Broadview, 2005); I thank Julia Gaunce, Barbara Conolly, Leonard Conolly, and Colleen Franklin for their help in bringing that project to completion. Thanks also to Matthew McAdam, my acquiring editor at the Johns Hopkins University Press, and to George Roupe for his meticulous copy editing.

Peter Sabor and William H. Epstein were kind enough to read drafts of the first three chapters, and I am grateful both for their comments and for their pioneering work on Cleland, which has inspired my own. Thomas Keymer read the entire manuscript and made invaluable suggestions for improving it; the faults that remain, of course, are my own. For giving me the opportunity to present this work to diverse audiences, I want to thank Monika Fludernik, Greta Olsen, and Jan Albers (University of Freiburg); Tim Hitchcock (Institute for Historical Research, London); and Shohini Chaudhuri (University of Essex). For advice, solidarity, conversation, and other forms of moral or intellectual support, my thanks to Hans Turley (much missed), Lúcia Sá, George Haggerty, John Richetti, Noelle Gallagher, Brian Ward, Jill Campbell, Kathryn King, Bette London, Tom DiPiero, Ruth Mack, Rachel Ablow, Laura Rosenthal, Corrinne Harol, Morris and Georgia Eaves, Victoria Myers, Max Novak, and Ruth Yeazell. Although I can't name them all here, colleagues at the University of Rochester and, now, the University of Manchester have provided warm and intellectually vibrant environments to work in.

Through the whole writing process, Laura Doan, Marlene Mussell, and Janet Wolff cheered me on and celebrated every tiny milestone. Far away though they are, I want to send this out to my family: Anne Morgan; Glenn and Dale Gladfelder; and Kari and Tobbe Johansson. Closer to home, Oliver, Emilia, and Sophie played a vital creative (and sometimes destructive) part in the writing: ideal collaborators. The most vital part, though, was played by Jeff Geiger, writing away in the next room while I wrote this, and who came with me to walk around Cleland's old haunts.

1710   Born, probably late summer, Kingston-upon-Thames, near London; first child of William Cleland, former army officer and civil servant, and Lucy DuPass Cleland; christened 24 September.

1721   Enrolls as student at Westminster School, January; withdraws, for reasons unknown, in 1723.

1728   Arrives in Bombay as a soldier in the service of the British East India Company and lives there until 1740, advancing to the position of junior merchant and becoming secretary to the governing Bombay Council.

1730   According to his own later statements, begins writing *Memoirs of a Woman of Pleasure* in collaboration with Charles Carmichael (born ca. 1712).

1733   Death of Charles Carmichael, 24 July.

1734   Becomes embroiled in two legal cases: one initiated by William Boag, seaman, who charges JC with abducting Boag's female servant, Marthalina (decided in favor of JC in September 1735); the second initiated by Henry Lowther and Robert Cowan, members of the Bombay Council, who lodge complaints against JC for injurious language (December 1734; case sent to the Company Directors in London for adjudication; decided in favor of JC, 1736).

1736   Arrival in Bombay of sister, Charlotte Lucy (or Louisa) Cleland, listed as a resident from 25 October. The following year, on 24 June, she marries George Sadleir, and on 3 October 1739 their son John is born; by 4 December 1739 he had died of "flux." Charlotte would continue to live in Bombay until September 1740 and from October 1743 until her death (in Surat) in October 1747.

1738   Appointed secretary for Bombay Public Consultations in January, having been appointed secretary for Portuguese affairs the previous year; promoted to junior merchant in July.

1740   Petitions Bombay Council for permission to return to London, probably because of his father's poor health; states his intention to return at the earliest opportunity. Sails from Bombay in September, probably accompanied by his sister.

1741   Reports his arrival in London to company directors on 26 August; death of William Cleland, 21 September. Introduced to Sebastião José Carvalho e Melo (later Marquis de Pombal) by WC in this period.

1742   Writes a "*mémoire*" offering his services to the king of Portugal for the creation of a Portuguese East India company (included in letter to Cardinal da Mota from Carvalho e Melo, dated 19 February).

1743   Visits Lisbon in May to discuss plans for East India company with Cardinal da Mota and others; meets Carvalho e Melo there on latter's return from London but soon after leaves Lisbon, when plans for company are put on hold.

1748   Arrested for a debt of £800 allegedly owed to his former friend and probable literary collaborator Thomas Cannon and confined to the Fleet Prison, 23 February; remains in prison until March 1749. First volume of *Memoirs of a Woman of Pleasure* published in November.

1749   Second volume of *Memoirs of a Woman of Pleasure* published on February 14; the week before, Thomas Cannon had sworn an affidavit against JC for harassment, JC having written a note in which he accused Cannon of sodomy and attempted murder. In April, Cannon's *Ancient and Modern Pederasty Investigated and Exemplify'd* advertised. In May, JC begins writing review articles for the *Monthly Review*, as he would continue to do off and on through 1774. On November 7, publishes *The Case of the Unfortunate Bosavern Penlez*, a pamphlet critical of the prosecution and execution of an accused rioter. On November 8, arrested for obscenity, along with the printer and publisher of the *Woman of Pleasure*. All are examined by the secretary of state but apparently never prosecuted. While under arrest, Cleland denounces Cannon to the secretary of state for publishing a work "in defence of sodomy"; legal action would be taken against Cannon the following year.

1750   Cleland's expurgated and restructured abridgement of the *Woman of Pleasure*, now titled *Memoirs of Fanny Hill*, published in March; JC arrested again, along with the printer and publisher, and again examined, but apparently never prosecuted. Publishes *The Œconomy of a Winter's Day*, a parody of Robert Dodsley's *The Œconomy of Human Life*.

1751   *An Historical and Physical Dissertation on the Case of Catherine Vizzani*, a medical treatise on a lesbian cross-dresser and adventurer, translated from the Italian and with a commentary by Cleland, published in March; *Memoirs of a Coxcomb* published in September.

1752   Cleland's translation of Charles Pinot-Duclos's fictional *Memoirs Illustrating the Manners of the Present Age* published in May.

1753   Publishes *The Dictionary of Love*, translated and adapted from J. F. Dreux du Radier's *Dictionnaire d'amour*.

1755   *Titus Vespasian: A Tragedy*, based on Metastasio's *La Clemenza di Tito* (which would later provide the libretto for Mozart's opera), and *The Ladies Subscription: A Dramatic Performance*, a short satirical piece, published together; neither was ever produced on stage.

1757   Begins to write political commentaries in the form of letters to the *Public Advertiser*, as he would continue to do through 1787. John Henry Grose's *Voyage to the East Indies* published, likely ghost-authored by JC.

1758   *Tombo-Chiqui; or, The American Savage*, a three-act comedy adapted from the French *Arlequin Sauvage*, published; like JC's other plays, it was never produced. Death of JC's aunt, Lady Allen, in March. On this occasion, JC sends letter of condolence and recrimination to his mother, his last known communication with her.

1759   *The Times! An Epistle to Flavian*, published in September.

1760   Second *Epistle to Flavian* (like the first, a satirical commentary on contemporary political themes) published in April; *The Romance of a Day*, a comic-sentimental novella, published in September.

1761   Publishes *The Institutes of Health*, a medical-dietary treatise.

1762   Publishes *The Romance of a Night*, a second comic-sentimental novella.

1763   Death of Cleland's mother, Lucy DuPass Cleland, in May.

1764   Publishes *The Surprises of Love*, a collection of four novellas, including *The Romance of a Day* and *The Romance of a Night*, and adding to these the previously unpublished *Romance of a Morning* and *Romance of an Evening*.

1765   Publishes his second medical treatise, *Phisiological Reveries*.

1766   First of three works on etymology and the origins of language, *The Way to Things by Words, and to Words by Things*, published.

1767   Following the success of the first three volumes of letters written by Lady Mary Wortley Montagu and published posthumously in 1763, *An Additional Volume to the Letters of the Right Honourable Lady M——y W——y M——e* published, containing five spurious letters often (but unverifiably) attributed to Cleland—who was often accused of involvement in such literary forgeries.

1768   Publishes *The Woman of Honor*, a three-volume novel, and apparently his last work of fiction, and a second linguistic study, *Specimen of an Etimological Vocabulary*.

1769   Publishes *Additional Articles to the Specimen of an Etimological Vocabulary*, the last of his writings on language.

1778   Visited at home (in the Savoy) by James Boswell, who had recorded earlier meetings with him in 1769 and 1772 (describing him as "a fine sly malcontent").

1779   During another visit from Boswell, JC tells him about the origins of *Memoirs of a Woman of Pleasure*.

1781   Visited at home in the Savoy by Josiah Beckwith, who later records rumors of Cleland being a "sodomite" and political renegade.

1782   Moves to Petty France, near St. James's Park, where he lives till his death.

1787   Last known letter on political topics published in the *Public Advertiser*, 21 July.

1789   Dies at his house in Petty France, 23 January.

FANNY HILL in BOMBAY

"Old Cleland"

On a Sunday afternoon in 1778, James Boswell paid a visit to John Cleland, although he had not really meant to. "The day," he writes—it was late April—"was charming."[1] After calling on Sir Joshua Reynolds, he had planned to go on an outing with a friend, but "was too late"; he then tried to call on Dr. Johnson, only to find him "not at home." So he had another thought:

> Called on old Cleland. Found him in an old house in the Savoy, just by the waterside. A coarse, ugly old woman for his servant. His room, filled with books in confusion and dust, was like Dupont's and old Lady Eglinton's, at least old ideas were suggested to me as if I were in a castle. He was drinking tea and eating biscuits. I joined him. He had a rough cap like Rousseau, and his eyes were black and piercing . . . He had resolutely persisted. There was something *genteel* in his manner amidst this oddity.

Boswell's sketch of Cleland in an old house by the river, amid "confusion and dust," served by a "coarse, ugly old woman," juxtaposes the cozy and the weird, the mundane and the fantastic, in a curious tableau. "Curious," in fact, was the word Boswell used to describe Cleland when he met him nine years earlier: "Cleland, curious figure."[2] Now visiting him at home, Boswell draws Cleland as a "figure" out of time, out of place in the modern world. His repetition of the word "old," which he uses five times in four sentences, though at first it seems just to refer to Cleland's age, comes to locate him in an archaic, fantastic other world, like the setting of a fairy tale: "old ideas were suggested to me as if I were in a castle." Even the ordinary domestic detail—"he was drinking tea and eating biscuits"—contributes to the overall "oddity" of the scene, in which "old Lady Eglinton's" moldering Scottish castle has been transported to the busy Savoy, complete with a fairy-tale crone whom Boswell initially described in his diary as "a horrible old woman."[3]

At the center of this scene sits Cleland himself, a visually striking figure with a "rough cap" like that worn by Jean-Jacques Rousseau in the portrait Allan Ramsay painted in 1766 and "black and piercing" eyes.[4] This is the only surviving glimpse of Cleland's physical appearance, and it seems to fit with Boswell's otherwise unexplained assertion that "he had resolutely persisted": there is a kind of fierceness in this old man drinking tea and eating biscuits, a resolve that has enabled him to persist as if beyond his allotted time. Even the "something *genteel* in his manner" conveys a sense of anachronism. The "oddity" Boswell is struck by is that of a figure at odds with the ways of the late eighteenth-century London world, despite having lived almost his whole life there.

By the time Boswell knew him, John Cleland had largely brought his authorial career to a close, though he continued to haunt the newspapers in the persona of "A Briton," writing letters on political themes to the *Public Advertiser* and perhaps other papers until nearly the time of his death in 1789. But while Boswell knew something of Cleland's political writing and owned at least two of his later fictional works—*Memoirs of a Coxcomb* and *The Surprises of Love*—in his accounts of a handful of meetings with Cleland over the years, it is Cleland's first book that he keeps circling back to. Published under duress in 1748–1749, when Cleland was in prison for debt, his *Memoirs of a Woman of Pleasure*, or *Fanny Hill*—"that most licentious and inflaming book," as Boswell called it— was the most scandalous literary debut of that or any period.[5] In its way it was an incredible success; but its notoriety brought Cleland so many legal troubles and so much moral opprobrium that he soon came to dismiss it as "a Book I disdain to defend, and wish, from my Soul, buried and forgot."[6] Yet Boswell, among many other readers more or less clandestine, refused to forget it: he even got Cleland to tell him how he worked up the story in cahoots with a friend when they both were young and living in the British East India Company settlement in Bombay.

However ardently Cleland may have wished it, Fanny Hill's *Memoirs* have never been "forgot"; indeed, his own name has always been overshadowed by that of his heroine. For all his efforts to disown it or diffuse its impact, his first novel *branded* him as an author, then as now. Where would he be if it had been "buried and forgot"? In an obituary published in the *Gentleman's Magazine* the month after Cleland's death, the literary chronicler John Nichols wrote that the book "brought a stigma on his name, which time has not obliterated, and which will be consigned to his memory whilst its poisonous contents are in circulation."[7] But of course the stigma it brought on his name is the source and sign of his literary immortality, "which time has not obliterated." If Fanny's *Memoirs* were "buried and forgot," the stigma would disappear, but so, Cleland must have known, or feared, would his name itself. Nichols did not need to give the book's title in his obituary, for it was "too infamous to be particularised," and his refusal to name it just confirms its fame, while all the other books Cleland wrote in an authorial career of forty years were, by the time of his death, becoming lost in "confusion and dust." Why then this study, in which I look as closely at the whole range of Cleland's writing—not just published texts but also letters, private notes, and newly discovered transcripts of his testimony in legal trials—as others have at the work and writing lives of such undeniably major, well-remembered figures as Hume, Johnson or Pope?[8]

The answer, perhaps necessarily, is double sided. On one side, I try over the course of this book to show that the whole corpus of Cleland's work rewards close attention—that even the forgotten texts are striking, audacious, aesthetically and intellectually daring and complex (but also idiosyncratic, frustrating, bizarre). On the other, it is precisely his marginality and oddness, the unsuccess of his struggle for authorial renown and respectable immortality, that makes him worth studying—not just because the very qualities that have barred his work from the literary canon may be those we find most interesting today, but because his history of failure emphasizes the historicity of authorship itself. Cleland's writing was enabled and constrained by specific historical conditions, some common to all authors of the period (new print technologies, copyright law, changes in readership and literary fashion), others unique to him (financial pressures, family troubles, his own "history" of travel, work, and reading). But beyond that, his combative relationship to the literary market and to the times in general, and his permanent state of alienation, make him exemplary of the modern author as self-exiled outsider.

Boswell's "old Cleland" is an almost allegorical figure of failure, a resolute survivor whose literary career was nevertheless undermined by the scandalous success of his own creation, and who was disappearing, even as Boswell visited him, into a kind of oblivion. In that respect, he could be seen as representative of the legions of failed literary aspirants in a period that Samuel Johnson sardonically labeled "the Age of Authors": dunces, hacks, distressed poets, and neglected visionaries; the marginalized and misunderstood; the outsiders; the maligned.[9] All of these are implicated, Johnson writes, in an "epidemical conspiracy for the destruction of paper" (458); all are contributing to "the depravation of taste and the corruption of language" (461). All, perhaps needless to say, will be forgotten, if indeed they were ever known.

It is true that Cleland made his way through the commercial and ideological battlegrounds of the eighteenth-century literary market with only fitful success: his best-selling work made him a pariah, and some of his most cherished projects, as I discuss in the later chapters of this book, went unfinished, unperformed, or unread. But if his travails were those of everyone who shared his "low abject condition, that of a writer for bread," Cleland is also a singular figure whose body of work is compelling, extravagant, perverse.[10] From the start the pornographic excess of his first novel rubbed off on the persona of its author. While the equation of authors with whores was a commonplace of the period (as the use of the word "hack" for both suggests), in Cleland's case this equation was more pointed, as when, in Archibald Campbell's satire *The Sale of Authors* (1767), a group of young male "Bucks and Bloods" in a London bawdy house shift their gaze from the women at work there to Cleland, who writes down their lives. "Mr. Cl——d," the young bucks swoon, "has a most luscious pen, he possesses infinite *Powers*, he describes the thing so feelingly: in short, we must have him and will give you any money for him."[11] It is as if Cleland, by writing about whores, becomes a whore himself, the reader's illicit object of desire.

Roland Barthes, having in his most celebrated essay proclaimed "the death of the author," later admits that "in the text, in a way, I *desire* the author: I need his figure . . . as he needs mine."[12] This book grows out of a similar desire (similar insofar as I can untangle Barthes's). That is, not to put Cleland as capital-A transcendental Author-God or Author-King back on his throne, or, as Barthes put it in "The Death of the Author," to "impose a limit on [the] text, to furnish it with a final signified, to close the writing" (147), but rather the obverse: to reopen the writing in all its messiness of being written. Such recent theorists of "the author" as Seán Burke and Andrew Bennett have drawn attention to the playfully (or mournfully) conflicted character of Barthes's relationship to the author whose death he announced but whose textual presence he continued, as a reader, to desire, even to need.[13] The desire Barthes discloses in *The Pleasure of the Text* is akin to that of the "Bucks and Bloods" in *The Sale of Authors*, who want Cleland not just as a writer of "infinite *Powers*" whom they wish to claim for their own, but also, metonymically, as a lover or whore, whose "luscious pen . . . describes *the thing* so feelingly." What they desire is not a disembodied text but the very body of its author, and this is also, impossibly, the object of biographical desire.

Why do we care about authors' lives? Biographical desire is driven partly by curiosity and partly by identification, although as Andrew Bennet and Nicholas Royle point out, "the author" with whom the reader identifies is a fiction, a phantom. "Never fully present or fully absent, a figure of fantasy and elusiveness," they write, "the author only ever haunts."[14] All the more so in the case of a writer like Cleland, whose material remains are a modest corpus of published texts and a smattering of manuscript traces—"haphazard fragments," as his first biographer, William H. Epstein, put it, "scattered remnants."[15] The only "life" such an author can have is as an anthology of texts that have outlived him. Cleland in fact is far more a phantom than his fictional persona Fanny Hill. He has reached that state of attenuation implicit in Barthes's definition of writing as "the destruction of every voice, of every point of origin . . . that neutral, composite, oblique space where our subject slips away, the negative where all identity is lost, starting with the very identity of the body writing" ("Death," 142). In writing this book I was haunted by that image of the text as a "space where our subject slips away . . . where all identity is lost," for it calls into question the value of looking for the author even as it offers, by negation, a model for doing so. I wanted to follow a line of thought Barthes's words opened up: that Cleland, in writing, and later writing about, the *Memoirs of a Woman of Pleasure*, was plotting multiple points of origin, and that writing leads not to the loss but to an assaying and multiplication of identity. The authorial subject we retrace when as readers and biographers we move back through the skein of archival and published texts linked to the author's name is far from a fixed point or final signified; biography should if anything make literary texts *less* stable.[16]

My work on this book was impelled by biographical desire, but it is not a biography in the usual sense of the word. I have not tried to replace Epstein's *John Cleland: Images of a Life*, on which I have very often relied, but have tried to construct a history or case study of the writer writing. But why Cleland? I suggested above that he could be seen as representative of the conditions of authorship in the latter half of the eighteenth century, insofar as his authorial career was a continual struggle to stay afloat financially, to stay out of prison (for crimes of writing and for debt), and, more idealistically, to teach readers "to pursue good, and to avoid evil, to refine their morals, and to detest vice." Cleland's relationship with his audience, however, was often hostile, at least on his part, and in the same essay where he declared his aim to teach readers "to pursue good," he blamed the "declension of wit and taste" of his own day on "the public," absolving "the authors who have been forced to consult, and con-form to, its vitiated palate."[17] While literary success required Cleland to please the paying public, he was more prone to scourge it. In doing so, he set himself, like Johnson, against "the depravation of taste and the corruption of language" endemic to "the Age of Authors." Yet his fascination, over the course of his writ-ing career, with sexual "deviance" and excess, and with unstable, fluid, or dissi-dent gender identities, marked him as a renegade even as he pursued the most conventional sorts of cultural authority and respectability. Despite his patrician origins and his seeming political conservatism, the audacity of his writings on sexuality and desire, and his "sarcastical," even nihilistic treatment of the monarchy and of whichever political party happened to be in power, led another author who visited Cleland late in life to remark, "It is no Wonder, in this Age, that he lost his Place or Pension . . . or that he should pass under the Censure of being a Sodomite, as he now does."[18] The coding of Cleland's authorial persona as "sodomitical," in any of the different senses that word could assume in the eighteenth century, is a measure of his defiance and estrangement, the qualities that both made and unmade him as an author.

The one overtly sodomitical passage in Cleland's work, late in Fanny Hill's *Memoirs,* was suppressed after the book's first edition and only restored to the text in Peter Sabor's and Peter Wagner's invaluable Oxford and Penguin edi-tions of 1985. In the intervening years, whenever (rarely) it was mentioned, it was usually attributed to the curiously named Samuel Drybutter, a shop-keeper who was perhaps one of Cleland's friends, and who was later killed by a mob as a sodomite; Cleland's authorship was only put beyond doubt by David Foxon in 1965.[19] But even excised, the passage lingered like a kind of phan-tom limb, shadowing Cleland's authorial reputation. So if Cleland is exemplary of the problems and opportunities would-be authors had to negotiate in the period—from censorship and political pressures to shifts in cultural vogues and audiences' tastes—his willful "perversity" often set him against prevailing commercial norms and canons of taste. This could provide him, as with the semi-underground success of Fanny's *Memoirs,* with a commercial edge, for no one else of his day was daring enough to risk such a publication. But it could also mark him as another eccentric in an age of eccentrics: Boswell's "Cleland, curious figure."

Rather than harmless eccentricity, Cleland's "strangeness" as an author can be seen as a form of dissidence or defiance, not just in terms of the work's overtly sexual or political content, but also in terms of its language and form. Reviewing Cleland's *Memoirs of a Coxcomb*, Tobias Smollett wrote that "certain French idioms have crept into the language; a trespass for which the author is the less excusable, because he seems to be a master of the *English* tongue . . . nor is the performance free from stiff, compounded epithets, quaint terms of expression, that debase the stile, and new words affectedly coined."[20] A decade later, William Rider agreed that "Mr. *Cleland* has been not unjustly censured for the Affectation of his Stile, in particular for adopting too many foreign Idioms."[21] Such criticisms of Cleland for allowing too many foreign idioms to "cre[ep] into" his language or for "affectedly coin[ing]" too many new words are interesting both for the anxiety they reveal about the contamination of "the *English* tongue" and for drawing our attention to the traits that make his writing distinctive. There is a foreignness to Cleland's sentences, a figural complexity, lexical inventiveness, and rococo profusion that draw attention to themselves and that do often suggest the influence of French or Italian models. But foreignness is also integral to his work in another way: many of his most important texts are translations, while others, including *Memoirs of a Woman of Pleasure* and *Memoirs of a Coxcomb*, freely adapt plot lines and narrative strategies from continental, especially libertine writing, whose skeptical self-reflexivity became the keynote of Cleland's own fiction.

Cleland engaged with the literary, scientific, and philosophical innovations reshaping the intellectual contours of continental Europe, from Crébillon's experimentation with open-ended narrative forms to the atheist materialism of La Mettrie's *L'Homme machine*, at the same time as he sought, using the authorial persona of "A Briton," to found a radical critique of the present political order on his own semihistorical, semimythic ideal of an original, uncorrupted ancient Britain. His work positioned him as both foreigner and native, but even as native he was out of step with the world he inhabited. He was also out of step with himself: in his later work he attempts to reclaim his authorial self by repudiating the book that brought down scandal and shame on his head. Fanny Hill's *Memoirs* not only made him—won him lasting fame, showed off his stylistic virtuosity, gave him an entrée into the profession of author—but also unmade him: set him against the law, overshadowed his later work, reduced him to a parasite on his own fictional "creature." He is only remembered, after all, as the ghost author of Fanny's autobiography.

But there are other ghosts haunting her text. In some ways they are the key to retracing not only how that first book came to be written but Cleland's practice of authorship throughout his career. When he was arrested for obscenity eight months after his first novel appeared, Cleland wrote a letter to an official in the secretary of state's office, part confession and part disavowal. In a passage that provides the jumping-off point for this study's first chapter, he writes that "the plan of the [novel's] first Part was originally given me by a young Gentleman of the greatest hopes that ever I knew . . . above eighteen years ago, on an occasion immaterial to mention here." Thirty years later he told Boswell the young gentleman's name: Charles Carmichael, Cleland's friend when they both lived in Bombay.[22] Of course in part he was trying to shift blame for the offending book onto another: as the phrase "of the greatest hopes that ever I knew" suggests, Carmichael had died young, in 1733, and who better to blame than a ghost? But actually what is interesting about Cleland's letter and his later remarks to Boswell is that he does not simply shift responsibility for the work onto Carmichael; rather, he insists on the text's collaborative origins, in a challenge Carmichael set him, to write "about a woman of the town without resorting to the coarseness of *L'École des Filles*," a notorious erotic dialogue they had been reading together.[23] The text Cleland sold for publication did not originate with him but took form dialogically: not just in conversation with Carmichael but in answer to the "coarseness" of its precursors. Read in this light, the novel is thick with half-hidden allusions to the scenes of its own origins. The search for an author, far from reducing or closing off the text, leads to a proliferation of intertexts, for Cleland is not only himself but a medium who transmits the voices of the dead.

Hauntings, ghosts, and the spectral are useful figural resources for literary study because they evoke the ways in which the absent—the dead, the past, the imagined—nevertheless live on, in some way, in texts.[24] So, for Cleland, with the dead Charles Carmichael. And so, in a very different but equally impassioned way, with another ghost in the text, that of Thomas Cannon, author of a work even more scandalous than Cleland's novel, a paean to same-sex desire titled *Ancient and Modern Pederasty Investigated and Exemplify'd*. In the same jailhouse letter that invoked Carmichael as coauthor, Cleland, trying to evade prosecution for his book, denounces Cannon, without naming him, as one who "was mad and wicked enough to Publish a Pamphlet evidently in defence of *Sodomy*."[25] The tactic must have worked: Cleland was never prosecuted but

Cannon was, or rather was forced to flee the country on the eve of prosecution. But what makes Cleland's invocation of Cannon so interesting in this context is that he too had been one of Cleland's intimates. It was Cannon who had him arrested for an £800 debt, and it was only after he had been rotting in prison for nearly a year that Cleland sold his copyright to the text of Fanny's *Memoirs*. My search for Cleland led in turn to a search for Cannon and to the discovery both of the text of *Ancient and Modern Pederasty* and of archival evidence that the two had for some time been collaborators and friends, though their friendship had been volatile, verging on murderous. It's no coincidence that they simultaneously produced the only two explicit accounts of male same-sex desire in English before the late nineteenth century, published just a month apart in 1749. Indeed relations between the two, authors and texts, form the crux of my reading of Cleland's career, for collaboration is just the most overt instance of the ways in which all writing is caught in webs of personal and textual relatedness: translation, imitation, parody, repudiation, attack.

Calling on old Cleland on a spring afternoon in 1778, Boswell found someone other than the author of the "licentious and enflaming" book he had most likely read at about the same age Cleland and Carmichael had been when they dreamed it up in a burst of adolescent bravado and excitement. (When Cleland told him of the novel's origins, Boswell said that he "wondered he kept it so long; that it did not burst out.")[26] Over thirty years Cleland had experimented with, or conjured up, a variety of authorial personae, and these personae—memoirist, sodomite, hack, man of feeling, Briton—are the focus of this book's chapters. Cleland, Boswell wrote, had "resolutely persisted." The figure who lived "with books in confusion and dust" was of course dust himself and returned to dust not long after, but he loiters, or persists, as a guest (to use another of Barthes's terms) in the writing into which his identity long ago "slip[ped] away."[27]

MY ACCOUNT OF CLELAND'S AUTHORSHIP comprises seven chapters, broadly corresponding to stages of his writing career, though these are not always chronologically discrete. Particularly in the later chapters, the personae I have identified— the hack, the man of feeling, "A Briton"—do not follow each other in dutiful succession but come and go, overlapping, jostling for preeminence. Because this is not a strictly linear chronicle of Cleland's life, I've placed a skeletal chronology at the start, including the titles of all the known works. In the chapter summaries that follow, I have not provided references for the passages I cite from Cleland's texts, as these can be found in the chapters themselves.

In my first chapter, "Fanny Hill in Bombay," I explore the colonial origins of the text that both established and tainted Cleland's name. His years in the East India Company's Bombay colony, where he worked from the ages of eighteen to thirty and wrote the first draft of the *Woman of Pleasure*, constitute an exemplary colonialist success story, as he advanced from foot soldier to attorney to the Mayor's Court and secretary of the Bombay Council. His skill in writing and mastery of languages allowed him to rise rapidly through the ranks, but there is no evidence he had any plans for a literary career. Yet some traces of his life in Bombay reveal a flamboyant, contrarian authorial persona—above all when he speaks in the public forum of the Bombay courts. In one case, he had to defend himself from accusations of acting against the company's interest for his too-zealous representation of a Hindu client, "notwithstanding Personall Revilings and Insults . . . and being hooted at in open Court." In a second case, which I discovered in the India Office archive, he was accused of persuading a slave woman to leave her master's house—the implication being that he had done so to make her *his* sexual slave. The case exhibits striking parallels with the *Woman of Pleasure*'s focus on sexual objectification, economic inequality, and male violence—indeed the London-set novel locates the sexual morality of the slave market in the heart of the middle-class home. Cleland in Bombay was both colonialist slave owner and renegade champion of those whom the colonials cheated, raped, and enslaved, and the writing self that began to emerge in those years is similarly divided. Fanny Hill's voice is simultaneously female and male, hetero- and homoerotic, moralistic and obscene, just as the Cleland on trial in the Bombay public records is simultaneously colonialist and anticolonial.

When Cleland set off for London in 1740, he meant just to settle some family business before resuming his career as a Bombay merchant, but his father's death led to a radical change of plan, and he resettled in the metropolis. The period between his return and the publication of his first novel is sparsely documented, but the betrayals and frustrations of those years forced him into authorship and infused his later works. In my second chapter, "Down and Out in Lisbon and London," I focus on two episodes from an unsettled decade, each linked to a long-lost text. The first was an abortive scheme to set up a Portuguese East India company to rival that of the British, which led to secret meetings with King João V's highest ministers in Lisbon. His clandestine plot of treason and mercantile espionage was an act of revolt against his former masters and prefigures his political and cultural estrangement in later works. The second episode, to which I have already referred, was Cleland's friendship with a fellow would-be writer, Thomas Cannon. Everything we know of this dates from the bitter aftermath of their falling out, when Cleland was imprisoned in the Fleet for debt and mounted a campaign of libel and harassment against Cannon and his mother. In one handwritten note Cleland called Cannon an "execrable white-faced, rotten catamite, who joined with his own mother to consummate the murder of an unfortunate gentleman who had saved his life, and whom, in return, he poisoned five times with common arsenic." Accusing Cannon of sodomy and murder, Cleland signals that they were intimates—indeed betrays that they had once been collaborators. When affection turned to hatred and Cannon threw the friend "who had saved his life" into prison, the destitute Cleland was driven to sell the *Memoirs,* and so became an author by accident.

In my third chapter, "Sodomites," I offer close readings of Cannon's *Ancient and Modern Pederasty* and Cleland's *Woman of Pleasure.* All copies of Cannon's pamphlet vanished after his arrest (thanks to Cleland's denunciation), while Fanny's account of a sodomitical romp in the *Memoirs* was suppressed after the first edition. I discovered the sole surviving transcription of Cannon's lost text in the King's Bench records at the National Archives, so it is possible for the first time to compare the two works. Both authors break with the moralistic discourse of eighteenth-century antisodomite and anti-molly writing but make ironic use of its rhetorical conventions, allowing them to produce their own double discourse, conveying contrasting messages to different potential readerships. Cannon's "Wicked Lewd Nasty Filthy Bawdy Impious and Obscene" pamphlet is a miscellany of Latin translations, scraps of gossip, philosophical debates on natural versus unnatural desire, dirty jokes, misogynist asides, and an amatory fiction of cross-dressing and seduction set in contemporary London. The text's formal variegation corresponds to the varied meanings of "pederasty" itself, which becomes a figure for the undermining of any fixed category or role. Cleland too is at odds with the antisodomitical stance his narrator Fanny assumes. When she, in her rage to denounce the youths she has spied on, trips on a floorboard and knocks herself out, she earns our laughter and contempt and calls down mockery on the law she invokes. Asserting that sodomy is "a taste, not only universally odious, but absurd, and impossible to gratify, since . . . it was not in nature to force such immense disproportions," she actually subsumes all desire under the title of sodomy, for "disproportion" is also the keynote of her accounts of other-sex desire. Confounding any distinction between natural and unnatural, possible and impossible desires, Fanny's sodomitical encounter forms part of a larger pattern in the text of *unsexing* the body, unmooring it from any single sexual identity, female or male.

The success of Cleland's first novel created a commercial opportunity, and it was followed by *Memoirs of a Coxcomb*, whose title signals its claim to be a masculine partner to its precursor. Like Fanny's memoirs, Sir William Delamore's constitute a novel of education, and their plots are structurally the same: the narrator falls in love with an idealized partner of the other sex; the beloved disappears; the narrator is prevented from seeking out the beloved; (s)he enters into a life of wanton but unfulfilling sexual indulgence; the beloved is accidentally found; the lovers are reunited. But if both narrators move from innocence to experience, naïveté to worldliness, the country to the city, virginal singleness to heterosexual union, in social terms they are antithetical, as different as male from female or plain Fanny from Sir William. In my fourth chapter, "Three Memoirs," I read the texts comparatively, arguing for their importance to the history of the new, open-ended, self-critical, and self-reflexive form of the novel. Cleland took energetic part in debates on the moral and aesthetic aims of fiction, and in both *Memoirs* he experiments with narrative form, constructing the *Woman of Pleasure* as a set of variations and the *Coxcomb* as a suspended romance that frustrates the very expectations it instills. In this it owes a debt to the libertine novelist Crébillon, whose *Égarements du coeur et de l'esprit* also withholds the resolution its plot demands, and to Charles Pinot-Duclos, whose fictional *Mémoires* Cleland translated. Like Pinot-Duclos, Cleland uses the first-person history of moral education to challenge both narrative form and readers' expectations. Writing their own stories, Fanny and William fashion themselves as literary, as well as moral and social, subjects. But they are no less constrained in this than they are in terms of their social position: both have to insert themselves into preexisting narrative roles and forms, to narrate their experience in keeping with familiar forms of life story.

In my fifth chapter, "The Hack," I explore the work Cleland produced in his first decade as a "writer for bread," compassing fiction, translations, parodies, reviews, essays on legal and political controversies, medical histories, satirical verse epistles, and plays both comic and tragic. In the fluctuating and unstable literary marketplace of the mid-eighteenth century, he sought to maintain a stance of independence, neither a supplicant for patronage nor a hack for hire but a new kind of cultural producer, engaged with but not engulfed by the market. Of the work Cleland produced in this decade, I focus on his account of three days of bawdy-house riots in the Strand, *The Case of the Unfortunate Bosavern Penlez* (1749), an antigovernment polemic stinging enough to prompt Henry Fielding, who as magistrate had examined the rioters, to issue his own defensive riposte, and the lurid *Case of Catherine Vizzani*, Cleland's version of an Italian medical history of a cross-dressing "Lesbian" seducer who, armed with "a leathern Contrivance, of a cylindrical Figure," eloped with a series of young women until she was gunned down and anatomized to seek the origins of her willful and perverse desires. Along with his other translations, from Pinot-Duclos's *Mémoires* to Dreux du Radier's *Dictionnaire d'amour* (which as the *Dictionary of Love* was one of Cleland's greatest successes), the Vizzani text exhibits such strong continuities with his "own" or original writing as to call into question Edward Young's distinction between the originality of a true author and the hackwork of "other invaders of the Press" whose work is "a sort of *Manufacture* wrought up . . . out of pre-existent materials not their own." All of Cleland's work is caught up in networks of rewriting, imitation, and translation. Its originality consists precisely in the imagination and energy with which "pre-existent materials" are adapted to new occasions for writing.

On the evidence of a newly unearthed cache of letters, the middle to late 1750s was the most distressing period of Cleland's life. The combination of financial insecurity, verging on penury, and family antagonisms, verging on hatred, spilled out in his correspondence, in which his emotions are laid barer than in any of his other writing. Violent, excessive, extravagant, his language in these letters conveys Cleland's emotional volatility while narrating the Cleland family's breakdown in the style of melodrama. In my sixth chapter, "The Man of Feeling," I set the late fiction—*The Surprises of Love*, a collection of romances, and *The Woman of Honor*, a three-volume epistolary novel—against the private correspondence to explore the different registers of feeling in his private and public writing and the role of sentiment in his later work. If Cleland's trajectory as a novelist is understood as a movement from satirical and enflaming to sentimental and chaste portrayals of love, such a trajectory ignores the defiant oddness of the *Woman of Honor*, which shows him pushing against the boundaries of romance in a wittily alienating way, as if to expose "the imaginary spaces of fiction and chimæra." The late fiction bristles with the spirit of what Edward Said has called "late style": a "nonharmonious, nonserene tension . . . a sort of deliberately unproductive productiveness going *against*."[28] In the "pretty tale[s], prettily told" of *The Surprises of Love*, as in the almost paralyzed romance of *The Woman of Honor*, Cleland continually worries away at his own fictional inventions, producing a sense of estrangement that aims by turns to unsettle and amuse.[29]

In his later authorial career, Cleland turned from presenting himself as a writer for bread to adopt the persona of gentleman-amateur, as he shifted from fiction to three other areas of enquiry: politics, physiology, and language. Disavowing all interest in fame, he issued his work in a deliberately rough state. As he writes in the first of three studies on the origins of language, *The Way to Things by Words*, "In order to sound the opinion of competent judges, on the probability of my ideas . . . I threw them together in the loose undigested manner in which they now appear"—his nonchalance signaling that he had left behind the anxieties of professional authorship. Cleland's approach to his three fields of inquiry took the form of a search for origins: the foundations of bodily health, national identity, and the true meanings of words. His concern with the vigor and integrity of the body parallels his call to revive the integrity of the political constitution. He appeals in his political essays to the myth of an original, uncorrupted Britain, an appeal embodied in the pseudonym he adopted as their author: *A Briton*. And it is clear from his works on language—the "Ancient Celtic" he took to be the "primitive" or original "language of Europe," coextensive with "the ancient Laws of Britain"—that the word "Briton" denoted not just a political but a cultural ideal counter to the degeneracy of his own time. The emblem of that ideal is the maypole, an image of phallic authority that was also, he insists, the symbolic center of the ancient British government. Cleland's linguistic texts bring his authorial career full circle, evoking the same idealized past as Fanny does in her portrait of the virile Mr. H——, whose body incarnates "a system of manliness, that might pass for no bad image of our antient sturdy barons . . . whose race is now so thoroughly refin'd and fritter'd away into the more delicate modern-built frame of our pap-nerv'd softlings, who are as pale, as pretty, and almost as masculine as their sisters." In the search for origins of his late work, Cleland returns to his own origins, to the imaginative world of the book that first unmade him.

CHAPTER ONE

Fanny Hill in Bombay
(1728–1740)

For John Cleland, the paradox of authorship was immediate and acute: the same book that delivered him from one prison led to his confinement in another and, in time, both made and unmade his reputation. To his enduring shame and disgust, Cleland was famous in his own life for only one—the first—of the many books he produced over a career of more than forty years: the scandalous 1749 *Memoirs of a Woman of Pleasure*, better known today by the name of its first-person narrator, Fanny Hill. Published in two parts in order to pay off the debts for which he had been confined to the Fleet Prison more than a year before, Cleland's novel led to both freedom and subjection: he was released from the Fleet, but he was also trapped, in his own words, in the "low abject condition" of "a writer for bread," in a state of commercial dependency on the novel's shadow publisher, Ralph Griffiths.[1] His condition was soon to become more abject still, for on 8 November 1749 Cleland was arrested and confined to the house of Samuel Gray or Grey, messenger of the press, the government's agent for detecting "unauthorized and undesirable" publications.[2]

In his outrage and fury at this new incarceration, Cleland at first appealed to vague rumors that the *Woman of Pleasure* had been written by someone else, but in a letter to Lovel Stanhope, law clerk to the secretary of state, written on 13 November, he offered a franker, if still guarded, account of how the book had come to be written. "The plan of the first Part," Cleland writes, "was originally given me by a young gentleman of the greatest hopes that ever I knew, (Brother to a nobleman now Ambassadour at a Foreign Court) above eighteen years ago, on an occasion immaterial to mention here."[3] Cleland left the young gentleman nameless—a gesture of discretion or perhaps, as David Stevenson argues, a threat to bring down scandal on a diplomat and his noble family if provoked—and it was not until recently that evidence of his identity came to light, with the publication of a volume of Boswell's journal in which he records a conversation with Cleland, then almost seventy.[4] "Cleland said he had wrote his *Woman of Pleasure*," Boswell reports, "to show the Hon. Charles Carmichael that {one} could {write} so {freely about a} wom{an of the town without resorting to t}he {coarseness} of [*L'École*] *des filles*, which had quite plain words. What is strange, he kept it five-and-twenty years, that is, the first part and half [the] second, which was all wrote by the time he was twenty. The last was done when he was older. I said I wondered that he kept it so long; that it did not burst out."[5]

Charles Carmichael, then, is the young gentleman of great hopes who gave Cleland the "plan" for his book around 1729 or 1730, before Cleland turned twenty. Memory plays tricks, of course, and the letter and journal entry differ in some details, but Carmichael *was* brother to "a nobleman now Ambassadour"— John Carmichael, third Earl of Hyndford (ambassador to Russia in 1749)—and would have been of the right age and circumstances to have become Cleland's friend and to have spurred him on to a piece of adolescent bravado like the writing of a whore's life with no coarse words.[6] And the place they were living then, where the *Memoirs* were first written, was the East India Company's trading settlement at Bombay.

Cleland arrived at Bombay as a soldier in the company's service in August 1728, just turned eighteen. His dozen years in the company's Bombay colony offer an exemplary colonialist success story, as he advanced from foot soldier through the positions of writer, factor, junior merchant, secretary for Portuguese affairs, and attorney to the Mayor's Court to secretary of the Bombay Council. His skill in writing—he was described by one member of council as having a "poinant and ready pen"—and mastery of languages enabled him to move rapidly through the ranks and might be seen retrospectively to mark him out as an author, but there is no evidence he had any thought then of a literary career.[7] On the other hand, the traces that survive of Cleland's life in Bombay show him very self-consciously elaborating a flamboyant, contrarian authorial persona—not in published texts, but in the public forum of the Bombay courts. In this chapter I explore the colonial origins of Cleland's *Woman of Pleasure* and the literary career that ensued after its dangerous success. It is possible, of course, that Cleland was lying when he claimed that the novel originated with Carmichael's challenge or plan: Carmichael was long dead when the novel appeared, and the mature Cleland had good reason to distance himself from the text that provoked his arrest for obscenity. But he had no reason to lie to Boswell, and in any case the literal reliability of Cleland's statement is less important than the crucial figural and thematic correspondences one can trace between Cleland's public authorial "performances" in Bombay and the authorial persona he constructs, inhabiting Fanny's voice, in the novel.

Had he wanted, Cleland in his jailhouse letter could have assigned much more of the blame for the offending text to Carmichael. What stands out, in fact, both there and in Boswell's journal, is Cleland's emphasis on the novel's collaborative origins: the ways in which, "at my leisure hours, I altered, added to, transposed, and in short new-cast" the lost Carmichael source, as he writes to Stanhope or, as he tells Boswell, his taking-up a kind of challenge Carmichael set him, to find a figural language, neither coarse nor "quite plain," for the representation of sex. One should not overlook the homoerotic subtext (at least) of this boyish collaboration, for in the same years, and despite his career success, Cleland was more than once branded as morally dissolute. In what follows, I situate his collaboration with Carmichael in relation to two hard-fought legal cases that induced Cleland to articulate an embattled, sometimes overwrought public self. In the second, which has never before been published, he was accused of the kidnapping and seduction of a slave woman, and his testimony exhibits striking parallels with the novel's exploration of the links among sexual objectification, economic inequality, and male violence. In his clandestine fiction writing, he coupled these themes with the challenge of writing from the vantage point of a whore who lusts after men's bodies and describes them rhapsodically—thus initiating the "perverse" authorial persona that would color, or by his detractors be read into, all his later work.

Cleland and Carmichael

Although Cleland embarked for Bombay aged seventeen as a common foot soldier, his lineage was impressively patrician, and his parents' social and political connections, as well as his own brief early education at the Westminster

School—which was, along with Eton, one of the most prestigious of elite public schools in the period—would in the regular course of things have marked him out for university and a career in one of the professions, church, army, or law.[8] He had been selected within a year of matriculating at Westminster (at age ten) for a King's Scholarship, but a year later he withdrew from the school for reasons unknown. Nor does any trace survive of his life over the next five years, before his embarkation. Whatever the reasons that led to his enlistment with the East India Company, he was evidently ambitious and skilled, and quickly maneuvered his way out of what could have been a dead-end post. In a letter written on Cleland's behalf in early 1731, when he was petitioning the company to be appointed writer (the lowest civil service position), the steps of his early progress are put on record. In 1729, "Governor Cowan approving of his behaviour . . . advanced him into the Gun Room," where he soon headed the list of "montrosses," or gunners' assistants. Soon after, a Mr. Page, secretary of the Bombay Council, "finding him well qualify'd in Book keeping, writing, & languages, sober, faithfull, and diligent employ'[d] him to write under him." In August 1730 he was chosen to fill a vacancy as attorney to the Bombay Mayor's Court, "the fittest person for that Employ" because he was "allready somewhat acquainted with the business."[9] By July 1731 he had been appointed as a writer, which not only gave him a sure foothold on the bureaucratic ladder but allowed him to engage privately in trade in his own behalf.[10]

Meanwhile, Charles Carmichael, youngest son of the second Earl of Hyndford, had also come to Bombay. If Cleland's father was the lineal descendant of an ancient Scottish family that had been forced to sell off its estate and lived in a condition of near constant economic insecurity, Carmichael's was a Scottish peer whose four eldest sons took up their allotted places in the ruling class: John, the third earl, and envoy or ambassador to Prussia, Russia, and Austria; William, Church of England cleric and archbishop of Dublin; James, member of Parliament for Lanark Burghs; Archibald, page to George II and captain in the army.[11] As fifth son, Charles was sent farthest from the centers of power but must have been expected to extend the family's dominion into the burgeoning sphere of colonial trade. He is listed as writer in the company's register of civil servants for January 1731 and appears with Cleland on the next six semiannual lists.[12] Although it used to be thought that he died in Bombay aged twenty in 1732, he in fact died on 24 July 1733 (of "Fever") and was buried the next day.[13]

Cleland and Carmichael would have known each other, then, from the second half of 1730, around the time Cleland was appointed attorney, and their friendship would have been compassed in the three years before Carmichael's death. When they met, Carmichael was seventeen or eighteen, Cleland two years older. Although the Cleland family's fortunes had been in decline for some time, his parents were on close terms with many among the political and social elite of the period, from the Duchess of Marlborough to Richard Steele and Alexander Pope, a quite close friend of Cleland's father, William.[14] So the two young men in Bombay came from the same social world, from well-connected families with roots (if not estates) in Scotland, although both had been thrown into the rough and tumble and high mortality rates of colonial life in South Asia in the hopes they'd be able to make their own ways, since nothing would be left them to inherit. Remembering his friend, years later, as "a young gentleman of the greatest hopes that ever I knew," Cleland catches something of the sense of exhilaration and risk they must both have felt at such distance from their own native land.

Exhilaration and risk marked their collaboration on the *Memoirs* as well. It started with their reading of *L'École des filles*, an erotic dialogue of 1655 in which an older woman instructs a younger in the secrets of sexual anatomy and practice, which they may have read in the French original or in an English translation, *The School of Venus*, first published in 1680.[15] Sixty years earlier Samuel Pepys had been so fascinated by this "idle, rogueish" book when he came across it at his booksellers that he returned to buy it later, although he was "resolve[d], as soon as I have read it, to burn it . . . that it might not be among my books to my shame."[16] Carmichael and Cleland may not have felt the same sense of shame, but evidently did feel a similar fascination, and set to work on their imitation-with-a-difference "on an occasion," as Cleland writes in his letter to Stanhope, "immaterial to mention here." Despite Cleland's reticence, it would be interesting, and perhaps even material, to know what the occasion was. Not knowing, one can only try to reconcile the discrepant accounts Cleland later offered of the novel's origins. In the first, he writes that Carmichael gave him "the plan of the first Part." It's not obvious what this means: is the plan the plot in detail or an overall idea, or is it the claim Cleland put to Boswell, that one could write a harlot's story freely but avoid the "quite plain words" of *L'École*? Did Cleland then plan the second part (and are the "plans" of the two parts really separable)? Did Carmichael actually write any of the book as eventually published? To claim that he gave Cleland just a plan might suggest no, but to state (in the same letter) that Cleland later only "altered, added to, transposed, and in short new-cast" a lost original might suggest yes. None of these questions can really be answered, but the opacities and differences in the two accounts confirm what is most significant in both, that the text does not originate with or belong only to Cleland—that it took shape as a series of exchanges, challenges, borrowings, revisions, and dares between Carmichael, Cleland, and the books they were secretly reading.

Apart from these recollections of his friendship with Carmichael, Cleland's time in Bombay has to be reassembled from a range of public documents now held in the Oriental and India Office Collections at the British Library. Along one axis, as recorded in one set of records, his career was exemplary: he made steady and rapid progress through the ranks, from his appointment as writer in 1731 to factor in 1734 (two years ahead of the normal pace) and to junior merchant in 1737; by 1740 he headed the list of junior merchants and was first in line for promotion to senior merchant, the highest civilian rank.[17] He was evidently valued highly enough for his acuity and diligence that he was appointed to other positions of responsibility: attorney to the Mayor's Court (1730), secretary for Portuguese affairs (1737), and secretary for the Bombay Council (1739), among others.[18] By these measures, Cleland appears a capable and thoroughly conventional figure, having outgrown, perhaps, the unrespectable sexual high spirits of his writing with Carmichael—perhaps even having been sobered into respectable industry by Carmichael's early death.

Yet along another axis, the Cleland that emerges from the public documents in the company archives is a more reckless, combative, rebellious figure, gambling his future with the company by taking on the whole council on behalf of a Hindu merchant he had been assigned to represent and risking accusations of sexual impropriety by harboring a slave woman in his house in defiance of her putative master. Both these incidents are fully documented in the company's records, and both are compelling not least because they put Cleland on a public stage, the object of others' representations and the subject of his own, forcing him to construct and defend what I have called a public authorial persona, on which his later literary work would build.

First Case: Cleland versus Lowther

The first case arose directly from Cleland's appointment as attorney, though in this instance his "sober, faithfull, and diligent" carrying-out of his duty set him against those who had appointed him, in part because it laid bare a streak of aggressive defiance in him that overrode any deference to authority.[19] In November 1734 Cleland was called on to prepare a bill of complaint on behalf of Lollaboy Susunker Ballanauth Vossontroy, a merchant based in Surat, against

Henry Lowther, chief of the company's custom house at Surat and member of the Bombay Council.[20] Lowther had borrowed 40,000 rupees (ca. £5,000) from Vossontroy at Surat, about one hundred miles up the coast from Bombay, and had then refused to repay it. Believing, as Cleland later wrote, that Lowther's influence in Surat would be prejudicial, Vossontroy sued in the Bombay Mayor's Court for redress, presenting Lowther's signed IOU with the bill Cleland drew up. Against this, Lowther claimed, first, that because Vossontroy was "born an Alien, & a Subject of the Great Mogull," he was not entitled to plead before an English court and, second, that because the debt was incurred at Surat, Vossontroy's complaint should not be heard in Bombay.[21] Although Cleland argued cogently against them, Lowther's claims were upheld and Vossontroy's bill rejected. In the end, Vossontroy took his case to the Mughal emperor, as Lowther had indirectly suggested, and won it.[22]

What is interesting in the case is not the injustice of the Bombay court's decision but the rhetorical violence of the representations on both sides. It was risky enough for Cleland to argue in earnest against a member of council, but it was much more so to characterize the case in almost Manichaean terms, as when he writes, "I am not to be awed & frightened from pleading the cause of the poor or weak, against Power or oppression," or suggests that were Lowther's claims to be granted, this "wou'd effectually tear up all publick faith & credit by the Roots, fundamentally destroy the whole English Trade in these Parts & convert our Island into an Asylum or Sanctuary only sacred to Pillage & Rapine."[23] Although he later denied that he meant to impugn the integrity of the council, Cleland had in the course of his argument implied that the court would be guilty of hypocrisy if it found for Lowther, for as he reminded the court, the council had recently permitted Lowther himself to use the threat of military force to recover a debt from the governor of Surat. If Cleland meant just to urge that the principle of reciprocity should apply in cases of debt, his reference to this incident was read by Lowther and his fellow councillors as an act of "criminal disrespect" and his whole case on Vossontroy's behalf as an almost treasonous attack on the company itself.[24]

Despite having won the case, Lowther was indignant enough at what he regarded as Cleland's attacks on his character to file a complaint against him, joined in this by another councillor, Robert Cowan, who denounced Cleland in a supporting letter as "this common Assassin of Men's Characters and Reputations." The figure of Cleland as assassin pervades Cowan's letter, as for example when he asserts that "my impotent Adversary, arm'd with nothing but villainy and Malice, attempted to wound my Character" or writes that "the Stab" of Cleland's argument "was design'd at my Reputation."[25] The most mystifying and damning of Cowan's charges comes halfway through his letter, when he writes that he would not be suing for redress

> had the affront been offer'd me by any man that bore the character of the smallest
> share of Honour or honesty, which I hope will not be allow'd by any impartiall Judge
> to one who not many years since deserted his King, Country & even the Colour Nature design'd him, & was sent to me from Mahim (when I was Second in Council)
> as a pinion'd Slave;—Circumstances indeed that best suit his Principles & Practices,
> but render him unworthy of even my Horsewhip.[26]

It is hard to know what to make of this, given that Cowan had three years earlier testified to Cleland's good behavior and supported his appointment as writer, and given the absence of any other evidence in the company's records of such an incident. Cowan's assertion that Cleland had "deserted . . . even the Colour Nature design'd him" is arresting but cryptic, as is the image of Cleland sent from Mahim to Bombay "as a pinion'd Slave." If the story is not a wholesale fabrication, it seems to offer a sort of garbled or truncated captivity narrative with Cleland a willing captive, deserting his own race—as if only this could account for the treason of his exertions on behalf of Vossontroy.[27] Cowan's portrait of Cleland as a criminal against nature whose unspecified "Principles & Practices . . . render him unworthy of even my Horsewhip" is just the most extreme instance of a vein of commentary that dogged Cleland for most of his life, much of it characterizing him, more or less explicitly, as a sodomite. Perhaps Cowan is also hinting at this. Resistant as his anecdote is to decoding, it stands as the antithesis to that other narrative of Cleland as model young colonialist striver that emerges from other parts of the archive.

Cleland gives no response to Cowan's charge of having deserted "the Colour Nature design'd him," and it is likely that he had not seen Cowan's letter when he wrote his answer to Lowther's complaint. But it is clear from what Cleland writes that he was just as jealous of his reputation as Lowther or Cowan were of theirs, and there is no trace of deference to his superiors' higher standing in the Bombay colony. He too figures his antagonist as an assassin, as when he writes, "The low dishonourable Stabs Mr. Lowther is pleas'd to aim at me, in his expressions of 'a Person of Mr. Cleland's known Reputation and Character'—'my usual Front'—'& audaciousness' with other Language equally decent & well bred, only deserve my solidest, & coolest Contempt."[28] If Cleland's alternately aggressive and contemptuous treatment of Lowther was risky, validating Lowther's charge that his rhetoric during the trial itself constituted an attack on Lowther's character, open public defiance may have seemed the only real option, both to vindicate his own character and to ensure that the case would not simply be silenced. Cleland presents himself as the unjustly injured party, suffering for his dutiful adherence to the company's interests: Lowther's "unjust and iniquitous" claims, he argues, "inevitably engaged me in the cruel and grevious [sic] Dilemma of drawing this Persecution upon me, or basely giving up the most sacred regards, whether I am consider'd as an English Gentleman, a Servant of the Hon Companys, or an Attorney acting for my Constituent."[29] And this "persecution," he repeatedly notes, has been in the public eye. Near the end of his answer to Lowther's complaint, Cleland writes, "He may oppress me: & under the name of taking other Satisfaction as he has threatned publickly Injure my person by open violence, or my Character & Fortune by open Injustice," while in an earlier passage he notes that he spoke on Vossontroy's behalf "notwithstanding the Personall Revilings & Insults from Mr Lowther & being hooted at in open Court by some Gentlemen equally Members of this Hon.ble Board & of the Court of Appeals who composed part of that greatest Audience that was ever known."[30] Cleland's insistence on the public nature of these "revilings" sets him in defiance of not only Lowther but "some" of the very "Gentlemen" who are judging his case. If he thereby risks alienating his listeners, he does so not just to portray himself as a lone and thus rather heroic figure, justice's champion, but also to remind them that the case has already attracted the attention of the whole colony, "the greatest Audience that was ever known" in the Mayor's Court. It was too late simply to hush the whole affair up.

Such a reminder was crucial, for Cleland was under threat from two different forms of violence: the lesser, overt form was the violence of injurious language; the greater, covert form the violence of erasure and exile. This, he knew, was what the council intended: to banish him to a subordinate outlying "factory" or station and to expunge all record of the dispute from the register the council sent monthly to the company's Court of Directors in London. This "Silent Escape," as Cleland called it, would effectively have killed his career, and would have consigned both the arguments in the original Lowther-Vossontroy case and the subsequent war of words between Lowther and Cleland to oblivion.[31] In fact the council had voted unanimously to this effect, but one of the councillors, John Bradyll, changed his mind some hours later, deciding that "the Matters that appear in [Cleland's] Answer are of too Important a Nature to be stifled in this manner."[32] That Bradyll came to this conclusion was probably due to the defiant, impassioned language in which Cleland expressed both his legal arguments and his self-defense, so that a dispute over the terms of a debt became a debate on the principle of equity in colonial affairs, and the insulting barbs of a "diminutive & empty Chatterer" (as Cowan called him) were recast as an expression of "due abhorrence and resentment" of the sort of double-dealing that would "spread an alarm dishonourable to our Nationall Character & Laws."[33] The very extremity of Cleland's (and Lowther's) rhetoric meant that the case could no longer be "stifled": it called into question the very bases of the company's presence in Bombay and elsewhere.

And, luckily for Cleland, it did so at a time when his two accusers had already come under scrutiny for their irregular business practices. Cowan had recently been dismissed as governor of the Bombay colony for his questionable financial dealings, and Lowther was under investigation for corruption related to his excessive indebtedness—one year later he would be dismissed by both the Bombay Council and the company's London office for "gross mismanagement."[34] It seems, from a passing remark in Cleland's answer to Lowther's complaint, that he was already involved in the inquiry that would lead to Lowther's demise: "He may make an Example of me," Cleland writes, "or procure me to be transported to a Subordinate Factory at a time too I have another cause of importance against him under my management."[35] Within a year, Cowan would also be thoroughly disgraced, the Bombay court refusing his request to be invited in and publicly thanked for his good services to the company.[36] Nevertheless, even if Lowther's and Cowan's reputations were under a cloud, their fellow councillors' first, automatic impulse was to side with them against attacks either from outside (Vossontroy) or from below (Cleland), as if the very principle of hierarchical governance was at stake. For Cleland to take them on with such "inveteracy and Venom," as Lowther put it, and in doing so to portray himself as valiantly speaking truth to power while "being hooted at in open Court" by the "Gentlemen" of the council, was an enormous risk.[37] But in making a public *affaire* of a private dispute, he raised the stakes to such a degree that Bradyll, in the end, saw that his own and the company's interests would be more damaged by suppressing than publishing the case, and so he presented a letter of dissent to the council. Once this was accepted, the council had no choice but to gather all the documents in the case and enter them in its minutes for review by the company's directors in London. In a striking instance of archival irony, the very action by which Lowther aimed to expunge all record not just of the case against him but also, in effect, of Cleland himself—sending him off to the oblivion of a subordinate factory—led to the preservation of the documents in the register of council proceedings and thus to a kind of immortality for Cleland as author, his answer to Lowther's complaint becoming the earliest of his writings now held in the British Library, no less.

Even so, the council's original decision to rebuke and expel Cleland from Bombay would most likely have been upheld by the company had Lowther and Cowan not brought ignominy on their own heads—even if, back in London, Cleland's father was simultaneously enlisting support for his own campaign to vindicate his son's reputation and "to protect" him from "arbitrary" treatment.[38] Whatever the relative weight of the different factors, by March 1736 the company's directors in London gave official notice of Cleland's exoneration: "As to Mr Cleland's Case, and the disputes concerning him," they ordered, "what he hath done should not prejudice him in your Esteem."[39] The gap of more than a year between the decision to send the Lowther-Cleland documents to London and the directors' judgment in Cleland's favor—owing in large part to the length of the sea voyage, but also to the ongoing investigation of Lowther—left Cleland in a doubtful state, and his father's campaign suggests how worried he really was. In fact, things were worse than has so far appeared, for Cleland was at this same time embroiled in another legal battle that could have damaged him even more than the Lowther affair. Indeed the use of the plural in the directors' judgment on "Mr Cleland's Case, and the *disputes* concerning him" may allude to this second trial, which has never before been brought to light, and which, like the first, grew out of "the faithfull Discharge of his Duty as an Attorney in the Mayor's Court."[40]

Second Case: Cleland versus Boag

In the second case, it was Cleland himself on trial. According to the complaint of William Boag, sea captain, recorded in the Register of Proceedings of the Bombay Mayor's Court for 10 September 1735, Boag had gone to Cleland in August 1734 for legal advice. The matter on which Boag consulted Cleland was to do with a man named "King, who with one or two more persons, had Enterr'd your orrator's [that is, Boag's] house, and committed a rape upon the Body of one Marthalina his Servant or Slave."[41] According to Boag, Cleland

did prevail on your orrator, under a pretense of serving him . . . to send her Marthalina to his the said John Cleland's House, where your orrator that day dined, and where thro' the perswasions of the said John Cleland he did give his Consent she

shou'd live for some time; But some time afterwards a differance arising betwixt the
two Friends . . . your orator did desire that he woud send home the said Marthalina
again. (f. 123)

At this point, Cleland gave Boag "some unbecoming Language," and instead of
returning Marthalina, he sent her "to a certain Justice of the Peace, who under
a misrepresentation, that your orator had given her Freedom, did set her at
Liberty, telling her she might go and live where she pleased, by which means yr
orator hath been deprived of his right and property, and thereby greatly preju-
diced in his Estate" (f. 124).

Boag's complaint is terse to the point of obscurity. What, for example, were
the circumstances under which King and his companions entered Boag's house?
What motives would Cleland have had for "pretense" or "misrepresentation"?
What was the "differance" that arose between "the two Friends"? The story has a
certain unfathomability or starkness, and Boag makes no great effort to explain
or connect the different events, although there is a semantic affiliation among
the words he uses to describe Cleland's actions: "did *prevail*," "under a *pretense*
of serving," "the *perswasions* of the said . . . Cleland," "a *misrepresentation*." All
of these involve a mixture of linguistic cunning, seduction, and deceit, thus
configuring Cleland as a trickster or tempter but assigning no particular motive
for his temptations.

Cleland's answer to Boag's complaint, by contrast, is a far more circumstantial and connected narrative that makes use of the novelist's strategy of
presenting itself as "a plain, and Impartiall account." In fact Cleland starts by
"observ[ing]" that Boag has applied to the court "*under the colour* of a plain
honest man," setting up a contrast between Boag's pretended and his own authentic honesty, but also foregrounding the interpretive task that confronts the
reader of these discrepant texts. Boag had indeed come to him, Cleland begins
his narrative, for legal advice "concerning a horrid outrage Committed on the
Body of a Woman that cohabited with him in his house by one John King,
in Conspiracy with two others to this defendant unknown." After listening to
Boag's story, Cleland advised him, as the case was "very heinous," to prosecute
the offenders, but Boag objected "that he shoud be obliged to go to Sea very
soon," and if he had to wait in Bombay for the next quarter sessions, his business would suffer. To this Cleland responded that "there cou'd be no remedy
or Punishment of the Crime without he prosecuted himself, as he believed the
person that had sustain'd the Injury was a Slave, and consequently depriv'd of
the right of suing, prosecuting, or doing any Legal act" (ff. 124–125).

Faced with this dilemma, Boag took a surprising tack: yes, Marthalina *had* been his slave, but "she had been a free Woman for some time"; specifically, she had been "cleard and freed from Bondage by himself about a month before, by an authentick Gift of her Liberty under his hand Executed in form, and deliver'd her before witnesses." In fact, Boag said, he had meant to bring the document with him that day, but "was afraid he had mislaid it, though he wou'd go home and make a stricter search among his papers than he had hitherto done" (f. 125). With that assurance, Cleland agreed to take Marthalina as his client— an act that "wou'd have been inconsistent with his duty, to have done, and highly criminall in him, had she not been free" (f. 126). As for taking Marthalina into his house, Cleland asserts that Boag told him "that his house had been broke upon"—presumably by the alleged rapists—"and that there was a false key to the Room where the said Woman lay, and that he was afraid she might have her Throat Cutt, or have some mischief done to her whilst he was absent upon his Business . . . having already suffer'd such a violent abuse." So, out of compassion, "moved with the account [Boag] gave of the distress and danger of the unhappy Creature," Cleland "offer'd him the shelter and protection of his house for the said Woman" (f. 126).

To Cleland's "Answer" to his original "Complaint," Boag then gives a "Reply," which is followed by Cleland's "Rejoinder" and the depositions of witnesses on both sides of the case. The one voice missing is Marthalina's, precisely because it is the question of her right to speak in court that the court has to determine. Indeed her story is almost incidental to the struggle the trial stages between the two men for social and sexual prestige. The case at law is an agon between two male-authored narratives. In Boag's, Cleland has stolen—raped in the sense of abducted—what is properly his. Marthalina is his property, although in a complex and equivocal way, as it turns out: a quasi wife, a voluntary slave. A month before he had consulted with Cleland, Boag had learned from Marthalina that "she was with child by him" (f. 131). In response, according to one of his witnesses, Boag stated that "he was desirous of giving her her Liberty but with conditions that she shou'd not Live, or be kept by any other person so long as he lived, nor likewise woud he sell her but provide for her, and maintain her so long as she lived" (f. 139). He had not drawn up a document of manumission, then, but a certificate of liberty "with conditions"—the liberty, that is, of a slave (which has a certain resemblance, as Boag describes it, to marriage).

But even this was more than Marthalina desired: offered this paper, she refused it, according to Boag, "telling him she desired to Live, and Die with him in the Condition or state she then was, from which plainly appears the grateful sence she then had of her masters favours" (f. 132). Another witness confirms that Boag "offer'd the said Marthalinah the said certificate of her freedom, which she refused accepting of tho' much pressed thereto by her said master, telling her said master that she was his Slave, and wou'd forever continue so, upon which Captain Boag immediately tore said paper" (f. 140). Marthalina's torn certificate is almost too obvious a symbol of the flimsiness and precariousness of her place in the world, and her putative renunciation or refusal of the paper "freedom" it offers marks not her internalization of subservience but her sense of how little that freedom is worth that can so easily, in view of her confinement to Boag's house, be taken away. When the paper is first referred to, Cleland reports Boag's statement that when he handed it to Marthalina, she, "having no place to keep it in but what he might come at when he pleased, returned it into his custody and care" (f. 125). Whether Boag then "mislaid" it, as Cleland says he told him, or "tore" it, the proffered "freedom" is in either case his to withdraw, as within his house—where, under the terms of her "Liberty but with conditions," she has to remain—he can "come at it when he pleased." In such a state of affairs, under such constraints, it would have been more politic for Marthalina, especially before witnesses handpicked by Boag, to protest her desire to stay with him.

Marthalina, in Boag's narrative, has a voice, but it only speaks through his report of it, and then only to renounce any legal right to speak for herself. In Cleland's account, she speaks as a free woman—though again, given the focus of the trial, only through him. But if she can't speak in her own behalf, Cleland grants her considerable authority: it is her will he agrees to carry out as her legal representative in the rape case, and more important, it is her wish to stay in his house rather than go back to Boag's. As soon as she had taken refuge with him, Cleland declares, she "threw herself at this defendant's Feet and implored him in the most moving manner, to take pitty of her, and hear her case" (f. 127)—at liberty for the first time to tell her story. Having heard it, he "used his sincere and hearty Endeavo[r] to persuade her to replace herself under her former master"—uneasy, perhaps, at the prospect of antagonizing Boag—but this "she refused absolutely, saying she wou'd throw herself into a well, with other Expressions of Dispair, rather than be forced into his power again" (f. 128). There is a tension, in this last characterization of Marthalina, between firmness of will ("she refused absolutely") and an emotionalism linked to vulnerability or weakness ("she wou'd throw herself into a well . . . rather than be forced into his power"), but it is this latter quality that Cleland tends to emphasize in his account, the familiar narrative pattern of virtue in distress.[42] He notes from the start that he acted out of "charitable compassion for a woman's Distress" (f. 126), and in telling her story he creates a series of pathetic tableaux, as in the scene just cited, in which she "threw herself at [his] feet and implored him in the most moving manner, to take pitty of her."

Yet if Cleland might be said to be drawing on conventional narrative motifs in order to solicit his listeners' sympathy, he combines this with an unsparing circumstantial account of the violence of slavery in a British colony in 1734. Boag, Marthalina avers, "used her in so Barbarous and inhumane a manner, whilst she was his slave, and afterwards, that ever since she knew the meaning and priviledges of her Freedom & Liberty"—the same freedom she "renounced" before witnesses—she determined "to Embrace the first opportunity to rid herself from her Insupportable misery under him." As an example of such "misery" she tells of Boag's

> often striping herself stark naked and then tying her up by the hands, and beating her with a thick cane, of which she had the marks upon her Limbs . . . He used to hold a naked Sword to her Breast, and threaten to stab her, with other numberless outrages and crueltys, insomuch that she had pass'd some months with him in the utmost anguish and misery, and in perpetual fear of her Life from his Extravagancies . . . He kept her so close Locked up, from any person that she cou'd take advice of for Relief, that till then she had been destitute of all human help and assistance, which she therefore now cravd and begg'd of this defendant. (f. 127)

Cleland, then, in accordance with both narrative conventions and Marthalina's real state of civil abjection, becomes her champion, the protector of distressed femininity, a sentimental hero. Even in making the case for her legal autonomy or independence of will, Cleland has to draw on narrative conventions that emphasize her dependency—conventions which serve to *feminize* and thus constrict her.

As the feminized protagonist of this narrative-in-process—that is, the narrative under contested construction within the documents in the case—Marthalina has a limited number of roles available to her: concubine, serving girl, victim (of rape and unlawful confinement). By drawing the court's attention to the third of these, Cleland, or Marthalina through him, means to assert another identity, that of free woman, which could actually release her from sexual subjection. For within the economy and ideology of slavery, sexual availability is coextensive with her position in Boag's household. No one finds it curious that she is "with child by him" or asks if their sexual relations were voluntary or forced: What could it mean for a slave's actions to be voluntary? And how could

sexuality be outside or untainted by the logic of slavery? The link between domestic habitation and sexual submission is so taken for granted that Boag need
not state outright his accusation that Cleland's motive in taking Marthalina into
his house must have been to make her *his* sexual slave. As Cleland protests,
Boag "has forged a vile and scandalous story, as if [I] had offer'd her a Harbour
for Ends and purposes too Low and scandalous to take the Liberty of mention-
ing to this Honourable Court, altho' [I] had never seen the said woman in [my]
life even when [I] made him the offer" (f. 126). The story Boag told in his complaint was elliptical because he took it for granted that Cleland could have had
no other motive for his "expropriation" than sexual competition for possession
of Marthalina.

In Cleland's narrative, by contrast, her presence within his house is actually
a sign of her freedom: his house is a refuge she has chosen in the context of a
public assertion of her legal rights, which will permit her to leave Boag's house
and prosecute her attackers; in fact, she could prosecute Boag as one of her
attackers. For not only would any violence against her in his own house have
been criminal after his assertion of her freedom before witnesses (whether or
not she refused the paper itself), but according to Cleland, Boag "committed an
assault and Battery upon the person of said Woman, within the defend[ant]'s
own house, which wou'd have been an unsupportable Insolence even had she
been his slave" (f. 128). In this last sentence Cleland actually conflates two offenses, one against Marthalina—an assault and battery—and one against himself: Boag's "insolence" in striking Marthalina while inside Cleland's house and
thereby challenging Cleland's authority as master within that domestic space.
Indeed the most piercing irony of the whole case is that while he allowed Marthalina to sojourn with him in order to vindicate her status as free, Cleland's
was a slave household, and she lived with him there as if a slave. "Having
several Female Slaves his Domesticks at that time," he writes, he "readily" took
in Marthalina, since "she might live in Company with the rest, without either
Trouble or Expence" (f. 126). Living "in Company with the rest," she is both
absorbed into and radically distinct from the community of slaves.

Cleland insists that she is "as free as the Complainant himself, and absolutely at her own disposal" (f. 126)—yet she has neither social nor economic
standing to live in anything but a state of dependency. By the time Cleland gave
his "Answer" (2 October 1734), he had "placed the said woman in a Service at a
house and family, intirely at present depending upon this defendant, where she
has a subsistence, and from whence she is at full Liberty to remove" (f. 130).[43]
This summary of her position suggests both how much and how little her des-

ignation as free meant: the dependant of a dependant, she is "at full Liberty to remove," yet even though she is no longer subject to sexual violence or abuse, her liberty is bounded by her need to earn a subsistence in service to another's family. The distinction between slave and free is momentous, yet her choice of life, even free, is severely constricted: in a slave economy, a subsistence is all she is ever likely to gain. As a free woman, however, she is entitled to leave Boag's house and empowered to prosecute her own case, which is why Cleland draws attention to Boag's attempt to blur the categories of slavery and freedom. In the case at law, Boag is caught in a logical trap: once he has declared Marthalina free in order to allow her to prosecute King for rape, he cannot invoke his right as her owner to compel her return to his house. Accordingly, he lost the case: the complaint was dismissed, Boag was ordered to pay costs, and Marthalina evidently pursued her case against King and the others "in vertue of her said Freedom" (f. 142)—although I have found no record of that case or any other traces of her later life.[44] Cleland was vindicated, yet the case leaves the logic of the slave system intact, for of course Marthalina's freedom was, however much he may have come to regret it, entirely Boag's gift.

Little Families of Love, Markets of Flesh and Blood

Cleland, a slaveholder himself, makes nothing like an abolitionist argument, but his testimony registers his uneasiness with the abuse of women integral to the system, founded as it was on sanctioned violence. The slave trade between East Africa (notably Zanzibar and Kilwa) and India (especially the Gujarat and Deccan regions north of Bombay) started with Arab traders in the twelfth or thirteenth century and had been taken up by the Portuguese in the sixteenth; around the time Cleland worked for it, the East India Company was taking over the trade in its turn. The trade went in both directions, and by the eighteenth century its victims included not only East and West Africans but Indians, particularly female domestic and sexual slaves, who were then sold in the Persian Gulf and elsewhere. Nothing is said in the Mayor's Court proceedings about Marthalina's ethnicity or place of origin, just as nothing is said of her age, appearance, family, or other aspects of her identity. But if the evidence lacks detail, it confirms Indrani Chatterjee's argument that "the violence borne by slaves" was "the founding principle of intimacy in 'the family'"—that is, in the domestic space inflected by slavery.[45] Boag's "family" or household is a flagrant instance, mixing literal, brutal violence with sexual intimacy and a sort of forced conjugality, but even Cleland is complicit in the same system, his domestic comfort founded on the tacit, taken-for-granted violence—violence not outwardly enacted but understood as his to enact—of female subjugation.

Complicity, however, does not diminish Cleland's unease (though it may expose his blindness to the contradictions of his own stance); rather, it throws that unease into sharper relief. For if the case, as he repeatedly insists, turns on his assurance of Marthalina's status as free, he also states that he acted "from the common Ties of humanity and compassion, Especially for persons of her sex in Distress"—"Ties" that in this formulation override distinctions of social status. He even asserts that, as a lawyer, it is "the duty of his Profession to procure Justice, and the relief of the Laws Indifferently to all people" (f. 128). Of course such rhetoric can coexist—historically has coexisted, however illogically—with slavery. Yet the evidence of Cleland's other writing suggests that he was persistently troubled by the fact of coercion and violence against women integral to the domestic realm—and not only within a slave economy.

While it's impossible to know how much of the *Memoirs* as eventually published Cleland and Carmichael might already have written before Cleland wrote his statements in the Marthalina case, the areas of convergence between the two texts—despite their obvious dissimilarities—are striking. The novel, of course, has been both celebrated and attacked for conjuring a "pornotopia" of willing feminine confinement and endless sexual availability, the commodification of female sexuality taken to a fantastic extreme.[46] In this respect it could be seen to reproduce the sexual ideology of such precursors as *L'École des filles* or the 1683 *Vénus dans le cloître* (*Venus in the Cloister*), translated and published in English versions in 1683 and 1724.[47] But if Fanny's authors adhered to pornographic conventions, they also (again, from the evidence of the text Cleland published in 1748/49) used the whore's-story formula to insinuate that sexual exploitation, analogous to that found under slavery, was rife even within the domestic realm of midcentury England. Mrs. Cole's brothel, in which Fanny lives for most of the novel's second half, is idealized by her as housing "a little family of love," and its proprietor calls the women who work there her "daughters"—and if this serves to gloss over or glamorize the prostitute's life, it also undermines the sanctity of eighteenth-century family values: a mother seeking a respectable marriage for her daughter is no different from a bawd.[48] In an earlier passage Fanny denounces the landlady of a "fine" house in St. James's—shouting distance from the house where Cleland himself grew up—for selling her daughter, "for not a very considerable sum neither, to a gentleman, who was going an *Envoy* abroad, and took his purchase with him" (51).[49] The landlady, Mrs. Jones, "though she was worth, at least, near three or four thousand pounds" (52), was nevertheless "base enough to make a market of her own flesh and blood" (51)—yet of course this is the very same "market" that Mrs. Cole makes of her "daughters" every day. For Fanny, to treat a whore like a daughter is good, to treat a daughter like a whore wicked, but the effect of the juxtaposition of these two households (the wickeder located almost literally in the Clelands' back garden) is to exhibit the sexual morality of the slave market in the heart of the middle-class home.

In a pamphlet published the same year as the *Woman of Pleasure*, Cleland devotes a dozen pages to a vitriolic attack on London's bawdy-house owners, who keep the women they profit from "in a State of Slavery . . . scarce less cruel, and much more infamous, than that of a Captive in *Barbary*." A woman trapped in such a house, he writes, is "enslaved in short so thoroughly, that nothing, no, not her own Person, is her own Property, or at her own Disposal."[50] As both these later texts and his statements in the Marthalina case reveal, Cleland was keenly aware of the connections among sexual commodification, economic dependency, and violence both physical and moral—from rape to the coercion even found in "little famil[ies]of love." These are the real-world corollaries of the familiar pornographic fantasy of sexual gratification linked to female subservience, and it seems he learned about them in Bombay.

But just as it would be misleading to present Cleland, based on his arguments in the Marthalina case, as a proto-abolitionist, so it would be to read the *Woman of Pleasure* as a protest against sexual exploitation, even if the text is less oblivious to the real conditions of a prostitute's life than has sometimes been claimed.[51] If Cleland in Bombay was divided between colonialist, slave-owning householder and renegade, reckless champion of those whom the colonials cheated, raped, and enslaved, so the writing self was divided: on the one hand, as in much of the *Woman of Pleasure*, playful, coruscating, cheerfully "inflaming"; on the other, as in the court cases and pamphlets, truculent, self-dramatizing, grandiloquent.[52] Yet perhaps more salient than these divisions is Cleland's authorial dexterity or doubleness (two-facedness, double-voicedness). He can move, as in the court cases, from a meticulous, circumstantial narrative in keeping with both legal conventions and the emerging discourse of novelistic realism to an oratorical, theatrical eloquence suited to the public performance of an embattled subject. Such eloquence may verge on the bombastic, but his advocacy on behalf of Vossontroy and Marthalina is genuinely stirring and impressive, not least because in both cases he put his own career and reputation on the line. This authorial doubleness is still more pronounced in the *Memoirs*, not only because it was the product of an authorial double act but owing to the virtuosic construction of Fanny's voice, simultaneously female and male, hetero- and homoerotic, moralistic and lubricious, decorous and obscene. Her voice is both Cleland's and another's. Enter, Janus-masked, the author.

Coda

It is strange that for the rest of his authorial career Cleland published nothing that refers to the dozen years he spent in Bombay.[53] But there have long been rumors of his involvement in a work published under another name. In *Glimpses of Old Bombay and Western India* (1900), for example, James Douglas writes, "It is stated that 'Grose's Travels,' 1750–64, in two volumes, were written out by [Cleland] from notes received from Grose."[54] The work in question, *A Voyage to the East Indies, with Observations on Various Parts There*, is credited to John Henry Grose, a former writer for the East India Company who served in Bombay from 1750 to 1753. Published in 1757, it was recently described as "the most popular source for information on India" for most of the 1760s, and it was republished in 1766 and 1772.[55] Although it is impossible to know exactly how much of *A Voyage* is Cleland's work, he was certainly a key collaborator—perhaps the text's ghostwriter.

Douglas's claim most likely reflects rumors still current in Bombay when he wrote. More specific evidence appears in the "Avertissement" to the 1758 French translation of *A Voyage*, in which the translator, Philippe Hernandez, writes that Grose,

> the author of this work, has included nothing of which he was not well assured, and often an eyewitness. He was, in addition, aided by the observations of Mr. Cl——, a man celebrated in England for his works, his style, and his taste. He had made the same voyage before Mr. Grose, and communicated to him all that he had gathered on the Indies. Thus we have, in a single work, the results of the research of two learned travelers, who have neglected nothing to make the best use of their sojourn in faraway lands.[56]

Hernandez was one of the editors of the *Journal Étranger*, in which excerpts from a French version of the *Woman of Pleasure* had appeared in June 1755, translated by Cleland's friend Claude-Pierre Patu, so his claim that *A Voyage* represented a collaboration between Cleland and Grose has some authority. The clincher is a letter Cleland sent his mother's lawyer, Edward Dickinson, on 18 February 1757. "As you are to me then the only channel of communication with my family left unstopped," Cleland writes, he asks a favor:

A gentleman, one Mr Grose of Richmond[,] applying to me for some materials towards a treatise on the East-indies, my mother has got some papers of mine relating
thereto, and especially to the island of Salset which would be of infinite use to me
on this occasion, and of which she cannot surely refuse me the delivery, as she has
heretofore done, if you at your best leisure and opportunity, for I am in no hurry, will
be so good as to convey to her this hardly an unreasonable request.[57]

Cleland's request was evidently successful, for when *A Voyage* was published
eight months later, it included material that echoes his preoccupations and experience. There is much emphasis on the origins of names of places, gods, and
rituals, in keeping with Cleland's etymological studies of the 1760s. The concluding "Summary Reflections on the Trade in India" reflect both his interest
in the political effects of trade and his gloomy forecast of the "extinguish[ing of]
the antient English spirit of discovery and extension." There are descriptions of
the "cleanliness and suppleness" of "Orientalist" bodies, "which they perhaps
not absurdly conceive conduce even to the pleasure of the mind," that anticipate his approach to issues of hygiene in the 1761 *Institutes of Health*, and the
extended accounts of Mogul seraglios and the dancing girls of Surat are akin to
passages in the *Coxcomb* and *Dictionary of Love*.[58]

Such echoes, of course, are impressionistic, and do not prove that any particular passage in *A Voyage* is by Cleland. But the fact that Grose never wrote
anything else of his own—the passages he added to later editions were taken
from other sources—suggests that he relied on Cleland to fashion the text as
published, and this is all the more likely as Grose had been sent home after only
three years in Bombay, "having been deprived of his senses for some months
past, and there being no hope of his recovery."[59] However the labor of producing *A Voyage* was divided, one small story in a chapter titled "Miscellaneous
Observations" is unquestionably Cleland's, and returns to the period when he
was embroiled in the legal cases that threatened to destroy his career in Bombay.[60] This story, unexpectedly, is a kind of romance, and it features Cleland's
old antagonist William Boag. Indeed the story can only have come from Boag
himself.

It begins in the forests of the Carnatic region of southeast India, where a
"singular species of creatures" (365) who were "exquisitely cunning and shy"
(367) could at that time be found. A Carnatic merchant sent two of these creatures as a gift to John Horne, governor of Bombay, on "a coasting vessel, of
which one captain Boag was the master" (365–366). Cleland describes the creatures thus:

They were scarcely two feet high, walked erect, and had perfectly an human form. They were of a sallow white, without any hair, except in those parts that it is customary for mankind to have it. By their melancholy, they seemed to have a rational sense of their captivity, and had many of the human actions. They made their bed very orderly in the cage in which they were sent up, and on being viewed, would endeavor to conceal with their hands those parts that modesty forbids manifesting. (366)

Melancholy, modest, very orderly: they are sentimental creatures lamenting their lost freedom but still preserving their delicacy of conduct. Despite manifest signs of humanity—their "perfectly human form" and "human actions," their orderly bed making and modest concealment—the very fact of calling attention to these signs places them outside the boundaries of the human: no actual human would be said to have "perfectly an human form." Nevertheless, their "resemblance to the human species" is reiterated twice more before the story resumes its "pathetic" course. It turns out they are a male and a female, a loving couple held captive, and their distress is the index of their sensibility: "whether the sea-air did not agree with them, or that they could not brook their confinement, or that captain Boag had not properly consulted their provision, the female sickening first died, and the male giving all the demonstrations of grief, seemed to take it to heart so, that he refused to eat, and in two days after followed her" (366–367). If their "*resemblance* to the human" denies them actual membership in the human species, their refinement of feeling, the quintessence of humanity, also sets them apart from the ordinary humans around them, in particular Cleland's old enemy Captain Boag. Still sparring twenty-three years after their legal fight, Cleland shows Boag failing to fulfill his duty of care, thus exposing his own inhumanity. His coarseness of feeling is clearest after the creatures' deaths. When asked, upon his return to Bombay, "What he had done with the bodies? He said, he had flung them over-board"; both the action and his use of the verb "flung" attest to a lack of sympathy, an inability to be affected by the creatures' heartbreaking, heartbroken display of constancy. In this secret coda to his eventful life in Bombay, Cleland offers his most touching affirmation of love.

CHAPTER TWO

Down and Out in Lisbon and London
(1741–1748)

f Cleland's dozen years in Bombay saw both his rapid rise in the colonialist ranks and his sometimes clandestine, sometimes contested emergence as an author, the name he had begun to make for himself was shadowed by intimations of scandal or danger. Even though he prevailed in the Lowther and Marthalina cases, he only got caught up in them in the first place out of a rather dashing and reckless disregard for his own interests; a more cautious servant of the company would have deferred to his compatriots and left the "native" merchant and slave to fend for themselves. An outlaw aura seems to have grown up around him: in a work of antiquarian and local history from 1900, *Glimpses of Old Bombay and Western India*, James Douglas includes a biographical sketch of our subject under the title "John Cleland, Desperado."[1] To some extent, of course, the bad reputation is owing to the later fame of the *Woman of Pleasure*, but in Douglas's portrait Cleland comes across as a ne'er-do-well in all his pursuits. "He left Bombay," Douglas writes, "in a destitute condition, somewhat hurriedly, and for unknown reasons connected with a quarrel he had had with members of Council there. For many years he wandered in obscurity over the cities of Europe."[2] None of this is quite true, yet the sense it conveys of

Cleland as a shady, combative character, an uprooted cosmopolitan, hits close to the mark.

Nevertheless, when Cleland left Bombay in late 1740, the outward signs pointed to his return in due course to resume his colonial career. His younger sister, Charlotte Louisa (or Lucy), had joined him in Bombay in the fall of 1736 and had married one of his fellow writers, George Sadleir, in June 1737. Charlotte had given birth to a son, christened John, in October 1739, and although the child died within two months (of "flux"), Charlotte and her husband remained in Bombay and could have offered a sort of domestic stability to the otherwise deracinated Cleland.[3] In a letter requesting leave to return to England, Cleland expresses his intent to resume his place in Bombay at the earliest opportunity. Addressing the members of council, he writes:

> Certain concerns of the utmost Importance to my private Fortune requiring my personal Attendance in England, I am obliged to request your Hon[ours'] Leave to proceed thither on the first Ship. The Share I have the Honour of having in the Hon[oura]ble Company's Business is now up, and I am in Readiness to deliver up my Charge, though I am extremely willing to give all the Assistance in my Power to the Dispatches now in Hand, and hope this Step will not deprive me of the favourable Indulgence of my Hon[oura]ble Masters on a Reclamation of their Service, Which Nothing could oblige me to leave at this Juncture, but an indispensible Call Home.[4]

Cleland's tone is suitably deferential, but his letter withholds more than it tells. Both the "indispensible Call" and the "concerns" bearing on his "private Fortune" are left discreetly unspecified, as one would expect in such a petition, but the words "personal," "private," and "home" point to family pressures, as does other evidence. Having lost her first and only child nine months before, Charlotte accompanied her brother, probably to recuperate from the double strain of childbirth and mourning; and their father's health, poor for some years, had worsened enough in his late sixties—his sinecure as commissioner of taxes under Walpole's patronage now in danger—that his elder son felt obligated to help sort out his family's affairs.[5] The younger son, Henry—christened thirteen months after John and, according to Pope, his father's "Favorite Son"—was probably then living in the West Indies, endeavoring to write his own colonialist success story; but almost no traces have been found of him, and he seems to have died without returning to London, sometime before the early 1750s.[6]

Caught up in the worries and griefs of family life, Cleland still seems, on the basis of his letter to the council, to intend a "Reclamation" of his career, even if the covenant he signed in 1732 was "now up," so that he was no longer indentured to the company.[7] Certainly he gives no sign of disaffection or of the destitution, hurry, and rancor suggested by Douglas. The council approved his request, and John and Charlotte sailed for England, probably on the *Warwick*, which left Bombay on 23 September 1740.[8]

Nothing further, no other documentary trace, appears until eleven months later, when he reported his arrival in London to the company's directors (26 August 1741). After that, apart from vague notes in the watch rate and poor rate account books (that is, in tax collectors' records), the evidence of his activities or even whereabouts before 1748 is fragmentary and elusive. Until recently, nothing seemed to have survived from the period between his father's death (September 1741) and Cleland's imprisonment for debt (February 1748) other than unattested rumors of his "wander[ing] in obscurity," as Douglas puts it, "over the cities of Europe."[9] Yet these were years that marked a radical change in his life's direction, and the betrayals and frustrations that infuse and perhaps disfigure his later work all lead back to this period when Cleland—in the words Samuel Johnson wrote of his scapegrace friend Richard Savage—"having no Profession, became, by Necessity, an Author."[10] In the rest of this chapter I focus on two key episodes from a trying, tumultuous decade, each one linked to a long-lost text of Cleland's. The first, his involvement in an abortive scheme to establish a Portuguese East India company to rival the British, signals a decisive turn away from, or against, his former masters—almost an acting out of Cowan's charge years earlier that Cleland had "deserted his King [&] Country," and a prefiguration of his political and cultural estrangement in later works.[11] The second, Cleland's volatile, even murderous relationship with a fellow would-be writer, Thomas Cannon, can only be reconstructed from the bitter aftermath of their falling out, but its effect was to force Cleland into authorship in the face of misery and shame; and while publication relieved his misery, it only augmented his shame, and for life.

The Portuguese Scheme

Cleland must have brought the manuscript of the coauthored *Woman of Pleasure* with him when he sailed on the *Warwick*; but the Bombay Fanny Hill is a phantom, a conjectural urtext whose relation to the published text is unknowable. There is no way of knowing, either, if it had been kept a shared secret or if Carmichael and Cleland circulated it among friends or more widely still. A curt note in the minutes of a Scottish phallic gentleman's club, the Beggar's Benison and Merryland, states that at a meeting on St. Andrew's Day, 1737, "Fanny Hill was read," just after, or perhaps during, a spirited session at which "all frigged," but apart from some question as to the reliability of the minutes, reconstructed from memory after the originals had been destroyed, the note itself is ambiguous. Is this "Fanny Hill" the Carmichael-Cleland text or a generic name, a common Englishing of the Latin *mons veneris* (hill of Venus)? If the former, how did a copy end up in Anstruther in Fife at a time when Cleland was working his way up to the position of junior merchant in Bombay? The fact that a "Robert Cleland" was listed among the Beggar's Benison's members in 1739 is intriguing, but the degree of his relationship, if any, to John is unknown.[12] Whatever the case, there is nothing to suggest that Cleland imagined publishing the text or imagined authorship as a possible life.

His appearance before the company directors in August 1741, soon after his arrival in London, suggests an intention to keep the way open for a return to Bombay, but this seems to have been the last contact he had with the company, and by the next year he was engaged in a secret mission to create a rival company to serve the mercantile and imperial aims of a nation that, if not an enemy to Britain, was not exactly a friend. From 1739, Britain was at war with Portugal's chief rival in the Americas, Spain (the curiously named "War of Jenkins's Ear"); and the British government had proposed an Anglo-Portuguese convention that would offer British protection to Portuguese assets in exchange for trading access to Brazilian ports. Such gestures of solidarity, however, masked a deeper antagonism. As the recently appointed Portuguese ambassador to the court of George II wrote in July 1741, "The envy of our Brazil[,] so strong in British hearts . . . would eventually lead them to an attack on Portuguese America."[13] The author of these words, Sebastião José de Carvalho e Melo, would in later years, as the Marquês de Pombal, occupy a position in Portugal comparable to Walpole's in Britain. As ambassador in London from 1738 to 1743, he was elected a Fellow of the Royal Society and sought out men of political influence and learning who could enlarge his knowledge of mercantilist economics and the practicalities of trade.[14] One such person, with whose family he became close soon after arriving in London, was William Cleland, and it was through the father that Carvalho came to know the son.[15] More than this, it was William Cleland's fall from political grace, and his death just a month after Cleland's homecoming, that turned Cleland from a loyal servant of the company and Crown to the principal actor in a plot to challenge their growing power abroad.

William Cleland, aged sixty-eight when his son returned from Bombay, had served for ten years in the army, rising to the rank of major around the time of John's birth. When the Peace of Utrecht of 1713–1714 brought an end to the War of the Spanish Succession, in which he had seen battle, William turned from the military to the civil service, first as a commissioner of customs for Scotland and from 1723 as a commissioner of taxes in England, a post he held for eighteen years.[16] These positions were well paid (£400 and £500 per annum, respectively) but depended on ministerial patronage and were thus vulnerable to calculations of political interest, so in the spring of 1741, when Walpole's government needed shoring up, William Cleland's sinecure as commissioner went to a more useful ally. To add insult to injury, he only found out by a back channel: as he wrote to the Duke of Newcastle on 22 May, late the night before, his wife had received "an Anonimous billet in a Counterfeit hand advising her that there was a resolution of takeing her husbands employment from him and a promise of it given to another."[17] For all the cloak-and-dagger intrigue of warnings delivered under cover of darkness, there was no countermove for William to make, and the news seems to have shattered him. As he wrote in the same letter to Newcastle, "My heart is so ffull that I am asham'd of it and I am affraid that if I said any more I should show so little manhood that you would be asham'd to espouse my cause."[18]

Even if John, from the evidence that reached him in Bombay, knew that his father was in trouble, the change for the worse by the time he reached London in August must have been distressing: his father had been "cruell[y] strip[ped] of [his] fortune" and was approaching his death—which, if not directly caused by his dismissal, was surely hurried on by it.[19] Such was Carvalho's sense, at any rate, when he undertook to explain to the powerful Cardinal da Mota the younger Cleland's reasons for offering his help toward the establishment of a Portuguese East India company: the family had been "brought into disgrace" and William destroyed by heartbreak when his post was taken away at Walpole's behest.[20] In the same letter, Carvalho maintained that the British East India Company's directors were also Walpole's "creatures" and had provoked Cleland the younger's "disgust"—so linking the son's disaffection to the father's disgrace. For all his success in Bombay, John, as the Cowan case vividly shows, held at least some of his superiors there in contempt, and Walpole's sacrifice of his father to political expediency (never mind that his job security over the preceding twenty-seven years was also owing to political favoritism) could only have aggravated his sense of injustice. "Pricked by resentment at the injuries he had received," Carvalho reports, Cleland after his father's death was ready to shift his allegiance from Britain to Portugal, and to a scheme commensurate with his ambition and sense of his own abilities.[21]

Carvalho held Cleland in high esteem, describing him as a "man of distinction" and, like his father, "a person . . . of honor and well-known integrity," and he consistently presents Cleland as the "author" of the plan for a Portuguese company, the only person with the precise mix of "natural abilities" and knowledge born of "years of tireless study and curiosity" needed for the successful realization of such an ambitious undertaking.[22] If Carvalho on his posting to London was initially most concerned with what he saw as "the unfair advantages the British enjoyed in Lisbon and Oporto" and the threat posed to Portuguese interests in Brazil, his friendship with Cleland kindled an interest in reviving Portugal's fortunes in India and the East Indies, notably weakened by war with the Marathas—a war tacitly endorsed by the British East India Company, which stood to profit from the Portuguese losses.[23] Carvalho's younger brother, José Joaquim, "a brother I raised and whom I loved also as a son," had been killed during the Maratha attack on Goa in 1740, which suggests that, as with Cleland, personal motives were bound up with his political calculations: theirs was a plan driven, in part, by displaced filial and paternal grief.[24]

Carvalho presented the scheme in the long letter already cited to Cardinal da Mota, the Portuguese king's chief minister, dated 19 February 1742—just six months after Cleland's return to London. In his letter, Carvalho introduces Cleland as the project's author, presenting his background and qualifications but leaving him nameless (the main reason, of course, for his involvement remaining a secret for two hundred years). He then discusses the history of other European trading companies in the Indies and outlines the system of commercial education that would need to be introduced in Portugal for its merchants to be competitive with those of other nations, especially the British. In effect, during his four years in London he had been gathering commercial intelligence through conversations with merchants, as he writes in a 1741 text, the *Relação dos Gravames* (*Report on Grievances*): "In Portugal I could not have had the sources that I have here for research . . . Here we eat and drink with a merchant who is talkative after having drunk too much . . . What would be difficult in Portugal to discover directly, only requires patience to gather here."[25] In the 1742 letter, he summarizes those discoveries, building to his pièce de résistance, a *mémoire*, or memorandum, written in French, from Cleland to the king of Portugal, João V.[26]

In keeping with the secrecy of this early stage of the scheme, Cleland presents himself anonymously, as "the author of this *mémoire*," or simply "the author." Both he and Carvalho had good reason for secrecy: Carvalho because of enemies in the Portuguese court who meant to thwart (or hijack) his proposals, Cleland because his involvement verged (at least) on treason and mercantile espionage, especially as it featured what Carvalho describes as a "vast collection of manuscripts containing examples of all the British East India Company's practices in the administration of trade in Asia."[27] To use papers acquired as a result of his employment with the company in order to further the interests of the Portuguese—or as he puts it in his *mémoire*, "to increase His Majesty's revenue, to strengthen His Kingdom's Navy, to cause His colonies in the East Indies . . . to flourish"—was seriously risky, as British government policy in the area, dictated by the company, was aimed at nothing less than the expulsion of the Portuguese from the region.[28] Cleland's plan to found a rival company was not simply an entrepreneurial scheme but an act of defiance against his own late "Honourable Masters."

The *mémoire*'s intended audience—Carvalho, the cardinal, and the king—could not have missed the challenge to British interests implicit in the author's call for the Portuguese nation to recognize "the value and even necessity of restoring its Indian trading colonies and drawing from them all the profit and benefit which the cultivation of commerce cannot fail to produce" nor the larger, indeed global, geopolitical implications of this revival. Cleland writes that "even after the loss of many previously conquered properties and territories, there remain enough favorably situated settlements and valuable resources to form a plan of trade in the Orient which . . . will more than make up for past losses." Portugal, he asserts, enjoys "numerous advantages" over Britain, both geographical ("its colonial settlements well positioned along the East Indian trade routes") and cultural ("the Portuguese language, diffused throughout the East"), and these are part of a global fabric of colonial enterprise. The revival of trade in India, then, with its attendant benefits (the increase of the king's revenue, the strengthening of the navy) will lead, "indirectly and as a result," to the "flourish[ing]" of Portuguese colonies in Brazil. In light of Carvalho's fears that the British aimed not only to expel the Portuguese from India but to attack them in America, what Cleland held out was the prospect of a radical reconfiguration of imperial power relations.

Apart from outlining the strategic benefits of a revitalization of the Portuguese presence in India—benefits, he argues, that make this scheme "a matter of highest priority for the state," to which it should "dedicate . . . all its genius and power"—Cleland sets out his qualifications for the role of chief advisor. "The author of this memorandum," he writes,

> having resided for the span of many years in the East Indies, has long been in a
> position to learn a great deal about the situation and interests of the Portuguese na-
> tion in India, from the many dealings and conversations he has had on this subject
> with the most respectable persons of that nation, both ecclesiastical and lay, as well
> as by his endeavors to acquire all the knowledge necessary to maintain trade in the
> Orient, whether between India and Europe or within the Indies.

His knowledge of the place, of trade, and of the Portuguese is knowledge gained, although he can only say so indirectly, in the service of Portugal's enemies. What he has to offer is "the example of other nations which have well known how to profit" in India, "whose systems of administration can be instructive as examples." This is in keeping with Carvalho's claim, in his letter enclosing Cleland's *mémoire*—that "all European nations are benefiting and prospering by means of reciprocal imitation. Each one observes carefully the actions of the others"— with one difference: rather than information gleaned from careful observation of another, Cleland offers insider knowledge at first hand.[29] He doesn't explain his willingness to shift allegiance to a new master but simply notes that a new system of trade "necessarily requires the advice of some person or persons of sufficient experience, particularly in Indian affairs and the practice of trade there, in order to guide and steady its first steps, which otherwise could not help but be wavering and uncertain." For Cleland himself, the scheme would mark his elevation from a mere functionary (albeit a successful one) to a king's counselor, the author and architect of a comprehensive system.

Cleland concludes the *mémoire* by offering "to travel to Portugal in order to communicate, in person and in detail, all the necessary records, written in- structions and other information, in whatever manner and form are required, without setting any conditions in advance and seeking no reward other than as it pleases His Majesty." And that is the last we hear of the scheme from Cleland directly; no other account of it in his words has come to light. But a later letter of Carvalho, written in 1748 to his cousin Marco António de Azevedo Coutinho, the Portuguese secretary of state, cuts to the story's end. Just over a year after sending his letter and Cleland's *mémoire* to Cardinal da Mota, in May 1743, Carvalho returned from his ambassadorial posting in London to Lisbon and there met Cleland, who had been received by the cardinal at home, in the com- pany of Coutinho. It is not clear how long Cleland had been in Lisbon, but his secret meeting with the king's two highest ministers confirms their very strong interest in the scheme. Yet within a short time the proposal was dead. A number of different explanations have been suggested: the cardinal evidently told Cleland he "absolute[ly] lacked the means" to support the scheme; the king's faltering health made negotiations difficult; the secrecy of the proposals had been breached; Carvalho's enemies at court blocked the plan. It was probably a combination of the last two of these that sealed its fate: when Carvalho's rivals got wind of the scheme, they maneuvered to have him sent to Vienna—not because they opposed the East India plan, but in order to shut Carvalho out of its implementation. And in fact in late 1747, with Carvalho away, a new plan for a Portuguese East India company began to circulate in Lisbon, but this time without Cleland attached.[30]

According to Carvalho, the scheme's unraveling made for a very bad end to Cleland's stay in Portugal. Carvalho himself had to deliver "the final disappointment, which forced him [Cleland] to leave Lisbon when he least expected it, and in quite disagreeable circumstances."[31] Exactly what these were is unclear, but the phrase hints at something sordid, as if the project's failure carried some disgrace. The violence of this reversal—from secret talks at the highest levels of state to ignominious retreat—was not only, as Carvalho writes, shocking and disappointing, but seems to have had an enduring, traumatic effect. Cleland did not return to the company, or to India, where, whatever conflicts he had had with other members of the colonial establishment, he had laid the foundation for a flourishing career. If news of the secret Portuguese negotiations had got back to London, of course, he could hardly have picked up again where he had left off with the company, but there is no evidence of this; it seems more likely that the same "disgust" and "resentment" that led him to devise the Portuguese scheme in the first place barred him from asking to return to his former station. His sister Charlotte did return to her husband in Bombay, around the same time John was in Lisbon—her name is registered on the lists of European residents from October 1743—and remained there until her death in October 1747, of "dropsy."[32] But for John there seems to have been no more thought of going back.

Cleland and Cannon

Instead, he stayed on, or perhaps off and on, with his mother in St. James's Place, and all that is known of the period between May 1743 and February 1748 is that he fell into debt, to the tune of some £800. Such, at any rate, was the claim made against him by two men, Thomas Cannon and James Lane, whose charges led to Cleland's arrest and committal to the Fleet Prison, where he spent the next twelve and a half months.[33] There is no indication in the legal documents of how the debts were incurred or of how Cannon's and Lane's interests were linked. Both charged Cleland with "trespass" as well as failure to pay, but the nature of the trespass is unspecified. Lane sought payment of £20 damages (again unspecified), while Cannon sought the same in damages and repayment of the £800 Cleland allegedly owed him. Although it is notoriously tricky to establish what a particular sum of money in an earlier period would be worth today, £800 was a huge debt: almost double the very substantial salary William Cleland received as a high-level government tax official with over twenty years' service, and nearly thirty times the annual rent of the house on St. James's that Cleland's mother shared with John after her husband's death.[34] How Cleland could have owed such a sum to Thomas Cannon, whose own father's death in 1722 had left his mother and family in such "necessitous circumstances" that George I granted them a pension of £120 per year, is unclear.[35] But while much of what led up to Cleland's arrest is hopelessly murky, enough remnants survive from its aftermath to suggest that Cannon may have been, to Cleland's rage, the most important person in his life.

Cannon, born 1720, was ten years Cleland's junior and was, as Cleland noted in a 1749 letter, "the Son of a *Dean* and Grandson of a *Bishop*."[36] His father, Robert (1663–1722), though described by the controversial scientist and clergyman William Whiston as "one of the greatest Scepticks that ever was born," had a successful career in the church, becoming a prebendary of Ely, Westminster, and Lincoln and dean of the last—perhaps in part thanks to the influence of his wife Elizabeth's father, the bishop of Norwich and Ely, John Moore.[37] His father's skepticism may have dissuaded Thomas and his elder brother Charles (born 1713) from following clerical careers; in any case, they seem not to have done so, and Charles died at the Battle of Fontenoy in 1745.[38] Thomas, by contrast, evidently pursued literary interests, and seems by that route to have come to know Cleland in the mid-1740s, when they lived, with their widowed mothers, on opposite sides of St. James's Park.[39]

In the wake of the Lisbon debacle, and unwilling to go back to Bombay, Cleland might have expected to assume the role of head of family. Pope wrote in 1742 that William Cleland had lived just long enough "to receive his Eldest Son with great Satisfaction," adding, "I hear that this Son behaves himself very kindly to his Mother & is in a capacity of assisting her"—as if he had taken the father's place, and the mother now depended on her son's kindness.[40] But it was John who was powerless in the family home. Lucy was administrator of her husband's estate and was also well provided for by her older sister Margaret, Viscountess Allen. When Lucy Cleland in turn wrote her will in 1752, it was her sister and her niece Frances whom she named as executors, not her son: he was limited to a pension whose stringent conditions he railed against, fruitlessly, for years.[41] As he wrote to his mother's lawyer, Edward Dickinson, sometime later:

> Birth, Education, and a certain rank defend most real gentlemen from at least mean, and dirty distresses, but my gratious parent is *content!* yes *content!* that I should fall by such hardships, as Tinkers, Taylors, or an honest Washerwoman would not think of their children enduring if they could help it: and yet She, even she herself it is, whose rank obstinacy has brought them every one upon me. Can Lady Allen join in this execrably inhuman procedure? Can this be the spirit of our Family? if so: happy the Dead of it.[42]

Cleland's authorial voice in his letters—often peevish, self-pitying, theatrically reiterative ("she, even she"; "*content!* yes *content!*")—can be hectoring and unpleasant, but his tone of wounded outrage betrays a keen awareness of his own marginality and dependence, and it would be hard not to feel some sympathy for the sense of abandonment he expresses with such intensity. For whatever one thinks of the rhetorical posturing, the "hardships" by which he had fallen were not imagined: he spent twelve and a half months in the hell of the Fleet, and his family did nothing.

With no other help to sustain him, Cleland took up the "poinant and ready pen" he had been noted for in Bombay.[43] Two of his prison writings survive: the *Woman of Pleasure*, which in his "leisure hours" he "altered, added to, transposed, and in short new-cast," giving the text we know, and a handwritten note found "stuck to the outer Door" of Thomas Cannon's chambers in New Inn. The second of these survives thanks to Cannon's decision to submit it in support of a complaint he lodged against Cleland on 5 February 1749, taken down in an affidavit by W. Foster of Serjeants Inn (connected to the Court of King's Bench).[44] Cannon, accompanied to Foster's office by his servant Hannah Simpson, who found the note, begins by saying "that he is well Acquainted with the handwriting of John Cleland now a prisoner in his Majestys prison of the Fleet at this Deponents Suit" and goes on to assert "that since the said John Cleland has been confined in the said Prison . . . this Deponent has received diverse scurrilous and libellous papers from the said Cleland greatly reflecting upon and abusing this Deponent And this Deponent's Mother Elizabeth Cannon."

The morning before, Hannah Simpson had seen "the paper Writing hereunto annext" on Cannon's door and brought it in "before this Deponent was up"— although, judging by her use of an X rather than a signature on the affidavit, she would not have been able to read it. Cannon concludes by declaring that he "verily believes" the note "to be the proper handwriting of the said John Cleland[,] this Deponent having often seen him write." Attached to the affidavit by a wax seal is the note itself:

> Here lives that execrable white-faced, rotten catamite, who joined with his own mother to consummate the murder of an unfortunate gentleman who had saved his life, and whom, in return, he poisoned five times with common arsenic, which, it is probable, he will never recover the bloody effects of. Enquire for further particulars of his Mother in Delahaye Street. His name is Molly Cannon.
>
> N.B. The next shall be on every Post in London and Westminster.

The note does indeed "greatly reflect upon and abuse" him. In seventy-five words it manages to accuse Cannon of two capital crimes: the attempted murder of "an unfortunate gentleman" who is, presumably, the note's author, and sodomy, a crime implicit in the reference to Cannon as a "rotten catamite" and his rechristening as "Molly."[45] It also threatens the launch of a campaign of defamation, perhaps to pressure Cannon into dropping his charges against Cleland. For Cleland is certainly the note's author: it is his "proper handwriting," and it exhibits his signature rhetorical extremism. It presents a ghoulish portrait of Cannon—vampiric, riddled with corruption, oxymoronically linking the youth of the catamite to the rottenness of decaying age—and constructs a gruesome scenario of mother and son bound in a vicious compact against a virtuous "unfortunate" gentleman. Why the Cannons repaid his kind act, saving Thomas's life, with repeated attempts to kill him, Cleland leaves unexplained, perhaps to intensify the aura of monstrosity. Certainly he means to incite feelings of horror at the crimes he alleges, and terror in Cannon at the prospect of exposure.

Cleland's note was found on Cannon's outer door just short of a year after he had been confined to the Fleet. If it was just the latest of a number of "scurrilous and libelous" papers, as Cannon alleges, Cleland had been on the attack for twelve months and, if anything, was ramping up the levels of violence and menace, as this was the first time Cannon had gone to the law. There is no way of knowing if there is any truth to Cleland's allegation of a poisoning plot— certainly Elizabeth Cannon, the aging widow of the dean of Lincoln, makes for an unlikely murderess—but what stands out is the charge that they "poisoned

[him] *five times* with common arsenic," which implies that he saw them regularly over an extended period, presumably as their guest at home, plied with tea and cakes. Cannon's affidavit reinforces this suggestion of an ongoing relationship, as when he asserts that "he is well Acquainted with the handwriting of John Cleland . . . having often seen him write." If such words as "well acquainted" and "often" suggest intimacy over time, there is more: it is Cleland's *handwriting* with which Cannon is well acquainted, for he has "often seen him write." His words imply not just friendship but friendship centered on writing—that is, literary collaboration. This, in turn, might explain the otherwise astonishing coincidence that Cannon and Cleland, within a few weeks of this note, would separately publish the only two explicit descriptions of male same-sex desire in eighteenth-century English literature: the sodomitical episode from volume 2 of the *Woman of Pleasure* and Cannon's long-lost *Ancient and Modern Pederasty Investigated and Exemplify'd.*[46]

Both of these were published anonymously, and both got their respective authors into serious legal trouble when their identities were found out. Cleland's text was published about a week after Cannon's affidavit (appropriately enough, on St. Valentine's Day), whereas Cannon's was first advertised in the April 1749 issue of the *Gentleman's Magazine.*[47] Considering the risk he was taking in writing about "pederasty" at all, it was foolhardy of Cannon to bring Cleland's incriminating note to the law's attention so close to the time of his own pamphlet's publication, but it was equally reckless for Cleland to be broadcasting accusations of sodomy when his book was being readied for sale. Both seem more intent on ruining the other's life than on protecting their own, and it is the very excessiveness of their enmity that suggests a collaboration gone disastrously awry. When intimacy turned to hatred and Cannon had the person "who had saved his life" thrown into prison, the destitute Cleland, denied his family's help, could finally think of nothing but to show the long-gestating *Woman of Pleasure* to "some whose opinion I unfortunately preferred to my own, and being made to consider it as a ressource, I published the first part."[48] This appeared on 21 November 1748, after he had spent nine months in the Fleet; three months later, the second volume came out.

How Cleland first made contact with a person from the book trade whose opinion he unfortunately preferred to his own is unrecorded, and there were some efforts to mask the publisher's identity, but the key figure was the young and not risk-averse bookseller and author Ralph Griffiths, who dealt with Cleland either directly or via his brother Fenton.[49] When Ralph Griffiths was arrested for obscenity in November 1749 (that is, a year after the first volume of

Cleland's novel came out), he stated, when "asked whether he knows who is the Author, printer or publisher thereof,"

> That some time last Winter his Brother Fenton Griffith came to him & asked his advice whether it would be safe for him to Publish the said Book; That at that Time there was only one of the said Volumes finished & the said Fenton Griffith giving the Examinant a description of the said Volume the Examinant did advise him to publish it & the Examinant believes he did publish the same at his the said Fenton Griffiths Shop in Exeter Exchange in the Strand & supplied the Booksellers with it.
>
> The Examinant says that his Brother told him that he had the Copy of the said Work from one J. Cleeland who the Examinant believes, from what his Brother has told him, is the Author of the said Work.[50]

But while Ralph Griffiths's account is confirmed by Thomas Parker, the book's printer, it is almost certain that Ralph was the real publisher and Fenton largely a front. Fenton is not known for publishing anything else; indeed, as William Epstein notes, he "seems to have dropped from sight" almost immediately after Cleland's novel appeared, and there is no record of any examination of him when the others involved in the work's production were questioned.[51] He may have been his brother's agent in acquiring the text from Cleland; he certainly lent his name to the book's title page, which identifies the publisher as "G. Fenton." But it was Ralph who was arrested, who published (the next year, under his own name) an expurgated version of the novel he had commissioned from Cleland, and who took Cleland on as a writer for hire after his release from the Fleet in March 1749. It is probable, in fact, that Cleland's release from prison was arranged by Ralph Griffiths, and that in taking over or paying off Cleland's debts he engaged Cleland to work for him in a form of indentured servitude. Although Cleland was reputed to have sold Griffiths the copyright to the *Woman of Pleasure* for just twenty guineas, the fact that his creditors' complaint was dismissed within three weeks of the second volume's appearance seems to indicate Griffiths's mediation, and in fact Griffiths testified the following year that his motive for asking Cleland to prepare an expurgated text of the *Woman of Pleasure* "was that Mr. Cleeland owed him a Sum of money & as Cleeland was going abroad he thought it was the only Method to get his Debt paid."[52] His youthful collaboration with Carmichael gave Cleland his ticket of leave from the Fleet, but the freedom he gained was itself a new form of dependence.

In the course of a half dozen years Cleland had fallen from a "man of distinction" whom the Portuguese ministers of state looked to for advice to a man condemned to "the meanness of writing for a bookseller" and lamenting his "low abject condition, that of a writer for Bread."[53] In fact he was lucky in his bookseller: Griffiths was ambitious, energetic, a person of wide-ranging interests. Soon after Cleland's release he started up the *Monthly Review*, which offered Cleland a venue for some thirty critical articles over the next few years, and he gave Cleland what seems like a pretty free hand to choose his other literary projects. But like such later *Monthly Review* contributors as Smollett and Goldsmith, Cleland bridled at any hint of subordination—whether to a bookseller, theatrical producer, or parent—and Griffiths, who played a key role both in the dissemination of a new literary culture in the eighteenth century and in what these writers saw as the mechanization and prostitution of authorship itself, was one focus of their resentment. Goldsmith, who wrote for the *Monthly Review* from 1757 to 1763, complained in 1761 of "that fatal revolution whereby writing is converted to a mechanic trade; and booksellers, instead of the great, become the patrons and paymasters of men of genius."[54] Such complaints were in fact already a cliché, as was the equation of authorship with prostitution, going back many decades and given ludicrous form in Richard Savage's Iscariot Hackney, the title figure of *An Author to be Lett* (1728).[55] To a person as jealous of his reputation as Cleland, the reduction to a cliché, the stock figure of a "distrest poet" (as in Hogarth's engraving of 1737), would have been galling, and it was Thomas Cannon who had driven him to the step of "becoming the author of a Book I disdain to defend," as he wrote to Stanhope, "and wish, from my Soul, buried and forgot." His fault was not having written the book but the public misstep of "becoming [its] author"—that is, selling the text "for Bread."

While Cleland "new-cast" the Bombay manuscript in prison and placed his future in the hands of a bookseller, Cannon made arrangements to have his own manuscript printed. In late February or early March 1749, according to the politically dissident printer John Purser, "Mr Cannon, the Author, brought him a Copy of a Pamphlet, to print, intituled, Antient & Modern Pederasty, &c."[56] When Purser objected to the title, "Cannon assur'd him on his Honour, that the whole Pamphlet throughout was so far from encouraging the Vice, that it was Design'd to explode the Crime and make it hatefull to all Mankind; and that it was wrote in such a manner, that it could not offend the nicest Ear; and that he would justifie every Tittle it contain'd before any Court in England."[57] Despite his assurances, Cannon did all he could to conceal the work's contents from the printers, even correcting his own proofs, but Purser's assistant Hugh Morgan later told Purser he suspected it was "a bad Pamphlet," and Purser in turn accused Cannon of having lied to him. Cannon then "made an elaborate

Display of Learning, in which he talked of Petronius, Arbiter, and Aretine, and quoted other antient Writers Greek as well as Roman," but seeing this wasn't working, he returned to his earlier claim, that he was "so perfectly sensible of the just and lawful Intention and Execution of his Piece that he would put his Name to it." Purser, according to Morgan, was "in some sort pacified by what Cannon said," but he wanted as little to do with the inflammatory pamphlet as possible, and insisted that Cannon take all the copies away as soon as he had paid for Purser's paper and time.[58]

In these negotiations, Cannon presented himself as an independent scholar, a gentleman-amateur—a far cry from a writer for bread. He even left "an old Fashion'd Gold Watch" with Purser as security for payment—probably passed down from his father the dean or grandfather the bishop, a token of inherited gentility. Despite what he had told Purser, he did not "put his Name" to the text. It was published, like Cleland's, anonymously, but unlike Cleland's it lacked even a false publisher's name. It's unknown how many copies were printed or how many sold; a printer named Robert Swan bought "several," and Cannon hired a city porter named Robert Tomlinson "to carry the said Book to several Pamphlet Shops, in order to their being sold," but that is the last we hear of them.[59]

The work would have vanished entirely had it not been for Cleland's desire for revenge against Cannon for his year in prison (and for the poisonings, if they were anything other than a complete fabrication). Nine months after volume 2 of the *Woman of Pleasure*, eight months after Cleland's release, seven months after *Ancient and Modern Pederasty* was listed for sale, Cleland was arrested again, on 8 November 1749, for obscenity. In his self-exculpatory letter to Stanhope, he offered, in addition to an account of the pressures under which he had consented to the novel's publication, an argument against prosecution. The wisest course, he suggests, is simply to let the book fade into oblivion, to let it lie "buried and forgot." Convinced that the move to prosecute was the work of "my Lords the Bishops," Cleland counters that "they can take no step towards punishing the Author that will not powerfully contribute to the notoriety of the Book, and spread what they cannot wish supprest more than I do." Cleland supports his claim with a recent example: "It is not eight months," he writes,

since the Son of a *Dean* and Grandson of a *Bishop* was mad and wicked enough to Publish a Pamphlet evidently in defence of *Sodomy*, advertised in all the papers. This was perhaps rather overlooked than tolerated—What was the consequence? Why, it is at this instant so thoroughly forgot that few I believe know that ever such

a Pamphlet existed: Whereas, if My Lords the Bishops had been so injudicious as
to stir this stench they might have indeed provoked the public indignation, but its
curiosity too: and all to punish a crazy wretch, who would, I dare swear, not be un-
ambitious of taking Vanini for his Model.[60]

However apt the example, Cleland's goal was clearly to direct his readers' attention to a work that, without his intervention, would indeed have been "thoroughly forgot." By referring to Cannon indirectly, through his ecclesiastical lineage, Cleland takes an apparently irresistible dig at the clergy—more of whom,
he says earlier, "bought [the *Memoirs*], in proportion, than any other distinction
of men"—while also slyly fingering Cannon. He goes further, characterizing
Cannon's work as a "defence of *Sodomy*," and offers the judicial murder of the
freethinker and philosopher Lucilio Vanini (1585–1619)—burned at the stake,
after having his tongue cut out, on charges of atheism—as an appropriate
"Model" for Cannon's punishment.

In the short term his reminder had the desired effect: two months after Cleland's letter, the secretary of state called on the attorney general, Dudley Ryder,
to prosecute Cannon, the "Author of a most wicked, and mischievous Book,
intitled, 'Ancient, and Modern Pederasty investigated, and exemplified.' "[61] Cleland had successfully set in motion the machinery of legal persecution in which
Cannon would be caught for the next several years. In that sense he had the last
laugh, and there is no record of any further exchange between them. Yet if the
tail end of their relationship was a depressing call-and-response of cruelty, defamation, and threat, it had some unintended and beneficial (to us if not to them)
effects: Cannon, by hounding him over a debt, forced Cleland into professional
authorship; Cleland, by informing on Cannon, ensured the preservation of his
"wicked and mischievous" work in the legal archives, as the next chapter will
show. Each of them, by lashing out, secured the other's literary immortality.
Hatred, too, is a form of collaboration.

Sodomites
(1748–1749)

On 27 May 1781, when Cleland was seventy years old and living "in the Savoy," off the Strand near Somerset House, he was paid a visit by the lawyer and antiquary Josiah Beckwith. Beckwith had read Cleland's treatises on etymology and the origins of language and wanted to discuss some points with "the learned and ingenious Author." Cleland seems to have told him that he had had a government pension of £200 taken away "on Account of his Publications," and Beckwith, noting Cleland's "sarcastical" treatment of "Monarchical Government" in his writing, comments that "it is no Wonder, in this Age, that he lost his Place or Pension . . . or that he should pass under the Censure of being a Sodomite, as he now does, and in Consequence thereof Persons of Character decline visiting him."[1] Beckwith's note, written on the end paper of a volume of Cleland's linguistic tracts now in the Cambridge University Library, comes as a revelation, for it seems to preserve a "knowledge" that is ordinarily lost: the intimate knowledge transmitted in gossip, rumor, whispered asides. The "truth" of gossip may not always be true, but it gives access to what is thought to be hidden, and of all such secrets, the secret of prohibited sexual desires or acts—even if the secret is a lie, but especially when it confirms

what we already suspect—is the most thrilling. Cleland a sodomite! How could such a revelation not profoundly affect our sense of his position in eighteenth-century culture, or not lead us to read his texts in a different light?

Beckwith's note certainly marks Cleland as an outcast: the author as pariah. But its final sentence is at the very least ambiguous. At first glance it seems simply to mean "it's no wonder people think he's a sodomite," as if there were something in Cleland's appearance or conduct that fit Beckwith's preconceived notion of what a sodomite is like. But in context, the sodomite remark is subsidiary to Beckwith's larger point, which pertains to Cleland's contrarian political stance, his "sarcastical" derision of the monarchy. The "no Wonder" Beckwith expresses applies to the contention that "*in this Age*" such political unorthodoxy can lead to a loss of place, or the strategic circulation of socially damaging rumors. Far from in any straightforward sense "outing" Cleland, Beckwith's note might instead offer an instance of the ways in which the *accusation* of sodomy could be deployed as a device to discredit other forms of marginality, as if political and sexual deviation were akin.

In practice, of course, they often are. It is no accident that when he needed a printer for his pamphlet on pederasty, Thomas Cannon approached the accused seditionary John Purser, for Purser had handled dangerous texts, had battled the censors, and might relish (or at least not fear) such a moral provocation. Under the law, seditious, blasphemous, and obscene libel were types of a single crime, all held to be threats to "the peace of the king," as Attorney General Sir Philip Yorke contended in the trial of the bookseller Edmund Curll in 1728. Moral crimes (sodomy, obscenity) *are* political crimes, Yorke argued, "for government is no more than public order which is morality."[2] For that reason, sodomy, the most egregious of all crimes against not only morality but also nature, could stand in figurally for a host of other offenses, from antimonarchism to atheism (of which Cleland also was accused, according to Beckwith), which means that "the Censure of being a Sodomite" might not reflect the intimate or hidden truth of the subject in question but rather act as a kind of libelous shorthand, a way of discrediting or silencing a contrarian voice.

Yet in Cleland's case, this "Censure" was not just politically expedient or figural but closely bound up with the course of his authorial career. The rumors of sodomy that bedeviled him for much of his life—starting, perhaps, with Cowan's allusion in Bombay to unspecified "Principles & Practices" that made the young Cleland "unworthy of even my Horsewhip," and persisting to Cleland's dying years, as the Beckwith anecdote clearly shows—point to something real. Not that, as things stand, the biographical question of Cleland's sexual practices or desires can definitely be answered: lacking a journal of Boswell-ian candor, one can only make likely inferences from a range of frequently tendentious, ambiguous, multiply voiced texts, his own as well as others'. But what I argue in this chapter, in juxtaposed readings of Cleland's and Cannon's forever-conjoined first books—*Memoirs of a Woman of Pleasure* and *Ancient and Modern Pederasty Investigated and Exemplify'd*—is that the texts themselves are sodomitical in precisely the ways that the dominant *anti*sodomite discourses of the period warned readers to beware. They are unnatural, in that they question settled notions of what "nature" is; disruptive, in that they challenge fixed cat-egories of identity; preposterous, in that they elicit and embody "impossible," absurd desires. Both authors thus explode the moralistic lexicon of antisod-omite and anti-molly writing, though they both make canny use of its rhetori-cal conventions, masking their lubricious and playful depictions as evidence gathered in order to condemn what Cannon calls "the *Detested Love*."[3]

Such masking, however, was not actually all that effective, to judge from the harassment and threats of prosecution both authors suffered. If both aimed to disguise their "inflaming" or impassioned accounts of same-sex desire as stringent denunciations, the texts were immediately understood as fanning the very fires they pretended to put out.[4] In that respect, the censorial readings of eighteenth-century moralists are more persuasive than those of some of the *Woman of Pleasure*'s more recent critics, who argue that the novel represses or condemns the sodomitical or otherwise deviant desires that Fanny narrates.[5] As for Cannon, the suppression of *Ancient and Modern Pederasty* has meant that no one, it seems, even saw it between 1750 and 2007. But Cleland's text, too, was dismembered and suppressed for almost as long, something its recent familiarity tends to make us forget. Despite its clandestine, underground cir-culation, the *Woman of Pleasure* was only legally cleared for publication in New York State in 1963, in the rest of the United States in 1966, and (tacitly) in the United Kingdom in 1970. The sodomitical episode I discuss in this chapter was largely unavailable until the publication of the Oxford and Penguin texts, edited by Peter Sabor and Peter Wagner, respectively, in 1985; before then, the scene, if cited at all, was attributed to the little-known sodomitical bookseller Samuel Drybutter (so little known, in fact, that because of his curious name, he was thought by some scholars to be an invented figure). Both Cleland and Cannon, in the midst of their legal travails, expressed the wish that their sod-omitical texts might be "buried in Oblivion," and their wishes were very nearly granted.[6]

Detestable Practices

Virtually every moral commentator on the supposed growth of sodomy in the early to mid-eighteenth century justifies the campaign against it on the basis of the danger it poses to Britain: it is a crime not just against nature but nation. Sodomy may be suited to the unnatural inhabitants of other nations, but it has, or should have, no purchase in Britain. Yet it flourishes, having been "translated," in the words of one author, "from the *Sadomitical* [sic] Original, or from the *Turkish* and *Italian* Copies into *English*."[7] In another text, the figure of transplantation is used in place of translation:

> Since that most detestable and unnatural Sin of *Sodomy*, which but rarely appears in our Histories, and that among Monsters and Prodigies, has been of late transplanted from the hotter Climates to our more temperate Country, and has dared to shew its hideous Face among a People that formerly had it in the utmost Abhorrence; it is now become the indispensable Duty of the Magistrate to attack this horrible Monster in Morality, by a vigorous Exertion of those good Laws, that have justly made that vile Sin a Capital Crime.[8]

But if sodomy is not only unnatural but naturally un-English—if it has always been held in the "utmost Abhorrence" in Britain—what can account for this modern infestation?

Whether transplanted or translated, sodomy is represented in all the antisodomite texts as a form of contagion, a plague whose primary mode of transmission is not bodily but cultural. It comes from the East, from Sodom itself by way of Turkey and, almost always, Italy. In some texts it comes uninvited, an insidious and contaminating vice; in others, more commonly, it comes as the bad effect of cross-cultural emulation. This model is implicit in the notion of *translation* either from an ancient original or "from the *Turkish* and *Italian* Copies into English," and is fully elaborated in the 1749 *Reasons for the Growth of Sodomy*:

> But of all the Customs *Effeminacy* has produc'd, none more hateful, predominant, and pernicious, than that of the Mens *Kissing* each other. This *Fashion* was brought over from *Italy*, (the *Mother* and *Nurse* of *Sodomy*); where the *Master* is oftner *Intriguing* with his *Page*, than a *fair Lady*. And not only in that *Country*, but in *France*, which copies from them, the *Contagion* is diversify'd, and the Ladies (in the *Nunneries*) are criminally *amorous* of each other, in a *Method* too gross for Expression.[9]

Kissing is not only repellent in itself (the pamphlet's author equates it with "slavering" and "slopping") but is "the first *Inlet* to the detestable Sin of *Sodomy*" and thus a vehicle for the corruption of youth. If the custom were abolished, "the Sons of *Sodom* would lose many *Proselytes*, in being baffled out of one of their principal Advances; for under Pretence of extraordinary Friendship, they intice unwary Youth from this first Step, to more detestable Practices, taking many Times the Advantage of their Necessities, to decoy them to their Ruin."[10] As with the broader "translation" of sodomy from the Middle East to Turkey to Italy to England, the mode of transmission within England is emulation: the neophyte imitates the customs he sees and insensibly falls into more "detestable Practices."

The fashion of men kissing one another, compared to the "more manly, more friendly, and more decent" custom of shaking hands, is a predatory form of initiation or schooling in vice, and the schoolboy often appears in antisodomite texts as a figure of moral vulnerability. Sometimes the threat was from dissolute schoolmasters or tutors: the future attorney general Dudley Ryder, who would later be assigned the prosecution of both Cannon and Cleland, wrote in 1716 that "it is dangerous sending a young man that is beautiful to Oxford."[11] In other cases the threat came from men who loitered in the vicinity of schools, as in the 1760 trial of Richard Branson, found guilty of attempted sodomy against a "poor scholar" at God's Gift College in Dulwich. In his summation to the court, the council for the Crown "demonstrated the fatal Consequence of this wicked Attempt": had Branson "prevailed with this Lad, now Sixteen Years old, to commit this horrid and most detestable Crime, he would have infected all the others; and, as in Course of Years they grew big enough, they would leave the College to go into the World and spread this cursed Poison, while those left behind would be training the Children to the same vitious Practices."[12] Sodomitical inclination is infectious and irresistible once it gains a foothold; it passes from schoolboy to schoolboy and friend to friend or older to younger, but while transmission involves bodily intimacy, the inclination itself is imitative rather than rooted in bodily anomaly. There's nothing about this crew of schoolboys that marks them as specially susceptible; the presumption is that, once exposed, every schoolboy is a sodomite.[13]

The notion of universal susceptibility coexists uneasily with an essentializing discourse that configured the sodomite as not only perverse but of a different species or race—from the use of such phrases as "the Sons of *Sodom*" to the notion of sodomy as a transplant "from the hotter Climates to our more temperate Country." This unstable mix of tendencies to read sodomy as alien to or, contrarily, latent in our nature is a notable feature of English eighteenth-century antisodomite writings, whose very incoherence only adds to the anxiety aroused by a propensity both far-reaching and outwardly undetectable.

Cannon's "Curst Pederasts"

In the text of his indictment of John Purser, printer of Cannon's *Ancient and Modern Pederasty Investigated and Exemplify'd*, Attorney General Dudley Ryder deploys the full range of antisodomite rhetoric to convey the danger Cannon's writing poses to the nation—in particular, to the nation's (male) youth. Purser, he thunders, "being a Person of a Wicked and Depraved Mind and Disposition," printed the work in order to "Debauch Poison and Infect the Minds of all the Youth of this Kingdom and to Raise Excite and Create in the Minds of all the said Youth most Shocking and Abominable Ideas and Sentiments beneath the Dignity of Humane Nature" (39). As Ryder explains, the mere act of reading such a work not only instills novel and illicit desires in readers' minds but also inspires them to emulation: it brings them "into a State of Wickedness Lewdness and Brutality and more Especially into the Love and Practice of that unnatural detestable and odious crime of Sodomy" (39–40). As in the case of the Dulwich schoolboys cited above, sodomitical desire is characterized as imitative, infectious, and irresistible: the reader experiences an apparently uncontrollable arousal or excitement and is impelled to enact the perverse desires unleashed by the text, ineluctably drawn into "the Love *and Practice*" of what Cannon's work represents. Ryder's argument, tellingly, is as incoherent as those of other antisodomite screeds, for while it represents all of Cannon's potential readers as helplessly susceptible to the text's seductive power, it also describes the "Ideas and Sentiments" that reading "Raise[s] Excite[s] and Create[s]" as "beneath the Dignity of"—contrary to—"Humane Nature," which the text thus seems able to counteract.

When Ryder presented his case before the Court of King's Bench in Trinity term (June–July) 1751, the author in question had been out of the country for over a year—"stung," according to a later statement by his mother, "with the utmost remorse of Conscience at the heinousness of his guilt, and not daring to throw himself upon the Justice of his offended Country, whilst the Memory of his Crime was yet recent."[14] Once the secretary of state, alerted by Cleland's jailhouse letter, ordered Ryder to begin legal proceedings against Cannon and his printer in January 1750, Cannon wisely took flight, probably after destroying any copies he had of the work, and remained abroad for three years. The only copies of the pamphlet known to have survived are two that Newcastle sent to Ryder with the order to prosecute; these would have been needed in order to copy the offending passages into the indictment itself, consistent with the practice in other obscenity cases of the period.[15] These copies may have been kept with the indictment and other documents in the case for a time but at some point were lost, so all of Cannon's text that does survive does so in the form Ryder's clerk or clerks transcribed it in the indictment of Purser, whose trial went ahead in 1751 after Ryder decided not to wait any longer for Cannon's reappearance. The text as presented in the indictment probably comprises the bulk of the original pamphlet, and given its evidentiary role, the transcription would need to have been reliable, although we are necessarily at some remove from the text Cannon saw through the press.[16]

After summarizing the gist of the charge against Purser, for printing Cannon's "Wicked Lewd Nasty Filthy Bawdy Impious and Obscene Libel" (40), the indictment then gives the first of several excerpts from the original. Cannon frames the text—rather slyly, considering his family's connections to the church—by contrasting the Christian present to the pagan past: "Among the many Unspeakable Benefits which redound to the World from the Christian Religion, no one makes a more conspicuous Figure than the Demolition of Pederasty. That celebrated Passion, Seal'd by Sensualists, espoused by Philosophers, enshrin'd by Kings, is now exploded with one Accord and Disown'd by the meanest Beggar" (40). The opposition seems orthodox enough, but a certain teasing ambiguity is apparent from the start. Why, for example, are the benefits of Christianity "Unspeakable"? That word seems to allude to the stock description of sodomy as a crime "not to be named among Christians," as if to invert the relationship between the crime and the religion that condemns it. "Pederasty" itself is almost always conjoined with terms of admiration: in this sentence Cannon calls it a "celebrated Passion" and links it favorably to philosophers and kings, whereas only "the meanest Beggar" disowns it. Even if he claims that it has been "exploded with one Accord," the sentence nevertheless sets the beggar and those others into separate camps, associating the first with terms of violent destruction ("demolition," "exploded") and the second with terms of cultivation and civility ("celebrated," "espoused," "enshrin'd").

Developing this contrast between ancient and modern, Cannon writes that now, "since Fashion discountenances, Law punishes, God forbids, the *Detested Love*, we may sure discuss it with Freedom, and the most philosophical Exactness . . . free from any Apprehension of exciting in any Breast so preposterous, and Severe-treated an Inclination" (40). In claiming this, he disavows the possibility that delineating perverse desires might also excite them. Yet when he proceeds to inquire "what Charm then held so many Sages and Emperors, clear Heads and hale Hearts" among the ancients, he slips into a lascivious reverie on the male form that in its sensual extravagance betrays his own arousal as it seeks to arouse the reader:

> Inform me, what was that which like a chrystal expanded Lake drew all Mankind to bathe entranc'd in Joys, too mighty every one for our poor Utterance? . . . Was it the Perfection of a gradually lessening Shape? or, you in turn demand, was it the Firmness, yet Delicacy of Masculine Limbs? Hush; the Beauty-engrossing Sex will over-hear us. In Time, was it the more equally close Pressure, a certain Part afforded? (40)

Cannon builds on his initial association of "the Detested Love" with philosophers and kings by affiliating it here with "Sages and Emperors, clear Heads and hale Hearts," but now there is no one in the antisodomite camp; instead, "*all* Mankind . . . bathe[s] entranc'd" in unutterable "Joys," in contrast with which the Christian "Demolition" looks decidedly unalluring. As he will do repeatedly in later passages, Cannon praises male bodies at the expense of female, mocking the latter as "the Beauty-engrossing Sex," which is represented here as spying on the "us" of his all-male audience. So rhapsodically is the male form described that it is other-sex desire that begins to look perverse and unaccountable.

In the first part of his pamphlet, then, while Cannon makes use of a well-worn authorial gambit—moralistically framing his text as a denunciation of the practices and pleasures he goes on to "investigate" and "exemplify"—his voluptuary language and ironic asides give the game away, so that phrases such as "Detested Love" or "abominable Practice" become themselves objects of ironic deflation. When he writes, "With wond'rous Boast curst Pederasts advance, that Boy-love ever was the top Refinement of most enlighten'd Ages; or, never in Supreme Degree prevail'd where liberal Knowledge had not fix'd his Seat, and banish'd crampsoul Prejudice" (40), the single word "curst" is rhetorically overbalanced by the pederasts' language of enlightenment, setting "liberal Knowledge" against the "crampsoul Prejudice" that pronounces curses in the first place. Despite the obligatory execrations, there is no mistaking where the author's sympathies lie: with "polish'd Greece" and "all-subduing Rome" and the "proud Streams of Learning, Taste, and Pederasty" (41) that flowed from one to the other.

Cannon's rather perfunctory moral posturing is also belied by his editorial choices. By beginning his anthology of ancient texts with Lucian's "most witty" dialogues on Ganymede, he signals his real aim of amusing the reader: the two dialogues are "so extremely entertaining, I make no Doubt, they will be with Pleasure accepted" (41). This is why he adapts his sources so freely: "I paraphrase, or, use ancient Writers only as a Basis: If you like what you meet with, is it not enough?" (41). Instead of following through on his earlier claim to examine "the Detested Love" with "philosophical exactness," he admits here that he aims only at pleasure. An earlier translator of Lucian, Thomas Heywood, prefaced his 1637 version of the Ganymede story with the statement that "Jove's Masculine love this Fable reprehends."[17] Cannon, by contrast, leaves the moralizing to Jupiter's jealous wife and luxuriates in the "Masculine love" Jupiter expresses to his shepherd boy. "It shall be my seeking to fire you with fervid Kisses," he tells Ganymede, "to glue to you my pressing Limbs; to mix, and make one common Essence with you. Mercury, pledge him Immortality in a Cup of Nectar, that invigorated he may meet the nervous Joy. Now and but now, I find myself in Heaven" (43). Moral judgment is beside the point; instead, Cannon lingers over the refined sensuality of Lucian's scenario, the deliquescence or fluidity of desiring bodies.

After the second of the Lucianic dialogues, the transcription of Cannon's text is broken into by a drab legal refrain that serves to join one excerpt to the next in the indictment: "And in another part thereof according to the tenour following (to wit)," here followed by a passage that reads like a bawdy snippet from a medical advice column on whether or not it's acceptable for a man to "mingle" with a pregnant woman. (The answer is no, and the implication is that since this would be a waste in reproductive terms, he might just as well scatter his seed elsewhere.) After this, the refrain, and then an extended passage from Petronius's *Satyricon*. These shifts in register exemplify the interpretive problems posed by the document as a whole. It is impossible to know how the various fragments quoted in the indictment might have been arranged in the original or how much is missing or, on another level, what principle of selection led to the incorporation of some parts but not others. The effect of a chaotic miscellany is surely more pronounced than it would have been in the original pamphlet, but in any form, it must have been a hodgepodge, with passages from Lucian and Petronius next to one-liners about the Duchess of Cleveland and the Duke of Orleans's confessor, veering in style from erotic rhapsody to scholarly essay to dirty joke. The three chief narrative sequences—Lucian's Ganymede, Petronius's story of Eumolpus and the insatiable boy, and the London-set narrative of Amorio and Hyacinth—are separated by bits of gossip, a report by Lucian of

a philosophical debate on same-sex desire, misogynistic commentaries about
Lucian, possibly by Cannon himself, and sniggering schoolboy asides. False
endings and passages transcribed twice increase the effect of randomness, and
when the legal formulas are repeated toward the end of the document, it is as if
the scribe thought he had finished, only to be told to tack on another fragment.
But if the text is formally incoherent, so is the category of "pederasty" itself,
which assumes a multiplicity of historical and aesthetic shapes over the course
of Cannon's literary meanderings.

The Jupiter-Ganymede and Eumolpus-pupil narratives embody the classic
pederastic relationship between a mature male (tutor or god) and a youth whom
he initiates into sexuality. The difference in age and maturity corresponds to a
difference in power, a difference in sexual role (penetrator versus "pathic," or
catamite) and, at least at the outset, a difference in desire: the older is drawn
to the beauty of the younger, whom he designs to ravish or seduce.[18] But, as
Cannon notes, the Eumolpus story offers a twist on the traditional pattern: "We
commonly conceive the Pathic's Part disagreeable; But Petronius, whose Experience is hardly questionable, represents him sharing in the accurst Rapture"
(45). Eumolpus at first thinks of the boy as a passive object of desire, and over
three nights he vows to Venus that if, while the boy sleeps, she allows Eumolpus
first to kiss, then touch, then "enjoy" him, he will give the boy a series of more
and more extravagant gifts. The reader, however, knows that the boy only feigns
sleep. On the second night, Eumolpus relates, "the sweet Youngster hearing
what I bid for the Joy, moves Insensibly towards me, afraid, I suppose, of my
falling asleep in Reality: But I quickly reassure him, and slide my Hand over
his delicious Body: 'till grasping Love's Bolt, [I] spurt myself away, plunging in
a Gulph of unutterable Delight" (45). The next morning, Eumolpus observes on
the face of the boy "a new Soul-stealing Desire, raised by my rambling Touches,
[which] makes itself felt within and diffuses over him a Strength of Lustre beyond Description" (46). Although he only recognizes it retrospectively, Eumolpus has by this point ceded the dominant desiring role to the boy, who at the
story's comic denouement so wearies his older lover that the latter threatens to
tell all to the boy's father if the boy doesn't let him sleep.

Playing with the classic pederastic paradigm, Cannon notes the variability of
desire and its objects, the way desire can multiply and migrate from one subject
to another, unsettling the distinction between active and passive, subject and
object, male and female.[19] As if to emphasize this last point, Cannon includes
two anecdotes of "pederastic" other-sex desire as commentaries on the Eumolpus narrative. In both, a woman appropriates for herself the role of catamite,

assuming by witty and perverse inclination the place of a subservient boy and thus making a hash of the binarisms presumed to operate in both other-sex and same-sex relations. Taking on the ostensibly passive, or "pathic," role, she asserts her own authority, assuming the power to dictate to her male lovers the terms of their sexual interactions and to articulate for herself what counts as pleasure. The "rampant Duchess of Cleveland," in the second anecdote, after what Cannon calls "a usual Bout" (that is, "normal," nonpederastic sex), "wou'd turn her . . . Rump to the rapturous Spark [her lover], and say; you have pleas'd yourself; now please me" (47). In doing so, she literally embodies the characterization of sodomitical desire as "preposterous," in that she turns the body back to front (*prae/posterus*) and reverses "natural" expectations of who takes pleasure where, and in what actions.

Over the course of the text, the category of pederasty opens up to accommodate a range of nonnormative, upside-down expressions of desire. But even if, in some passages, Cannon allows for a pragmatic distinction between "extraordinary" and "ordinary" desires, he uncouples this from any concomitant belief in a meaningful boundary between the unnatural and the natural. In one later passage an unidentified speaker recounts meeting "an abhorred, and too polish'd Pederast" who, "attack'd upon the Head, that his Desire was unnatural, thus wrestled in Argument; Unnatural Desire is a Contradiction in Terms; downright Nonsense. Desire is an amatory Impulse of the inmost human Parts: Are not they, however constructed, and consequently impelling, Nature?" (54). The Pederast, to be sure, is "abhorr'd," his rhetoric "too polish'd"; Cannon is careful to observe the posture of moral denunciation. But this posture is only fitfully assumed, whereas with each new episode or anecdote the distinction between natural and unnatural becomes less secure. Rather than referring to a single, insistently hierarchical model of male-male sexual relations, pederasty in Cannon's incoherent anthology becomes a figure for the undermining or vacuation of fixed categories and roles.

This is nowhere more vivid than in the story of Amorio and Hyacinth, which, fittingly, begins at a masquerade. In this playground of malleable and imaginary selves, the "young and blooming" Amorio is struck by lightning in the form of "a Lady," who without much need for prompting tells Amorio her "Brief and sorrowful Adventures" (47) as a virtuous Devonshire farm girl seduced by an aristocrat and abandoned by him in London without money or friends. One day, she says, she was accosted by a "genteel Fellow" in Somerset Gardens to whom she told her tale of seduction. The fellow responded "with Transport" and prevailed on her to become his mistress, but he proved a tyrant. She has resolved to leave him, but "Honour and Justice" require her to stay for the three weeks that remain of the "engag'd Time" for which he has paid her fifty guineas. Still, as her "fondling Tyrant is now in the Country," her sense of honor is not so restrictive that she cannot invite "the agreeable Amorio" to supper at her chambers. Amorio finds her story "transporting," as had her tyrant before, and inflamed, in equal parts, by "a delicious Repast, in which yet Elegance prevails over Luxury, inspiring French Wine, and the [Ladies] Face where every Moment a new Charm is quickening," he carries her to bed, "where Incumbrances quickly off, he finds in his Clasp a Body past Imagination delicate; but of Gender masculine" (49–50).

At this point, the reader's surprise is likely equal to Amorio's, but for Cannon this twist is only a prelude:

> Surprize invades; yet more predominates Desire; which becomes absolute, when Hyacinth (so let's name the guilty Boy) mortify'd at the Deliberation, then speaks in a Voice, to which every Melody lends it's [sic] Aid; My dear *Amorio* does not enfold a Woman; but one, who more than Woman *Grasps*, and *Binds*. Penetrating *Love* takes the Meaning; and the most libidinous Fire ever felt by our wondring Glower, seizes his panting Frame. He is quickly piloted into a Streight whose potent Cling draws all the Man in clammy streams away. (50)

Amorio is happy to transfer the desire he thought he felt for "a Lady" to another object. Indeed, it seems as if the highest degree of "libidinous Fire" is aroused by the surprise of Hyacinth's sex as a sort of riddle ("who more than Woman *Grasps*, and *Binds*"). In this respect his desire runs parallel to ours as readers: similarly piqued by a surprising turn in the story, we too are drawn further in. "Penetrating *Love*," which is both the phallus and the insight gained from desire, allows Amorio to "take the Meaning" of Hyacinth's riddle, but as he enacts the "pederast" to Hyacinth's "pathic," Cannon's imagery and language reverse their roles, or at any rate the erotic dynamics between them. Hyacinth takes the active verbs ("grasps," "binds"), while Amorio's "panting Frame" is emptied of agency, turning him into a sort of dummy. Seized by libidinous fire, "piloted" into Hyacinth's body, "the Man" is at length drawn away "in clammy streams" by Hyacinth's "potent Cling." Amorio's unmanning is integral to his rapture, and not just at this moment. He has been under Hyacinth's control from the start, in relation both to her/his performance of the travesty role of "a Lady" and to his/her narrative authority—for it is primarily through narration that Hyacinth exerts his power over Amorio. Casting himself as the distressed heroine of a seduction narrative, Hyacinth seduces Amorio into seeing him both as a suitable object for compassion and as a kept, and therefore sexually available, woman. Amorio is only the more uncontrollably aroused when he discovers he has been misled in the object of his amorous pursuit.

The riddle that Hyacinth presents—active or passive, desiring or desired, female or male—finds an echo in Amorio's longing to be taken out of himself, embodied in Cannon's strange periphrasis for sexual climax: "draws all the Man in clammy streams away." While the idea of sexual passion as a dissolution of the self is ancient, Cannon makes it new by once again emphasizing the (even literal) fluidity of desire, which allows not just for the dissolution but for the multiplication of selves.[20] Accordingly, the next morning, Amorio, "hugging Hyacinth, crys; Now let me towzle the dear Creature, who so perfectly imitated a Woman. And now Hyacinth says, let me clasp that charming Amorio, who wou'd touch nothing, but a Woman." Both are now other than they were, or other than they thought they were. We might conclude that Amorio was tricked into pederasty by Hyacinth's powers of imitation, or perhaps that other-sex desire, for him, was itself an imitation. Either way, the imitation leads to pleasure, which is precisely the danger that Cannon's pamphlet poses. In its first appearance in the indictment, the Hyacinth-Amorio story ends, charmingly enough, with: "They love away an Hour or two; then rise and recruit with a long Breakfast" (50). But when the later part of the story is repeated some lines later, this is followed by the words "The Lady's Story is the Subject of much Laughter" and then by the two youths preparing to go out "to Billiards" (56). This curious little coda suggests that the whole "Adventure" (47), not just Hyacinth's imitation of a lady, has been a piece of playacting, that they have chosen together to put on this comedy whose effect is to refresh desire. This is never spelled out, but their laughter might be read as a sign of their complicity in devising this amorous playlet, and their pleasure in trying on fictional selves. Their story is "pederastic" not according to the classical model, which their actions seem to parody, but by virtue of its confounding of both sexual and narrative conventions—not only that of pederast and pathic, but those of virtue in distress, the country girl corrupted, and the unfaithful mistress. Pederasty, for Cannon, is just this unfixing of sexual and narrative roles in the pursuit of pleasure—primarily, although not exclusively, between men.[21]

In the absence of more information on Cannon and his milieu, it is impossible to know if he had a particular audience in mind, a coterie of known or imagined readers. The pamphlet does read, however, like a gossipy and in some sense group enterprise. Cannon introduces one passage as "an Anecdote, I have heard"; avers that Amorio himself, now an "antiquated Beau . . . who at this day creeps about St. James's" (47) told him his story; and writes that he encountered the too-polished Pederast who derided the notion of unnatural desire "in a Company where I happen'd" (54) and where others were arguing the point. None of this may be true, but it evokes a subcultural milieu in which certain stories and texts might be passed from hand to hand as shared jokes, vehicles of seduction, or markers of affiliation.[22] If Cannon and Cleland were indeed literary collaborators, they may have been in one another's coterie or moved in overlapping circles, perhaps centered near their houses in the same district, St. James's, where the antiquated Amorio crept about. One might even speculate, given the similar emphasis on sexual riddling and indeterminacy in Cleland's sodomitical writing, that he was the model for Cannon's creeping Amorio and that "antiquated" is targeted insultingly by the younger writer at the middle-aged Cleland. Neither of the two authors can have been far from one another's private thoughts in the period when these two texts took their eventual public form.

Young Sparks Romping

However variegated and mutable Cannon's conception of pederasty may be, everything in his text exemplifies some form of sodomitical practice: unnatural, disruptive, preposterous.[23] In that sense, all the passages belong together. The sodomitical scene from Cleland's *Memoirs of a Woman of Pleasure*, by contrast, strikes many commentators—not least Fanny Hill herself, who narrates it—as anomalous. Of all the licentious scenes Fanny takes part in or observes over the course of her story, this is the only one for which she reserves the language of criminal law, testifying, "All this, so criminal a scene, I had the patience to see to an end, purely that I might gather more facts, and certainty against them in my full design to do their deserts instant justice" (159). It is also, as Kevin Kopelson and Lee Edelman have noted, a singularly destabilizing and disorienting moment for Fanny as narrator, the one scene where she literally loses the plot, for it ends, famously, with Fanny knocked unconscious and so unable to narrate the youths' escape from her punitive clutches.[24] Fanny herself, as Cameron McFarlane has observed, wraps up her report by dismissing the scene as extraneous: "here washing my hands of them, I replunge into the stream of my history" (160).[25] Yet as these and other critics have argued, while the episode is in many ways incongruous, striking for all the ways it departs from the portrayals of other-sex desire that dominate the text, its very incongruity throws into relief what Donald Mengay has called its "structural and thematic centrality."[26]

Although Fanny presents it as the great exception, the scene in effect sodomizes everything that has come before, transforming normality into its deviant other.

Fanny crosses paths with the sodomites by accident: en route to visit her friend Harriet at Hampton Court, her carriage breaks down, and she is forced to wait for the next stagecoach in a public house. There, from a window, she sees two "young gentlemen, for so they seem'd" alight from a horse chaise, and when they come into the room next to hers, she idly decides to spy on them, prompted, she claims, "without any particular suspicion, or other drift, or view, to see who they were, and examine their persons and behaviour" (156–157). But if the encounter is accidental, Fanny's curiosity is actually *not* idle, for she has earlier expressed her bafflement about sodomy to her matronly bawd, Mrs. Cole, asking "how it was possible for mankind to run into a taste, not only universally odious, but absurd, and impossible to gratify" (156). It is only her thirst for a solution to this puzzler that can justify the really quite laborious preparations she has to make in order to keep her eye on the youths: first scrutinizing every inch of the movable partition dividing their rooms to find a "peep-hole," then "oblig'd to stand on a chair" to reach "a paper-patch of the same colour as the wainscot," "pierc[ing]" this "with the point of a bodkin," and "post[ing]" herself with her eye to the opening to keep "the light from shining through" and betraying her. Fanny, that is, is *looking for* sodomy, and Cleland has ensured that the reader is looking for it, too, for this is only the last in a series of scenes in which the narrative moves ever closer to a direct encounter with this odious, absurd, impossible taste.[27]

In the first of these, Fanny, "under the dominion of unappeas'd irritations and desires" provoked by her "wanton" but impotent lover Mr. Norbert, is picked up in the street by a young sailor, "tall, manly-carriag'd, handsome of body and face" (140). Taking her to a nearby tavern, he brings out his "splitter," which she struggles to accommodate: "I took part of it in too," she writes, "but still things did not jee to his thorough liking," so "he leads me to the table, and with a master-hand lays my head down on the edge of it, and with the other canting up my petticoat and shift, bares my naked posteriours to his blind, and furious guide: it forces his way between them, and I feeling pretty sensibly that it was going by the right door, and knocking desperately at the wrong one, I told him of it: 'Pooh, says he my dear, any port in a storm'" (141). Cleland evokes the familiar association of sodomy and sailors for the sake of a joke, but one of the effects of his substitution of figural language for the "plain words" of other, coarser texts is to pose riddles. Which is the "right door," which the "wrong one"? One can take it for granted that the answer is obvious, or that there is an answer, but the sailor's joke calls such certainties into question. In a passage largely composed of nautical metaphors, the sailor's remark prefigures Mrs. Cole's observation a few pages later "that for her part, she consider'd pleasure of one sort or other, as the universal port of destination, and every wind that blew thither a good one" (144): there is no meaningful distinction to be made between one part of the body and another as long as pleasure is served. On the other hand, Fanny's configuration of the body as a kind of house, with closed doors to be knocked at for admission, insists on a distinction between "right" and "wrong" but leaves us to guess which is which.

Meanwhile, the sailor is arranging things in a way that muddles terms that Fanny seems anxious to keep clear. At first, he bares her breasts with "keenness of gust" and starts to have sex with her face to face, but he soon finds this not "to his thorough liking," and repositions Fanny so as to block her face and breasts from view, an occlusion emphasized by her use of the word "blind" to describe his "guide" (the blind thus leading the blind). His repositioning introduces an element of indeterminacy: Is the body of which only the naked posteriors are visible female or male? Is the door the right one or the wrong? In this ostensibly other-sex encounter, admission at the wrong door threatens to turn Fanny into a boy, inverting the more familiar pattern of boys' school, prison, and pirate narratives in which the "pathic" male is feminized by sodomitical penetration. While the caddish Mr. Norbert, interested only in women, is "flimzy" and "wrack'd" and boasts a "machine, which was one of those sizes that slip in and out without being minded" (132, 133), the "manly-carriag'd" sailor with his "splitter" needs to cast Fanny as his Ganymede to get "snug into port" (187), as Fanny later says of herself.

In the second quasi-sodomitical scene, Emily, one of Fanny's fellow whores, attends a masquerade in the guise of a shepherd boy and is accosted by "a gentleman in a very handsome domino" (154). As Fanny observes of Emily, "Nothing in nature could represent a prettier boy than [she] did," but Emily fails to realize that the domino "took her really for what she appear'd to be, a smock-fac'd boy" and so assumes "all those addresses to be paid to herself as a woman, which she precisely ow'd to his not thinking her one" (154). Fanny describes this double confusion as a "joke," and the laugh is on Emily and the domino alike, for both exhibit a confidence in their ability to distinguish natural from unnatural which turns out to be misplaced. Emily fancies that the domino feels natural desire for her as a woman; the domino imagines that she is naturally the boy she appears to be. Both are wrong, but their mistakes owe as much to the inadequacy of the category of the "natural" as to their inadequacies of judgment. Emily is a better ("prettier") boy than any produced by nature, while to the charge that his desire is unnatural, the domino might respond, with Cannon's "too polish'd" pederast, "Desire is an amatory Impulse of the inmost human Parts: Are not they, however constructed, and consequently impelling, Nature?" (54). So it seems, at any rate, as the scene unfolds. For a surprise awaits: "when they were alone together, and her *enamorato* began to proceed to those extremities which instantly discover the sex . . . no description could paint up to the life, the mixture of pique, confusion, and disappointment, that appear'd in his countenance, which join'd to the mournful exclamation, 'By heavens a woman!'" (155). The moment is the precise mirror image of that when Amorio discovers Hyacinth to be "of Gender masculine." Unlike Amorio, however, of whom Cannon writes, "Surprize invades; yet more predominates Desire" (50), the domino is at first put off by his discovery, and it is only when, like the sailor, he positions Emily so as to conceal her natural sex that he can press on, short-circuiting his awareness that she is not the boy she plays.

Yet this, not surprisingly, creates a new problem: as Fanny writes, "He was so fiercely set on a mis-direction, as to give the girl no small alarms for fear of losing a maiden-head she had not dreamt of"—exactly the danger Fanny had to sidestep with the sailor. And Emily's solution is much the same: "her complaints, and a resistance gentle, but firm, check'd, and brought him to himself again; so that turning his steed's head, he drove him at length in the right road" (155). In this scene, too, the ostensible "normality" of the encounter is thoroughly undermined by our apprehension that the "right road" of other-sex desire is only a simulacrum: the would-be sodomite can only be "brought to himself again"—by which Fanny actually means the opposite, that is, brought to impersonate a man who desires women—by an imaginary substitution of the boy Emily seems to be for the woman she naturally is, and of the "wrong road" for the right. As Fanny concludes, "His imagination having probably made the most of those resemblances that flatter'd his taste, he got with much ado whip and spur to his journey's end" (155–156). The domino's performance of normal masculinity is as flagrant a travesty as Emily's shepherd-boy getup.

The unnaturalness, in this scene, of "natural" desire fails to register with Fanny when she hears Emily's report. Instead, she responds, as we have seen, with bafflement, asking "how it was possible . . . to run into a taste, not only universally odious, but absurd, and impossible to gratify." Or, put another way: how can the impossible be possible? Sodomy, for Fanny, is impossible in that it must violate the limits of the body, "since, according to the notions and experience I had of things, it was not in nature to force such immense disproportions" (156). Bodily "proportion" is the standard by which the natural and unnatural can be distinguished. But if her logic is clear, this only makes sodomitical desire all the more baffling, as it can never be satisfied. Such is the quandary Fanny aims to clear up, some months later, when she puts her eye to the peephole.

What she sees, at first, is just "my two young sparks romping, and pulling one another about, entirely to my imagination, in frolic, and innocent play" (157). That she thinks of the two as *her* young sparks might help to explain her outrage when it turns out they only have eyes for each other, but it also might suggest a sense of affinity or likeness, especially given the feminine and sexual connotations of "romp" and "romping" in the period.[28] The elder of the two "sparks," Fanny guesses, is "towards nineteen, a tall comely young man"; the younger "could not be above seventeen, fair, ruddy, compleatly well made, and to say the truth, a sweet pretty stripling." (Is it impertinent to recall here that Cleland was "towards nineteen" and Carmichael seventeen when, "on an occasion immaterial to mention," they came up with the plan of Fanny's history?) Fanny herself is eighteen, of the same social background as the younger ("a country lad, by his dress") and, like both of them, still "in the rashness" of youth, as her imprudent escapades, around this time, with the sailor and "Good-natur'd Dick" confirm. Although for the moment they only romp "in frolic, and innocent play," her close attention to their "comely," "pretty" looks implies an erotic fascination that both she and the reader may expect will lead, as in many previous scenes, from voyeuristic arousal to rapturous gratification. Yet she has already framed the scene as an "occular demonstration" of the "infamous passion" she finds it impossible to imagine (156, 159). Nothing sodomitical seems to be happening, but soon "the face of things" alters: "For now the elder began to embrace, to press, to kiss the younger, to put his hands in his bosom, and give such manifest signs of an amorous intention, as made me conclude the other to be a girl in disguise, a mistake that nature kept me in countenance in, for she had certainly made one, when she gave him the male stamp" (157).

With this last, tortuous sentence, Fanny scrambles to make sense of the scene she has so assiduously sought out, putting forward a number of different potential answers to the riddle of sodomy ("How can the impossible be possible?"). Perhaps the younger boy is really "a girl in disguise": as in the anecdote of Emily at the masquerade, the female's "natural" sex is concealed behind a false male costume. This would still leave the older boy's desire ambiguous— does he, like the sailor and the domino, only desire females he can imagine as male?—but it would allow Fanny to bypass the worrying "impossibility" of sodomy in favor of a game of let's pretend still anchored in the "natural" intercourse of other-sexed bodies. The answer to the riddle would be that nothing impossible is taking place: what looks like sodomy is not. Yet within this same sentence Fanny advances another, contrary idea: perhaps there is an indeterminacy in nature as to "female" and "male." As soon as she concludes the younger "to be a girl in disguise," she reverses course, calling that conclusion "a mistake," but it is "a mistake that nature kept me in countenance in, for she had certainly made one, when she gave him the male stamp." What does this mean? Is the "one" that nature has made "a girl" or "a mistake"? The first option seems nonsensical: how could nature have made "a girl" by giving "him" the "male stamp"? Yet this might be thought of as a very similar hypothesis to that offered by the nineteenth-century sexologists who proposed that the male "invert" was effectively a female in a male body.[29] This would not totally solve the riddle, as "immense disproportion" would still be a problem, but it would neutralize the perversion or threat of sodomy by making it really an expression of other-sex desire with some scrambling of body parts. On the other hand, if "one" refers to "a mistake"—so that "nature had certainly made [a mistake] when she gave him the male stamp"—the sentence is perhaps even more puzzling, for what other stamp could she have given "him"? It would be hard to be more ambiguously sexed than this sentence makes the young lad, whose gender indeterminacy is not deplored as unnatural but explicitly attributed to nature, thus subverting the typical appeal to "the natural" as the standard by which sodomy was condemned. By this logic, the solution to the riddle is that the impossible is not impossible—just a cock-up, so to speak, of nature on an off day.

Nevertheless, whatever the origin of sodomitical desire might be, the problem of bodily disproportion persists, and so Fanny remains with her eye to the peephole. As the older spark begins to undress the younger, she describes their bodies and gestures with a closeness we may read as forensic or desiring (or of course both). There were a number of sodomy trial reports in circulation in the 1740s in which the witnesses' testimony prefigures key elements of Fanny's account. In the trial of Richard Manning and John Davis from 1745, for instance, one witness, an innkeeper's wife, testifies, "There is a wainscot partition between the 2 rooms [her own bedroom and one adjoining], about 5 feet high, and the rest is glass, and a curtain to part of it. I looked through the glass, and saw them sitting facing one another with their knees jammed in together . . . Then I looked through a thin curtain and saw them kissing one another. A little after I looked in again, and saw Manning's hand in Davis's breeches . . .

I looked again, and saw them acting as man and woman."[30] The witness, like Fanny, has first to explain how she gained visual access to the scene and then report what she saw in coherent narrative sequence in order to secure conviction. A similar partition played a role in the 1722 trial of John Dicks (reprinted in the widely circulated *Select Trials* of 1742), in which the key witness states that "I saw the Prisoner and the Boy come in together, and go into an Apartment by themselves. There was but a thin Partition between them and me . . . I look'd thro' a Slit in the Partition. I saw the Prisoner in the very Act of Sodomy, making several Motions with his Body, and then I saw him withdraw his Yard from the Boy's Fundament."[31] In this case, the witness and an unnamed "Woman, who was in the same Room with me," act as agents of the police in precisely the way Fanny attempts: "It was not long before [Dicks] began to repeat his unnatural Leudness; and then the Woman, who had been peeping all the while, cry'd out, *I can look no longer,—I am ready to swoon—He'll ruin the Boy!* We both rushed in and seized the Prisoner, as he lay upon the Boy's Backside."[32] Fanny's case, of course, ends calamitously for her but well for the sparks, who, "alarm'd, I suppose, by the noise of my fall"—for in her attempt to seize the miscreants she trips on a nail, knocking herself out—"had more than the necessary time to make a safe retreat" (159).

But if Fanny emulates these witnesses in her forensic attention to the details needed for legal prosecution—averring, in a passage cited before, that she was able to keep watching "purely that I might gather more facts" (159)—the language of her report also reveals a rather breathless erotic attraction. So when the older lad begins "playing" with the "white shaft, middle-siz'd, and scarce fledg'd" of the younger, she observes that this was "all receiv'd by the boy without other opposition, than certain wayward coynesses, ten times more alluring than repulsive" (158). In a later passage, Fanny writes that as with one hand the older "diverted himself" with the younger's "red-topt ivory toy," with the other "he wanton'd with his hair, and leaning forward over his back, drew his face, from which the boy shook the loose curls that fell over it, in the posture he stood him in, and brought him towards his, so as to receive a long-breath'd kiss" (159). As with Cannon's sexual descriptions, Cleland's "luscious pen . . . describes the thing so feelingly," in the words of a 1767 satire, as to solicit the reader's arousal, too.[33] Of course the language of erotic arousal alternates with the language of moral condemnation, as when Fanny writes, of the older youth's "engine," that it "certainly deserv'd to be put to a better use," but her sniffy disapproval is quite complexly enmeshed with other, more ambiguous discursive threads. In this passage, for example, after declaring that the "engine . . . deserv'd to be put to a better use," she proceeds to assert that it was "very fit to confirm me in my dis-belief of the possibility of things being push'd to odious extremities, which I had built on the disproportion of parts" (158). Not only is there a hint of personal jealousy in her reproach—picked up on later by Mrs. Cole when she complains that sodomites "take something more precious than bread" from the "mouths" of "woman-kind" (159)—but she connects her repudiation of sodomy as "odi-ous" to her belief in its impossibility owing to the necessary "disproportion of parts." Yet as the scene plays out, this belief is exploded, from two different angles.

First, the two sparks demonstrate pretty unmistakably that their desire is anything but "impossible to gratify." When the older "introduces" his "instru-ment" into the younger, she writes that "the first streights of entrance being pretty well got through, every thing seem'd to move, and go pretty currently on, as in a carpet-road, without much rub, or resistance" (158).[34] There is no sense of struggle or difficulty; even her characterization of "the writhing, twisting, and soft murmur'd complaints of the young sufferer" is far gentler than her usually violent reports of her own sexual response. Second, even if there is some valid-ity to Fanny's belief that "it was not in nature to force such immense dispropor-tions," in asserting this she actually subsumes all desire under the heading of sodomy. For immense disproportion has been, from the beginning, the keynote of her representation of other-sex desire as well: the more immense, the more strongly desired.[35] The novel's first scene of sexual intercourse is witnessed by Fanny through a partition very much like the one in the Manning-Davis sodomy trial, so that "seeing every thing minutely, I could not myself be seen" (24). Initiating the pattern of voyeuristic arousal that runs through the text and culminates in the sodomite episode, Fanny in her "dark closet" feels "every vein of my body circulate liquid fires" (25) as she watches. But afterward, asked for her reaction to the spectacle, she tells her bedmate Phoebe that "having very cu-riously and attentively compared the size of that enormous machine, which did not appear, at least to my fearful imagination, less than my wrist, and at least three of my handfuls long, to that of the tender, small part of me which was framed to receive it, I could not conceive its being possible to afford it entrance there, without dying" (27). And this inconceivability, articulated in almost the same terms as in her diatribe against sodomy, remains a constitutive part of her experience of desire as such.

When, for example, she first undresses the "clever-limb'd" young footman Will (second only to Charles as an object of sexual pleasure), she beholds "with wonder and surprize, what? not the play-thing of a boy, not the weapon of a man, but a may-pole of so enormous a standard, that had proportions been observ'd, it must have belong'd to a young giant . . . and it now fell to my lot to stand his first trial of it, if I could resolve to run the risques of its disproportion to that tender part of me, which such an over-siz'd machine was very fit to lay in ruins" (70, 72–73). If immense disproportion is the mark of the unnatural, Fanny's accounts of other-sex desire repeatedly denaturalize it, recast it as another kind of sodomy.[36] And this is the case not only when she explicitly refers to disproportion but also when she makes figural use of the lexicon of violence. Will's "machine" is "very fit to lay [her] in ruins"; Charles is "the sweet . . . murderer of my virginity" (41); the sailor penetrates her with a "splitter"; Fanny's friend Louisa, in their escapade with Good-natur'd Dick, is "torn, split, wounded . . . she was tied to the stake, and oblig'd to fight the match out, if she died for it" (164). This current of violence in the novel may be disturbing or comically exaggerated or both, but the one thing it's not is literal. The desiring body is pushed to its limits, or in some sense beyond, but Louisa is not actually tied to the stake, nor is Fanny murdered or split. Instead, death, ruin, and agony are figures that Fanny deploys to convey the extremity of her own or another's sensations of pleasure, just beyond what can "naturally" be borne. So when she first experiences sexual pleasure with Charles, she bursts out, "What floods of bliss! what melting transports! what agonies of delight! too fierce, too mighty for nature to sustain" (43). Desire and delight are out of proportion to the body through which they're felt; other-sex desire is as unnatural as sodomy, indeed is a form of it.[37] Hence Fanny's "burning . . . with rage, and indignation" (159) after she spies on the scene that she has, after all, taken some pains to see. In confounding any distinction between natural and unnatural, possible and impossible desires, the "young sparks romping" in the next room have made a mockery of the moralistic pretensions that, incongruously enough, structure her narration.

The Mount-Pleasants of Rome

Like Fanny's sailor and Emily's gentleman in a domino, the older of the two sparks positions the younger to face away from him, with his head against the back of a chair, so that "slipping then aside the young lad's shirt, and tucking it up under his cloaths behind, he shew'd to the open air, those globular, fleshy eminences that compose the mount-pleasants of *Rome*, and which now, with all the narrow vale that intersects them, stood display'd, and expos'd to his attack" (158). Here, too, the effect is to introduce a degree of sexual indeterminacy (is the body thus displayed male or female?)—an effect underlined by Fanny's periphrasis for the young lad's buttocks, "the mount-pleasants of *Rome*." She has once referred to her own mons veneris as a "mount-pleasant," when Phoebe first explores her body with "lascivious touches" (11) in the novel's early pages. In returning to (almost) the same phrase—which is synonymous with the name Fanny Hill itself—Cleland draws attention to the likeness between Fanny and the lad at the same time that he emphasizes the shift from front to back of the body.[38] If Fanny's name is in one way a joke at her expense—a reduction of her self to her sex, so that she is nothing that is not sexual corporeality—in another way it just affirms the primacy of the body as a source of pleasure, the centrality of eros to her experience of the world. In that sense, the movement of the mount-pleasant from Fanny's front to the lad's rear, while it can be read as simply a way of feminizing him, and thus reinforcing his role as the older lad's catamite or "Ganymede" (158), also forms part of a larger pattern in the novel of *unsexing* the body—that is, unmooring it from a single sexual identity, male or female, to reconfigure it as an unfixed, polymorphous locus of desire, one's own as well as others'.

Migrating from Fanny to the lad, from female to male, front to back, Cleland's "mount-pleasants" embody the variability and multiplicity of desire, its openness to transformation and substitution—as the domino and the sailor have already shown with their artful construction of the tableaus that allow each to get to "his journey's end." That the lad's are "the mount-pleasants of *Rome*" alludes both to the Latin origins of the phrase itself and to the hackneyed antisodomite claim, cited earlier, that Italy is "the *Mother* and *Nurse* of *Sodomy*."[39] Fanny's (and of course Cleland's) increasing emphasis in the novel's second volume on "naked posteriors" (141)—in the scenes discussed here as well as the extended episode in which Fanny whips Mr. Barvile's "pair of chubby, smooth-cheek'd, and passing white posteriours" (146) and has her own flogged in turn, leading to "such violent, yet pleasingly irksome sensations . . . that I scarce knew how to contain myself" (151)—points to an increasing, if wary, fascination with sexual "inversion" as well as with indeterminate or ambiguous bodies. None is more ambiguous, as I've already argued, than that of the younger lad, most vividly when the older boy takes hold of the younger's "red-topt ivory toy, that stood perfectly stiff, and shewed, that if he was like his mother behind, he was like his father before" (158). *Like* his mother, *like* his father: he is in one sense both, in another sense neither. He is also like the pupil in Cannon's version of Petronius, who, far from finding "the Pathic's Part disagreeable," shares (and then some) "in the accurst Rapture" (45). Neither biological sex nor positions of pleasure are fixed; the body, at least to the desiring imagination, is plurally and malleably sexed.[40]

Perhaps Fanny's subsequent pratfall and lapse into unconsciousness are produced by the shock of this moment. But the figure of the body unsexed by desire continues to haunt her, even in the novel's climactic scene, when she is reunited with the long-lost Charles. As they reach the culminating moment of rapture, she writes, he "took me so much out of my own possession, whilst he seem'd himself so much in mine, that in a delicious enthusiasm I imagin'd such a transfusion of heart and spirit, as that coaliting, and making one body and soul with him, I was him, and he, me" (184). Fanny here imagines a wholesale transfusion of bodies, impossibly both a merging and an exchange of selves, such that neither of them retains any marks of a specific, separate, individual sexual identity. Once is not enough, though, and soon after, "we play'd over-again the same opera" (185). This time, the only way she can express what she experiences is to reconfigure Charles himself as female, "lavish of his stores, and pleasure-milk'd," his "instrument of pleasure" imagined as "the nipple of Love," which she "thirstily draws and drains"—likening herself to "infants at the breast . . . extract[ing] the milky stream prepar'd for their nourishment." The conceit is comically outrageous, but fittingly brings to a close the motif of sexual reversibility or lability by showing this to be integral to even the most "conventional" of other-sex relationships.[41] Fanny and Charles are no less engaged in a "project of preposterous pleasure" (157) than the lads in the next room, for eros turns the body topsy-turvy.

When Fanny, back home, tells Mrs. Cole about her sodomitical misadventure, the latter tries to reaffirm her faith in an impermeable border separating the deviant from the normal, declaring, "whatever effect this infamous passion had in other ages, and other countries, it seem'd a peculiar blessing on our air and climate, that there was a plague-spot visibly imprinted on all that are tainted with it" (159). But all the evidence Fanny has amassed from her own and others' observations belies this: nothing marks the sodomites out, any more than the Dulwich schoolboys in danger of imitative "infection."[42] There is no bodily imprint by which the sodomite can be known and cordoned off.[43] Indeed there is nothing to distinguish the lads in the next room from the two youths, Will and Charles, who are the objects of Fanny's most lustful gaze, and who are consistently portrayed as desirable precisely for their androgynous beauty. Charles is first labeled, like the younger sodomite, "a fair stripling" (34), and Fanny's descriptive blazon, while referring to his "manly graces," lingers over features most often treated as feminine: "his eyes closed in sleep, displayed the meeting edges of their lids beautifully bordered with long eye-lashes, over which no pencil could have describ'd two more regular arches than those that grac'd his fore-head, which was high, perfectly white and smooth; then a pair of vermillion lips, pouting, and swelling to the touch, as if a bee had freshly stung them" (35)—and so, adoringly, on. Will is singled out for "his maiden bashfulness (for such it seem'd, and really was)"—an odd parenthesis that turns him into a girl—and even his "may-pole" is feminized, as Fanny recalls "its skin, whose smooth polish, and velvet-softness, might vye with that of the most delicate of our sex" (72). In another paean to Charles, she writes, "Think of a face without a fault, glowing with all the opening bloom, and vernal freshness of an age, in which beauty is of either sex" (44), so representing him as another Ganymede (as she calls the younger sodomite), and even, I would say, as one of those "unsex'd male-misses" (160) that Mrs. Cole deplores.[44]

This phrase comes at the end of her tirade to Fanny, in which she insists that sodomites "were scarce less execrable than ridiculous in their monstrous inconsistency, of loathing and contemning women, and all at the same time, apeing their manners, airs, lisp, skuttle, and, in general, all their little modes of affectation" (160). Again, none of the sodomites we have seen fit this bill, and Mrs. Cole seems here to be conflating two quite distinct eighteenth-century types: the "fribble," an effeminate, more or less asexual fop, and the sexually desiring sodomite proper with whom Fanny struggles to come to terms.[45] The first of these types is "unsex'd" in the sense of impotent or sexless, lacking desire; the second, by contrast, in the sense of desiring with such ardor that the body is transformed. The younger sodomite is an unsex'd male-miss in this latter sense, "perfectly stiff" but at the same time androgynous: "like his mother behind . . . like his father before." Will and Charles are similarly polymorphous, their awesome phalluses fantastically, perversely feminized, and their "beauty . . . of either sex." Nothing, really, accounts for their not being sodomites themselves except that they have never been schooled in the practice.

For as Fanny demonstrates in her memoirs, and as Cleland would go on to contend in a number of later works, all desire is an effect of imitation, voyeuristically aroused and then acted out. Fanny, as a novice in Mrs. Brown's brothel, is first exposed to the "luscious talk" of the other girls, which "highly provok'd an itch of florid warm-spirited blood through every vein" (23); her "bed-fellow" Phoebe next "artfully whetted" her curiosity and "explain'd to me all the mysteries of *Venus*"; but the decisive step in the creation of desire is her voyeuristic observation of two sexual encounters. "From that instant," she writes, "adieu all fears of what man could do unto me"—that is, the fears inspired by disproportion—"they were now changed into such ardent desires, such ungovernable longings, that I could have pull'd the first of that sex that should present himself, by the sleeve, and offered him the bauble" of her virginity (31–32). And in fact this is precisely what she does, for the next man she sees is Charles. Nor does the two-step process of arousal followed by imitation end here, as is shown, for example, in the long opening sequence of the novel's second volume, Fanny's "ceremonial of initiation" (95) at Mrs. Cole's, at which she first listens to each of the other girls tell the story of her first sexual experience, then watches each in turn have sex with one of four "young gentlemen" (95) Mrs. Cole has provided for the purpose, and finally has sex with her own "particular-elect" (120). "Now," she writes, "all the impressions of burning desire, from the lively scenes I had been spectatress of . . . throb'd and agitated me with insupportable irritations: I perfectly fever'd and madden'd with their excess: I did not now enjoy a calm of reason enough to perceive, but I, extatically indeed! *felt* the policy and power of such rare and exquisite provocatives as the examples of the night had proved towards thus exalting our pleasures" (123). Desire is never original, always an imitation—which is not to say inauthentic or ungenuine, but learned from what we hear and see.

Reading too is a sort of voyeurism, exposing us to otherwise unsuspected behaviors and desires and so prompting us to enact them. Such at any rate was Dudley Ryder's concern in the indictment of Thomas Cannon's printer: what we observe or read has the power to "Debauch Poison and Infect the Minds of all the Youth of this Kingdom and to Raise Excite and Create in the Minds of all the said Youth most Shocking and Abominable Ideas and Sentiments" (39). This is why Fanny's argument that "all young men" should be taught the dangerous "snares" of sodomy just as she was (158)—that is, by spying on (or reading about) other comely young men having sex—is such a snare itself. She calls for suppressing immorality by pornographically multiplying its representations. But such a strategy, as her own example illustrates, would only engender new legions of sodomites. Perhaps this was Cleland's intention; certainly it is what his and Cannon's would-be prosecutors accused them of intending, and explains why they sought to suppress their books. Reading infects the soul.

Luscious Pens

As things turned out, neither Cannon nor Cleland was ever prosecuted. When the legal machinery against him was set in motion, Cannon, as I've mentioned, disappeared. According to John Ibbutt, who in June 1750 had been sent to serve notice to Cannon's bails that he had been summoned to court the following week, when he went to "the late Dwelling House of Mrs Cannon Mother of abovenamed Defendant in Delahaye Street Westminster," he found the house shut up and Elizabeth Cannon "retired with her family into the Country." But Thomas, the neighbors told him, "went beyond Sea sometime since and still continues there."[46] He spent three years abroad "and then returned to England," as his mother later stated when she sought pardon for him, "partly constrained by Necessity (having neither property nor any other means of Subsisting himself) but principally in order to make the only Atonement in his power to the Publick, by Printing and Publishing his Retraction or Recantation."[47] This retraction, long supposed lost, was recently found, "prefix'd" to a rare text published in 1753, *A Treatise on Charity*, which is credited on its title page to "Mr. Cannon."[48] John Purser, of course, *was* tried for having printed the text, found guilty during Trinity term 1751, and sentenced to be fined, imprisoned for one month, and pilloried at Charing Cross and the Royal Exchange. He was also required to provide security for good behavior for a period of seven years. According to a note added to the register, Purser was afterward pardoned and "the Rule was never drawn up," that is, the sentence was never fully carried out, though he may have served part of it.[49] Cannon, at the time of his mother's petition for pardon (ca. 1755), was said by her to be living "the most recluse life at Windsor" with her and his sisters, "abstracted from Society, and almost wholly dedicated to Religious Offices," his cleric father's son at last. In his premature and "indigent" retirement, according to Elizabeth, he looked ahead to "a future course of Life Expressive of his utter abhorrence and detestation of the Principles which have unhappily fallen from his Pen but never yet descended into his heart."[50]

Cleland, meanwhile, although arrested and examined, managed to avoid prosecution, but it is unclear how or why, as the secretary of state did convey "Directions to prosecute" to the attorney general on more than one occasion, both for the *Woman of Pleasure* and for its expurgated 1750 abridgement, the *Memoirs of Fanny Hill*.[51] Cleland's obituarist, John Nichols, circulated the unlikely story that "for this publication he was called before the Privy Council; and the circumstances of his distress being known, as well as his being a man of some parts, John Earl Granville, the then president, nobly rescued him from the like temptation [that is, of writing an obscene work for money] by getting him a pension of £100 a year, which he enjoyed to his death."[52] Cleland evidently did enjoy a government pension for some or much of his life—although he told Josiah Beckwith it was for £200 and was taken away "on Account of his

Publications" (but which? and when?)—but this would have been for what he did write (such as progovernment articles), not for what he didn't. In any case, both he and Griffiths must have decided that the sodomitical material of the first edition was too dangerous, and it was severely cut back in later editions, all of which retain the seven paragraphs in which Fanny leads up to the scene but omit the two long paragraphs in which the lads undress and actually have sex, bringing the curtain down, in effect, after Fanny writes, "They now proceeded to such lengths as soon satisfied me, what they were" (158).[53] The abridged text adds, "And O! what a shocking scene ensued," but when the curtain rises again, the action (whatever the reader may imagine it to have been) is over. Cleland was careful in the abridgment to expunge every teasing sodomitical hint from the earlier scenes as well: in it, the sailor does not knock at the wrong door, turn Fanny back to front, or say "any port in a storm," while the gentleman in a domino, although labeled "an old S——te" in the chapter heading, does not go through any of the substitutions and repositionings that allow him to turn Emily into the boy she imitates, instead leaving her with "a confus'd apology" when he discovers her sex.[54]

So while Cannon and Cleland were both able to avoid prosecution, the heavy-handed censorial machinery of arrests, interrogations, and threats did lead to the suppression of what was evidently seen as most disruptive or ambiguously enticing in their texts—which in Cannon's case amounted to the whole of it, in Cleland's just to those passages in which the antisodomite surface was troubled by insinuations of sexual dissidence or laughter. The absence of the two explicit paragraphs from all but one (the first) of the novel's early editions led to speculation in later years that those paragraphs were someone else's work: specifically, in the most influential of such speculations, the work of Samuel Drybutter, a shopkeeper, sometime bookseller, and accused sodomite who was also, it turns out, a friend, or at least a friend of a friend, of Cleland. It was the bibliographer Henry G. Bohn who in 1864 wrote that after the novel first appeared "the language was considerably altered for the worse by Drybutter, the bookseller, who was punished for it by being put in the pillory in 1757."[55] Drybutter's curious name and comparative obscurity led a number of scholars to conclude that there was no such person, but in 1992, Rictor Norton established not only that he was real but also that he was a friend of the playwright and actor Samuel Foote, a longtime friend of Cleland's who was himself later accused (and acquitted) of sodomy.[56] Whether Drybutter, Foote, and Cleland were part of a sodomitical or otherwise suspect coterie is impossible, without further evidence, to know, just as it is impossible to verify that there was a 1757 edition of Cleland's novel including the suppressed paragraphs or that Drybut-ter was pilloried for it. But it is quite interesting that Drybutter, who was used, after Bohn's attribution, to distance Cleland from the taint of sodomitical incli-nations by acting as the fall guy for the text's most incriminating passage, now connects Cleland, albeit indirectly, to a largely hidden sodomitical demimonde, lending some support to the rumors of sodomy reported by Beckwith in 1781.

Shorn of its most daring passage, Cleland's work nevertheless continued to be scourged by moralists and sought out by immoral readers (the unexpurgated text was far more popular than the expurgated).[57] In a satirical Lucianic dialogue of 1767, *The Sale of Authors*, attributed to Archibald Campbell, "Mr. Cl——d" is portrayed as a figure who "haunts" the bawdy houses and bagnios of London to enjoy the company of "fine jolly, buxom, Wenches."[58] The premise of the dia-logue is that Apollo and Mercury are discussing various contemporary authors whom they can put up for sale to customers in a kind of mock slave auction. Apollo asks Mercury if he has "any Authors in your Collection . . . who instead of being praised and rewarded for their works, deserve to be hanged for them. I mean such Authors as inflame the passions of mankind, and stimulate them to vice, lewdness and debauchery; or instruct them in Arts and practices not only pernicious and destructive to themselves, but to society in general" (130). Such authors are the most likely to fetch a good price. Cleland's name comes up, linked to that of "Mr Harris the Pimp," author of *The Man of Pleasure's Kalendar*, a guide to London's prostitutes. Cleland has already, as it happens, been "bespoke" by "a worthy and pious Lady" (131), but a group of "Bucks and Bloods" want to buy Cleland and Harris together—for, in Apollo's words, "after the one has raised and inflamed their passions, they will be obliged to consult the other how to gratify and allay them" (132).[59] So far, so conventionally bawdy, but the young male "Bucks and Bloods" put it rather differently. Fired up by his writing, they paint Cleland as "our most curious and delicious author" (142), whose body they want for themselves: "C——d," they declare, "has a most lus-cious pen, he possesses infinite *Powers*, he describes the thing so feelingly: in short, we must have him and will give you any money for him" (139). It is as if Cleland, by whoring and writing about whores, becomes a whore himself, and an object of sodomitical desire to his male readers.

If Cleland's "luscious pen" can transform him into one of the whores he portrays, or his hot-blooded readers into sodomites, the moralists and censors had good reason to warn against the dangers of unrestricted publication. It may be that Cannon's writing posed a still greater potential threat, for Cannon is far more interested than Cleland in the subjective experience of desire and even love between men, and unlike Cleland's voyeuristically observed youths in the next room, Cannon's "pederasts" speak feelingly of their desires and in spirited defense of their practice.[60] After his brief moment of notoriety and his pained public retraction, he seems, as his mother wrote, to have lived a "most recluse life." I have only found one other trace of him—if it is him—from 1779 or 1780, around the time of Beckwith's visit to Cleland. In the autobiographical *Life* of the radical playwright, actor, and novelist Thomas Holcroft, Holcroft's friend, the musician William Shield, ventures one day into a "dark, dirty-looking" cook-shop in an alley off St. Martin's Lane called Porridge Island—"a mean street," according to Hester Thrale Piozzi, "filled with cook-shops for the convenience of the poorer inhabitants."[61] There he meets "a grave, elderly looking man" pre-siding at the head of a table at which "philosophy, religion, politics, poetry, and belles letters were talked of, and in such a manner, as to shew that every person there was familiar with such subjects, and that they formed the ordinary topics of conversation" (208). The elderly man turns to Shield, "telling him that he seemed a young man, and by his countenance shewed some grace," and urging him not to mind the "rather free turn" the conversation sometimes takes (208–209). The person "who thus assumed the office of a censor" is named Cannon, said to be "the son of an Irish bishop" (209). Shield is "so much amused with this old gentleman" that he tells Holcroft about him, and with a couple of other friends they form what they call "The Cannonian Society," even though Can-non is "rather tenacious of his opinions, and impatient of contradiction" and frequently argues with the outspoken Holcroft (210–211).

This Cannon, to whom Holcroft never assigns a first name, "was a man of letters, and had traveled. He spoke a very florid language, full of epithets and compound words, and professed to be engaged in an edition of Tibullus" (210). Albius Tibullus, who died young in 19 BCE (the same year as Virgil), was one of the greatest Latin elegists, his work addressed both to male and female lovers. No extant edition has been attributed to Cannon, Thomas or otherwise, but it is not hard to imagine that the same "man of letters" who in his late twenties produced "spirited" English versions of Petronius and Lucian might at sixty still pursue an amateur interest in classical erotic writing, especially the work of an author concerned with the lability and changeability of desire.[62] As to "very florid" language, the phrase calls to mind the sinuous, ornamental style of *Ancient and Modern Pederasty*: "when polish'd Greece bow'd her once laurell'd Head to all-subduing Rome" (40–41); "the all-surpassing Beauty of my Host's son" (45); "Love-inspiring Goddess, by thy heart-bowing Divinity I swear" (45); "the Star-glowing Sky" (46); "the dissolving lovely Dissolver" (46); "Nature with wonder-working Hand" (47); "the joy-ravishing Amorio" (47); "this bank-scorning Torrent" (48); "with forceful Tears, and heart-bled Sobs, I vent the high swoln Passion" (57); or, in the last words preserved of the original, "I, a Mortal, thus extacy'd begin to know the closing Dissolution" (58). This final phrase, in which sexual pleasure foreshadows the "dissolution" of the self in death, is from the younger Cannon's version of a passage from Petronius, "one of the finest Raptures," as he wrote then, "ever pour'd from mouth" (58). It can stand here as the last word both of the younger Cannon, whose life was turned upside down by his spirited pamphlet, and of the elder, with his affectionate interest in the graceful-countenanced young William Shield. Despite Elizabeth Cannon's well-meaning denials, it seems that the "Principles" which had "fallen" from Cannon's "Pen" had also, perhaps not "unhappily" for him, "descended into his heart."

CHAPTER FOUR

Three Memoirs
(1748–1752)

n form, the *Memoirs of a Woman of Pleasure* is an uneasy hybrid of two common types of eighteenth-century narrative: the fictional autobiography and
the novel in letters. Its hybridity is uneasy because it apes the format of both
narrative genres without fulfilling the expectations usual to either. It deviates
from the conventions of "epistolary verisimilitude"—the illusion of a plausibly motivated, real-seeming correspondence—and the effects of emotional or
temporal immediacy that had come to define the novel in letters as practiced
by Aphra Behn and (recently and decisively) Samuel Richardson, and Cleland
leaves unexplored the potential play or clash of contesting voices that Richardson had orchestrated so effectively in *Clarissa* (published 1747–1748).[1] For
Richardson, the essential "Nature of Familiar Letters" is that they are "written,
as it were, to the *Moment*, while the Heart is agitated by Hopes and Fears, on
Events undecided"; but this link between temporal open-endedness and affective intensity is disregarded in Cleland's text, whose events are narrated by an
older Fanny from a perspective of sheltered "ease and affluence" (1).[2] Cleland
did later write an epistolary novel in a more Richardsonian vein, *The Woman of
Honor* (1768), but the *Woman of Pleasure* largely bypasses or ignores the techni-

cal and expressive possibilities of epistolary fiction that Richardson, Behn, and others had opened up.

Similarly, while Cleland's first novel exhibits the retrospective form and end-driven claims to meaning typical of eighteenth-century autobiography—as when Fanny, at the outset, promises to "recall to view those scandalous stages of my life, out of which I emerg'd at length, to the enjoyment of every blessing in the power of love, health, and fortune to bestow" (1)—those moral claims are so relentlessly pummeled by Fanny's unintended and ridiculous double entendres that her pretended structure of meaning collapses into burlesque. This is especially glaring in her concluding moral reflections, in which, lying in "the bosom of virtue," she writes: "Looking back on the course of vice, I had run, and comparing its infamous blandishments with the infinitely superior joys of innocence, I could not help pitying, even in point of taste, those who, immers'd in a gross sensuality, are insensible to the so delicate charms of VIRTUE, than which even PLEASURE has not a greater friend, nor than VICE a greater enemy" (187). The view she espouses here is similar to that offered by Cleland himself in a number of other texts, but Fanny seems to be unaware of the ways in which the very language she deploys casts doubt on her smug moral distinctions. In such phrases as "the bosom of virtue" and "this tail-piece of morality" (as she labels this summing-up) her words insist on the bawdy second meanings she seems not to notice, as has been true from the novel's very first page.[3] There, Fanny writes, "Truth! stark naked truth, is the word, and I will not so much as take the pains to bestow the strip of a gauze-wrapper on it, but paint situations such as they actually rose to me in nature"; and as she continues in this half-knowing, half-oblivious vein of obscene double meaning, Cleland does not so much hold her up to ridicule as underline the inescapable ambiguity of all first-person accounts, with their mixture of insight and blindness, authenticity and self-deceit.

By simultaneously adopting and dismantling these familiar novelistic forms in his own first novel, Cleland was acting as both practitioner and critic; he thus exemplifies the degree to which, at least in the mid-eighteenth century, to write a novel was in itself to engage in a critique of the still-emerging genre (or ragbag of genres, as it may better be described). Although he evidently worked on some version of the *Woman of Pleasure* as early as 1730 and continued to write fiction into the late 1760s, Cleland's most intense period of engagement with contemporary debates over the aims and effects of fiction was from 1748 to 1752, during which period he wrote his two most successful novels—*Memoirs of a Woman of Pleasure* and *Memoirs of a Coxcomb* (1751)—reviewed fiction for Ralph

Griffiths's *Monthly Review*, and translated an important French libertine novel, Charles Pinot-Duclos's *Mémoires pour servir à l'histoire des moeurs du XVIIIe siècle* (1751), the third of the three memoirs on which I focus in this chapter. These *Mémoires* were published in English as the second of a two-volume set, titled *Memoirs Illustrating the Manners of the Present Age*, whose first volume consisted of Pinot-Duclos's *Considérations sur les moeurs de ce siècle* (*Observations on the Manners of the Present Age*), a collection of moral reflections, not translated by Cleland.[4] Pinot-Duclos's novel was written as a sequel and narrative fleshing-out of the "detached Maxims and Reasonings," as Cleland calls them, of the *Considérations*, and in it Pinot-Duclos focused on "l'amour, la galanterie, et même le libertinage" (love, gallantry, even libertinism).[5] There are, then, as this last phrase suggests, strong thematic connections between Cleland's two *Memoirs* and the *Mémoires* of Pinot-Duclos.[6] Both authors make use of narrative genres that readers expected to unfold in familiar ways—in particular, the first-person history of moral education—in order to interrogate both narrative form and the moral assumptions that readers (and, usually, authors) bring to particular kinds of texts.

Although the *Woman of Pleasure* presents itself as a story of moral education, there is still pretty sharp disagreement as to how seriously we're meant to take this claim. In what follows I propose that it is precisely to the extent he laughs (and invites us to laugh) at it that Cleland takes (and invites us to take) this claim most seriously. As their parallel titles suggest, *Memoirs of a Woman of Pleasure* and *Memoirs of a Coxcomb* are counterparts, and in this chapter I read them comparatively, arguing for their importance to the fashioning of the self-consciously new, open-ended, self-critical, and self-reflexive form of the novel. I consider Pinot-Duclos's *Memoirs* more briefly, focusing on Cleland's translator's preface as, in Roger Lonsdale's words, his "most sustained and serious statement about the nature of fiction."[7] Like Pinot-Duclos, but more brazenly, Cleland in his two *Memoirs* experiments with narrative form, constructing the *Woman of Pleasure* as a set of variations and the *Coxcomb* as a suspended romance that teasingly frustrates the expectations it creates. In that respect, the latter work may owe a debt to another libertine novelist, Crébillon fils, whose 1738 *Les Égarements du coeur et de l'esprit* (literally "the wanderings of the heart and spirit," translated by Barbara Bray as *The Wayward Head and Heart*) similarly withholds the closure its plot seems to promise.[8] As a habituated cosmopolitan—well-traveled, skeptical, "understanding most of the living languages, and speaking them all very fluently"—Cleland drew at least as much from French as from English literary and philosophical writing, and if this set

him against the prejudices and tastes of a good part of the English reading public, it led his fiction into some novel *égarements*, or wanderings, from the literary
mainstream of midcentury London.[9]

Presenting themselves as novels of education, both the *Woman of Pleasure*
and the *Coxcomb* (like Pinot-Duclos's and Crébillon's works) carry their pro-
tagonist-narrators from innocence to experience, naïveté to worldliness, the
country to the city, virginal singleness to heterosexual union. Sir William Delamore, like Fanny Hill, claims to have learned, over the course of the life his
narrative retraces, the difference between real and sham pleasures, love and
mere sex, virtue and vice. In Cleland's work, even more than in the libertine
texts he drew from, the protagonist's education is not just sentimental or moral
but also social—that is, a preparation for insertion into a determinate place in
the hierarchies of gender and class. For Fanny, this is the state of a wife and
mother in an apparently conventional bourgeois marriage; for the aristocratic
Sir William, the state of a wealthy landowner, heir to a vast fortune and member
by birth of the ruling class of Britain. If the social gulf between them is deep,
however, Fanny and William share one key trait: both are authors, not only the
memoirists but, in some measure, the makers of their own lives. Writing their
own stories, they fabricate themselves as literary as well as moral and social
subjects. But they are no more free, no less constructed, in this role than they
are in terms of their social position: both, that is, have to insert themselves into
preexisting narrative roles and forms, to interpret and narrate their experience
in keeping with familiar forms of life story.

Among Women: Fanny Hill's "Expressions of Extasy"

The first word of Fanny's memoirs, "Madam," comprises a pun and a puz-
zle: she addresses her unnamed correspondent both politely, as a respectable
gentlewoman, and contemptuously, as a whore or bawd (the word was in common use in both senses). Nothing later in the text gives us any clue as to who
"Madam" is, and the very few remarks Fanny makes (as when she refers to
"such unreserved intimacies as ours" or notes that "you have too much sense,
too much knowledge of the *originals* themselves"—that is, the facts or personages of Fanny's life—"to snuff prudishly, and out of character, at the *pictures* of
them" [1]) tend to uphold the implication that Madam may well be a woman of
pleasure herself. How "unreserved" is their intimacy? How much "knowledge"
of the originals might she have? It would evidently be "out of character" for her
"to snuff prudishly," so is she a regular consumer of pornographic "pictures"?

Certainly she is very keen for what Fanny, who presents herself as a reluctant author, has to write: it is only because she regards Madam's "desires as indispensible orders" that Fanny undertakes the "ungracious . . . task." Indeed this characterization of Madam as an importunate customer is taken further at the start of the second letter, when Fanny writes that she has "delay'd the sequel of my history" in the "hopes that, instead of pressing me to a continuation, you would have acquitted me of the task of pursuing a confession, in the course of which, my self-esteem has so many wounds to sustain" (91). But Madam insists, and Fanny has no choice but "compliance with a curiosity that is to be satisfied so extremely at my expence."

Madam, of course, is also Cleland's stand-in for the reader, his own importunate customer, and the implications of this are also puzzling. Does he imagine a female readership? Most critics take it for granted that this is not the case, that the novel can only be read as a text addressed by its male author to a male readership—the usual pornographic contract. In that case, we would have to read not only Fanny as a "drag" persona of Cleland but Madam as a drag persona of the necessarily male reader.[10] The question of the novel's readership, intended or real, does not have a simple or obvious answer, but even granting that it was directed at an exclusively male audience, what is the effect of addressing this audience as if it were female? This question has not gone unanswered either, in a variety of ingenious and well-argued ways, by such critics as Nancy K. Miller, Julia Epstein, Madeleine Kahn, Rosemary Graham, Felicity Nussbaum, Lisa L. Moore, and David M. Robinson, but taken together, what is perhaps most telling is how stubbornly the questions of gender identity and identification persist.[11] If, with Nussbaum, we read Cleland/Fanny "not as a 'man' who puts on a 'woman,' but as an ambiguously gendered human embodiment that may resonate with recognized sexualities but may also invent others," this should also apply, a fortiori, to the reader/Madam.[12] The novel's first word unsettles every possible reading because it throws our own position into doubt while assigning responsibility for the text to our "curiosity" and "desires," whoever we are.

Fanny yields to Madam's "pressing" (91) and starts to write some eighteen years after the last scene she narrates, her acceptance of Charles's proposal of marriage.[13] But while the narrative thus has the retrospective form of such fictional autobiographies as Defoe's *Moll Flanders* and *Colonel Jack* (both 1722), it scrupulously avoids their penitential moral structure. Fanny describes herself as having "emerg'd" from the "scandalous" earlier stages of her life, but although she retires from prostitution, she experiences no moral awakening even of the ambiguous kind narrated by Moll and Jack. Her memoirs contain no warning and proffer no lesson, nor do they express regret. She does, in passing, describe herself "looking back on the course of vice, I had run, and comparing its infamous blandishments with the infinitely superior joys of innocence" (187), but as Fanny uses them, even the terms "vice" and "innocence" are not really moral, but affective—based, that is, on her affective preference of Charles, the source of those "superior joys," to all her other sexual partners. Innocence in a prelapsarian sense, as virginity, or ignorance of the ways of the world, is laughable or pitiable, and she never regrets its loss. In any case, it is clear from the start that Madam the reader neither wants nor expects "the history of a wicked life repented of," as Moll Flanders's "editor" puts it in Defoe's novel; instead, Madam has asked Fanny "to recall to view" only the "scandalous stages of my life." And Fanny offers "no farther apology, than to prepare you for seeing the loose part of my life, wrote with the same liberty that I led it" (1). She is quite happy to flout any censorial standard, "careless of violating those laws of decency, that were never meant for such unreserved intimacies as ours"— implying, of course, that their intimacy is itself indecent, however the reader might choose to interpret this.

If the *Woman of Pleasure* deviates from the moral pattern of Defoe's first-person accounts, which value "the penitent Part" far above "the criminal Part" of the narrator's life (notwithstanding the complexity of Defoe's treatment of this pattern), it strays even more flagrantly from the pattern popularized in Richardson's *Pamela*, as intimated in its subtitle: *Virtue Rewarded*.[14] Cleland's novel has often been identified as a product of the "anti-Pamelist" faction, whose most notable exponents were Henry Fielding and Eliza Haywood, and of course "virtue" in the narrowly sexual sense is not rewarded in Fanny's narrative, but blithely disregarded or mocked. Cleland signals his awareness of the Pamela-Shamela conflict early on, when Fanny's townswoman Esther adopts the misspelling of "virtue" as "vartue" by which Fielding derided what he represents as the real, mercenary, motivation underlying Pamela's virtuous pretenses. Urging Fanny to come with her to London, Esther offers a Shamelan spin on the *Pamela* plot to lure her, telling her "as how several maids out of the country had made themselves and all their kin for ever, that by preserving their VARTUE, some had taken so with their masters, that they had married them, and kept them coaches, and lived vastly grand, and happy, and some, may-hap, come to be Dutchesses" (3). Fanny, however, is neither Pamela nor Shamela, neither chaste nor a mercenary marriage hunter, and Cleland, as Peter Sabor astutely notes, has produced "a novel that is anti-Shamela as well as anti-Pamela, a critique and an imitation of both works."[15] That the practice of novel writing was for Cleland a form of both imitation (albeit allusive, refracted) and critique (albeit playful, ambivalent) is borne out by the resistance of both *Memoirs* to any resolution of the conflicts their plots, or their narrators' desires, set in motion. Not that the *Woman of Pleasure* is inconclusive: it ends, like *Pamela*, with its heroine happily married to a man of higher social origins, and mother to his children, living in "ease and affluence." Indeed it even follows, in an affective or romantic sense, the model provided by the Richardsonian subtitle "Virtue Rewarded," for while Fanny is no tenacious defender of virtue-as-virginity, it is her constant devotion to her first love, Charles, that earns her her happy ending. In that respect Cleland's novel may act as evidence for the defense against Richardson's detractors, for it serves to remind us that Pamela's virtue is not only—not even mainly—virginity, but integrity, an articulated sense of her own moral agency and worth.[16] Yet if Cleland, like Richardson, brings the narrative to a close by linking romantic fulfillment to social advancement as fitting rewards for moral or affective integrity, he also pulls the rug out from under the complacent domesticity to which his protagonist imagines herself to have arrived, exposing it, like Fielding, as at least in part a sham.

Fanny's origins are as unpromising as those of any protagonist in eighteenth-century fiction. "I was born," she writes, "at a small village near *Liverpool* in *Lancashire*, of parents extremely poor, and I piously believe, extremely honest" (1–2): her father a disabled net maker, earning a "scanty subsistance," and her mother the keeper of "a little day-school for the girls in her neighbourhood" (2). If this last detail suggests a belief in the value of education even for girls of very low social rank, Fanny notes that her own instruction, "till past fourteen, was no better than very vulgar; reading, or rather spelling, an illegible scrawl, and a little ordinary plain-work, composed the whole system of it: and then all my foundation in virtue was no other than a total ignorance of vice" (2). Fanny's own education is neglected because the social possibilities open to her are so negligible: a little sewing, an illegible scrawl, and a general ignorance of the world are sufficient to her prospects, even in her mother's eyes. It is only when she is orphaned by the loss of both parents to smallpox that her real education begins, with her setting out for London.

Fanny Hill is even more disconnected, deracinated, than Moll Flanders or Hogarth's Moll Hackabout, the country girl corrupted of *The Harlot's Progress* (1732). She has no kin, no friends, no village connections: her father was an uprooted "Kentish-man" whose settling in Lancashire was "accidental." Abandoned by her guardian Esther the moment they arrive in London, Fanny is left "stupified, and most perfectly perplex'd how to dispose of myself" (5). "Distitute," directionless, she has reached the first of her story's narrative cruces or crises. In the scenes of her arrival in London and her visit to an "intelligence-office" to find a "place," Cleland works through many of the same motifs found in the first plate of *The Harlot's Progress*, in which Hogarth stages the corruption and demise of a rural innocent snared into prostitution. All the elements are in place: the stage wagon (from Chester or York); the inn (unnamed in Cleland, The Bell in Hogarth); the "rustic wardrobe" of "a young country-girl, barely fifteen" (6); and of course the ensnarer, "a lady (for such my extreme innocence pronounc'd her)" whose "grave and matron-like" (7) air conceals her profession of bawd, and whose flattery and solicitous attention to the welfare of "an artless unexperienced country-maid" convinces Fanny that she "was by the greatest good luck fallen into the hands of the kindest mistress, not to say friend, that the *varsal* world could afford" (8). It soon transpires that this Mrs. Brown is acting as procuress for a depraved and brutal "monster" (16) with a penchant for virgins—analogous to the gentleman lurking in the inn doorway in Hogarth's image (hand to crotch, leering at Moll), who has been identified as the notorious Colonel Francis Charteris, convicted in 1730 of the rape of his servant Anne Bond.[17] Through all these allusions to the well-known components of Hogarth's engraving, Cleland both identifies one narrative genre to which the text belongs and prepares for the deviations from Hogarth's plot that will mark the *Woman of Pleasure* as a radical departure from the traditional, monitory form of whore narratives, which end with chastisement, confinement, or death.[18]

The scenes Fanny witnesses at Mrs. Brown's are the real beginning of her education, comprising disillusionment, erotic awakening, and dawning awareness of her own social place. Fanny is groomed as a virgin sacrifice to the "shocking hideous" (16) elderly gentleman Mrs. Brown calls her cousin, and to that end she is taken in hand by Phoebe Ayres, "one of [Mrs. Brown's] favourite girls, a notable manager of her house, and whose business it was to prepare and break such young Fillies as I was to the mounting-block" (9). Phoebe, too, is called "cousin" by Mrs. Brown, a parody of kinship analogous to Mrs. Brown's assumption of the place of mother (repeated by the more genteel bawd Mrs. Cole in the novel's second half). Throughout the novel, the satirical equation of brothels with loving family homes has the double effect of glamorizing prostitution and unmasking the sexual exploitativeness of the respectable bourgeois household—thus laying the groundwork for the cynicism or ambiguity of the novel's final pages. In these early scenes, Fanny is still too "simple, and silly" (13) to perceive herself as an object of exploitation, and even after the

old "monster" Mr. Crofts tries to rape her, obviously with Mrs. Brown's conniv-
ance, Fanny notes that "I sought to deceive myself with the continuation of my
good opinion of her . . . sooner than being turn'd out to starve in the streets,
without a penny of money, or a friend to apply to" (19–20). Here, the disillusionment integral to a moral or sentimental education is half-knowingly held
at bay in consequence of Fanny's still rather inchoate sense of her own social
powerlessness and alienation. Expelled from Mrs. Brown's "family" (however
monstrous or ersatz) Fanny would become just one more of those poor "wandering" the London streets whom Henry Fielding argued should be sent back
to their "Habitations" and compelled "to starve or beg at home."[19]

The focus of Fanny's education at Mrs. Brown's is eros. Phoebe, her "tuter-
ess elect" (9), acting at the behest of Mrs. Brown to ensure her submissiveness
to her clients' desires, takes a powerful sexual interest in Fanny herself and
elicits Fanny's sexual curiosity and desire in ways that threaten to bypass the
logic of patriarchal control—which Mrs. Brown, although an entrepreneurial
woman, serves by constantly replenishing the marketable stock of young wom-
en enslaved to a system that ruthlessly commodifies female sexuality. A woman
caught up in such a "household," Cleland wrote in another text the same year,
is "enslaved in short so thoroughly, that nothing, no, not her own Person, is her
own Property, or at her own Disposal."[20] This is the abject state to which Fanny
is to be reduced or broken, and as Cleland writes in his *Case of the Unfortunate
Bosavern Penlez*, "This is effected commonly by indulging and humouring the
giddy, wild, thoughtless Turn, natural to that Age, till [the bawd] fixes a good
round Debt upon her; the imaginary Terrors of which, keep her in a State of
Slavery" (8–9). Indulging Fanny's wild side is Phoebe's task. On Fanny's first
night at Mrs. Brown's, Phoebe, "who was never out of her way when any occasion of lewdness presented itself, turned to me, embraced, and kiss'd me with
great eagerness. This was new, this was odd" (10), Fanny writes, but nonplussed
as she is at first, she soon experiences "a strange, and till then unfelt pleasure
. . . a new fire that wanton'd through all my veins" (11). It is striking that Fanny's
experience of a "till then unfelt pleasure" is not especially pleasant, and produces a sense of self-estrangement: "I was transported, confused, and out of
myself," she writes. "Feelings so new were too much for me; my heated and
alarm'd senses were in a tumult that robb'd me of all liberty of thought; tears
of pleasure gush'd from my eyes" (11–12). The sensation of pleasure provokes,
undoes, overwhelms, but doesn't prepare her to be tractable or to submit pas-
sively to male desire. Indeed, having "caught," as she puts it, "the first sparks of
kindling nature, the first ideas of pollution" (12) at the "licentious" hands of the

sapphically inclined Phoebe, Fanny learns to desire at least as much through her relations with other women as through her encounters with men.[21]

Although Fanny finally dismisses her sexual activities with Phoebe as "this foolery from woman to woman" and as "rather the shadow than the substance of any pleasure" (34), I agree with John Beynon and Lisa L. Moore that female same-sex desire persists as an essential component of Fanny's experience as prostitute, kept woman, and wife.[22] Fanny is perplexed, not to say disturbed (and aroused), by Phoebe's "fierce and salacious" (11) attentions, and speculates that Phoebe, "to whom all modes and devices of pleasure were known and familiar," finds

> in this exercise of her art to break young girls, the gratification of one of those arbitrary tastes, for which there is no accounting: not that she hated men, or did not even prefer them to her own sex; but when she met with such occasions as this was, a satiety of enjoyments in the common road, perhaps too a secret byass, inclined her to make the most of pleasure, where-ever she could find it, without distinction of sexes (12).

As Moore observes, Fanny runs through a range of possible sexual identities and hierarchies of desire in this passage—imagining by turns that Phoebe "prefer[s]" men, that she has a "secret byass" for women, that she makes no "distinction of sexes"—attributing to her not an androgynous body but an androgyny of desire that becomes the keynote of her representations of sexuality itself. In chapter 3 I argued that, in Fanny's *Memoirs*, all desire can be subsumed under the heading of sodomy; here I focus instead on Fanny's construction of other-sex desire as a by-product of her desire for women.

If Phoebe, her hands "like . . . lambent fire" (11), is the first to awaken Fanny to the "tumult" of pleasure and desire, her professional motive for doing so is to prepare her for her "deflowering" by the hideous Mr. Crofts. But Fanny feels so powerful an aversion that when she's left alone with him she struggles against his "attack," and his "hot fit of lust" ends with a premature "effusion" (19) on his part and "a nose gushing out blood" on hers (20). In the aftermath of his assault, Fanny falls into "a violent fever" (22), and while this buys her a temporary reprieve, it also induces Mrs. Brown to send the other girls of the house to visit, with an eye, Fanny writes, "to dispose me, by their conversation, to a perfect resignation of myself to Mrs. *Brown's* direction." The plan proves effective, and in short order "the being one of them became even my ambition: a disposition which they all carefully cultivated; and I wanted now nothing but to restore my health, that I might be able to undergo the ceremony of the initiation." In the company of whores, Fanny wants nothing else than to be a whore herself—not out of desire for or even curiosity about men, but to be part of this community of women. "Conversation, example, all," she writes, "contributed, in that house, to corrupt my native purity, which had taken no root in education, whilst now the inflamable principle of pleasure, so easily fired at my age, made strange work within me" (22–23). If the first stage of Fanny's education was tactile—Phoebe's "lascivious touches light[ing] up a new fire that wanton'd through all my veins" (11)—the second and decisive stage is effected by language: the other girls' "luscious talk, in which modesty was far from respected, their descriptions of their engagements with men, had given me a tolerable insight into the nature and mysteries of their profession, at the same time that they highly provok'd an itch of florid warm-spirited blood through every vein" (23). Conversation, luscious talk, stories, and descriptions all produce powerful physiological effects, and if their stories concern "engagements with men," Fanny asserts that she is "indebted only to the girls" for her corruption: whatever sexual interest she develops in men is mediated and prompted by the "luscious talk" of other women.

Accordingly, Phoebe, while continuing to "exert her talents in giving me the first tinctures of pleasure," also builds on the other girls' spoken lessons or lectures, rather Socratically "leading" Fanny "from question to question of her own suggestion" and so "explain[ing] to me all the mysteries of *Venus*." From Socratic dialogue Fanny proceeds to visual demonstration, first spying on Mrs. Brown having sex with her "favourite," a young horse grenadier (26), and then secreted in a dark closet by Phoebe to observe Polly Philips, one of the girls whose luscious talk so "provok'd" her, with her "keeper," a young Genoese merchant. In these episodes Fanny sees, for the first time, what she calls "that wonderful machine" (25), the penis, and she does immediately give it pride of place, writing after the first scene of "the rekindl'd rage and tumult of my desires, which all pointed to their pole, man" (27). From this point on, the phallus becomes the object of Fanny's most ardent descriptive attention and desire. I would, accordingly, not contest the critical claim that the text is phallocentric, but while Fanny attributes her fixation on the phallus to "the instinct of nature" (25), she acknowledges that it was her companions who taught her to see: "Prepared then, and disposed as I was by the discourse of my companions, and *Phoebe's* minute detail of every thing, no wonder that such a sight gave the last dying blow to my native innocence."[23] The wonderful machine "rekindl[es]"—reproduces—the desire that Phoebe has already "kindl[ed]" (12), and Fanny is drawn by "instinct" to the male "pole" in light of her companions' earlier discourse of pleasure. The "instinct of nature" takes effect within a social context that in many ways prioritizes (privileges and places first) same-sex affective and erotic bonds—and in any case, as with Phoebe's "secret byass," that instinct may not be other-sex centered.

When Fanny spies on Polly and "the young *Italian*" (30), what inflames her desire is not so much his body—for "luscious" as her description of it is, her description of Polly's is no less so—as "*Polly's* expressions of extasy" (31): both the words she utters as they have sex, and her gestures and facial expressions. The voyeuristic scene is structured by Phoebe as a demonstration in response to Fanny's anxious question about the "imaginary disproportion" (28) of female and male "parts." So, when Fanny sees the Italian naked, she writes that his "grand movement" was "of a size to frighten me, by sympathy, for the small tender part, which was the object of its fury" (30), and Phoebe, ever vigilant, asks Fanny "whether I thought my little maiden-toy was much less" than Polly's. Fanny, by her affective "sympathy" and Phoebe's express invitation, watches the whole scene in light of her identification with Polly and is attentive above all to Polly's responses, as when "she gave a deep sigh, which was quite in another tone than one of pain" (31), or when, afterward, "she gets up, and throwing her arms round him, seemed far from undelighted with the trial he had put her to, to judge at least by the fondness with which she ey'd, and hung upon him." Of this last tableau, Fanny writes, "From that instant, adieu all fears of what man could do unto me; they were now changed into . . . ardent desires . . . ungovernable longings." It is Polly's pantomime of delight that turns fears into desires. Fanny follows up her admission that from this moment she "could have pull'd the first of that sex that should present himself, by the sleeve, and offer'd him the bauble" (31–32) of her virginity, by doing precisely this with the next man she sees. Of course, this is the beloved Charles, but in light of Fanny's admission, their relationship loses a little of the romantic luster with which she labors to invest it. Any man would have done, for what Fanny "ardent[ly] desires" is just to feel what Polly felt.

Nonetheless, her sighting of Charles marks another of her story's cruces, a narrative turning point that also marks an apparent shift in genre, from whore narrative to romance.[24] Their chance meeting leads to their plotting Fanny's escape from Mrs. Brown's still a virgin, no longer the would-be whore but a personification of virtue in distress, whose getaway from her mistress's house she narrates in the breathless language of her adopted genre. "It came at last," she writes, "the dear, critical, dangerous hour came"—this even though no one else in the house is awake to stop her and the key to the front door lies where it always lies, on the chair next to her bed—"and now supported only by the courage love lent me, I ventur'd a tip-toe down stairs . . . Love that embolden'd, protected me too: and now, got safe into the street, I saw my new guardian-angel waiting at a coach-door ready open" (37–38). The passage exemplifies the doubleness of Cleland's writing, in that it both produces a certain excitement or suspense—similar to the excitement of those scenes from Richardson's *Clarissa* (1747–1748) in which the heroine tries in vain to escape from Mrs. Sinclair's London brothel—and makes fun of such hackneyed narrative effects.

The same is true of Fanny's instantaneous outpouring of love for this young man she finds sleeping off the previous night's "drunken revel" (34). She writes, "No term of years, no turns of fortune could ever eraze the lightening-like impression his form made on . . . my ravish'd eyes," before launching into a catalog of his beauties, and if on the one hand her portrait is sensually alluring, on the other her haste in ascribing the "passion" she then felt not to "gross lust" but to "new-born love, that true refiner of lust" (35) is faintly absurd, even by the laws of love at first sight. By the start of the second paragraph after she first sees him, his health—she is worried he might catch cold with his shirt collar unbuttoned—"began to be my life's concern"; by the next page she asserts that "I could, at that instant, have died for him" (36); a page further in, she exclaims, "The seeing, the touching, the being, if but for a night, with this idol of my fond virgin-heart, appeared to me a happiness above the purchase of my liberty or life. He might use me ill! let him! he was the master! happy, too happy even to receive death at so dear a hand" (37). Yet for all the clichéd and masochistic extravagance of Fanny's rhetoric—the very stuff of romance—the love plot is really only playing out in her own imagination. Charles doesn't see her as virtue in distress or suppose her a virgin; he assumes she is "one of the misses of the house" (35) and asks her to have sex with him on the spot, "assuring me that he would make it worth my while." The best approximation of love he can offer is to tell her later that he "lik'd her as much as he could think of liking any one in my suppos'd way of life" (36), and he "ask'd me briskly at once, if I would be kept by him," not because he is love struck but because "in his fears of the hazard of the town"—that is, venereal disease—"he had been some time looking out for a girl to take into keeping." Although Fanny writes that "it was by one of those miracles reserv'd to love, that we struck the bargain in the instant," from her own evidence there's nothing miraculous about it: her "person happen[ed] to hit his fancy," he took her for a whore, she played along, and they "struck the bargain." From this more disenchanted or cynical perspective she has simply moved on to the second stage of "The Harlot's Progress," that of being kept by a gentleman, and the "miracle" of love proves, in truth, a commercial transaction.

None of which is to say that Fanny as narrator is either insincere, hypocritical, or deluded, as it is she who registers the dissonances and discrepancies of this crucial scene. But she wants, like any narrator, to make such scenes intelligible in the light of a meaning-giving plot: intelligible, that is, in terms of its outcome or ending, which in her case, by her reading—as will also be true of Sir William in *Memoirs of a Coxcomb*—is the happy ending of romance. The two memoirs' romance plots are the same: the young protagonist falls in love with an ideal or idealized partner of the opposite sex; the beloved disappears; the protagonist is prevented from seeking out the beloved; he or she thereupon enters into a life of wantonness and extravagant but emotionally unfulfilling sexual indulgence; the beloved is accidentally rediscovered; and the lovers are reunited, this time for life, and of course happily. But if William and Fanny want to write their memoirs in the form of romance, these are not the only plots at work in their texts, and a scene such as Fanny's meeting with Charles may mean quite different things in the different plots it is part of. As a scene from romance, it is a fateful, predestined encounter: love is immediate and undying, the story's beginning and ending, which every obstacle, interruption, or digression along the way can only defer, never alter. To her mind, Fanny has no say in the matter: "love itself took charge of the disposal of me, in spite of interest, or gross lust" (34). As a scene from a harlot's progress, however, it shows interest and lust in action: each of them has some good, economic or sexual, that the other wants, and a bargain is struck. The naïve Fanny may be "ravish'd," but in fact she is only following the familiar path of Polly and Hogarth's Moll, taken into keeping at an early stage of their eventual, inexorable downfall. As a scene from Fanny's education in desire, it puts to the test her resolution to have sex with the first man she sees and thus to experience Polly's pleasure for herself. It is only when she has heard and seen what other women want, by their discourse and dumb show, that she begins to conceive what she wants herself. Charles is simply a means to an epistemological end: the knowledge of pleasure.

Fanny's departure from Mrs. Brown's clearly marks a new phase in the narrative, removing her from the woman-centered world in which her education began. Charles takes over as Fanny's teacher, "instructing me, as far as his own lights reached; in a great many points of life, that I was, in consequence of my no-education, perfectly ignorant of" (53), and taking control of her both economically and sexually. Fanny's lubricious account of their first hours together takes the clichés of erotic writing—"what floods of bliss! what melting trans-

ports! what agonies of delight!" (43)—to extremes of anguish and disembody-
ing, ecstatic liquefaction. Of Charles, she writes, "Born head-long away by the
fury and over-mettle of that member, now exerting itself with a kind of native
rage, he breaks in, carries all before him, and one violent merciless lunge, sent
it, imbrew'd, and reeking with virgin blood, up to the very hilts in me" (41).
But Charles's murderous violence only makes her love him more: "I arriv'd at
excess of pleasure, through excess of pain" (42), she writes, and this pleasure is
a type of death, "a delicious momentary dissolution" (43).[25] In Fanny's version
of the old metaphor of orgasm as dying, Charles, "he who now was the absolute
disposer of my happiness, and in one word, my fate" (41), is also her "murderer
. . . who hung mourning tenderly over me"—an image that fulfills her earlier
boast that she was "happy, too happy even to receive death at so dear a hand"
(37). In thus linking "real" sexual pleasure to utter, abject submission to male
authority, Fanny's "progress" appears to affirm Nussbaum's claim that "sexual
desire for the same sex . . . must be rechanneled toward men in order to be fully
satisfying"—leading, by the novel's end, to Fanny's transformation from whore
into "bourgeois matron" and validating "the moral superiority of monogamous
wedded love."[26]

This, of course, is the moral trajectory that Fanny herself insists on impos-
ing on her memoirs in the work's opening and closing pages. Her elopement
from Mrs. Brown's with Charles represents her passage from the "foolery from
woman to woman" offered by Phoebe to "more solid food" (34), from "the
shadow" to "the substance" of pleasure. Yet as I suggested in chapter 3, the
relationship between Charles and Fanny cannot be summed up or cordoned off
as heterosexual, for Charles is not (or not only) of one but "of either sex" (44),
and Fanny, too, as Donald Mengay first observed, repeatedly figures herself as
phallic—a point Nussbaum also makes, writing, "Cleland radically implies that
Fanny Hill's body is both male and female."[27] Charles and Fanny can thus be
read by turns as sodomites, as tribades, as man and wife—not only confounding the borders between same-sex and other-sex desire but calling into question
the very notions of same and other sexes. The novel's profusion of ambiguous,
androgynous, unreadable, unsexed bodies repels any critical effort to fix it as a
validation of something that would later come to be known as "heterosexuality,"
especially if this is assumed to be already normative or taken for granted at the
time Cleland wrote.[28] For if it's true, as Nussbaum writes, that "sexual desire for
the same sex is necessary but must be rechanneled toward men in order to be
fully satisfying," it is also true that desire for the "other" sex, to be fully satisfying, has to be redirected toward women.

The clearest examples of this are found in the novel's second part, when Fanny joins Mrs. Cole's "little Seraglio" (95)—a word that in itself, as John Beynon notes, carried sapphic overtones in the period.[29] The extended "ceremonial of initiation" with which the second volume begins repeats the pattern of Fanny's education at Mrs. Brown's: first the "luscious talk" of the other girls, as Emily, Harriet, and Louisa tell how they lost their virginity; then visual demonstration, as she watches each of the others in turn having sex, in a kind of genteel serial orgy; and then having sex herself, with the rest of the company looking on. Despite the orgy's ostensibly "heterosexual" structure, what is striking is the extent to which the action is orchestrated to comply with the interests of what Lisa Moore calls "a female homosexual gaze."[30] Again and again, Fanny draws attention to the care with which the women arrange their own and each other's bodies into tableaux of visible and reciprocal desire—reciprocal, that is, not just between the male and female of each couple, but between the female observer and observed. The most flagrant instance appears when Harriet's beau lifts her petticoats, "at which, as if a signal had been given, *Louisa* and *Emily* took hold of her legs, in pure wantoness, and yet in ease too, to her, kept them stretch'd wide abroad. Then lay expos'd, or to speak more properly, display'd the greatest parade in nature of female charms" (115). In part, of course, Louisa and Emily's action facilitates the beau's mastery by offering Harriet's body up to him, but Fanny stresses their sisterly interest in Harriet's "ease" as well as the "pure wantoness" that betrays their own desire to gaze on this "display" of "female charms." There is a continuity of desire among all those present: the "wanton" Louisa and Emily; the "enamour'd gallant," who stands "absorb'd and engross'd by the pleasure of the sight"; Fanny and the others looking, who benefit from the gallant's desiring gaze, since it holds him spellbound "long enough to afford us time to feast ours, no fear of glutting!" (115–116); and Harriet herself, who begins the scene by appealing to Fanny, "blushing as she look'd at me, and with eyes made to justify any thing" (114), in effect performing for *her* approbation and pleasure. This continuity of desire extends beyond the scene as well, to include Mrs. Cole—for although she discreetly leaves the room when the orgy begins, she later talks to Fanny about "the pleasures of the preceding night" (125), and Fanny learns "without much surprise, as I began to enter her character, that she had seen everything that had passed, from a convenient place, manag'd solely for that purpose, and of which she readily made me the confidante." The whole spectacle, in effect, has been "manag'd" for her voyeuristic pleasure, of which she "readily" enlists Fanny as "confidante," again privileging the circulation of pleasure and desire among women.

Mrs. Cole is thus the mirror of Fanny's Madam, and of the novel's reader, the offstage spectator to whose gratification the performance is devoted. Rather than take for granted that the text can only really be addressed to a male "heterosexual" readership by a male "heterosexual" author (ideologically heterosexual if not practically so), I would argue that the Mrs. Cole–Fanny dynamic here foregrounds instead the sheer range of possible desiring positions both inside and outside the space of narrative action.[31] Certainly the relationship between the two, which dominates the novel's second volume, offers a powerful sapphic counterweight to the linearity and teleology of the heterosexual romance plot, within which Charles is Fanny's alpha and omega, her master and natural husband. For while her eleven months with Charles represent a crucial stage in her formation, and his disappearance when she is "three months gone with child by him" (54) marks the third of her narrative's cruces—forcing her to become the "kept mistress" (66) of Mr. H——, her "first launch into vice" (65)—in the economy of the text as a whole, Charles is far more absent than present, and not even an absent object of desire for most of it.[32] So while it may be true that Fanny progresses from sapphic "foolery" to "more solid" phallic "food" when she passes from Mrs. Brown and Phoebe to Charles, she moves on again, after he disappears, to other men, other women—of whom Mrs. Cole has the greatest impact on her life. Just as she described Charles as "the absolute disposer of my happiness, and in one word, my fate" (41), so she refers to Mrs. Cole as "one to whom I had now thoroughly abandon'd the direction of all my steps" (92), stressing that theirs is not just a business partnership: "For Mrs. *Cole* had, I do not know how, unless by one of those unaccountable invincible simpathies, that nevertheless form the strongest links, especially of female friendship, won and got intire possession of me." Although Fanny gives no report of any "foolery" between them, she places considerable weight on the sympathy that "links" them, emphasizing its strangeness and "unaccountab[ility]."[33] The sympathy between them is so strong as to blur the boundary between "female friendship" and "intire possession," with its unignorable (in context) sexual connotation. This ambiguity colors much of the novel's second half and surfaces most suggestively at those moments when Mrs. Cole's voyeuristic presence is discovered: on the morning after the orgy, and in the midst of Fanny's whipping session with Mr. Barvile, when she is "rehearten'd" to let him whip her as she has whipped him, "especially, as I well knew Mrs. *Cole* was an eye-witness, from her stand of espial, to the whole of our transactions" (148). Later she writes that "this adventurous exploit had more and more endear'd" her to Mrs. Cole, and here again there is a blurring between Mrs. Cole's sense of Fanny's economic value, for Barvile has paid them both well, and the "endear[ing]" pleasures of watching her (153).

A similar sympathy, blending "female friendship" and "intire possession," links Fanny to her epistolary Madam, whose "desires" are the occasion of Fanny's writing, in violation of the "laws of decency" (1). Contrary to what some other critics have stated, Fanny does not leave off writing when she is reunited with Charles, even if that is the point where she brings her story to a close; indeed up to that moment she has never written a word. Instead, her writing originates in Madam's desires, and it is only in writing that the pleasure by which she identifies herself is fully realized. It is curious that Fanny never tries to write Charles, and more curious still that Charles never writes her, during the "two years and seven months" (176) of their separation—so curious, in fact, as to lead Gary Gautier to suggest that Charles, rather than having been kidnapped and "forc'd on a long voyage without taking leave of one friend" (55), as Fanny is told after he disappears, has ditched her to avoid being saddled with a child and the burden of supporting them both.[34] I return to this point in my discussion of the novel's ending, but the fact that Fanny writes of her sexual and affective experience only to another woman reinforces the pattern established during her time at Mrs. Brown's: the circulation of eros—as gazes, stories, confessions—among women. And this sapphic circulation of "expressions of extasy" (31), whether the bodies involved are same sex, other sex, or something else, displaces or decenters the operations of the novel's various ready-made or generic plots: romance, Bildung, the harlot's progress.

One of the critical problems the *Woman of Pleasure* poses is that of how to make sense of the tension between the end-oriented momentum of the novel's plot or plots and the very episodic character of the text's unfolding, consisting as it largely does of a repetitive series of sexual descriptions. Robert Markley, while acknowledging the overarching structure of "female Bildung" described by Nancy Miller and others, writes that "the novel often seems less an educative harlot's progress than a nearly paratactic series of sexual adventures and descriptive vignettes."[35] More recently, John Beynon has proposed that "the pleasure we derive from [this] text" does not lie "in the traditional narrative imperatives of fiction and its teleological drive" but in its "proliferation" of "self-contained moments presenting a variety of sexual propensities, situations, and bodily configurations."[36] Annamarie Jagose, decrying what she calls "the overvaluation of story and the undervaluation of sexual description" in "most critical discussions" of the novel, argues that these miss out on the novel's crucial ideological intervention: its role in "giv[ing] voice to an emergent sexual ideology," that of "heterosexuality" itself.[37] Finally, in an essay exploring "the interaction of male and female erotic dynamics of plot," Antje Schaum Anderson argues that the particular "female plot model" at work in Cleland's narrative undermines "the male, linear plot of Fanny's sexual initiation and education."[38] All these readings offer insights into the tension between linear progress and descriptive repetition in Cleland's text, and I want to follow up by looking at what Fanny, or Cleland, has to say on the inescapability of repetition in writing about eros. Author and narrator superimpose the form of variations on a theme on the intersecting linear plots I have been tracing: an experiment in narrative form analogous to the challenge originally set by Charles Carmichael in Bombay, to write about sex without using "plain words." How do you tell a story through repetition? Cleland uses the tension between repetition and plot as a way of testing or interrogating the *value* of plot, especially as this affects the formation of personal identity. In so doing he contributes his part to the fashioning of the novel as a genre that distrusts and does violence to the plots it depends on.

Circles of Pleasure / Poisonous Remedies: Cleland and the Novel Form

As Robert Markley writes, "Few novels stop in mid-course to tell you how boring they are," but Fanny's apology to Madam at the start of the *Woman of Pleasure*'s second volume raises the possibility or threat of boredom as integral to any story with sex at its center.[39] "I imagined indeed," she writes, "that you would have been cloy'd and tired with the uniformity of adventures and expressions, inseparable from a subject of this sort, whose bottom or ground-work being, in the nature of things, eternally one and the same, whatever variety of forms and modes, the situations are susceptible of, there is no escaping a repetition of near the same images, the same figures, the same expressions" (91). Fanny's apology, however, is also a boast disguised as a gesture of authorial modesty: if her subject is "in the nature of things, eternally one and the same," it is her ingenuity in devising a "variety of forms and modes"—inventing images, figures, and expressions that, if "near," are nevertheless not "the same"—that the reader has to thank for not being "cloy'd and tired." Quite the opposite: Madam has demanded a continuation of the narrative, and anyone who reads this passage has opted to pay for and plunge into the second volume (or at any rate, as when the two volumes are published together, to keep on rather than stop reading). So if

Fanny pays her obligatory respects to Madam's imagination and sensibility as necessary "supplements, where my descriptions flag or fail," Madam's "pressing" desire for a continuation demonstrates that Fanny hasn't failed at all.

Fanny's apology, indeed the text as a whole, plays with the dialectic between sameness and difference: if each scene of sexual description is, structurally, more or less the same—preliminaries, penetration, simultaneous orgasm—the variety of settings, body types, motives, emotional bonds, and visual or narrative perspectives is considerable. Apart from the two scenes Fanny spies on from a dark closet (once alone, once with Phoebe), the first volume ranges from the same-sex erotics of her initiation by Phoebe to the "pestilential" (18) Mr. Crofts's attempted rape; from the extreme physical pain of her defloration (which is nevertheless an expression of affective bliss) to the "lifeless insensibility" and subsequent "pleasure merely animal . . . struck out of the collision of the sexes, by a passive bodily effect" (60, 64) of her first encounters with Mr. H——; and it culminates in her "extacy, that extended us fainting, breathless, entranced" (83), with the bashful but "prodigious" footman Will. In the second volume, there are extended episodes in which the bodies on display are virtually interchangeable: the orgy at Mrs. Cole's, with its succession of couplings, or the edenic "party of pleasure" involving Fanny, Emily, and "two very pretty young gentlemen" (166) where, as Fanny writes of one couple, "as their limbs were thus amorously interwoven, in sweet confusion, it was scarce possible to distinguish who they respectively belonged to" (170). The couple's unsexed bodies affirm the lability of desire, but in thus depersonalizing it they also collapse every enactment of eros into a repetition, however pleasant, of the same—so that when Fanny and her spark in turn "finished our trip to *Cythera*, and unloaded in the old haven," she dryly notes that "as the circumstances did not admit of much variation, I shall spare you the description" (171). It was perhaps to offset an increasing sense of "the uniformity of adventures" that Cleland extended the range of proclivities in the second volume to include flagellation, fetishism, and of course sodomy.

Against this encyclopedic impulse to encompass the diversity of sexual practices and tastes, Fanny repeatedly expresses the sense that at bottom (to deploy her own pun) one scene is much the same as another. She suggests this in her very first description, writing of Mrs. Brown and the horse grenadier, at the end of their second go-round, "And thus they finish'd, in the same manner as before, the old last act" (26). The phrase is more suited to the mature, worldly writer than to the ingenuous, inflamed *voyeuse*, but repetition seems integral to desire from the very start. Later, Fanny uses similar terms to bring what she represents as sexual "freaks" (166) or "criminal scenes" (159) within the compass of the familiar: so Louisa, at the end of her "terrible sally" with the "soft simpleton" Good-natur'd Dick, "kept him faithful company, going off, in consent, with the old symptoms" (165), while at the end of the sodomitical scene she writes, "The height of the fit came on with its usual symptoms, and dismiss'd the action" (159). "The old last act," "the old," or the "usual symptoms": the wording seems to connote exhaustion, ennui, excitement recollected in weariness. But repetition has another sense in the novel: refreshment, renewal, the continued force of desire even after its satisfaction. If, as Steven Marcus writes, "fulfillment implies completion, gratification, an end"—that is, death—repetition acts as a sign of life, the inexhaustibility of pleasure.[40] So, when Fanny is reunited with Charles, as they launch into their second round of lovemaking, she writes that "we play'd over-again the same opera," which on its own might sound dismissive, but not as she goes on to develop the figure: "with the same delightful harmony and concert: our ardours, like our love, knew no remission" (185). Play, whether of music or games, makes repetition a condition of pleasure, and as Fanny spins out the musical metaphor, repetition becomes a necessary condition of love as well.

This association of repetition with play echoes Fanny's account of her first night together with Charles, "when after playing repeated prizes of pleasure, nature overspent, and satisfy'd, gave us up to the arms of sleep" (43). Nature is "satisfy'd," but unlike what Marcus calls "fulfillment," satisfaction doesn't imply an end, but a pause. And if orgasm and sleep have often been figured as little deaths, they are crucially unlike death in that life (waking, desire) keeps renewing itself in their wake. So in this first scene with Charles, Fanny extols "the fierceness of refreshed desires" (42) and, adopting a figure analogous to that of musical repetition, writes that "we spent the whole afternoon, till supper-time, in a continued circle of love-delights" (43). The circle is a figure for everything that doesn't count as, or doesn't advance, plot, but it does advance, does count as time: time spent "playing repeated prizes of pleasure." The same image recurs in the "party of pleasure" episode, where Fanny concludes "that what with a competent number of repetitions, all in the same strain, (and by the bye, we have a certain natural sense that those repetitions are very much to the taste of) what with a circle of pleasures delicately varied, there was not a moment lost to joy all the time we staid there, till late in the night" (171). Joy unfolds in and over time, like music; and like the sapphic circulation of pleasure, the "circle of pleasures delicately varied" does not just delay the forward motion of plot but offers an alternative model for structuring time and text alike. The novel, of course, has a plot, or rather multiple generic plots—whore biography, romance, heroine's progress—which Cleland follows, deviates from, parodies; Fanny, too, uses such plots to make sense of the experiences she narrates. But to say the text is involved in plot is not to say it's governed by plot—not unless we privilege the novel's last two pages over the roughly two hundred that precede them. Instead of (or while also) reading the *Woman of Pleasure* as a romance or progress punctuated or stalled by sexual descriptions that, as Markley writes, "bring the ostensible narrative action . . . to a standstill," it needs to be approached as a set or cycle of variations on a theme: "the same strain," "the same opera," the "circle of pleasures delicately varied."[41] Partly through differences in external features (sex, age, beauty, locale, love), partly through "variety of forms and modes" ("expressions," "images," "figures"), the text draws variegation from sameness. Rather than a simple contrast between static episodes and temporally progressive story line—between dilations and the drive to an ending—the variation form registers the unfolding of experience in time while loosening this from the teleological grip of the plot's terminus or outcome. Narrative action doesn't come "to a standstill" in these episodes, but Cleland shifts the text's emphasis away from ready-made patterns and endings and toward a more open-ended, plural, or diffuse model of novelistic plot.

Cleland's interest in questions of plot is evident not only in the self-reflexive play of his first foray as a novelist but in his critical essays on the self-consciously experimental form of the novel at midcentury. In his review of Henry Fielding's last novel, *Amelia* (1751), which he was unusual in considering perhaps the best of Fielding's fictions—calling it "the boldest stroke that has been yet attempted in this species of writing"—Cleland suggests that Fielding's "original turn" is clearest in his deviation from the conventional romance plot:

> The author takes up his heroine at the very point at which all his predecessors have dropped their capital personages. It has been heretofore a general practice to conduct the lover and his mistress to the door of matrimony, and there leave them, as if after that ceremony the whole interest in them was at an end, and nothing could remain beyond it worthy of exciting or keeping up the curiosity of the reader.[42]

His remark is astute even if it overlooks one obvious precursor: that is, Richardson's *Pamela*, close to a third of which follows Pamela after she has walked through the "door of matrimony" with Mr. B. But what is significant in Cleland's observation is not whether he is correct that Fielding diverges from "all" his predecessors but, first, his implication that boldness and originality—that is, novelty—are essential to "this species of writing"; second, that they are best measured by an author's departure from received or conventional plots; and third, that the challenge implicit in such a departure is to find other ways of "exciting or keeping up the curiosity of the reader." Indeed, "he who does not peruse" *Amelia*, Cleland writes, "will hardly imagine how the relish of such conjugal endearments, as compose the basis of it, could be quickened enough to become palatable to the reader."[43]

As this last remark suggests, if *Amelia* and the *Woman of Pleasure* are alike in the challenge they face of "exciting" or "keeping up" the reader's curiosity, they differ radically in their "subject": in Fielding's case, "the history of two persons already married"; in Cleland's, the "circle of pleasures" prior and alien to marriage (for in Fanny's narrative, sexual pleasure stops at the "door of matrimony"). This difference is all the more striking in that Cleland's statement of Fielding's moral aims in *Amelia* is almost identical to the "tail-piece of morality" (187) with which Fanny concludes her memoirs. According to Cleland, "the chief and capital purport" of *Amelia* "is to inculcate the superiority of virtuous, conjugal, love, to all other joys; to prove that virtue chastens our pleasures, only to augment them; that the paths of vice, are always those of misery, and that virtue, even in distress, is still a happier bargain to its votaries, than vice, attended with all the splendor of fortune."[44] For her part, Fanny asserts of her married state that "in the bosom of virtue, I gather'd the only uncorrupt sweets" (187) and offers her condolences to "those who, immers'd in a gross sensuality, are insensible to the so delicate charms of VIRTUE, than which even PLEASURE has not a greater friend, nor than VICE a greater enemy" (187). But if Fanny espouses the same moral views that Cleland finds praiseworthy in *Amelia*, should we conclude we are meant to take her "tail-piece" straight? Rather than offering guidance in how to read Cleland's fiction, his critical writings on the novel, I would argue, complicate rather than clarify our relationship to the fictional text, drawing attention to the distance between the pronouncements Cleland makes in his own voice and their ironic or ambiguous effect as fictional utterances.

Cleland took energetic part in contemporary debates over the moral and aesthetic aims of fiction, both in the pages of the *Monthly Review* and in his practice as translator and novelist, and if the relationship between theory and practice is slippery and complex, his work in both domains exhibits a sophisticated critical intelligence informed by his familiarity with developments in French as well as English literature. Like the *Woman of Pleasure, Memoirs of a Coxcomb* offers itself as a work of moral instruction: Sir William Delamore describes his narrative, on its first page, as the "history of my errors, and return to reason."[45] And in his critical writing, Cleland, like Samuel Johnson in his famous *Rambler* essay on fiction, asserts that the novelist's project is fundamentally instructive, as in his review of Smollett's *Peregrine Pickle*:

> There are perhaps no works of entertainment more susceptible of improvement or public utility, than such as are thus calculated to convey instruction, under the passport of amusement. How many readers may be taught to pursue good, and to avoid evil, to refine their morals, and to detest vice, who are profitably decoyed into the perusal of these writings by the pleasure they expect to be paid with for their attention, who would not care to be dragged through a dry, didactic system of morality; or who would, from a love of truth universally impressed on mankind, despise inventions which do not at least pay truth the homage of imitation?[46]

Like Johnson the year before, who had memorably declared, of works of fiction that "exhibit life in its true state," that "these books are written chiefly to the young, the ignorant, and the idle, to whom they serve as lectures of conduct, and introductions into life," Cleland ties the efficacy of the novel's moral instruction to its convincing imitation of truth, its verisimilitude.[47] But whereas Johnson held that the semblance of reality was necessary in order to reinforce the exemplary value of fiction—"for what we cannot credit we shall never imitate"[48]—Cleland aligned himself with such authors as Cervantes, Sarah and Henry Fielding, and Smollett, who tried, as he wrote in his review of *Amelia*, to "[paint] the corruptions of mankind, and the world, *not as it should be, but as it really exists.*"[49] If for Johnson the purpose of fiction is, above all else, to provide the reader with virtuous models for imitation, for Cleland its proper aim is to expose folly and vice through ridicule.

This argument is most fully developed in the translator's preface he wrote for his version of Charles Pinot-Duclos's *Memoirs Illustrating the Manners of the Present Age* (1752), in which he bolsters his defense of contemporary fiction by linking it to the aesthetic principles advanced by the Roman lyric poet and satirist Horace and rediscovered in the sixteenth century, as Cleland argues, by Cervantes. There are three main strands to Cleland's preface: an introduction to Pinot-Duclos and the moral aims of the *Memoirs*; a discussion of "Ridicule" as "the surest Method of attacking [the] Errors . . . of the human Heart"; and a brief history of "this Branch of Writing" to which the *Memoirs* belongs, that of "Romances, Novels, and Novel-Memoirs," in which Cleland argues on behalf of those "Authors, who naturalized Fiction, and employed it in the Service of the most useful Truths," among whom he names Cervantes, Fénelon, Scarron, Le Sage, Marivaux, and Crébillon (234, 236). This last group, along with the Fieldings and Smollett in English, stand as the culmination of an evolutionary process that began with "the old Romances, full of imaginary, unnatural Characters, all of [which] deserved the Motto prefixed to one of the most noted of them, *Amadis of Gaul, Lis et oublie* (Read and forget)" (236). It was the "great Physician *Cervantes*" who "disenchanted or dispossessed his Nation" of the "endemial Madness" of readers' taste for "false Heroism and Knight-errantry" and in so doing made "a Revolution in the Ideas of his Age" (236–237). But such is the perversity of readers that "to this Vein of Romance succeeded another as silly, and surely more tiresome," the romances of Honoré d'Urfé, La Calprenède, and Madeleine de Scudéry, "in which Love, tortured, and sophisticated a thousand Ways, and ever out of Nature, formed a flimsy Web, unmercifully spun out to ten or twelve Volumes" (237). This "Depravation of Taste" was soon "exploded," and these works succeeded by "Romances at least less voluminous, and in which the Passion of Love was treated with more regard to Probability, but with still not enough to Nature"—the best being Madame de La Fayette's *La Princesse de Clèves*. Such "Novel-Romances" were popular enough to furnish "whole Libraries," but as "Amusement nearly constituted all the[ir] Merit," they were in time supplanted by works more natural, and so more useful. Apart from Fénelon, whose didactic romance *Télémaque* is rather out of step with the others, the authors Cleland favors are affiliated to either the picaresque-satirical (Cervantes, Scarron, Le Sage, Smollett) or libertine (Marivaux, Crébillon) modes. Richardson does not figure in his criticism at all, although it is intriguing that he finds much to praise in the arguably Richardsonian *Amelia*. But for the most part, Cleland associates "Nature" and "naturalized Fiction" with the comic and erotic rather than the exemplary, sentimental, or tragic.

Pinot-Duclos's *Memoirs* fits in with the other works Cleland admires not so much because of its topic, "the Provinces of Love and Gallantry," as because of Pinot-Duclos's aggressive manner of treating it (which Cleland compares to that of a physician "point[ing] out the Rankness and Malignancy" of his patient's "Symptoms" [236]). "His Plan and Design are sensibly to explode that egregious Mixture of Vice and Folly which the *Gayloves* of the Age had erected into a Sort of Fashion, and which consisted in debauching as many Women as they could come at, and in triumphing over the Spoils of Virtue and Innocence" (233). Pinot-Duclos's vehicle for this "explosion"—a key term in Cleland's critical lexicon—of vice and folly are "the Intrigues and Procedure of a sprightly young Nobleman" (232–233) who, just like Sir William Delamore in *Memoirs of a Coxcomb*, has a series of sexual liaisons until he is "brought at length back by the Strength of his own Reflections on the Emptiness and Vanity of such a Course, to the Simplicity of Virtue and domestic Happiness" (236). Cleland's and Pinot-Duclos's novels are almost identical in plot and moral message, and utterly conventional in their opposition of domestic virtue to the "infamous blandishments" of vice, as Fanny puts it in her tailpiece. Yet if the "lesson" of all three memoirs is trite, almost tautological (surely "virtue" is a word that already praises itself), the aesthetic strategy of "sensibly . . . explod[ing]" what they mean to condemn puts both authors in a tricky spot. In order to explode the vice he condemns, Pinot-Duclos has to bring it "sensibly"—vividly, feelingly—to the reader's mind. Or, as Cleland puts it in another passage of the preface: "In Attention then to the Necessity of *discovering* the Enemy before he fires at him, our Author paints, with great Vivacity of colouring his Hero, carried impetuously down the Stream of false and fashionable Pleasure, making Butterfly-love to the whole Sex" (236). A "sprightly young Nobleman," "great Vivacity of colouring," "making Butterfly-love to the whole Sex": both content and style, as Cleland describes them, are alluring. As he put it in his review of *Peregrine Pickle*, the reader is being decoyed by pleasure. But he also knows—it was already a commonplace in eighteenth-century arguments on the moral dangers of fiction—that a reader decoyed by pleasure may not want to renounce it, and that a text that presents itself as morally therapeutic may entice readers to imitate the very vices it represents so "sensibly":

> There are, it is true, some worthy and well-meaning Persons who disapprove this Way of handling of Vice, and who think that its Sores are of the *noli me tangere* Sort, not to be touched for Fear of inflaming and irritating the Itch of them: That even the End aimed at in presenting the Situations of it, does not atone for the Indecency of the Means; that it is holding the Light too near the Magazine; that in short they corrupt oftner than they instruct. (235)

Here, the metaphorical explosion—what happens when a "Light" is held "too near the Magazine"—is not a purgation but an inflammation of vice: the light of public exposure via literary representation ignites illicit desires. Cleland acknowledges the danger: "Such an History" as Pinot-Duclos's *Memoirs*, he writes, "could not but imply certain ticklish Situations, in which austere Morality at least had some Reason to complain . . . but our Author has treated them with all imaginable Regard to Decency and Modesty" (236). Like the physician, the author needs to calibrate the dosage precisely: just enough "Vivacity of colouring" to bring the attractions of "false and fashionable Pleasure" alive, not so much as to make the work itself indecent or immodest.

Readers, however, make bad patients. In a passage toward the end of the preface, Cleland acknowledges that his endeavors may be futile. If the value of

fiction is to provide vivid examples in order to impress moral truths more forc-
ibly than "Volumes of the finest Reasoning," still, "how few [readers] are there
whom their Passions suffer to benefit by them!" (239). In much of Cleland's
critical writing, readers and authors are locked in a kind of fatal embrace, bringing out each other's most vicious tendencies. Surveying the literary marketplace
at the start of his review of *Peregrine Pickle*, Cleland asks, "What are so many
worthless frivolous pieces as we constantly see brought out, but the marks of
that declension of wit and taste, which is perhaps more justly the reproach of
the public than the authors who have been forced to consult, and conform to,
its vitiated palate?"[50] Aiming to please, authors and booksellers have issued a
"flood of novels, tales, romances, and other monsters of the imagination, which
have been either wretchedly translated, or even more unhappily imitated, from
the *French*, whose literary levity we have not been ashamed to adopt, and to
encourage the propagation of so depraved a taste." But Cleland's lashing out,
as here against translators and imitators from the French, is self-incriminating,
even as he seeks to lay the blame elsewhere. When he wrote this, he was in the
midst of writing his own imitation of French libertine fiction, the *Memoirs of
a Coxcomb*; he had just published his explicit translation of the medical case
history of the cross-dressing lesbian seducer Catherine Vizzani, full of "flagrant
Instances of a libidinous Disposition"; he was soon to translate Pinot-Duclos's
libertine *Memoirs*; and in the preceding sixteen months he had been arrested
and threatened with prosecution twice for having written the *Woman of Pleasure*. Who exemplified the wretched and unhappy state of authorship better
than Cleland? Even when he draws a clear line of moral demarcation, he places
himself on both sides of it. In his preface to Pinot-Duclos, he writes,

> As to the Objections which are made against this Branch of Writing in general, that
> is to say, against Romances, Novels, and Novel-Memoirs, they can certainly take
> place only against the Abuse of them. Every thing obscene, or tending to corrupt
> the Morals of the People, cannot be too severely animadverted upon, though even
> those Poisons have their Use, when their Distribution is properly guarded and re-
> strained. (236)

Having made a clear distinction between literary forms and their abuse, and
having unreservedly condemned "every thing obscene, or tending to corrupt
the Morals of the People," he then switches to an apologist for the corrupting
and obscene: they can be useful, too, as long as they are properly administered.
But useful for what? In the right physician-author's hands, in an especially
severe or desperate case, perhaps such poison is useful as medicine, a purga-

tive or emetic. Or perhaps, if the case is desperate enough, the only cure is the reader's death. What cures one may kill another, but given "the Rankness and Malignancy of the Symptoms" (236), the risk has to be run.

The same antagonistic relationship between author and reader—a hostile confrontation of depraved tastes and poisonous remedies—finds its most lurid expression in Cleland's discussion of ridicule, the second principle, along with realism, of his theory of fiction. Cleland credits this "surest Method of attacking [the] Errors . . . of the human Heart" to Horace, and compares it to a form of artillery, tapping into the metaphorical vein of military bombardment that runs through the text (234). But when he turns to examine Pinot-Duclos's use of ridicule, Cleland adopts a different but equally murderous metaphor, that of a knife:

> Our author has given the Ridicule he has employed so exquisite an Edge, by making it proceed even from the Hero of his Piece himself, in a Strain of unaffected Self-Condemnation . . . that he entirely gets the laugh on the Side of Virtue, which is the most shrewd Way of breaking the Heart of Vice. It is effectually turning its own Arms against itself; for Vice can less stand before a Laugh than before all the Artillery of grave Arguments, or Maxims of Morality. But especially when Folly is forced to laugh at itself, it dies, well-pleased, and licking the Knife that cuts its Throat. (234)

Cleland, having praised the "exquisite Edge" of Pinot-Duclos's ridicule, turns that purely figural edge into an actual knife, a keener, more intimate form of "Arms" than bombastic artillery. It would be hard to devise a more gruesome, more perverse emblem for the moral aims of fiction than this of Folly—a figure for the reader in need of a cure—licking the knife that cuts its throat, "well-pleased." The extreme degree of sexualized violence is startling—sadistic and masochistic at once. Folly takes such avid pleasure in its own murder that it licks the bloody knife that is killing it, even as we register that the hand that wields the knife is its own. The "Edge" of ridicule "proceed[s] even from the Hero . . . himself"; Vice "turn[s] its own Arms against itself." In this emblem Cleland gives us Virtue cutting the throat of Folly, the author cutting the throat of the reader, and Pinot-Duclos's self-condemning, self-murdering hero cutting his own throat, and laughing. Thus an emblem of moral correction is also a symbol of the author's hatred for his audience and a self-lacerating acknowledgment of his own folly and vice, exemplified in his "propagation" of the very "depraved taste[s]" he condemns.

In Cleland's critical writings on the novel, then, his forceful if rather conventional argument that the purpose of fiction is "to convey instruction, under the passport of amusement" is unsettled by images and admissions that reveal the real transactions between authors and readers to be more hostile and disorderly than that of wise tutor and docile pupil. Readers may want vicious pleasures, not well-meant lessons in virtue; indeed Cleland's own history of the novel's development suggests that while there has been an overall progress toward the more probable and natural, readers keep backsliding, hungry only for "monsters of the imagination." Authors, in response, have flooded the market with wretched, imitative works that only encourage more depraved tastes, and even those who endeavor to expose, and thus explode, vice run the risk of inflaming illicit desires by their skill in representing them.

Matters are further complicated in Cleland's two "Novel-Memoirs," the *Woman of Pleasure* and the *Coxcomb*, by his experimentation with narrative form and his deployment of sometimes egregiously unreliable narrators. Just as the variation form loosens the teleological grip of the *Woman of Pleasure*'s romance and education plots, thus calling the ready-made moral lessons of those plots into question, so the *Coxcomb*'s suspended ending, and its narrator's self-absorption and dim-wittedness, challenge his characterization of his own text as a "history of my errors, and return to reason" (39). Unlike Fanny's memoir, Sir William's is structured as romance from the start. In its first scene, the nineteen-year-old Delamore (the name itself announces the genre) meets the beautiful and secretive fifteen-year-old Lydia, on the run for reasons unknown from her family. He falls immediately in love; she flees him when he starts to inquire into her identity; he vows to find her. Only a letter warning him that any further inquiries will endanger her, he writes,

> hindered me from setting out that instant, and acting the part of a true knight-errant, in pursuit of a wandering princess. And indeed there was something so singular, and out of the ordinary road of things, in my meeting, falling in love with, and losing of Lydia, that did not make the less impression on me, for carrying a spice of the romantic through the whole adventure: I found, it seems, something flattering, in the idea, that such a peculiarity was reserved for me. (72–73)

From the first, Sir William interprets his experience according to romance conventions, although his very awareness of these *as* conventions—that in pursuing Lydia, for example, he would be "acting the part of a true knight-errant"—registers a certain ironic distance between William as narrator and William as romantic hero. Having set in motion this plot of love, disappearance, and pursuit, however, he pretty quickly drops it, and the novel shifts into an episodic account of William's various sexual liaisons as he makes his entry into society. The first of the novel's three parts concludes with two affairs he has while living at his aunt's house in Warwickshire—with a lecherous widow, Mrs. Rivers, and Diana, a chambermaid—while in the second and third parts the theater of operations moves to London. With each of his three subsequent affairs William becomes vainer of his own charms and more scornful of the women with whom he's involved, all wealthy, and two titled: Miss Wilmore, Lady Oldborough, and Lady Bell Travers. As these affairs become more and more frustrating and entangling, his memoirs degenerate from libertine romp to misogynist rant. "I declared war within myself," he writes, "against the whole sex" (193), and he sets off on a series of "conquests" of women he doesn't even bother to name: the "immemorables" (194). But having "obtained the honour of passing for the most splendid, happy, dangerous coxcomb in town," he grows "cloyed and sick of my successes," leaves off seduction, and suddenly remembers Lydia, who "once more rose to my rescue, triumphantly, and dispelling the clouds and fumes of a debauched imagination, resumed a flame which was to burn the purer and fiercer for its victory over the fewel of a grosser fire" (195). Restored to his proper narrative genre, "in this violent reflux of the tide of love, I determined nothing so strongly as repairing my failure, and going personally in quest of her, with a diligence that should leave no hero of a romance, in pursuit of his princess, the odds of comparison to his advantage" (196). In short order he finds her, and . . .

"At this interesting conjuncture," Smollett writes in his review of Cleland's novel for the *Monthly Review*, "the curtain is drawn so abruptly, as to leave the reader impatient of the disappointment, and eagerly desirous of seeing in another act, Sir *William* happy in the arms of the beauteous *Lydia*."[51] James G. Basker has argued that Smollett's remark means that the work as published is unfinished and that Smollett "clearly perceived it as the first volume of a multi-volume novel."[52] Basker also cites the final sentence of the review—in which Smollett calls it "one of those few productions, which . . . a discerning reader may peruse to an end, without yawning, and even rise from it, with a wish, that the entertainment had been prolonged"—as evidence of Smollett's "desire [for] a continuation."[53] As I read them, neither of Smollett's statements really supports these claims: the second offers blandly polite praise of Cleland's ability to sustain the reader's interest, while the first expresses irritation with the ending's abruptness and a sense of frustration at the absence of a suitably fulfilling final image of conjugal happiness. Smollett evidently disapproves of what he sees as the novel's inconclusiveness, and in this sense may have described it as unfinished, but I don't find evidence in his review of any belief that a further volume was planned.[54] Basker's own remark that "the sudden reversal at the close of the book not only invites continuation, but lacks the material that would resolve the plot and balance the novel's structure," is astute, and I take up his argument in the final section of this chapter, in which I discuss the three memoirs' endings. But whether or not the text of the *Coxcomb* has been cut off prematurely, it clearly corresponds to the *Woman of Pleasure* in its use of the romance plot as a vehicle for unifying, if not resolving, the narrative of the protagonist's education.

Specters of Masculinity: William Delamore's Education

The theme of education is introduced in the opening pages of the novel, as Sir William complains of the shortcomings of his own upbringing at the hand of his "over-tender" aunt: "for that a woman who had from her infancy constantly lived in the country, and of course had been but little acquainted with the world, could not be the fittest person in it, to superintend the bringing up of a young gentleman of my pretensions to make a figure in it, both from my birth, and my fortune" (40). His complaint displays William's characteristic arrogance but also his understanding that the education he requires has less to do with Latin and Greek than with acquiring the manners needed to "make a figure" in the world in accordance with his wealth and social rank. William, like Fanny, is orphaned; both are thus free (or compelled) to make their own ways in the world. Yet if, as I've suggested earlier, their narrative trajectories are similar, taking each from the country to the city, innocence to experience, ignorance to worldliness, and the like, their social positions, from the start, are antithetical, as different as "woman" is from "man," or plain Fanny from Sir William. By contrast with the dirt-poor Francis Hill, Sir William Delamore has inherited, along with his absent parents' wealth, a place in the world, and this literal place—"two of the best estates in two of our richest counties in England" (39)—corresponds to his inherited social position as a member of Britain's ruling class. Possessing as his birthright the prerogatives associated with both halves of the term *gentleman*—the prerogatives of masculinity and gentility—Sir William needs to learn, either by instruction or experience, how best to assume the responsibilities that go along with those prerogatives.

Cleland's novel thus poses, from the outset, the same problem addressed in John Locke's influential treatise *Some Thoughts Concerning Education* (1693), in which Locke declared that "the principal aim of my Discourse is, how a young

Gentleman should be brought up from his Infancy."[55] Like Pinot-Duclos's protagonist, who states that "I owe much to my Experience; but to my Education
nothing" (2), William complains that his fortune "was secured to me much
more effectually, as it happened, than a good education: For to say that I had not
a bad one was barely all that I dare venture, and keep any measures with truth"
(39–40). William does at the outset have a tutor who makes a start on educating
him in keeping with the Lockean idea that "the great Principle and Foundation
of all Virtue and Worth, is placed in this, That a Man is able to *deny himself* his
own Desires, cross his own Inclinations, and purely follow what Reason directs
as best, tho' the appetite lean the other Way."[56] But because his education is interrupted at a crucial point, "just as the heat and impetuosity of my age, barely
turned of seventeen, most required the guidance and direction of a governor"
(41), he veers off course, and his regret at his tutor's departure is "soon dissipated by the pleasure of thinking that I should have a greater swing of liberty."
In this sentence, "liberty" is affiliated with "dissipat[ion]" and "pleasure," the
antithesis of the self-denial for which Locke argues. Here, on the novel's third
page, William's formal instruction ends, and here, with a swing away from
Lockean self-control over his inclinations and appetites, his story proper begins.
At liberty, about to fall into "errors," if he is to "return to reason" by the close
of his memoirs, he has to find his own way of making "a young Gentleman" of
himself and so acquire an appropriately masculine and patrician identity. The
question his memoirs raise, for all his preemptive claims in the affirmative, is
whether he succeeds.

   The vacuum opened up by his tutor's departure is first filled by "the pleasures of the chace" (41) and, when those wear off, by "the ferment of desire for
objects far more interesting than horses and dogs." These "objects," of course,
are women—or, rather, phantasmal images of the abstraction "woman," as William seems to have encountered few actual women in his life. In fact "the ferment of desire" is not an effect of encountering any other person, but a kind of
spontaneous combustion or outpouring of the self. It is as if his "unbounded
pursuit of hunting" animals triggers some interior thermal reaction, for as soon
as satiety "put an end to the violence of my passion for [hunting]," he writes,
"my blood now boiling in my veins, began to make me feel the ferment of
desire" for those other as yet unseen "objects." His own body, not another's,
dictates desire:

   And a robust, healthy constitution, manifest in the glow of a fresh complexion, and
   vigorous well-proportioned limbs, gave me those warnings of my ripening man-

hood, and its favourite destination, by which nature prevents all instruction, and suggests the use of those things that most engage our attention, without putting us to the blush of asking silly questions . . . But now, those transient desires inspired by this rising passion, began to take a more settled hold of my imagination, and to grow into such tender pantings, such an eagerness of wishes, as quite overcame, and engrossed me intirely. Woman it was, that I may say, I instinctively knew, was wanting to my happiness; but I had as yet no determined object in that sex, but yearned, and looked out for one every where. (41–42)

The natural history of desire outlined here is almost the opposite of Fanny's voyeuristic, imitative training in the *Woman of Pleasure,* even if the outcome— both are primed to have sex with the first man/woman they see—is the same. In sharp contrast to Fanny's carefully graded lessons in eros, proceeding through "luscious talk" and visual demonstration, William explicitly sets "nature" in opposition to "instruction" and posits other-sex desire as instinctive, naturally dictated by the body.[57] But if the body's "boiling," "ripening," and "rising" come over him spontaneously and unbidden, they take hold, as he writes, of his "imagination": it becomes the crucible where physiological sensations "grow into . . . tender pantings" and eager "wishes." At the same time he asserts the instinctive nature of desire, then, he also acknowledges the transformative effects of imagination, by which an inchoate (and not even species-specific) "ferment" is turned into the wish for a woman, which he invests with all the "tender[ness]" and "yearn[ing]" suitable to a young man of sensibility.

As this passage suggests, the dynamics of erotic desire in William's first-person account are complex: on one hand the pure instinct of boiling blood and vigorous limbs, on the other a "tender melancholy" by which, as he writes, he "was really mastered," such that "this passion had a contrary effect on me to all others . . . from fierce and insolent, I was now I may say, transnatured to somewhat a more civilized savage" (42). Nature is itself subject to transformation, and desire, which is initially associated with animality—horses and dogs, the chase—becomes, by way of imagination, a civilizing force. There is, then, from the very beginning of William's narrative of the origin of erotic desire, a splitting off of the affective from the bodily, even if the former is also described as an effect of the latter. This splitting off is taken a step further in the same paragraph—which acts as a prelude to the scene in which he meets Lydia— when, having described the softening and civilizing effects of eros, William writes, "Yet, strong as this youthful passion ever is, it was fated for some time at least to give way to a stronger and a nobler one, even love itself." Fanny makes a similar claim just before she meets Charles, and just after confessing she was ready to sleep with the first man that offered, writing that "love itself took charge of the disposal of me, in spite of interest, or gross lust" (34). But Fanny's distinction between love and "gross lust" is crucially different from William's distinction between the passions of love and eros. Love, for Fanny, burns away the grossness but is inseparable from lust—indeed is unimaginable apart from it. For William, by contrast, sexual desire, even in its softened and civilizing form, has to be displaced onto another object from the beloved, while she, as a sign of her idealized status, is regarded as asexual. So, after recounting his first meeting with Lydia, William writes that "all the desires I had hitherto felt the pungency of, were perfectly constitutional: the suggestions of nature beginning to feel itself. But the desire I was now given up to, had something so distinct, so chaste, and so correct, that its impressions carried too much of virtue in it, for my reason to refuse it possession of me" (47). Love passes the Lockean test by carrying the imprimatur of reason, and this underlines how utterly distinct it is from the "Inclinations" and "Desires" that William, as proof of his love's and of his own "virtue," has to make a parade of denying himself.

From her first appearance, then, Lydia is made to embody a distinction be-tween two types of desire: one "constitutional," bodily, "pungen[t]," the other rational, virtuous, "chaste." As an object of the second type of desire, she comes to embody, for William and the reader alike, a specifically, stereotypically, femi-nine model of virtue. Significantly, however, she has nothing to say for herself: "In all that time," as William admits, she "had scarce opened her mouth, and that only in monosyllables; but with such a grace of modesty, such a sweetness of sound, as made every string of my heart vibrate" (46). This last observa-tion gives the game away. Incapable, for all he knows or cares, of forming a sentence, she does not present herself to him as a rational being capable of conscious virtue but instead as a source of pleasing vibrations, a purely sensual creature. Similarly, William's occasional proto-Freudian slips make a mockery of his hymns to virtue. When he declares, for example, "Nothing was truer than that I had never once harboured a thought about [Lydia] inconsistent with the most rigid honour" (59)—or, later, when he writes, of the cottage she has fled, that "so far from the paradise my raptured ideas had once erected it into, it now wore to me the aspect of a cold, dreary, disconsolate desert" (72)—the silly, obvi-ous sexual puns create a gap between narrator and author, between William's account of his own motivations and Cleland's ironic deflation of his claims. The effect is to put in question the binary opposition on which the moral and narrative structure of the *Coxcomb* rests: between (virtuous) love and (vicious) gallantry, or sexual pleasure for its own sake. Failing to see that, at least in his own case, love and desire are all confusedly entangled, he conceives of Lydia not as a person but an abstraction, a figure out of the romance and amatory fictions in whose light he reads his own experience. And because the real women he encounters after Lydia's disappearance choose, for reasons of their own, not to follow the models of feminine behavior he has learned from fiction, William swings wildly between extremes, one moment a lovesick swain, the next a heartless roué, by turns over-idealizing love and cynically exploiting the women he compulsively pursues.

William's immersion in the clichés of romance is signaled by the occasional self-conscious allusion, as when he describes himself as "more romantically in love than all the Celadons that ever owed their existence to fiction," Celadon being the archetype of the despairing, devoted lover, from the French pastoral prose romance *L'Astrée* (1607–1627) by Honoré d'Urfé. Here, William is being ironic at his younger self's expense, and in such passages he presents himself as one who has grown out of his youthful naïveté, having exchanged romance for realism, error for reason. But Cleland is less easy on William than William is on himself, for just when he most emphatically repudiates the clichés of romance, as after his first meeting with Lydia, he betrays how thoroughly they have ensnared him:

> I cannot here refrain from observing, that, not without reason, are the romance, and novel writers in general, despised by persons of sense and taste, for their unnatural, and unaffecting descriptions of the love-passion. In vain do they endeavour to warm the head, with what never came from the heart. Those who have really been in love, who have themselves experienced the emotions, and symptoms of that passion, indignantly remark, that so far from exaggerating its power, and effects, those triflers do not even do it justice. A forced cookery of imaginary beauties, a series of mighty marvelous facts, which spreading an air of fiction through the whole, all in course weaken that interest and regard never paid but to truth, or the appearances of truth; and are only fit to give a false and adulterated taste of a passion, in which a simple sentiment, is superior to all their forced productions of artificial flowers. Their works in short give one the idea of a frigid withered eunuch, representing an Alexander making love to Statira. (47–48)

It is perhaps unsurprising that William, in the grip of his "ripening manhood," should equate aesthetic merit with sexual potency, so that the "unaffecting descriptions" of literary "triflers" are likened to the ridiculous exertions of "a frigid withered eunuch" vainly pretending to be the virile Alexander; but the comparison not only emphasizes the blurring of sexual desire with the chaste "love-passion" he claims to feel for Lydia, it also raises doubts about the authenticity of his regard for her. For the name "Statira" is effectively a symbol for the interchangeability of female bodies and identities under male domination, referring as it does to two different women, mother and daughter, who became Alexander's lovers in turn—the second taking her mother's name when she took her place.[58] The historical allusion suggests a parallel between "Alexander making love to Statira" and William making love to Lydia, and if the parallel flatters William's nascent masculinity, it also suggests that Lydia has no identity of her own but simply "is" whatever William chooses to see her as.

William's larger point in this passage is similar to Cleland's own observations on the "imaginary, unnatural" conventions of romance in his critical essays on fiction.[59] The first principle of any writing worthy of "persons of sense and taste" is realism: "truth, or the appearances of truth." The fictional context of William's literary-critical tirade damagingly compromises his authority, however, even if the views he espouses are also Cleland's, for his attack on "novel writers" follows his own "forced productions of artificial flowers." Lydia, for example, is described as exhibiting "the shape of a nymph, an air of the Graces, features such as Venus, but Venus in her state of innocence, when new-born of the sea" (44), and so, formulaically, on. The hackneyed comparisons put him firmly on the level of the romance writers he berates; indeed the last image, equating Lydia with the naked Venus, could have come from the pen of *Shamela*'s Parson Tickletext, fantasizing Pamela "with all the Pride of Ornament cast off."[60] Similarly, when William turns to look back at the cottage where he has just met her, he writes, "Then! then I perceived all the magic of love. I saw now every thing with other eyes. That little rustic mansion, had assumed a palace-air. Turrets, colonades, jet-d'eaus, gates, gardens, temples, no magnificence, no delicacy of architecture was wanting to my imagination, in virtue of its fairy-power, of transforming real objects into whatever most flatters, or exalts that passion" (46–47). It is characteristic of Cleland's complex rhetorical effects that we are invited at once to enjoy the artificiality and elegance of Sir William's language and to observe how he deceives himself into believing that his own descriptions of "the love-passion" are more "natural" than those of other novel or romance writers.

In fact the phrase by which he condemns earlier, rival love narratives, "a forced cookery of imaginary beauties," stands as a fair encapsulation of the *Cox-comb*, especially those parts dedicated to the romance with Lydia—not because William (or Cleland) is a bad writer, but because love, like writing, is an act of

imagination. Nothing, for example, really distinguishes Lydia from the vacu-
ous mannequin Agnes, whom William unsuccessfully pursues in the novel's
second part, except for his imaginative investment of her with all the qualities
of a heroine of romance. Like Agnes, she is virtually mute during their scenes
together; as with Agnes, William can only approach her through the intermediary of a vigilant female guardian, to whom in effect he is compelled to make
his addresses. Lydia has an air of "sweetness and gentle simplicity" (44) and
a nice complexion; so has Agnes. If Sir William writes, of Agnes, that "she
was, in short, in point of understanding, little better than a beautiful *pantin* [a
marionette], of which Lady Oldborough directed the motions, and played the
wires as best suited her views of interest or pleasure" (118), he notes of Lydia
that, even as he is thunderstruck with love for her, she "had scarce opened her
mouth, and that only in monosyllables" (46). As he writes later, "One could
have indeed wished she had spoke more" (66), but in fact her silence, her essential blankness, allows William to project onto her the emotional qualities
required of a love object—required, that is, by the codes of romance fiction,
which as narrator he both mocks and (involuntarily) emulates.

Reading the story of his life according to the conventions of romance narrative—as a series of adventures and misadventures set in motion by the loss,
and subsequent pursuit, of the original and only beloved—William serves for
Cleland as a kind of test case in an inquiry into the adequacy of fictional forms
as models for imitation or self-understanding. Despite his ironic awareness of
his own susceptibility to the attractions of romance—as when, in the passage
above, he describes the tricks his imagination played on him, "in virtue of its
fairy-power, of transforming real objects into whatever most flatters, or exalts
that passion [of love]"—he nevertheless remains in thrall to it in his essentially
arbitrary idealization of Lydia, the infant incognita. "Fifteen was her utmost,"
he writes on first meeting her (44), and when he observes that "her native
modesty suffered her to say but little, and that only on subjects proper for her
age," he only underlines the limits of her childlike or doll-like allure. But those
limits are really William's, not Lydia's. We see only what he relays, so if she is
more than "a beautiful *pantin*," if his "love-passion" is different in kind from
his indiscriminate "panting" after interesting "objects," the onus is on him to
furnish the "appearances of truth" needed to sustain such distinctions. Failing
that, he joins the company of literary "triflers" he condemns.

Samuel Johnson, in his *Dictionary of the English Language* of 1750–1755, defined a *coxcomb* as "a fop; a superficial pretender to knowledge or accomplish-
ments" and a *fop* as "a coxcomb; a man of small understanding and much

ostentation . . . a man fond of show, dress, and flutter." Yet despite the seeming interchangeability of the two words, the coxcomb Sir William is no fop as that term had come generally to be applied in literature of the period, for if both figures were portrayed as vain and "superficial pretender[s]," only the fop was derided as effeminate. A case in point from the *Coxcomb* is the "pale meager, spectre-like, young man of quality" whom Miss Wilmore "drag[s] after her" (103) when William first meets her at the theater. "As for her poor conductor, who had the air of a figure of straw stinted in the stuffing," William writes,

> he was it seems one of those insignificant danglers by trade, whom she could take and leave without consequence, and who was not absolutely without some merit, since he did himself justice enough to pretend to none, and humbly contented himself with handing the ladies to public places, and held it for the greatest honour, if they would let him fancy a suit of ribbons for them, or play with their monkeys, and to say the truth he looked as if favours of another sort would have cursedly embarrassed him. (106)

William's close attention to this nameless figure who plays no further part in the story is a sign of his hunger for reassurance as to his own masculinity: this bloodless, asexual hanger-on lacks what William most emphatically, even insistently, has. He serves, as Cleland punningly suggests, as a straw man whose effeminacy shores up, by contrast, William's vigorous, heterosexually rapacious masculinity. Unlike this "insignificant dangler," whom the aptly named, assertive Miss Wilmore "rather dragged after her, than she was led by," William is primarily concerned, during the affair that soon follows, to demonstrate his power over her: the power to compel her, if she cannot have William's love, to renounce sex altogether. As he observes, "The idea of being the first to inspire her with sentiments of love, to fix her, to show her all over the town as my captive, and ty'd as it were to my triumphal car, carried with it something so soothing to my vanity, that I could not help giving it a dominion over me" (109). By forcing Miss Wilmore to renounce her "rakish" and promiscuous ways—the prerogative of aristocratic males like himself—Sir William asserts his own masculine dominance and differentiates himself from the beaus, fops, and fribbles whom Cleland satirically delineated two years later in his *Dictionary of Love*.

If the connection between masculinity and power is the subject, implicit or explicit, of every major episode of the *Coxcomb*, William's anxiety about a possible breakdown in that connection is brought to an extreme of what Isobel Grundy calls "dread and disgust" in the episode detailing his affair with "the celebrated lady Bell Travers" (171).[61] The final scene of this episode is certainly among the most bizarre in eighteenth-century fiction. Hiding in Lady Travers's closet one day in order to surprise her, William instead witnesses a perverse sort of primal scene: the unexpectedly maternal Lady Travers cradling her "ghastly" foreign manservant Buralt while a reluctant country woman, hired for the purpose, nurses him. The whole scene is marked by a descriptive excess that only accentuates its mysteriousness. "It is hardly possible to figure to one's self," Sir William writes,

> a more ghastly spectre than what this wretch exhibited, wrapped in a kind of blue coat, that sat on him yet less loosely than his skin, which was of a dun sallow hue. His eyes goggled from sockets appearing sunk inwards, by the retreat of flesh round them, which likewise added to the protuberance of his cheek-bones. A napkin in the shape of a night cap covered all his hair, (except a platted queue of it, and some lank side-locks) the dull dingy black of which, by its shade, raised, and added to, the hideousness of his grim meagre visage. (188–189)

As if to reinforce the feeling of horror this "spectre" provokes, William writes that once he begins nursing, he "looked more like a sucking demon, or a *vampyre* escaped from his grave, than a human creature" (189). But if this last phrase—perhaps the first appearance of the word "vampyre" in an original work of English fiction—emphasizes Buralt's alterity, his foreignness and unlikeness to William, the words "meagre" and "spectre," which were earlier used in the portrait of Miss Wilmore's fop, imply that the threat is close to home, and that William's horror is a reaction not to monstrous otherness but to self-recognition. In Buralt he sees a reflection of himself unmanned, his masculine authority ceded to Lady Travers.

The threat Lady Travers poses to that authority was, however, what drew William to her in the first place. Reporting his first impressions of her, he writes that "she displayed, in fine, a sort of imperiousness much after my own heart, which began by awing, and ended by captivating, me. I conceived now that I had met with my match, and promised myself, without looking further, that I would try what was to be won, or lost, with one, whose reduction was however with me rather a point of ambition than of love" (173). Confronted with a strong and sexually assertive woman, as earlier with Miss Wilmore, William is driven, by an "ambition" that amounts to a compulsion, to plot her "reduction." But unlike Miss Wilmore, Lady Travers beats William at his own game, and even "absorb[s]" his love for Lydia "in this ruling passion of my senses" (186). Ruled by, rather than ruling over, his desire for Lady Travers, Sir William begins to come undone. "My constitution," he writes overdrawn upon by the fierceness of my desires, and even by the vanity I took in the pleasure I gave, began to give signs of suffering by my unmoderate profusion . . . All my sprightliness, vigour, and florid freshness, the native attendants of healthy youth, began to give shew of drooping, and flagged under the violence of the heat, with which the constancy of fire in my imagination melted me down into current love (186).

It is not so much the overtaxing of his body by sexual excess as the loss of control over his own desires that threatens a breakdown in William's constitution, a breakdown that would make of him another "sucking demon," a vampiric "babe of delight" (189) utterly and abjectly dependent upon Lady Travers.

She, meanwhile, remains altogether in control of her own pleasure as well as his; she does nothing without a careful calculation of its effects. As William writes, she "joined to the charms of her person, a consummation in all the mysteries and science of voluptuousness, [and] employed such successive varied refinements of it, that she appeared a new mistress to me upon every re-approach" (186). Her disciplined self-regulation shows up his own inability to govern his desires: "Lady Travers indeed, from reasons of self-interest, and of an experience not unfamiliar to her, often recommended moderation to me, but while she preached that necessary virtue, her presence made the practice of it impossible." It is this recognition of his powerlessness to resist "the absolute dominion of an unremitting gust for her" (187) that leads to William's absurd, misogynistic rantings after he sees Lady Travers with his shadow self, Buralt. Buralt acts as a nightmarish foreshadowing of his own emasculation—that is, the stripping away of his "natural" masculine authority—at the hand of a woman who coolly assumes the prerogatives traditionally linked to masculinity. Cleland's ironic distance from his narrator is nowhere clearer than in the aftermath to this episode, when Sir William turns from rage to condescending pity:

I soon came to see lady Travers in no other light, than as one of those unfortunate characters, constitutionally subjected by the violence of their passions, to those weaknesses which too often debase those of the highest intellects, beneath their own notions and principles; and who, by this means, become lessons of humility to man in general, by shewing him, in the examples of others, to what excesses intemperance, and mis-rule of appetite, are, at times, capable of carrying even the wisest. (192)

It is, of course, William himself who has shown, in "the violence of [his] passions," every sign of "weakness," "debase[ment]," "intemperance," "excess," and "mis-rule of appetite," while Lady Travers has consistently maintained her "penetration, and acuteness of sense" (172) as she caters to her own pleasure. In the light of this episode, in fact, one might think back over William's accounts of his earlier affairs with some skepticism. While he consistently portrays himself as the dominant figure, masterfully manipulating to his own designs any woman who attracts his attention, one can read these relationships the other way round and see the female characters as controlling, rather easily, the conceited Sir William. From Mrs. Bernard and Lydia through the young widow Mrs. Rivers, the aspiring maidservant Diana, the lighthearted Miss Wilmore, the licentious Lady Oldborough, the money-grubbing brothel keeper Mother Sulphur, to Lady Travers herself, all the women Sir William encounters gain precisely what they are seeking from their dealings with him, from sexual gratification to financial security to the furthering of their fashionable (read scandalous) reputations. Faced with a parodic image of his own debility in the figure of the "chamber-satyr" Buralt (190), Sir William seems to sense how tenuous his presumed authority has been all along, and he lashes out indiscriminately. "I declared war within myself against the whole sex" (193), he writes, as if the battle between masculine and feminine has to be waged inside his own psyche.

In contrast to the self-divided, self-deluded William, it is Lady Travers, of all the characters in the *Coxcomb*, who best exemplifies Cleland's ideal of the "rational pleasurist," as Fanny Hill labels the wise, benevolent, still sexually attractive sixty-year-old gentleman with whom she lives for eight months in the *Woman of Pleasure*. As she writes of him, in words that apply equally well to Lady Travers,

> Age had not subdued his tenderness for our sex, neither had it robb'd him of the power of pleasing, since whatever he wanted in the bewitching charms of youth, he atton'd for, or supplemented with the advantages of experience, the sweetness of his manners, and above all his flattering address in touching the heart by an application to the understanding . . . He it was, who first taught me to be sensible that the pleasures of the mind were superior to those of the body, at the same time, that they were so far from obnoxious to, or incompatible with each other, that besides the sweetness in the variety, and transition, the one serv'd to exalt and perfect the taste of the other, to a degree that the senses alone can never arrive at. (174–175)

Lady Travers, with her "penetration, and acuteness of sense," has taken for her own both William's would-be sexually dominant role and his claims to superior reason; no wonder, when he realizes this, he "overflow[s]" with "gall and vinegar" (191). Of all the male characters in the *Coxcomb*, only Lord Merville,

William's epicurean mentor, comes close to this union of reason and pleasure, which was a recurrent theme in Cleland's writing and conversation. In one of his diary entries from 1779, Boswell writes, of a conversation he had with the then sixty-eight-year-old Cleland: "He said Epicurus was now well defended as not being a sensualist; that intellect and sense must unite in pleasure."[62] Merville, too, strikes the right balance: as William writes, "Even our most sensual gratifications were those of rational votaries to pleasure, and had nothing of the grossness of tavern-bacchanals, or brothel-orgies" (102–103). Yet Merville remains a rather shadowy figure in the text, an instructor who serves as little more than a foil to Sir William—graciously yielding the point, for example, whenever they find themselves in competition for the same "prize" (always, of course, a woman)—and lacking any independent existence apart from his friend.

Lady Travers, by contrast, emphatically leads her own life. Although married, she "hoisted" early on "the flag of independance, and made all her advantages of her irregular condition, being now, properly speaking, neither maid, widow, nor wife" (172). Her evasion of the settled categories of feminine confinement is one sign of her freedom; a second is her "noble indifference" (184) to scandal. "She had taken the lead in life, with so high a hand," William writes, "that she could very easily despise or dispense with the approbation of the rest of the world." Robert Halsband and Isobel Grundy have both argued that Lady Travers is based on Lady Mary Wortley Montagu, and while such an identification is conjectural, she corresponds to Lady Mary in intriguing ways.[63] Lady Mary spent time in Turkey as the wife of the British ambassador; Lady Travers is described by Sir William as "a seraglio of beauties" (186). Both eloped young with rich men whose love soon turned to indifference; both "had seen most of the courts in Europe" and were "flattered and consulted" by poets and political ministers (178). Lady Mary had a villa in the riverside suburb of Twickenham; Lady Travers has her own in the nearby riverside suburb of Chiswick. It may even be that Cleland had heard of Lady Mary's infirm Swiss servant Fribourg and based the grotesque Buralt on him: "He was by birth a Swiss," William notes; "she had picked him up abroad in her travels" (188).

In her biography of Lady Mary, Grundy contends that "Cleland's Bell Travers episode is deeply misogynistic" and suggests that it originated in Cleland's parents' friendship with several of Lady Mary's enemies: "Their son," she writes, "came honestly by his prejudice against Lady Mary."[64] To my mind, the biographical evidence is far from clear, interesting as the complex history of the Clelands' alliances and feuds may be. Cleland's father had been dead for ten

years, and relations between John and his mother were by this point frigid and
hostile by turns, so it is not obvious why he should want to take up his parents'
part in an old dispute. The one time Cleland does explicitly refer to Lady Mary,
in his *Institutes of Health*, he singles her out for extraordinary praise. Noting
her key role in promoting inoculation against smallpox in Britain (a practice
she had first observed in her travels in Turkey), Cleland writes, "Was merit to
be estimated rather by the nature of things, than by vulgar opinion, the British
lady who first introduced that practice in this nation, by which, in all human
probability, so many thousands of lives have been, and will be saved, certainly
deserved, and perhaps, in a more grateful age than this, would have had a statue
preferably to any of the illustrious destroyers of mankind."[65] For all William's
denigration of Lady Travers—he writes that she has no wit but only the "appearances of wit" and "the rage of being thought one" (178)—his memoirs make
clear that she is far more conversant with "the pleasures of the mind," (*Woman*,
174) in Fanny's words, than he is: "flattered and consulted" by poets, courted by
"authors who had read their works to her," familiar enough with the "courts of
Europe" to be the equal in her knowledge of politics of any "ten modern ministers" (*Coxcomb*, 178), she even knows enough of the world's prejudices against
learned women "to avoid making too great a display of her acquisitions" (179).
As Grundy observes, his text is full of "casual insults" against Lady Travers and
women in general, but instead of reading his misogynist screeds as the product
of Cleland's supposed animus against the real Lady Mary, they need to be read
as outbursts of impotent rage.

William's tirade echoes his earlier "impotent sallies of rage, and railing"
(149) after he catches on that he's been played for a fool by Lady Oldborough,
who not only induces him to have sex with her in the vain hope she will let him
sleep with her ward, the beautiful orphan Agnes, but tricks him into believing
he has been pipped at the post by a secret lover, whom she shows to William
lying with Agnes. In fact what he has seen is an artfully arranged tableau, il-
luminated by the light of a single candle, and the supposed farmer's son, who
lies "with his hand passed under her neck, and clasping her as it were to him"
(145), is really "a lusty country-girl, picked out, and disguised for the purpose"
(147). William later acknowledges that Lady Oldborough's trick was "a coarse
one enough employed on any but a novice" (147) and his inability to see through
her counterfeit tableau belies his supposed skills in gallantry. For "the most
splendid, happy, dangerous coxcomb in town" (194), as he styles himself, he is
pretty easily duped, and he knows it. Only a "novice" could be fooled as he was,
and it is precisely his recognition that he has been "reduc[ed]" by the women

he aimed to reduce that leads to his "copious expectoration of spleen, which I vented, in a ranting soliloquy, against the sex" (149).

The crisis that both Lady Oldborough and Lady Travers in their different ways provoke is one of power or, more precisely, the insufficiency of masculine authority. In both cases William is brought face to face with his own debility: his poor powers of sight, or insight, by Lady Oldborough and her tableau vivant; his "mis-rule of appetite" and imminent physical breakdown by the spectacle of his shadow self, Buralt. In both cases he "suppresse[s]" the truth to Merville so as not to lose face (150, 190–191), and in both he tries to compensate for his sexual humiliation by what he graphically terms a "copious expectoration of spleen." He is not unaware of his own ridiculousness, as when he describes himself embellishing his "ravings, with some scraps of poetry, theatrically tattered away," and he confesses that the rhetorical excess of his "ranting soliloqu[ies]" is an expression of his own weakness in relation to the women he attacks, "whose power never stands more sensibly confest, than in these impotent sallies of rage, and railing" (149).

William's constant anxiety to bolster his own sexual prestige and authority, so evident in his contempt and disgust for men like Miss Wilmore's fop, the broken-down rake Lord Melton, or the vampire Buralt, and in his compulsion to subjugate all the women he meets, points to his failure ever to achieve a confident sense of his own sexual and social identity. After his break with Lady Travers, he writes, "I set out then full speed in the same career, which I had seen pursued by a number of coxcombs, whom I heartily despised" (194). That he chooses to imitate "coxcombs" he despises shows how insecure his sense of himself and his desires still is. Lacking any clear sense of what he wants, he also lacks any models of exemplary masculinity. There is a near total absence in the novel of admirable figures of male authority, in either the public or private spheres: no fathers, judges, patriarchs; no political, religious, or military standard-bearers. His tutor, Mr. Selden, exits too early to have lasting impact, and Merville—who, "at an age when most young men are held to begin the world, [had already] exhausted all its variety"—is also governed by "a constitutional indolence, which would not suffer him to give himself the trouble of maintaining his dissent from the humours or inclinations of his acquaintance" (101). Affable and well-bred as William declares him to be, Merville is as exhausted morally as the vampire Buralt is physically. Apart from Merville, the novel offers an array of even more obviously ineffectual, dissipated, broken-down coxcombs, from William's four guardians, who dither inconclusively when he first arrives in London over whether he should be packed off on the grand tour, to the

"Mock-Machiavel" Lord Tersillion, whose repetition of a speech he had given in the House of Lords provokes William to ask, "What was this, however, but coxcombry, only of another species than mine?" (175–176).

The lack of any compelling figure of male authority leaves William with no one to emulate and no social responsibilities to assume. The inheritor of two of the best estates in England, he has no interest in managing or even visiting them, although he lives off their rents.[66] Similarly, he has no interest in either military or political affairs, the usual domain of a man of his station, and while this may make him more appealing as a person, it leaves him with nothing to occupy his time except "gallantry." At best he is an ornamental figure, at worst a parasite on the labors of others, and in either case soon to become one of the dissipated wrecks he has so mercilessly satirized.

But then, suddenly, everything changes. Lydia, like some fever-dream deus ex machina, "once more rose to my rescue, triumphantly, and dispell[ed] the clouds and fumes of a debauched imagination" (195). This quasi-religious vision of Lydia "rouzes" his heart and leads him to repent of his "follies" and resume his "quest of her" (196). The plot begins to accelerate as William decides to go abroad in search of her, meets a strangely alluring incognita at a masked ball, accompanies his aunt back to Warwickshire to retrace Lydia's steps, finds the boat on which she sailed from Bristol to Ostend, stops off in London to join Merville (his traveling companion) only to get caught up in Merville's new infatuation with the mysterious debutante Lady Gertrude Sunly—who turns out, of course, to be not only the incognita of the masked ball but Lydia herself, restored to her family and her true identity. All of this is shoehorned into just over ten pages of a novel that to this point has ambled along at a pretty leisurely tempo, and it produces a rushed, chaotic effect, as if the narrator has just noticed he is running out of time.

Lydia's visionary reappearance triggers the libertine Sir William's reformation and sets the romance plot back in headlong motion toward the outcome the reader surely expects: that is, in Smollett's words, "Sir *William* happy in the arms of the beauteous *Lydia*, who (by the bye) turns out a young lady of high rank and fortune."[67] But at the same time, nothing has changed, or changed convincingly, for as James Basker argues, "The sudden reversal at the close of the book . . . lacks the material that would resolve the plot and balance the novel's structure."[68] Despite William's assurances on the opening page that the story of his life has the shape of a fully "resolved" plot—the "history of my errors, and return to reason"—in the closing paragraphs he is in a state of "transition from a painful to a not unpleasing inquietude," his preparations to go abroad "countermanded in an instant" (220), leaving him waiting, in suspense, to hear if he will be allowed to present himself to the beloved Lydia. Of course, as he has just learned, there is no Lydia but rather a Lady Gertrude Sunly, and his discovery that he has known and pined for her under a false name only emphasizes how little he has known her at all. She is little more than a cipher he can invest with the sensibility and virtue of a heroine of romance, and for that reason his reinstatement of her as the be-all and end-all of his existence is rather a regression to a kind of boyish fantasy than an advance. For all his worldliness and his indeed often witty observations on the self-delusions of the people he has encountered in his passage through upper-class London life, he has no way of imagining love or the shape of his own life apart from the conventions of romance fiction—according to which, having rediscovered the lost beloved, he has arrived at the happy end of the story. But really he is only back to what he was at the beginning: a good-looking country bumpkin smitten with an untested and uninterrogated fantasy-ideal. Rather than a genuine novel of education, then, what Cleland has produced in the *Coxcomb* is a novel of *failed* education.

Tailpieces: Fanny's and William's Last Words

It could be objected that this reading of the *Coxcomb* overlooks the fact that the novel is simply unfinished. I agree that it is, in the same way that its protagonist is unfinished, but not, as Basker suggests, that the three-part text as it stands was intended to be just the first half of a two-volume novel published in installments, on the model of the *Woman of Pleasure*.[69] The argument either way is necessarily speculative, and the evidence of the text suggests that Cleland did alter his original plan. He probably intended at first for William to go on his grand tour, as several passages in parts 2 and 3 prepare us to expect. This would have allowed Cleland to enlarge the scope of his catalog of the manners and follies of high life and to show off his own cosmopolitan breadth of knowledge, even as William pursued Lydia from one fashionable resort to another. But if this was his original plan, he clearly changed it before the masquerade scene, where the masked Lady Gertrude makes her debut. The plot turns of the novel's last twenty-five pages—the hero's sudden conversion, the heroine's equally sudden return, the William-Merville love rivalry subplot (abandoned almost as soon as it is introduced), the formally awkward recitation by Mr. Withers of Lady Gertrude's backstory—do bring together the main strands of the narrative, and they leave little more work for the plot to do to bring about the foreordained union of William and his love. There is certainly no scope for another two hundred pages of misunderstandings and pursuits: if Cleland planned to keep the novel going, he surely would not have nipped the Merville-William rivalry in the bud or reconciled "Lydia" to her authoritarian father, who set the whole plot in motion by trying to force her to marry the odious Lord F. Instead, by removing every obstacle to Sir William and Lady Gertrude's union, Cleland leaves the narrative nowhere else to go even as he refuses to provide the ending he has so visibly prepared.

Cleland's closing off of these avenues of potential narrative complication suggests that as abrupt and unresolved as the *Coxcomb*'s ending is, he published it as a completed text. Unlike the first volume of the *Woman of Pleasure*, which ends with Fanny set up in new lodgings and promising Madam that "the number of adventures which befell me in the exercise of my new profession, will compose the matter of another letter" (89), there is no hint of a sequel at the end of part 3 of the *Coxcomb*.[70] It's true that the novel's closing sentence, in which Sir William calls off his trip abroad and tells his aunt, in the last five words of the text, about "the revolution in my schemes," invites the reader to wonder what happened next, in a quite different way than would the expected matrimonial finale. The effect is to reinforce Cleland's representation of William as a notably unfinished hero, appropriate not for romance but for the novel: half-educated at best; lacking any settled or mature sense of his place in the world; suspended, as he says, between hope and inquietude. If this seems anachronistic, too "postmodern" a reading, I'd suggest that, to the contrary, such a strategy of inconclusiveness is within the norms of the midcentury French libertine fiction Cleland clearly drew on as his model. Pinot-Duclos's *Memoirs*, for example, structured, like the *Coxcomb*, as a "Review" of the "Errors of my Youth" (4) in which promiscuous "Follies" are contrasted to rational "Pleasure" (2), concludes with a jarring and unexpected plot twist—unexpected by narrator and reader alike—that emphasizes the hero's state of doubtful irresolution. Having finally mustered the courage to propose marriage to his first and greatest love, the widowed Mme. de Canaples, Pinot-Duclos's narrator finds himself also in love with an orphaned ex-convent girl whom Mme. de Canaples has brought to live with her. Nevertheless, despite "this Division of my Heart" (189), when he honorably tells Mme. de Canaples of his conflicting desires, he seems to have reached that state of rational self-knowledge and self-control to which a reformed-libertine novel is meant to lead. As worthy as Mlle. de Foix may be of being loved, he says, "there can be no preferring her to you. My Reason in this Moment protests against a Moment of Surprise" (187). To his astonishment, however, Mme. de Canaples refuses to listen to his protestations, telling him it is her will that he marry Mlle. de Foix. The latter, when the hero asks her if she loves him, says only "that I have assured Madam *de Canaples*, that she is the absolute Mistress of my Disposal, and that whatever were her Designs for me, she might depend upon a blind Obedience from me" (193). Confused by this arrangement between the two women, the narrator is further astonished when Mme. de Canaples announces that she has settled her late husband's estate on him; when he protests against such an excess of generosity, she tells him he has no right to refuse: "Your Gratitude ought to make me no Answer, but by your Silence, and I dare add, by your Respect, and a perfect Submission to my Will" (197). Stunned into silence, as she commands, he is shepherded into marriage with Mlle. de Foix, and in the novel's last paragraph reports himself "happy and tranquil" (198).

Far from having attained self-knowledge or any degree of clarity on the distinction between coxcombry and love, Pinot-Duclos's narrator, like William at the end of his *Memoirs*, is caught in a state of bewildered disquiet. Uncertain what or whom he desires, Pinot-Duclos's hero gives up all control over his erotic and domestic life to Mme. de Canaples, his happiness an effect of numbed acquiescence. William is left hanging more visibly, unsure what awaits him. If Pinot-Duclos's text has an ending without a hero, Cleland's has a hero without an ending. Pinot-Duclos's *Memoirs* finishes with the promised happy ending of conjugal felicity at the cost of the protagonist's will and power of speech; Cleland's ends with a suspension of plot at the moment of the protagonist's greatest disorientation and emotional tumult. In that respect, the *Coxcomb* signals the influence of the most significant work of a novelist Cleland singled out in his critical writing: Crébillon's 1738 *The Wandering Head and Heart*, a novel that similarly comes to a halt before the promised ending of its reformed-libertine plot. Just as William, introducing the "history of my errors, and return to reason" (39), writes that "if I owed to that amiable and unaccountable sex [that is, 'the ladies'], my having been a coxcomb, I owe to a select one of it too the being one no longer," so Crébillon declares that while his hero, Meilcour, "simple at first and artless," lapses into "a man full of false ideas and riddled with follies," he is, "finally, in the last part, restored to himself, owing all his virtues to a good woman."[71] Meilcour, like William, falls in love with his "good woman" (Hortense) at first sight, not knowing her identity; as Catherine Cusset observes, and as is also true of William and Lydia, Meilcour "never finds Hortense when actively seeking her; he meets her always by chance, and her vision strikes him when he least expects it."[72] For both narrator-protagonists, the beloved embodies a categorical distinction between what William calls "the true love-passion" (195) and "the wantonness of a promiscuous chace" (194), yet in both cases the narrator inadvertently plants a seed of doubt as to the authenticity of "true" love by betraying how much this owes to the model of other romance narratives. As Meilcour writes of the emotions provoked by his first view of Hortense at the opera: "Full of agitation I returned home, all the more convinced that I was deeply in love because the passion had been implanted in my heart by one of those bolts from the blue that characterize all great affairs in novels" (788).

Reading his experience in light of the topoi of romance fiction, Meilcour casts his ensuing vacillation between the young, silent, melancholy Hortense and the forty-year-old libertine Mme. de Lursay as an inward struggle between true and false selves, the faithful lover and the vain coxcomb. But while the whole meaning of his text hinges on his eventual return to his true self after a period of *égarement*, or libertine errancy, Crébillon's novel ends with its hero more self-divided than ever. Having resolved to break with Mme. de Lursay, Meilcour nevertheless goes to her house in search of the elusive Hortense, but instead of leaving when he finds she's not there, he stays, "carried away by emotions that I did not understand and could not have defined" (894). In short order, Mme. de Lursay seduces him. Soon, however, he feels "an emptiness in my heart" (909), and in a moment that prefigures William's "redemptive" vision of Lydia, even as Meilcour lies in Mme. de Lursay's arms, "Hortense, whom I adored though so utterly forgotten, resumed her sway over my heart." Yet the effect of this triumphant return is not to recall Meilcour to virtue but instead to impel him "to drown in new frenzies a memory that continually plucked at my mind," so that "torn away from pleasure by remorse, snatched from remorse by pleasure, I could not be sure of myself for a moment" (910). Pleasure and remorse, figured as harpies that tear and snatch at the narrator, are linked metonymically to the two women he desires, and while the novel's preface seems to promise a moral awakening that will lead Meilcour to a conventional happy ending with Hortense, this final scene suggests that, for Meilcour, the condition of being "restored to himself" is just a keener awareness of his own unresolvable "contradictions" (910). "I was still far," he writes in the novel's penultimate sentence, "from resolving the conflict within me." This is confirmed in the text's final sentence, in which Meilcour writes, "I left [Mme. de Lursay], promising, in spite of my remorse, to see her early the next day, firmly resolved, moreover, to keep my word." The irony of this is not just, as Cusset argues, that Meilcour uses the lexicon of keeping faith ("firmly resolved"; "to keep my word") in the context of his infidelity and "incapacity to resist carnal pleasures and to be faithful to his genuine love for Hortense," but also that Meilcour's assertion that he was "firmly resolved . . . to keep my word" actually implies that he did not do so.[73] This would be in keeping with a pattern running throughout the novel, that whenever Meilcour resolves to do one thing (to find Hortense, to break with Mme. de Lursay), he does the opposite. It also leaves us, as readers, in the same position we're left in by the last sentence of the *Coxcomb*: face to face with our own frustrated expectations of a "real"—in other words, fictional—ending.

We readers, that is, expect romance. So do the narrators, Sir William and Meilcour. And Cleland, following Crébillon, provides romance, up to a point, while withholding and so inducing us to reflect on the satisfactions it pretends to provide.[74] By suspending the action just when readers are waiting for the loose ends of the plot to be tied up and the true lovers to be reconciled, Cleland and Crébillon not only draw attention to the artificiality of such plot structures but also call on us to question the narrators' claims to have reached some final understanding of themselves and of their own experience. William, like Meilcour, links self-understanding to love for the "right" woman, but both authors ironically undercut their narrators' representations of true love by showing them to be unconscious imitations of what they have read in other novels. In adapting Crébillon's device of the "suspended ending" (as Cusset terms it) to the *Coxcomb*, Cleland thus provokes broader questions about the relationship between incomplete narratives and unfinished selves.

No such questions arise, it seems, at the end of the *Woman of Pleasure*. Fanny is certainly married to Charles, in what she calls "this happiest of matches" (187), and is mother to a number of "fine children." She is living in "great ease and affluence" (1), and even if her occasional absurdities of language tarnish her moralistic summing up, she has clearly "got snug into port" (187) in a way that William and Meilcour emphatically have not. Enjoying "every blessing in the power of love, health, and fortune to bestow" (1), she seems, in a comically outrageous affront to Richardsonian ideals of sexual virtue, to offer a model for the formation of a married "bourgeois" female subject. Yet for all Fanny's material rewards and expressions of happiness, not every reader has been swept up in the celebratory spirit. Carol Houlihan Flynn has observed that "we leave the happy couple not hand in hand, but separated," Fanny at home writing letters while Charles trawls through brothels with their eldest son. Kate Levin has unpacked what she calls "the illusion of the *Memoirs'* happy ending," in which "middle-class morality" is revealed to be "infected" by the logic of prostitution.

Gary Gautier, more bluntly, has maintained that her "eloquent defense of virtue patently proves Fanny a fool."[75] The evidence to support such skeptical or contrarian views of the novel's ending is twofold: the economic motivation of Charles and Fanny's marriage, and Charles's habit of whoring, which he has bamboozled her into accepting as a vehicle for their son's moral education. As she writes to Madam in the text's penultimate paragraph:

> You know Mr. C—— O——, you know his estate, his worth, and good sense: can you? will you pronounce it ill meant, at least of him? when anxious for his son's morals, with a view to form him to Virtue, and inspire him with a fixt, a rational contempt for vice, he condescended to be his master of the ceremonies, and led him by the hand thro' the most noted bawdy-houses in town, where he took care that he should be familiariz'd with all those scenes of debauchery, so fit to nauseate a good taste. (188)

The more closely one looks at this passage, the more doubts it provokes. The educational method she approves of here is the same she called for in the heat of her confrontation with the sodomites, but as her whole memoir has shown, this is the way to excite, not curb, desire: far from inducing nausea, familiarization with "scenes of debauchery" leads first to arousal and then, inexorably, to an imitative acting out. Her failure to connect her husband's and son's activities to her own experience may prove Fanny a fool, but it may also betray a profound anxiety about the marriage in which she is trapped. For although she urges Madam to accept his claim that it is only because he is "anxious for his son's morals" that Charles "condescended to be his master of the ceremonies" on a whorehouse tour, her insistent repetitions ("You know . . . you know") and rhetorical pleas ("can you? will you . . . at least of him?") signal her own even more anxious need for reassurance.

And what, one might ask, is Charles's "estate"? He has none from his father, who "over-liv'd his income" (47), nor is anything left of his grandmother's annuity, "out of which she had laid up no reserves" (56). Charles "lost the little all he had brought with him" (180) from his colonial venture in the South Seas on his journey home, and he has no profession; so whether "estate" refers to land or social position, Charles's only comes from the wealth that legally became his the day he married Fanny. It is he who insisted on marriage, but the topic only arose when she told him the full extent of her fortune, built up over a career as prostitute ("a reserve of eight hundred pounds" she earned at Mrs. Cole's [173]) and concubine (the "vast possessions" she inherits after the rational pleasurist's death [176]). She ascribes his insistence to "the plea of love" (186), as she had already offered to give him her fortune as an "unreserv'd, unconditional dona-tion," but she does not consider (or allow herself to ponder) that only marriage can secure it to him by law and so make his real economic dependence on her disappear, as if by magic.[76] After marriage, she has no fortune, no estate, but his.

As with "estate," so with "worth": economically, Charles is worth what mar-riage brought him; in any other sense, his worth is questionable. It is as an object of sexual desire that he is most vividly present, and so worth most, in the text, but by the time Fanny writes, even that fire has died out. This is in fact *why* she writes. As she puts it in her account of their first day together, "Yes even at this time, that all the tiranny of the passions is fully over, and that my veins roll no longer but a cold tranquil stream, the remembrance of those passages that most affected me in my youth, still chears, and refreshes me" (42). With Charles and son off on their bawdy-house crawl, eros, for Fanny, can only be conjured in writing. This is nowhere more striking than in her account of her reunion with Charles, in which the temporal distance between the sexual scene and her writing of it collapses: "my thighs now obedient to the intimations of love and nature, gladly disclose, and with a ready submission resign up the soft gateway to entrance at pleasure: I see! I feel! the delicious velvet tip!—he enters might and main with—oh!—my pen drops from me here in the extasy now present to my faithful memory!" (183). Fanny's drift into the present tense—in a scene predominantly narrated in the past—effects a confusion between her body then and her body now, highlighting at this moment more than any other the power of writing to make sensations present, and thus to offer a medium for not only the expression but also the experience of "extasy."

Fanny's story, then, ends where her letters begin: she takes up a pen to write her memoirs, in answer to her reader's "desires." For that reason it might be more telling to describe her text, and William's, as artist's novels than simply as novels of education. Of course, every first-person narrator is, as the author of his or her own text, to that degree an artist, from Robinson Crusoe to Crébillon's Meilcour and the narrator of Pinot-Duclos's *Memoirs*. But Fanny and William are much more self-conscious than these other three about their own activity and aims as writers, and about the challenge of forging a literary style capable both of conveying the truth of their sensations of love and sexual desire and of triggering or evoking those sensations in the reader. While neither of them admits to designs of an authorial career, both set themselves in self-aware oppo-sition to the deficient productions of rival authors, as when William denounces "novel writers in general . . . for their unnatural, and unaffecting descriptions of the love-passion" (47), or when Fanny positions her work "between the re-voltingness of gross, rank, and vulgar expressions, and the ridicule of mincing metaphors and affected circumlocutions" (91). Indeed the challenge they take up is the same taken up by Cleland in Bombay: to "write freely" about eros "without resorting to the coarseness of . . . quite plain words."[77]

As Ruth Yeazell has argued, Cleland's, and his narrators', motive for shunning "coarseness" and "plain words" is double: to avoid revolting their readers with the "gross, rank, and vulgar," but in so doing, paradoxically, to give to their descriptions more of what Fanny calls "their due spirit and energy" (91).[78] Some thirty years later, in a conversation Yeazell cites to shed light on this paradox, Boswell reports Cleland saying that he found "Sterne's bawdy too plain" and that he had once told Sterne off for it. As Cleland tells Boswell: "I reproved [Sterne], saying, 'It gives no sensations.' Said he: 'You have furnished me a vindication. It can do no harm.' 'But,' [I said,] 'if you had a pupil who wrote c—— on a wall, would you not flog him?' He never forgave me."[79] It is no wonder that Sterne could not forgive Cleland for equating him to a dirty-minded schoolboy in need of a flogging. But the basis on which Cleland reproved Sterne is not, or not just, that his language is "gross, rank, and vulgar" but that "it gives no sensations"— that it is neither arousing nor affecting. Sterne twists this aesthetic reproof into a moral vindication, but for an author so attuned to sensation in all its forms, the criticism must have stung. Sir William faults his rival authors for the same deficiency: "In vain," he writes, "do they endeavour to warm the head, with what never came from the heart" (47). To "warm the head," however—that is, to excite the reader's imagination—is, as Sterne saw, to run the risk of doing harm: of inflaming or, as Cleland wrote in the preface to Pinot-Duclos, "holding the Light too near the Magazine" (235).[80]

It was Boswell who, reporting an earlier meeting with "old Cleland," referred to the *Woman of Pleasure* as "that most licentious and inflaming book."[81] In doing so, he paid tribute to Fanny's authorial success in finding the right stylistic register, a "mean temper'd with taste" (91) between the "gross" and the "mincing." Like William, she has taken to writing to show up other, inferior authors, as well as to give "the remembrance of those passages that most affected me in my youth" the clarity and shapeliness of art. Like William, too, she has cast remembrance in the form of romance and has cast herself as the protagonist of a narrative of moral education, but neither of them, by their stories' end, is in secure possession of the happy outcome to which their plotlines lead, and neither has disentangled the real from their fantasy-ideals. William's self-congratulation on his avowed but untested "return to reason" and Fanny's grandiloquent but self-deceiving "tail-piece of morality" may make them objects of the reader's laughter or contempt—Fanny does her best to head off precisely this reaction from Madam (187)—but such a response only confirms the seriousness of the novels' moral aims, in that both require the reader to gauge the distance between the narrators' claims and the truth that leaks through their representations. Judgment is only half the story, however. If we are invited by the ironic gap between Cleland and his narrators to assess the truth of their statements, we are also warmed by the sensations—of eros, love, and delight in the play of language—that the text inflames. To the extent that they succeed in this, Fanny and William have grown into authors who, like Cleland, can both give pleasure and do harm.

CHAPTER FIVE

The Hack
(1749–1759)

Trying to write his way out of the jail into which the *Woman of Pleasure* had landed him, Cleland painted his "present low abject condition" as that of "a writer for Bread" forced by economic necessity into "the meanness of writing for a bookseller."[1] The bookseller in question, Ralph Griffiths, most likely arranged to settle Cleland's debts to Thomas Cannon and John Lane, as their complaints were dismissed soon after the *Woman of Pleasure*'s second volume appeared. Cleland, as a result, was now in debt to Griffiths, and the only way he could pay the debt off was to serve as Griffiths's writer for hire. The clearest evidence of this comes in Griffiths's statement the following year to Lovel Stanhope—the same man, law clerk to the secretary of state, to whom Cleland had sent his jailhouse letter—as to his motive for asking Cleland to produce an expurgated version of the novel: "Mr Cleeland owed him a Sum of money & as Cleeland was going abroad he thought it was the only Method to get his Debt paid."[2]

Much outrage has been vented on Cleland's behalf concerning the advantage Griffiths took of his "low abject condition," notably by John Nichols in the obituary notice he wrote on Cleland for the *Gentleman's Magazine*. "Being without profession or any settled means of subsistence," Nichols writes, "he soon fell into difficulties; a prison, and its miseries, were the consequences. In this situation, one of those booksellers who disgrace the profession, offered him a temporary relief for writing the work above alluded to, which brought a stigma on his name, which time has not obliterated, and which will be consigned to his memory whilst its poisonous contents are in circulation."[3] An asterisk after "the work above alluded to" leads to this footnote: "The sum given for the copy [i.e., copyright] of this work was twenty guineas. The sum received for the sale could not be less than 10,000 £." The disproportion between those two figures says it all: the predatory bookseller, having taken advantage of an author "condemned to seek relief" by snapping up his work for a pittance, proceeds to rake in five hundred times what he paid for it. Not only that, but despite this staggering profit, he holds the impoverished author in a state of bondage for years after, forcing him, in the case of the expurgated *Fanny Hill*, to revisit a work that had already brought him humiliation and disgrace.

The odd thing about this complaint is that Cleland, never one to stifle his indignation or sense of injury, does not himself make it. He bemoans his abject state, the "meanness of writing for a bookseller," not because Griffiths has exploited him but, instead, to affirm his natural rank, that of gentleman, which should by rights preserve him from the necessity of laboring, even writing, "for Bread." In his first letter written after his arrest for obscenity, written to Andrew Stone, an under-secretary of state to Thomas Pelham-Holles, Duke of Newcastle, he portrays himself as "a weak, ruined, and unfortunate gentleman" and tries to benefit from his status as a fellow alumnus of the elite Westminster School: "I cannot imagine that your humanity, will permit you to refuse an old fellow-collegiate, and above all, a gentleman under most ungentlemanlike oppression, the favour of a private audience."[4] But this letter—in which he denied what was never in doubt, his authorship of the novel—went unanswered. So in his second letter, to Stanhope, Cleland acknowledges the novel as his, while both apologizing for the tone of the earlier letter and taking offense at Stone's silence, as treatment unbefitting a man of his rank:

> From the Messenger's House, in the heat of my resentment at being treated like a common malefactor, I wrote a letter to Mr Stone, and probably a very impertinent one, but I take for granted that he must be too much the gentleman to use it against me: Especially since his not vouchsafing me any answer, was, from one of his extream politeness, mortification enough to a gentleman, who measuring other hearts by his own, would pay ten times more tender respect to the natural Jealousy

of the distrest, than where, there is so little, and so vulgar a merit in paying it, to Fortune, and Power.[5]

Cleland himself, with his "tender respect" for the "distrest," is rather more a gentleman than Stone, who for all his "extream politeness" has behaved as a "vulgar" toady to fortune and power.

Given his readiness to attack Stone in writing to another official from the same department, it is unlikely that Cleland would have hesitated to shift blame onto Griffiths had he really resented his treatment. Instead, all he writes is that as a prisoner in the Fleet he showed the novel "to some whose opinion I unfortunately preferred to my own, and being made to consider it a ressource, I published the first part."[6] There is no claim of having been forced or even coaxed into publishing, just that "some"—Griffiths, or his brother, or other persons entirely—gave their opinion as to the text's potential value. Of course he regards the advice as "unfortunate" now he is under arrest, but he never suggests he was bilked or misled. On the contrary, he absolves the others arrested—Ralph Griffiths and Thomas Parker, the book's printer—of any blame. "It is really little more than Justice," he writes, "to acquitt, and deliver from longer confinement those poor People now under punishment for *my* fault: as they certainly were deceived by my avoiding those rank words in the work, which are all that they Judge of obscenity by."[7] Of course he is making a gesture here, "display[ing] his selflessness," as Epstein observes, and he might have expected this to weigh in his favor.[8] But Cleland had shown himself, as in the Bombay trials, willing to take risks on others' behalf, so his statement does not need to be read as disingenuous. Other authors, notably Smollett and Goldsmith, expressed genuine rancor against Griffiths, but Cleland never did.[9]

Almost all of Cleland's writing for Griffiths came in the five years following his release from the Fleet. Griffiths was just in his late twenties when he published the *Woman of Pleasure*, ten years or so younger than Cleland, and had only set up as a bookseller three or four years before.[10] He first comes to light in 1746, when he got into trouble with the law for two works that portrayed the Young Pretender and the Jacobite cause in a sympathetic light only a few months after the 1745 Jacobite rising had been put down at Culloden. When arrested, he, like Cleland, had written the secretary of state, and like Cleland he pleaded poverty as his excuse: "I am a young Man of no fortune, having a Family to maintain, and no means of subsisting but by my Pen."[11] In offering Cleland twenty guineas for the copyright to his first novel, he was not driving an especially hard bargain: the bookseller Thomas Lowndes paid the same to

Frances Burney in 1777 for her first novel, *Evelina*, and as James Raven notes, "Lowndes was neither poor nor uncharitable."[12] As it happens, Lowndes was also the publisher with William Nicoll of Cleland's third and last novel, *The Woman of Honor* (1768), for which Cleland was paid twenty-five guineas.[13] In that light, Griffiths's payment two decades earlier of twenty guineas to an unknown first-time novelist—at a time when he was just starting out in the trade, and for a text he knew could land him in more legal trouble—was unexceptionable.[14]

Moreover, the figure of £10,000 put forward by Nichols (ramped up to £20,000 in a later edition of his *Literary Anecdotes*) as "the sum [Griffiths] received for the sale" of the *Woman of Pleasure* is an utter chimera.[15] At a cost of six shillings per two-volume set, he would need to have sold over thirty thousand copies for gross earnings of that order. According to the book's printer, Thomas Parker, the initial press run was of 750 copies, and even allowing for multiple reprintings over the ensuing decades, such vast numbers are simply not credible. As James Basker has noted, editions of the *Woman of Pleasure* "continue[d] to circulate widely" to the end of the century, but "there is no evidence that Griffiths was responsible" for them—or, therefore, that they brought him any money. And the expurgated *Memoirs of Fanny Hill* seems to have been a commercial failure.[16] So while Griffiths likely did profit from sales of the *Woman of Pleasure*, those profits were liable to have been in the realm of hundreds rather than tens of thousands of pounds. And if Cleland only got twenty guineas for his labor, well, as Raven puts it, "Authors were the very last participants to benefit from the eighteenth-century book bonanza." Indeed "most authors and contributors to best-selling literature remained poor, powerless, and prolific" even as booksellers prospered.[17] Or as Catherine Gallagher expresses it, eighteenth-century authors consistently "portrayed themselves as dispossessed, in debt, and on the brink of disembodiment."[18] Charlotte Lennox, for instance, one of Gallagher's exemplary figures of authorship in the period, "called her steady employment 'slavery to the booksellers' . . . and her complaint is typical of 'independent' authors in the mid-eighteenth century."[19] Another writer cited by Gallagher, James Ralph, compared an author "who wrote for the booksellers to 'the Slave in the Mines': 'Both have their tasks assigned them alike: Both must drudge *and* starve; and neither can hope for Deliverance.' "[20] Intriguingly, Ralph made this comparison in a work published by Griffiths, *The Case of Authors by Profession or Trade, Stated* (1758). Whether or not he meant it as a reflection on his working relationship with Griffiths, it emphasizes the absence of any such personal reflections on Cleland's part. And while at times Cleland may have been on an alternating cycle of drudgery and starvation, the evidence suggests that his "tasks" were not mostly "assigned" him, but chosen.

The one task it is certain Griffiths initiated was that of cleaning up the *Woman of Pleasure*, for he said so under questioning after his arrest for having published it. Examined by Stanhope, he declared "that upon the Suppression of a Book Intitled the Memoirs of a Woman of Pleasure he applied to Mr. Cleeland the Author of it, & desired him to strike out the offensive parts of it & compile a Novel from it which might be inoffensive, which the said Mr. Cleeland did & called it 'Memoirs of Fanny Hill' which the Examinant is the proprietor and publisher of."[21] Cleland's lack of relish for the job is legible in the text's "impoverished" language and the weirdly pointless formal tinkering that sees the original two letters cut up into eleven, but even so, as Peter Sabor notes, he "took the opportunity . . . to make hundreds of corrections and revisions" to the first-edition text, so displaying a "careful attention . . . to stylistic accuracy" that Sabor calls "surprising" in view of the halfheartedness of his creative investment.[22] He seems, in this instance, to be approaching his work with a professional attention to detail even though he had written just a few weeks earlier that the *Woman of Pleasure* was "a Book I disdain to defend, and wish, from my Soul, buried and forgot." Indeed he asserted then that for all the fulminations of "my Lords the Bishops," "they cannot wish [the book] supprest more than I do."[23] Yet here he is, soon after, checking for "oddities of spelling and punctuation" to make it more presentable.[24]

Cleland's approach to the uncongenial task of scrubbing up the *Memoirs* reflects not only a professional ethos but a courtesy he felt he owed Griffiths, who had, after all, effected his release from the Fleet. Under questioning, Griffiths characterized the task not as an assignment but as a "Favour" he had "ask[ed] . . . of Mr Cleeland," as a way of paying off some part of his debt at a time when "Cleeland was going abroad"—which suggests not servitude but mutual obligation. If Cleland was in Griffiths's debt, he was not in his thrall: he produced work for other booksellers from the start of his career as a "writer for Bread," and the scraps that survive of their correspondence are amicable and frank.[25] Cleland's publication history suggests that from the time of his release from prison in March 1749 through November 1751, when Griffiths published *Memoirs of a Coxcomb*, Cleland did write primarily to work off the debt to Griffiths, but that after that they considered the debt paid, allowing Cleland to carry on as an independent author, with the risks as well as the freedom that entailed.

From 1749 through 1751 Cleland wrote about two dozen pieces for Griffiths's *Monthly Review*, starting with its inaugural issue of May 1749; these included reviews of fiction (Smollett's *Peregrine Pickle*, Fielding's *Amelia*, Francis Coventry's *Pompey the Little*) but also of works on subjects ranging from politics (Bolingbroke's letters, Montesquieu's *L'Esprit des Lois*) to medicine (*Observations on the Epidemical Diseases in Minorca*) and history (*Authentic Memoirs of the Christian Church in China*).[26] In these years, Griffiths also published *Memoirs of a Woman of Pleasure* (1748–1749), *Memoirs of Fanny Hill* (1750), and *Memoirs of a Coxcomb* (1751), as well as a short pseudomoral, pseudomedical burlesque, *The Œconomy of a Winter's Day*.[27] In this same period Cleland published two works with other booksellers: a polemical tract, *The Case of the Unfortunate Bosavern Penlez* (1749), published under the false imprint of "T. Clement near St. Paul's," and a sensational medical narrative, the *Case of Catherine Vizzani* (1751), "printed for W. Meyer."[28] It is not clear if these were commissioned by the booksellers that issued them or if Cleland sought out publishers after Griffiths had turned them down; both texts were potentially liable to prosecution, and Griffiths may have decided they were not worth the risk. In any case, from late 1751 Cleland stopped being a regular contributor to the *Monthly Review*, and while Griffiths did publish one more important work of Cleland's, the 1753 *Dictionary of Love*, Cleland could no longer be considered one of Griffiths's "house authors," those whom Norman Oakes calls the *Monthly Review*'s "corps."[29] For the rest of his authorial career Cleland shopped his work from publisher to publisher, trying out new genres, in some cases perhaps writing to commission but typically pursuing his own simultaneously eccentric and representative course.

If Cleland became an author by lucky or unlucky chance, the same could be said of many writers of the period. There were few useful models for an authorial career in the fluctuating and unstable literary marketplace of the mid-eighteenth century. What we tend to see as the golden age of the emerging novel—the years from 1740 to the early1750s, which saw the publication of most of the major novels of Richardson, the Fieldings, Smollett, Lennox, and Cleland—was actually a period of gradual decline for fiction, in which not only the number of new novel titles but the overall number of novels in print fell rather ominously.[30] As Gallagher observes, "It was not . . . a propitious time to begin a novel-writing career," and in fact no would-be professional writers could have thought of themselves as novelists in the way that later writers could. All professional authors at midcentury—all who depended on writing for their livelihood—were "miscellaneous writers," Fielding, Smollett, and Lennox no less than the famously eclectic Johnson, whose publications in his first ten years in London ranged from "London" and the *Life of Savage* to an annotated translation of a French commentary on Pope and, by some estimates, half a million words of semijournalistic, semifictional parliamentary debates written for the *Gentleman's Magazine*.[31] If neither he nor anyone else could rival the avowedly indolent Johnson's productivity, Cleland adopted a similarly diversified approach in his first decade as a hack, compassing fiction, translations, parodies, reviews, essays on legal and political controversies, medical histories, satirical verse epistles, and plays both comical and tragic. Of course "hack" is not a word that Cleland would have welcomed, seeing it, rightly, as a term of class disparagement, but if insultingly called a hack or "mercenary Scribbler," as he was by a pundit in a letter to the *Public Advertiser*, he stood his ground as a professional author:

> This term is really so stale so stinking an Oyster-Weed of the literary Billingsgate, that it hurts one the more in a Production of which the Stile would undoubtedly lead one to think the Writer superior to the Use of it either for Argument or Garnish . . . How frequently has not one poor Writer, poor in every Sense, while himself was languishing, under every Circumstance of [Want,] with so much of Wit and Humour as of Reason and Propriety, reproached some other Writer not more miserable than himself, with his white-limed Garret, his Farthing-candle, his Small-beer and his Lack of Credit at the next Chandler's Shop? [A] Senseless Scheme to raise a Laugh at the Expence of the Honour of Literature. Independently of the Inconsistence of which[,] they do not consider that they are only furnishing Matter of stupid Triumph to the common Enemy, the tasteless worthless Men of Fortune, those wretched Beings who with a Heart all rotten, and a Head all in Rags, affect to look down with great Contempt on Circumstances, which, at the worst, could not be a greater object of it than their own, a Poverty at once of Intellect and of Spirit.[32]

Such "Men of Fortune," Cleland writes later in the same letter, for all their advantages of birth and rank, themselves "never could rise so high as Scribbling, or but to common Orthography."

Cleland's defense of professional writers as upholders of "the Honour of Literature" does not try to conceal their material circumstances. Although he complains about "the meanness of writing for a bookseller," the writer's poverty becomes a sign of his cultural value in a period when Britain, as he would write at the end of his career, had been "debased and reduced . . . through her own follies, nearly to insignificance and nullity."[33] The general depravity of taste that Cleland saw all around him might turn one author against another in the hope of pleasing the public, but writers needed to recognize their common enemy and their common cause. Although in much of his private correspondence, as in the letters to Stanhope and Stone, Cleland took pains to portray himself as a gentleman in distress, his typical stance in his published work of the 1750s was that of an industrious jobbing author. In that respect he, like Johnson, resists fitting in to Alvin Kernan's claim that "most of the hacks, driven by their pride, tried to pretend that they were still gentleman-authors of the courtly tradition rather than the poorly paid print laborers they in fact were."[34] A courtly hanger-on was the last creature on earth Cleland would have been tempted to impersonate. Indeed he equates those he calls "the closetteers of St. James's" to "the Garretteers of St. Giles's": neither politicians for hire nor partisan hacks are distinguishable from "a nest of prostitutes."[35] Cleland himself was vulnerable to charges of being a hireling or "mercenary Scribbler," notably for his letters on political subjects in the *Public Advertiser*, which he was generally thought to have written at the behest of one or another ministerial faction. And he was often accused, during his lifetime and later, of being "an adept in literary fraud," a plagiarist, a literary pirate.[36] But in his first decade as a "writer for Bread" he sought ways of engaging with the literary marketplace that let him maintain a stance of independence—neither a supplicant for patronage nor a replaceable content provider, but a new kind of cultural producer, engaged with but not engulfed by the market.

Apart from the *Woman of Pleasure* and the *Memoirs of Fanny Hill*, it is uncertain how or why Cleland wrote what he did in the 1750s. Was he assigned books to review for the *Monthly*, or did he choose what interested him from books received? Probably some mixture of the two, and the degree of his interest probably corresponds to the length at which he comments on, instead of just summarizing or excerpting, the text. By that light, he was strongly invested in Bolingbroke's *Letters* and Fielding's *Amelia*, less so in a spurious sequel to *Tom Jones*.[37] Cleland's translations from the French—of Pinot-Duclos's *Mémoires* for a consortium of eminent London booksellers, and of J. F. Dreux du Radier's *Dictionnaire d'amour* for Griffiths—might have been commissioned by the publishers, or Cleland might have initiated them. Either way, both exhibit such strong continuities with the thematic preoccupations and narrative patterns of his first two novels that the translations should be read as no less his own work. Indeed Cleland's career calls into question the distinction made by Edward Young in his 1759 *Conjectures on Original Composition* between the originality of a true "Author" and the derivative hackwork of "other invaders of the Press," whose work is "a sort of *Manufacture* wrought up by those *Mechanics*, *Art*, and *Labour*, out of pre-existent materials not their own."[38] For Cleland, as also, emphatically, for Johnson—but also Richardson, Smollett, Fielding, Lennox, Eliza Haywood, and so on—the "art" and "labour" of writing, the "mechanics" of authorship, are not only visible in the text but are in some ways its subject, and their writings, whether they count generically as novels, reviews, burlesques, imitations, translations, essays, commentaries, or prefaces, are openly "wrought up" of "pre-existing materials not their own." This is not to say that none of these authors is original but that originality—and never more brazenly so than in the eighteenth century—consists precisely in the imagination and energy with which that "pre-existing material" is "altered, added to, transposed, and in short new-cast," to cite Cleland on how he reworked the lost Carmichael-inspired *Woman of Pleasure* into the novel whose copyright he sold.[39]

In the rest of this chapter I focus on two texts from this period of "mercenary Scribbling" in which Cleland brings his art and labor to bear on materials not his own and manages to make of them something new. The first, *The Case of the Unfortunate Bosavern Penlez* (1749), was stinging enough in its denunciation of the government's handling of the London uprising that came to be known as the Penlez riots to provoke a defensive jab from none other than Henry Fielding, who as magistrate had examined the rioters, including the hapless Penlez.[40] The second text is the *Case of Catherine Vizzani* (1751), Cleland's translation of and commentary on an Italian medical case history of a cross-dressing woman who, armed with a "leathern Contrivance, of a cylindrical Figure," seduced and eloped with a series of young women until her death led to the discovery and publication of her secret.[41] As with the *Woman of Pleasure* and the *Coxcomb*, intense curiosity about the sources of perverse desire drives Cleland's "Dissertation" on the Vizzani case, which culminates in a call for the suppression of "scandalous and flagitious books" such as, of course, itself—a call that echoes the ironies and instabilities of the two novel-memoirs.

I conclude with remarks on two other translations from French sources: Dreux du Radier's *Dictionnaire d'amour* of 1741 and Louis-François de La Drevetière Delisle's *Arlequin sauvage*, a comedy written in 1721 for the Théâtre-Italien of Paris. In turning the *Dictionnaire* into his 1753 *Dictionary of Love*, Cleland substantially "altered, added to, transposed, and in short new-cast" the original, in keeping with his understanding of translation as an act of cultural as well as linguistic reimagining. In his translation of Delisle's play, by contrast, Cleland stays close to the French, even though his title, *Tombo-Chiqui; or, The American Savage*, seems to offer something remote from the world of commedia dell'arte to which Delisle's "savage harlequin" belongs. Yet in strictly adhering to his source, Cleland produced a work that recapitulates many of the thematic concerns of his earlier fiction and anticipates some narrative motifs of his 1765 collection of novellas *The Surprises of Love*. Fidelity to another's text as expression of self: the paradox of the translator. When Cleland, in his review of *Peregrine Pickle*, assailed the "flood of novels, tales, romances, and other monsters of the imagination, which have been either wretchedly translated, or even more unhappily imitated, from the *French*, whose literary levity we have not been ashamed to adopt, and to encourage the propagation of so depraved a taste," he may have been venting some frustration at the wretched or unhappy necessity of selling his labor to produce salable English versions of someone else's work.[42] But this production is so integral to his literary corpus that it cannot be treated as marginal or secondary to his "own" or "original" writing. Instead, it allows us to see that all his work is caught up in networks of rewriting, imitation, critique, pastiche, and translation—or, as he once sourly defined the last of these, "forced and unnatural transplantation."[43]

The Unfortunate Bosavern Penlez

On Friday, 30 June 1749, a sailor was robbed "of a considerable Sum of Money" at a bawdy house in the Strand. When he "apply'd to the Keeper of the House for Satisfaction of his Loss," in Cleland's account of events, he was driven away "with foul Language and Blows."[44] It is indicative of the murky and conflicted state of the evidence in the case that while Cleland specifies one sailor, in more recent historical accounts the number is confidently given as two, or as three, and even the number of Portuguese moidores allegedly stolen varies from report to report.[45] But in every report, the sailors returned to ship, roused their mates, and came back en masse the next night for justice or revenge. Cleland, adapting the nautical jargon that also threads through the *Woman of Pleasure*, writes that the sailors "went to work" on the bawdy house "as if they were breaking up a Ship, and in a Trice unrigg'd the House from Top to Bottom" (18), throwing featherbeds and all into the street to make a great bonfire. All of this, Cleland writes, was done "with so much Decency and Order, so little Confusion, that, notwithstanding the Crowd gather'd together on this Occasion, a Child of five Years old might have crossed the Street in the thickest of them, without the least Danger." No surprise, this, given that when they first forced their way into the house, the sailors, "acting like true brave Fellows, suffer'd no Injury to be done to the poor Damsels, who got off safe and unhurt." In Cleland's account, the sailors are champions of virtue in distress—not at all the mob who, according to the *Gentleman's Magazine*'s report of the same events, "turn'd the women naked into the street; then broke all the windows, and considerably damaged an adjacent house."[46]

The Hack (1749–1759)   149

Whether the firing of this first bawdy house was an act of popular justice or of insurrection (as the *Gentleman's Magazine* and, later, Henry Fielding would assert), by the time soldiers arrived from Somerset House to quell the disorder, it was no longer just one bawdy house but all of them that the sailors and their allies aimed to pull down, and the troubles were to continue over the next two days, leading to the destruction of two more houses and attacks on agents of the police, among them Fielding himself. Bosavern Penlez, who was to give his name to the disorders, was in fact scarcely part of them. The son of an Exeter clergyman, he had lived in London since 1747, working first as a peruke maker and later as a gentleman's servant. On the second night of disorders, after a day of drinking with friends, he ended up among or around the crowd converging on the Star, a tavern-cum-bawdy-house near his home. He may or may not have joined them, but soon after one in the morning, just as soldiers were arriving at the Star to disperse the crowd and forestall another bonfire, Penlez was arrested a few streets away with what one watchman called "a great Bundle of Linnen" that was later identified as having come from the Star. That link to the scene of the riot led to Penlez's indictment under the Riot Act of 1715, and despite many questions about the evidence and the eventual guilty verdict—not least from the jurymen themselves—Penlez was executed on 18 October, the sole object of the law's vengeance for the sailors' bawdy-house rampage or crusade.

As the passages I have cited suggest, the Penlez Riots, as they came with grim inaptness to be called, provoked bitterly divided responses, most memorably presented in Cleland's and Fielding's warring pamphlets: Cleland's anonymously issued *The Case of the Unfortunate Bosavern Penlez*, published on 7 November 1749, and Fielding's avowedly corrective *A True State of the Case of Bosavern Penlez*, published eleven days later. Fielding being Fielding, his "frankly polemical and self-interested account," as Peter Linebaugh labels it, is probably the better known of the two, but the two pamphlets were regularly advertised together, and they are equally polemical, even if Cleland tried to put himself above the fray by presenting his as the work of "a Gentleman Not Concern'd." As the examining magistrate who committed Penlez to Newgate to await trial, Fielding was ineluctably "concern'd," not to say embroiled, in the extremely unpopular decision to proceed with Penlez's hanging despite pleas for mercy from the jury that had originally convicted him and from several hundred petitioners from local parishes—pleas even the king was said to favor.[47] In his pamphlet, Cleland expresses perplexity, or perhaps mock perplexity, at the refusal of mercy, hypothesizing "that there was some great and mighty latent Cause, that forbad the shewing of Mercy, where Mercy seems so much due, that it might even deserve the Name of Justice; some Cause above the Reach or Comprehension of those vulgar ordinary Understandings, which compose that common Sense of Mankind, which has not been a little *hurt* on this Occasion" (44). A few pages later, he concludes that "some deep abstruse Reason of State, in short, prevailed over an Occasion of gratifying large Bodies of Men, and indeed, the whole Town in general" (47), perhaps implying a position like that taken by Linebaugh in his essay on the case: Penlez was hanged, he argues, "so that the Government by the severity of its retribution could lend support to its characterization of the riot and to the decision to rely upon the military to suppress it, as if the seriousness of the punishment determined the gravity of the crime."[48] Penlez died, the argument runs, that the Pelham administration, to which Fielding owed his magistracy, might live—or at any rate that it might justify its arguably heavy-handed response to the disorders in the Strand by staging the exemplary punishment of Penlez as a symbol of Riot.[49]

But if Cleland's passing remarks imply suspicion that the decision to proceed with Penlez's execution, against the express will of the people, was politically motivated, his object in writing the *Unfortunate Penlez* was not to ask why the government acted as it did but to justify the sailors' and their supporters' actions, and to vindicate Penlez as a doubly traduced young man of "unblemish'd Character" (27). The ill-starred Penlez, in Cleland's account, was the victim, first, of "the Rage and Malice" of "a Wretch fit to taint the Air he breath'd in" (30, 37)—Peter Wood, keeper of the Star, hell-bent on revenge for the breaking of his house—and, second, of an unnamed slanderer who, aiming "to aggravate the Distress, and increase the Danger of a poor Creature under Sentence of Death" (26), spread the story, after Penlez had been convicted of riot, that he had been arrested holding the "great Bundle of Linnen" referred to above, and so was also guilty of theft. As Cleland writes, "No Notice, nor even Shadow of Notice, was taken of this Bundle at the Trial," so the motive of "whoever . . . made Report of it" was to furnish *"great Means of preventing Mercy from being extended to this unhappy young Man"* as it had been to the sole other person found guilty of riot, John Wilson, reprieved on the eve of his hanging. What Cleland does not write is that the slanderer in question was Fielding, who interceded, as he admits in his own pamphlet, with "some very noble Persons, in order to make some Distinction between the two condemned Prisoners, in Favour of *Wilson*, whose Case to me seemed to be the Object of true Compassion."[50] On the basis of the testimony of the watchmen who arrested Penlez, Fielding clearly believed that Penlez had stolen the bundle of linens from the Star. But Cleland is surely right to object that for Fielding to bring this, at the eleventh hour, to the attention of those with power to grant or withhold mercy, in a kind of end run around the broadly based campaign to win Penlez a reprieve—and to do so in private, so that Penlez had no chance to defend himself—was morally indefensible. As he writes, whoever circulated "this Story trumped up of a Bundle found upon *Penlez*" (28) was "not overloaded with good Nature, or common Humanity" (26).[51]

As for Peter Wood—proprietor, with "his Wife, or No-Wife" Jane (31) of the Star, and key witness for the prosecution in placing Penlez at the scene of the riot—Cleland asks, "But where was the Wonder or Improbability of his swearing *any Thing*, and against *any Body*?" (30). Nothing that either Wood swears can be taken for true: one witness at the trial, whom Cleland cites, declared that "for my part I would not hang a dog or cat upon their evidence, they keep such a bad house and other things," and the evidence Cleland marshals against them is damning.[52] Against Benjamin Lander, one of the three alleged rioters (along with Penlez and Wilson) whose cases went to trial, Peter Wood swore that half an hour before the guard came to disperse the crowd, "he was in the Passage of his house, assisting to break the Partition," and that "he broke the Window of the Bar with his Stick"; while Jane Wood (or as Cleland puts it, "the Woman who passed for *Wood*'s Wife, and may be might be so") swore "that *Lander* knock'd her down, and that she was beaten almost to a Jelly" (32). But Lander is able to prove that he arrived at the Star in the company of a soldier "who told him that they were going to disperse a Mob in the Strand" and whom, on the way there, he treated to a pint in a tavern (32). Providentially, when Lander is "collar'd . . . under the Notion of his being a Straggler left behind, of those concern'd in the Demolition of the House," it is at the hand of "the very identical Soldier whom he had the Instant before treated with a Pint of Beer," so that he "could not be guilty of those Facts sworn so positively against him by *P. W.* and his virtuous Consort" (33). Despite what Cleland rightly calls "this glaring Circumstance" (34)—which of course led to Lander's acquittal—the Woods' testimony against Penlez and Wilson was admitted. As Cleland writes, "Now unfortunately for poor *Wilson* he had treated no Soldier; he had No-body at hand to prove a Negative, against the point-blank Oaths of three thorough-pac'd Evidences [the third being the Woods' servant], the Weight however of all three of whom put together, one would have thought lighter than Air, in a Case where five Farthings should be at Stake, much more the Lives of honest Men" (35). As this passage reveals, Cleland is anything but neutral; instead, as in his statements before the

Bombay court, his language is by turns inflammatory, sarcastic, and figurally extravagant. Here, for example, is his explanation of Peter Wood's motives for testifying so positively against Penlez and the others:

> Bloodthirstily determin'd, at any Rate, to fix his grievous Complaint *somewhere*, and ready to run at every one, like a mad Dog, he was very indifferent who it was he hang'd by his Oath[,] since whoever he hang'd, if he was but an honest Man, stood in the Light of an Enemy to him. To this Keenness of Revenge may be attributed his seizing the first that were offer'd, or laid in the Way of it, whom the staunch hard-mouth'd Hound immediately fastened upon, and hunted some to Death, some to the Gates of it. (30–31)

Throughout the pamphlet, Cleland moves freely between this sort of dramatically colored, "Raw-head and Bloody-bones" (20) language and a more lawyerly, forensic discourse, as when he follows the above passage by writing, of Wood's bloodthirstiness, that "this will plainly appear on a Review of the Trial itself," even though no hellhounds can be found coursing through the documents Cleland urges the reader to consult.[53]

By contrast with the "mad Dog" Peter Wood, Penlez, who first appears in Cleland's text as "one of those who fell in with the Stream" of the crowd "being a little flustered with Liquor" and so "the more heated and imprudent in his Management" (25), by the end of the pamphlet has been ennobled by suffering—"the Hardships and Terrors of the long Imprisonment in *Newgate*" (48)—so that he goes to his death "with a Resignation and Composure worthy of a less deplorable End" (55). When his fellow convict Wilson is reprieved at ten o'clock on execution-day eve, Penlez is quoted saying, *"He was heartily pleas'd with it, whatever became of himself, and should be glad to be the first to wish him Joy of it"* (52). And "if to this is added what is equally true," Cleland writes, "that, on there being intimated to him some hopes of a Rescue" at the scaffold, "he express'd the warmest Disavowal of it . . . declaring, that though he was to suffer as a Rioter, he had so little of the Principles of one, that he did not even desire to owe his Life to a Riot" (53), Cleland's vindication of him as a person of "Sentiments that would have done Honour to a higher Condition of Life than his was" links up the personal and political strands of his text. Penlez is not just a person of "unblemish'd Character"; he embodies the "gentle and governable Sentiments" (45) of the "common People of *England*," giving the lie to those, like Fielding, responsible for "the Imputation of a riotous seditious Humour . . . among the People, and which had been the Handle made use of to urge the Necessity of this bloody Example" (54–55). It is because "the Condition of this young Man" was "low" in his lifetime that he can figurally embody the crowd of which he was, even if accidentally, a part. Since "a Lord and the meanest Craftsman are but Men alike, are but Subjects alike, and are, or ought to be, equally dear to the Laws of Society" (4), as Cleland asserts, Penlez is fully worthy of the reader's interest; and since he acts as a synecdochic figure for the London crowd, they are in turn worthy of justification as demonstrating by their actions "the old *British* Spirit" (54). So even if the pulling down of houses and destruction of their contents is "not . . . strictly justifiable" (17), the sailors who composed the core of the uprising were clear "of any premeditated Design to offer an Insult to his Majesty's Government, which their Body had been the greatest Support of, and which some of them had often ventur'd their Lives for" (18). It is they who manifest for Cleland the "antient Manliness" from which "the Spirit of the *English* is already too much broke, sunk, and declin'd" (46) nowadays.

Cleland makes the case for the sailors and those who joined them by narrating their actions so as to affirm their essential orderliness and restraint—as when, in a passage already cited, he asserts that the first bawdy house was dismantled "with so much Decency and Order, so little Confusion," that "a Child of five Years old might have crossed the Street in the thickest of [the crowd] without the least Danger" (18)—but also, rather contrarily, by presenting the uprising as a boisterous, carnivalesque spectacle, "which it is not easy not to look on in a ludicrous light" (41). This last phrase seems to have particularly rankled Fielding, who writes in the final part of his *True State* that "the Riot here under Consideration, was of a very high and dangerous Nature, and far from deserving those light or ludicrous Colours which have been cast upon it."[54] Cleland, however, repeatedly refers to the disorder as a "Frolic," asking why, if the riot was as "horrid" (20) as the authorities tried to make it appear, none of its ringleaders was seized early on. "But no!" he writes, "the Impunity or Neglect they met with in their first Attempt, begot a fresh one; The jovial Sailors imagin'd probably the Government look'd on their Frolic with the same Eyes that they did; and having got too high a Relish of the *Fun*, as they call'd it, the Demolition of one of these Dens was not sufficient to stay their Stomach, now it was well up" (21).[55] The local residents watching the action unfold are also moved by the spirit of fun, as Cleland portrays in a scene from the first night, mocking the lexicon of moralistic outrage that came to be attached to the events:

> The Neighbours too, though their Houses were not absolutely free from Danger of Fire, by the Sparks flying from the Bonfire, were so little alarm'd at this most

bloody outrageous Riot, this terrible Breach of the public Peace, that they stood at their Doors, and look'd out of their Windows, with as little Concern, and perhaps more Glee and Mirth, than if they had been at a Droll in *Bartholomew Fair*, seeing the painted Scene of the renown'd *Troy* Town in Flames. (19)

The neighbors' glee, however, is not simply a childish delight in the theatrical spectacle of mayhem and flames; it is also an expression of solidarity with the rioters' aims. Cleland offers an anecdote of one Mrs. L——, "who kept a Cheesemonger's Shop hard by, and who being a married Woman, had perhaps often seen with an evil Eye the Trade of those Houses" (19). Looking on the bonfire, she "happen'd to clap her Hands, and express her Joy too vociferously; which gave such Offence to some of the Runners, Imps, or Supports of these Houses, that she had an Action brought against her for encouraging the Rioters, which it is said she is not yet clear of." The neighbors share in the sailors' antipathy to "those obnoxious Houses" (23), whose keepers "not only live in a constant State of Elusion, or Contempt of the Law, but also in a Sort of State of Warfare with Mankind, preying on one Sex, and oppressing the other, and the weakest" (15–16). The rioters, Cleland suggests, were animated by the spirit of justice, even if the spirit of mirth at times overruns it.

As an instance of the former, Cleland offers the anecdote of "a little Boy, who perhaps thought [it] no great Harm to save a gilt Cage out of the Fire, for his Bird at Home, [and who] was discover'd carrying it off; when the Leaders of the Mob took it from him, and threw it into the Fire, and his Age alone prevented him from severer Punishment. Nothing in short," he offers by way of moral, "was imbezzled or diverted" (22)—and so confirms the ethical basis of the crowd's actions. Cleland acknowledges that there were also, among the hangers-on, "Numbers of thoughtless giddy People, young and old, with more Mirth in their Heads than Malice in their Hearts" (25); these, he surmises, were "probably taken with the Humour of the Thing, and thought demolishing a Bawdy-House was no such bad Joke." The spirits of justice and mirth, order and disorder, sit together uneasily here and throughout the pamphlet, but underlying even the most unruly of the mob's actions is a moral economy that held bawdy houses as legitimate targets of popular violence and mirthful demolition as a fitting expression of the "Odium and Contempt" (15) in which they were held.[56] Even the soldiers sent to protect the besieged bawdy houses and disperse the crowds are in sympathy with the riot:

One might see their Countenances, by the Light of the unexpir'd Bonfire, a little cast down and abash'd, at the Nature of the Service they were order'd upon: And

indeed their Behaviour shew'd yet more, that they were not much in Earnest about
the Matter; for instead of making any Bustle, to apprehend or secure the Ringleaders of the Riot, than which by the Way nothing was less difficult, they loiter'd about,
rang'd themselves on both Sides the Street, or stood very compos'd round the Remains of the Bonfire, as if that had been what they were sent to Guard, and not the
Bawdy-Houses. (20)[57]

This unanimity of aversion to the bawdy houses and their owners—but not
to the "poor Damsels" confined within them—is, for Cleland, at the heart of
the popular support of the sailors' crusade of destruction, and the *Unfortunate
Penlez* is structured to impress that sentiment on the reader from the start, so
that everything that follows has to be understood in light of it. For that reason,
the first quarter of the pamphlet is devoted to an impassioned denunciation of
"that Set of Men, vulgarly called *Cock-Bawds*" (4), by way of a somber exemplary
tale of the fall and wretched end of "one of those poor, young, tender Creatures" who has been "noosed, and intangled in [the bawd's] hellish Snares" (8).
If Cleland assumes here a stance remote from that of Fanny Hill's idealizing
portrayal of Mrs. Cole's "little family of love," his graphic account of the cock
bawd's corruption of one who was "once, probably, the Pride and Delight of a
fond Parent's Eye" (9) recalls certain elements of Fanny's own corruption at
Mrs. Brown's, but with no compensating pleasure. Like Mrs. Brown—and the
wicked landlady Mrs. Jones, who presents Fanny "with a bill for arrears of rent,
diet, apothecary's charges, nurse, &c." (57) in order to compel her into the arms
of Mr. H—— the cock bawd, modeled on the vicious Peter Wood, "indulg[es]
and humour[s] the giddy, wild, thoughtless Turn, natural to that Age, till he
runs her up a competent Score, at any Rate, true or false, till he fixes a good
round Debt upon her; the imaginary Terrors of which, keep her in a State of
Slavery to him, scarce less cruel, and much more infamous, than that of a Captive in *Barbary*." From then on, she is endlessly exploitable, and "nothing, no,
not her own Person, is her own Property, or at her own Disposal" (9).

The consequence of the young woman's economic abjection is corruption
both bodily and moral. The captives of the cock bawd's "Hackney-Seraglio of
wretched Women" (7) are "given up, at Discretion, to the Lust of every Ruffian
who can afford the Price he sets upon her, let his Person be never so loathsome
and infectious, to be touzed, and rumpled, like a Bit of dirty Paper": an image
in which venereal and other forms of infection are figured as the crumpling
or soiling of the woman's once spotless, unspoiled "tender delicate Person"
(9). Inwardly, she undergoes a similar transformation: "through the Ductility

and Aptness of that Age to take all Impressions, especially those which flatter the Senses, her Mind soon becomes tainted, and shares Corruption with her Person. Spirituous Liquors are resorted to, and employed to keep her Head hot, and indisposed to any Returns to Reason or Virtue; thus drowning all Memory of her former Condition, or Sense of her present one, in perhaps no better than the *Gin-Lethe*" (10). The young woman's ductility and aptness to take "impressions" again evokes paper, a surface that can be imprinted or stained, and conveys a sexual double entendre that links physical and moral "tainting."[58] Intoxication, too, at first a sort of sensory "flattery" or pleasure, leads in time to oblivion and a loss of self. That loss is also figured in a passage portraying the "poor young Women" as the "Spunges of an imperious Task-Master, who, if they have soaked up any Trifle, through the Generosity or Fondness of those they call so significantly their Cullies, are presently squeez'd, and oblig'd to give it up again, to the Cravings and insatiate Demands of the rapacious Pandar" (7–8). The obscene double meanings are closer to the surface here, "Spunges" evoking the vaginal sponges secreted in every bedpost of Mrs. Cole's house in the *Woman of Pleasure* for the purposes of counterfeiting hymeneal ruptures (by squeezing "a prepar'd fluid blood" between the thighs at the right moment) and of contraception (as was common practice in the period).[59] The sexual and financial are intertwined, from the use of "soaked up" to characterize the women's receiving of "trifles" from their "cullies"—victims or dupes but, etymologically, also testicles (Fr. *couillons*, It. *coglioni*), as Cleland well knew—to the "cravings" and "insatiate demands" of the bawd, exacting payment both in cash and in kind. It all ends badly, with the "amiable Creature," once "in pass to be a virtuous Wife, a happy Mother, and a Blessing and Ornament of Society," reduced to "an infected gangreen'd Member," ending "her miserable Life, either by public Justice, the Rottenness of Diseases, or the intrail-burning Fire of Spirits in a Gin-Shop" (14–15). There is symbolic justice, then, in the firing of the cock bawd's possessions, and in the sailors' chivalrous freeing of "the poor Damsels, who got off safe and unhurt" (18) from their house of captivity. By prefacing his account of the Strand riots and Penlez trial with the graphic tale of a young woman's destruction at the hand of one of these "Enemies to Mankind" (8), the bawdy-house keepers, Cleland endeavors to enlist us sentimentally, and thus politically, on the side of those the government denounced as seditious.

The Case of Catherine Vizzani

One might have expected that his arrests on charges of obscenity, in 1749 and 1750, would have deterred Cleland from undertaking as his next project an explicit account of female same-sex seduction involving cross-dressing, dildos, and detailed examinations of its protagonist's clitoris and hymen, but in March 1751, a year after his arrest for the *Memoirs of Fanny Hill*, the publisher W. Meyer issued Cleland's latest work, on this very subject. Titled *Historical and Physical Dissertation on the Case of Catherine Vizzani*, the sixty-six-page booklet was provided with an elaborate subtitle (probably devised, as was normal, by the bookseller) to attract potential buyers. It was said to contain "the Adventures of a young Woman, born at Rome, who for eight Years passed in the Habit of a Man, was killed for an Amour with a young Lady; and being found, on Dissection, a true Virgin, narrowly escaped being treated as a Saint by the Populace." Cleland's booklet, first attributed to him by Roger Lonsdale in 1979, is a translation of an Italian text of 1744 by Giovanni Bianchi, professor of anatomy at Siena, with extensive emendations and commentary by Cleland.[60] Bianchi's text, the *Breve storia della vita di Catterina Vizzani*, had been published, after some difficulties with papal censors, by Simone Occhi in Florence (albeit with the false imprint of Venice); it is not known how Cleland came across it or why he decided to translate it, but there are many connections with his other writing of the period.[61] As Cleland presents it, the Vizzani case resonates especially with the notion of "unsexed bodies" I have located in the *Woman of Pleasure*, a vision of eros as a force that unsettles and remakes the desiring subject.

Catterina Vizzani was born around 1719 in Rome "of ordinary Parentage, her Father being a Carpenter" (3). When she turns fourteen, "the Age of Love in our forward Climate," Catherine, as Cleland calls her, shows no interest in boys "but would be continually romping with her own Sex, and some she caressed with all the Eagerness and Transport of a male Lover" (3). One in particular, named Margaret, she falls in love with, and while she courts her during the days "under Pretence of learning Embroidery . . . scarce a Night passed, but she appeared in Man's Cloaths, under her Charmer's Window" for the sake of "viewing *Margaret*'s captivating Charms, and saying soft Things to her" (3–4). Discovered there one night by Margaret's father, who threatens "that the Governor of the City should learn of her Pranks," Catherine, now sixteen, is scared into running off to Viterbo "in a Man's Disguise," under the name Giovanni Bordoni. So begins the narrative of cross-dressing adventures and restless movement that Susan Lanser has affiliated with the "sapphic picaresque," a constellation of texts including work by Daniel Defoe, Eliza Haywood, Delarivier Manley, Jane Barker, Charlotte Charke, and others from the first half of the eighteenth century. In these texts, Lanser writes, "homo-affectional or homo-erotic behaviour is bound up with some form of adventuring: the women move out of their home spaces into a public space, a borrowed space, or a space of movement such as the road, as if no domestic frame can contain or sustain them."[62] Certainly Catherine's continual wanderings, taking in Rome, Viterbo, Perugia, Arezzo, San Sepolcro, Montepulciano, Anghiari, Librafatta, Florence, Lucca, Poggibonsi, and Siena, suggest an unwillingness ever to settle down, and when she is finally stopped, age twenty-four, she is on the lam with two runaway sisters.

For the most part, Cleland's English version stays close to the Italian original, but his style is both more discursive and more colloquial than Bianchi's. For example, if Bianchi writes "Costei essendo d'età di quattordici anni" (she, being fourteen years of age), Cleland adds, as an aside, "the Age of Love in our forward Climate," which draws attention to her precocity and plays on English notions of the erotic glamour of Italy.[63] Bianchi's Catterina "tenea dietro [alle fanciulle] ardentemente" (followed [the girls] ardently); Cleland's is "continually romping" with them. Bianchi's "amandole non come Fanciulla, ma come uomo stata fosse"(loving them not as a girl, but as if she were a man) becomes Cleland's "and some she caressed with all the Eagerness and Transport of a male Lover," making the physical expression of love explicit. When Catterina visits her beloved at night, Bianchi simply notes that she wishes to be near her ("vicino a lei si stava"), whereas Cleland presents her "viewing *Margaret*'s captivating Charms." But Cleland is also more prone than Bianchi to moralize, if often lightheartedly, as when he translates "amore" as "whimsical Amour," or when Bianchi's claim that the story of Catterina will serve to show "quanto mai strani sieno gli appetiti umani" (just how strange are human desires) is rhetorically pumped up so that the story becomes "a pregnant Example of the shocking Ebullition of human Passions" (2).

On the other hand, in a later scene Cleland both draws out the comic potential that Bianchi passes over and calls into question the idea that Catherine's conduct is against nature. A canon who recommended Giovanni for a post as gentleman's servant is informed that he has proved to be "a young Vagabond, and the most abandoned Whoremaster that ever seduced Woman" (12). Summoning Giovanni/Catherine's father to his house, the canon "con lui fortemente del difetto del figliuolo si lagnò" (complained strongly to him about his son's fault), to which "il Padre allora non molto turbato mostrandosi freddamente rispose, che il suo figliuolo era stato sempre a quell modo donnajuolo" (the father, not appearing to be very bothered, coolly replied that his son had always been a lady's man).[64] In Cleland's much-expanded version of this exchange, the canon begins,

> with the most serious Concern, to lay open to him the Particulars of his Son's scandalous Dissoluteness, **charging it upon the Want of timely Instruction and Chastisement, if not the Influence of a vicious Example.** The Carpenter, **who could hardly keep his Countenance during a Remonstrance delivered with a dictatorial Solemnity,** calmly answered, that, **to his and his dear Wife's inexpressible Grief,** their Son was a **Prodigy of Nature, and that, in his very Childhood, they had observed some astonishing Motions of Lust, which had unhappily gathered Vehemence with the Growth of his Body; that, however, since such was the Case, and the Vigour of his Constitution was not to be repressed by Words or Blows, Nature must e'en take its Course; and, as for the vicious Example you are pleased to insinuate, I hope I am no worse than my Neighbours.** (13–14; phrases in boldface added by JC)

Cleland uses Bianchi's report, which he translates more or less literally, as the jumping-off point for a duel between the two speakers: the canon accuses Vizzani not just of bad parenting but of having set a vicious example, while Vizzani can barely keep a straight face at the canon's misplaced remonstrance or his gullibility in taking Catterina for Giovanni in the first place. But in a way both speakers are objects of Cleland's irony, for while Vizzani enjoys playing off the canon's mistaken belief that Giovanni is a wicked lothario intent on ruining as many girls as he can, his answer—dramatically revealed later in the scene—is that "this same Child of mine, whose Irregularities have made such a Noise, is no Male, but as truly, in all Respects, a Female, as the Woman who bore her" (15). But this revelation, far from wiping away the accusation of sexual immorality, only makes it the more shocking (a Lesbian lothario!), although this seems not to have entered Vizzani's mind.[65]

Or perhaps it has: perhaps he is well aware that Catherine is a tireless seducer of women and, "vicious" as he is, takes pleasure in this. That could be in keeping with his mock expressions of grief at the child being "a Prodigy of Nature"—always an ambiguous phrase, hovering between monster and wonder, the unnatural and the perfection of nature. It is ambiguous, too, whether in referring to Catherine as "he" Vizzani is simply deceiving the canon or is identifying her nature as masculine. Were her/his childhood "Motions of Lust" astonishing tout court or only astonishing because of his/her real sex? Whatever he thinks Catherine "is," and whatever he feels about it, he links the vehemence or unruliness of his/her desires to the "Growth of his Body" and "Vigour of his

Constitution," suggesting that they are physiologically innate and that "Nature must e'en take its Course." Is Catherine's "Man's Disguise," then, a part of her nature? If so, it is not a disguise at all, but an expression of her inmost self. With its dramatic ironies and ambiguities, the scene Cleland elaborates from Bianchi's original is both more comic and more provocative in its foregrounding of questions of gender and sex, eros and the body. Even such phrases as "as truly . . . a Female as the Woman who bore her" or "I hope I am no worse than my Neighbours" raise unsettling questions: how female *is* the woman who bore her, then? And what other "prodigies" await discovery in his neighbors' houses? Through his expansion of such passages in Bianchi, Cleland raises questions about the origins of Catherine's desire and accentuates the erotic potential of the situations Bianchi renders in more neutral terms.[66]

After leaving home, Catherine-as-Giovanni becomes servant to a series of gentlemen, and while none can fault her for her work—"for, besides Reading, making of Chocolate, and Cookery, she was very dextrous at Pen, Comb, and Razor"—all reprove her "for incessantly following the Wenches, and being so barefaced and insatiable in her Amours" (8). She not only courts them as before, but "She had Recourse to several delusive Impudicities, not only to establish the Certainty, but raise the Reputation of her Manhood." And it is here, just when he has aroused our curiosity, that Cleland cuts, for the first and only time, something significant from Bianchi's text: symbolically enough, the description of a phallus. Here is the passage in Italian:

> Anzi per parere uomo da vero un bel Piuolo di Cuojo ripieno di Cenci s'era fatto, che sotto la camiscia teneva, e talora, ma sempre coperto a suoi Compagni per baldanza di soppiatto mostrava, per cui in Anghiari in poca d'ora corse fama che Giovanni nel fatto delle femmine più d'ogni altro valesse, la qual fama egli a caro grandemente avea che si spargesse.[67]

In my translation:

> Indeed, in order to seem like a real man, she had made herself a nice leather dildo stuffed with rags, which she wore under her shirt, and sometimes she dared to show it stealthily to her companions, though always half concealed, so that in a short time the rumor spread throughout Anghiari that when it came to pleasing women Giovanni had it over every other man, a rumor it was his dearest wish to have spread around.

Instead of translating this, Cleland launches into a rant, which has been the object of some critical attention, mostly negative.[68] "The Doctor," he writes indignantly of Bianchi, "enters into a nauseous Detail of her Impostures, which is the more inexcusable, they not being essential to the main Scope of the Narrative. These, if agreeable to the *Italian Goût*, would shock the Delicacy of our Nation" (8–9). Coming from an author who, the same month *The Case of Catherine Vizzani* was published, deplored the "vitiated palate" and "depraved . . . taste" of the English reading public in the pages of the *Monthly Review*, this appeal to "the Delicacy of our Nation" might ring some irony-alarm bells, and this editorial comment indeed proves disingenuous when checked against what Cleland has let into his own text, for he has left nothing material out.[69] It is true that he cuts this scene of Giovanni letting his friends have a look at his apparently impressive phallus, but since he describes the dildo in some detail later—"a leathern Contrivance, of a cylindrical Figure, which was fastened below the Abdomen, and had been the chief Instrument of her detestable Imposture" (34)—he cannot be said to have removed it from the text, only to have deferred its explicit portrayal. Cleland's cut here is not an expression of moral outrage but a ploy to fire the reader's imagination. He doesn't simply excise the passage, he thunders against it as nauseous, inexcusable, and shocking for a full page: who could resist the temptation to fill in such a blank? Feigning to spare us from details too obscene to translate, but translating them just the same, Cleland plays the part of zealous moralist even as he incites us to wonder about the "nauseous Details" he for the moment denies us. The effect is to produce a more dramatic scene of revelation when Giovanni is finally exposed and so actually to stress the importance of the "leathern Machine" (37) in the overall narrative economy, as the crucial marker of Catherine's masculine identity and desires.

After this deviation from Bianchi's text, Cleland falls back into line, recounting some of the other stratagems Catherine adopts: calling on surgeons "to buy Medicaments for the Removal of Disorders, which she pretended to have caught from infectious Women" (10), and deflecting her laundress's suspicions about the stains that appear on her shirt "at certain Times" of each month by saying these also result from venereal disease. Cleland goes Bianchi one better by having Catherine drop a hint to the laundress that the reason the girls won't let him alone is that they have heard "that Nature had been very liberal to him"—and one hint is enough to ensure "that within a short Time, it was whispered about that *Giovanni* was the best Woman's Man, and the most addicted to that alluring Sex of all the Men in that Part of the Country" (11). Such whisperings lead to a series of amorous adventures, culminating in Giovanni's elopement with "a very lovely young Gentlewoman, Niece to the Minister" of Librafatta. He, "knowing the Temptation of Beauty, and the Lubricity of Youth, kept a strict Guard over his Niece" (21). Weary of his vigilance, she plots to escape with Giovanni but cannot resist telling her sister. "This mettlesome Girl commended the Project to the Skies," Cleland writes, "but added, that she also, having long been tired of living with such an old Cuff, would take this charming Opportunity of freeing herself from him" (23). She threatens, in fact, to tell their uncle if she is not allowed to go with them—"and then, where is your Journey to *Rome?*" (24). Giovanni, when he learns he is to elope with two sisters, is delighted, and says, "It were Pity a Girl of so much Mercury should stay behind" (25), so they set out. Pursued by the uncle's chaplain and servants, the trio are soon run to earth, and the chaplain, to whom Cleland ascribes motives of jealousy (of Giovanni's erotic appeal) and greed (for monetary reward), orders the servants to fire on him:

> The Servants, pursuant to their Leader's Command, presented their Pieces at *Giovanni,* **who having a masculine Spirit, as well as masculine Desires**, not at all daunted at such a threatening Sight, drew a Pistol which hung at her Belt, and presented it **towards the Chaplain.** This unexpected Resolution put them to a Stand, and both Sides continued **watching each other's Motions, whilst the poor Girls were shrieking, and wringing their Hands.** (28; phrases in boldface added by JC)

The details Cleland adds to the scene heighten its tension—and its comedy. While in the original Giovanni aims his pistol at the servants, here he turns it on the chaplain, producing a more dangerously unpredictable crisscross standoff; accordingly, everyone freezes, watching and waiting for the least flicker of motion from the others. But in the background he adds the sisters' handwringing and shrieking, which can be read as comic or pathetic but in either case ratchets up the noise level and so the volatility of the scene. In the midst of it Cleland locates the undaunted Giovanni, characterized by "a masculine Spirit, as well as masculine Desires," thus returning to the questions of gender and nature, and of the origins of desire, that run through the text in its English reworking.

The spell of the armed standoff is broken when Giovanni, "considering that her Sex would secure her from any very bad Consequence of this Affair, and that one Girl's running away with two others might . . . be slightly passed over as a Frolick, rather than severely animadverted upon as a Crime" (29), decides to turn herself in, and lowers her pistol. Instead of defusing the threat of violence, however, her action only shifts its focus, for the chaplain, now safe from danger, compels one of the servants not to arrest Giovanni but to shoot him. Wishing to do as little hurt as possible, the servant aims at Giovanni's thigh and fires, but the gunshot unleashes havoc, not only wounding Catherine but killing a nearby hunting dog "and fracturing a Leg of a Boy of about twelve Years of Age, who happening to come by, had stopt, as it was very natural, to see what was the Matter" (30). Catherine and the boy are taken to a hospital in Siena, where, by chance, Bianchi's manservant happens to see her and "recognizes" her as Giovanni, whom he had met when they were both lodged in the same inn in Florence "for above forty Days, and Bed-fellows the greatest Part of that Time" (33). This servant tells Bianchi that Giovanni "desired, above all things, that I would be so good as to come and see him," which Bianchi promises to do, but as he admits, it slips his mind. Catherine develops a fever and an infection in her lungs and, anticipating the possibility of death, tells her secret to a kind nun: "that she was not only a Female but a Virgin, conjuring her . . . to let no Person whatever know it till her Death, and then to declare it publickly, that she might be buried in a Woman's Habit, and with the Garland on her Head, an honorary Ceremony observed among us in the Burial of Virgins" (35). It is a curious and poignant request, on which neither Bianchi nor Cleland offers any comment: that Catherine, who in life aimed at public fame as a cocksman, wishes in death to be publicly displayed as a virginal maid, her two gendered selves kept apart by the boundary between death and life.

It is only now, with his protagonist on the brink of dying, that Cleland reveals her "leathern Contrivance" to the reader, as it "became so troublesome, that she loosened it, and laid it under her Pillow" (35). The "nauseous Detail" of Catherine's "Impostures," which Cleland has withheld, acquires the status of a transcendental signifier, the phallus by which Giovanni's masculine identity was secured. But as is the fate of all such signifiers, it proves to be hollow. After Catherine's death, "the leathern Machine, which was hid under the Pillow, fell into the Hands of the Surgeon's Mates in the Hospital, who immediately were for ripping it up, concluding that it contained Money, or something else of Value, but they found it stuffed only with old Rags" (37). It is almost too perfect a symbol: the sign by which Catherine established her sexual, and thus social, status as a male, with all the prerogatives attending that status (freedom of movement and the like), is a simulacrum that exposes the illusory basis of all phallic authority.[70] But illusory as it may have been, Giovanni's phallic glamour and prowess bought Catherine eight years of sapphic-picaresque freedom, to adapt Lanser's term—or at least relative freedom, for Giovanni, of course, is always a servant and a dependent.[71] The phallus acts as a kind of passport; indeed it is not clear in either Bianchi's or Cleland's text whether Catherine/Giovanni puts it to sexual use or merely shows it off to sustain her vagabond-whoremaster persona.[72]

In any case, its discovery after her death by the hospital attendants, coinciding with that of "her prominent Breasts" when they begin to remove her body, leads to a closer scrutiny, and one of the surgeon's mates comes to Bianchi to tell him, "with a Blush" (38), that Giovanni has, "upon the Denudation of her Body, proved to be a Woman, with a fine sound Hymen, and other Tokens of an untouched Virginity." "Incited [by] Curiosity," Bianchi finally goes to the hospital to see her, and in due course conducts a postmortem. He verifies that "the Entireness of the Hymen incontestably proved her being actually a Virgin" (39), but this occasions a delay in the proceedings, for the news of her virginity leads the local religious leaders and townspeople to wish to proclaim Catherine "nothing less than a Saint, having preserved her Chastity inviolate, amidst the strongest Temptations" (40): the many times she shared her bed with male servants. But for Bianchi, the physiological fact of her intact hymen, while medically significant—he was engaged in a dispute with other Sienese doctors as to the existence of the hymen and had amassed a collection of them, to which in turn he would add Catterina Vizzani's—was morally insignificant.[73] He argues, rather, in Cleland's translation, "that her making Love, and with uncommon Protervity, to Women, wherever she came, and her seducing at last two young Women to run away from their Uncle, were flagrant Instances of a libidinous Disposition; Proceedings incompatible with any virtuous Principle, or so much as Decency"(41). There is no correspondence between literal virginity and feminine virtue.

After "the People's Ferment" (42), provoked by rumors of Catherine's sanctity, has calmed down, Bianchi returns to the hospital "and caused an Incision to be made in the Body, and the Parts of Generation to be dissevered with the nicest Exactness, which were carried to my House to be thoroughly examined by a regular Dissection." Having verified that her hymen is intact, Bianchi turns to the clitoris, as if to put to the test the early modern consensus that excessive female sexual desire, and especially desire for other women, is connected to bodily, specifically clitoral, excess—a consensus whose emblem was the monstrous and unruly figure of the tribade.[74] What Bianchi finds undermines the received medical wisdom: "The *Clitoris* of this young Woman was not pendulous, nor of any extraordinary Size, as the Account from *Rome* made it, and as is said, to be that of all those Females, who, among the *Greeks*, were called *Trib-*

ades, or who followed the Practices of *Sappho*; on the contrary, her's was so far from any unusual Magnitude, that it was not to be ranked among the middle-sized, but the smaller" (43–44). Again, there is no correspondence between the truth of the body and the identity of the desiring subject: bodily excess is not the origin of excessive or unruly desire.

And that is where Bianchi leaves the question of sexual or gender identity: it cannot be located in or mapped onto the body. The *Breve storia* continues for another half dozen pages, all scrupulously translated by Cleland, in which Bianchi examines Catherine's internal organs and takes issue with other scholars of anatomy. He assigns a cause of death—an infection of the lungs produced by gangrene—and ends with a brief account of the boy whose leg was shattered by the shot that killed Catherine. He too dies, and Bianchi concludes with a call for Italian surgeons to trust their manual skills rather than potions or drugs, suggesting that the boy's life might have been saved by "a timely and proper Amputation" (50). Nothing, it seems, could have saved Catherine's.

Having brought his translation to a close, Cleland now appends fifteen pages of "Remarks upon the Foregoing Dissertation" to the fifty pages of Bianchi's narrative. He begins by backhandedly defending Bianchi against charges of "bad Habits or vitiated Inclinations" (52) for writing on such a subject: it is, rather, Italy that is to blame. As before, when he contrasted the *Italian Goût* to "the Delicacy of our Nation" (8), Cleland offers a defensive model of national/cultural difference to account for the supposed immorality of Italian literature: "The Wits, and even the learned Men of *Italy*, have been long distinguished for their Inclination to Discourses of this Nature, which are frequently interpreted in such a Manner as to do no great Honour . . . to their Morals" (51). But this may be unjust, he suggests, "since, in a warm Country like theirs, where Impurities of all Sorts are but too frequent, it may very well happen that such strange Accidents may . . . arise as highly to excite both their Wonder and their Attention" (51–52). A text such as Bianchi's original case history, then, simply reflects the "Impurities" endemic to such a "warm" country as Italy and indeed demonstrates the author's "Skill in Anatomy" and "Acquaintance with human Nature" (52). Cleland's defense of Bianchi is genuine, but is also, of course, a preemptive justification for translating him into English. Yet the clichéd contrast between Italian "impurity" and English "delicacy" is at odds with Cleland's contemporaneous attacks on the vitiated and depraved tastes of his countrymen and, of course, with his own professional investment in bringing Italian, as well as French, works to the British reading public. If Italy is a place of impurity, should we not set up a system of quarantine to prevent infection from its cultural products? Such was the logic of the antisodomite texts quoted in chapter 3, whose authors advocated prohibiting such practices as that of "Mens *Kissing* each other," a "*Fashion* brought over from *Italy* (the *Mother* and *Nurse* of *Sodomy*."[75] By invoking the nationalist moralism of such texts, Cleland both hides behind its protective cover—a reaction to his practical experience of the dangers of flouting censorial authority—and undermines it from within, twitting the smug parochialism of English audiences and authors.

But if "the Case of this young Woman," Cleland writes, "is certainly very extraordinary, and may therefore justify . . . the Pains which this learned and industrious Man has taken about her" (52), he irritably notes that "it does not appear that he has assigned any Cause whatever, or so much as advanced any probable Conjecture on this extravagant Turn of her lewdness, notwithstanding it surprized him so much" (52–53). It is to make up for this deficiency that Cleland adds his concluding "Remarks" on Bianchi's text. The "irregular and violent Inclination" by which Vizzani "render'd herself infamous," he states, "must either proceed from some Error in Nature"—that is, some bodily malformation—or "some Disorder or Perversion in the Imagination" (53). Bianchi's detailed account of the dissection of Catherine's body has ruled out the first, so we ought "to acquit Nature of any Fault in this strange Creature, and to look for the Source of so odious and so unnatural a Vice, only in her Mind" (54). The logic of this is clear enough, but the distinction he posits between nature on the one hand and mind on the other is starker and more straightforward than emerges from what follows, or than Cleland implies in his comments in the text itself, as when he declares that Vizzani's story shows "that the Wantonness of Fancy, and the Depravity of Nature, are at as great a Height as ever" (2). Here, wanton fancy and depraved nature go together; no either/or is necessary or even possible. And so it proves from Cleland's speculative reconstruction of the origins of Catherine's perverse desires.

Echoing the canon's charge against Peter Vizzani that his son's dissoluteness was owing to "the Influence of a vicious Example" (13), Cleland writes that as "there was nothing amiss" (52) with Catherine's body, "it seems therefore most likely that this unfortunate and scandalous Creature had her Imagination corrupted early in her Youth, either by obscene Tales that were voluntarily told in her Hearing, or by privately listening to the Discourses of the Women, who are too generally corrupt in that Country" (54). Her "extravagant" desires were implanted or elicited not by seduction but by "obscene tales," by women's gossip—that is, by literature. "Her Head being thus filled with vicious Inclinations, perhaps before she received any Incitements from her Constitution,"

Cleland speculates, "might prompt her to those vile Practices" (55). Sexual desires, and the gender identity Catherine constructs in order to satisfy them, are products of cultural contagion, stories overheard, and are as unfixed by nature as a body that can "be" male or female at will. Cleland goes on to suggest that once perverse desire takes hold in the imagination, "this might occasion a preternatural Change in the animal Spirits, and a Kind of venereal Fury, very remote, and even repugnant to that of her Sex" (55)—unsexing the physical frame. He seems to be thinking along similar lines to those of the materialist Doctor Bordeu in Diderot's 1769 *Le Rêve de d'Alembert* (*D'Alembert's Dream*), who observes that "les organes produisent les besoins, et réciproquement les besoins produisent les organes" (our organs produce desires, and, conversely, our desires [or needs] produce organs).[76] Catherine prosthetically supplies the organ her needs or desires dictate, and this altered body is what her female lovers see, feel, and experience—or at any rate imagine—as well. After her death, that unsexed body is dismembered by the surgeon's mates, who tear apart the "leathern Machine," and by Bianchi, who "dissevers" her "Parts of Generation" from the rest of her body "with the nicest Exactness," and it appears that her "extravagant" actions left no imprint on the body. "Venereal Fury" is a fever of the imagination, not an organic disorder, but this does not make it any less real in its effects.[77]

As Cleland presents it, the Vizzani case is ultimately about the circulation of perverse desire as fantasy, as communal narrative, as moral contagion—not about deficient, excessive, or otherwise remarkable bodies. It is only when we become aware of what others want, by way of stories inciting desire, that we begin to conceive what we want ourselves. Certainly the reader's imagination is full, by the end of the text, of "flagrant Instances of a libidinous Disposition" (41), so that like the young Catherine—"her Head ... thus filled with vicious Inclinations"—we come away from reading with "Incitements" that "might prompt [us] to those vile Practices" (55). Those "Incitements" have been lodged in our English-reading heads by Cleland's writing. Yet he maintains that the Vizzani case

affords (if that were at all necessary) a new Argument for suppressing those scandalous and flagitious Books, that are not only privately but publickly handed about for the worst Purposes, as well as Prints and Pictures calculated to inflame the Passions, to banish all Sense of Shame, and to make the World, if possible, more corrupt and profligate than it is already. We are very certain that all Things of this Sort must have a very bad Tendency. (63–64)

But as Emma Donoghue asks, sensibly enough, "Is *Catherine Vizzani* not one of these 'scandalous books'?"[78] It is, and of course Cleland knows that it is. A writer as rhetorically supple and insidious as he shows himself to be in the *Woman of Pleasure* could hardly be unaware of how this book would be read. In fact, in the same issue of the *Monthly Review* to which Cleland contributed his review of *Peregrine Pickle, The Case of Catherine Vizzani* was duly noted (by Cleland? or by Griffiths?), but the work itself deemed unworthy of review: "We beg leave to decline any further mention of this article, for a reason that our readers will easily guess at; and we are sure that the female part of them will as easily pardon the omission."[79] Such a silence cannot help but provoke any potential reader's curiosity, and Cleland (or whoever wrote this notice) seems slyly to suggest that female readers in particular might find the book inflaming. Far be any such intention from the author's mind, of course. Indeed "the only Reason that can justify the making Things of this Sort public," Cleland writes, "is to facilitate their Discovery, and thereby prevent their ill Consequences, which indeed can scarce be prevented any other Way" (62). As was also true of the sodomitical scene in the *Woman of Pleasure*, the "making Things of this Sort public" is both an incitement and a warning, or more precisely a warning against the very incitement it provides. It is not only among Italian women but everywhere in this "corrupt and profligate" world that disorders and perversions of the imagination are liable to take root. And not only perverse desire, but desire itself, is secondhand, provoked as an involuntary effect of reading, listening, watching. A susceptibility to deviance is implicit in the capacity to desire at all.

Forced and Unnatural Transplantation

Cleland's "Remarks" on the Vizzani case end with a grouchy diatribe against what he alleges to be a common practice in his time, "that of Women appearing in public Places in Mens Cloaths; a Thing that manifests an extreme Assurance, and which may have many ill Consequences" (65)—none of which he specifies. Given the ironies and ambiguities of the whole work, it is unclear if cross-dressing is one of Cleland's bêtes noires or if he is mocking the moralism of antimasquerade and other reformers of manners, but in either case, he concludes by describing the practice as one of "those Alterations in our Policy and Manners, which have arisen from our Politeness, and our Desire to copy Foreigners in every Thing" (66). Cultural imitation was weighing on Cleland's mind, as in the complaint quoted before about the "flood of novels, tales, romances, and other monsters of the imagination, which have been ei-

ther wretchedly translated, or even more unhappily imitated, from the *French*,"
and he may have meant to incriminate himself for his part in unleashing this
flood.[80] For translations were a substantial part of his literary output in the
1750s. From the Italian came *Catherine Vizzani* and *Titus Vespasian: A Tragedy*
(1755), based on Metastasio's melodrama *La Clemenza di Tito* (later adapted as
the libretto for Mozart's opera); from the French, Pinot-Duclos's *Memoirs*, the
1753 *Dictionary of Love*, and *Tombo-Chiqui; or, The American Savage* (1758). The
last, a three-act comedy, may have been written with David Garrick in mind,
as *Titus Vespasian* was, but neither was ever produced, and they might be considered more or less complete failures—though he seems to wish to save face
in his "Advertisement" to *Tombo-Chiqui*, writing that readers "may be assured
it is not published under the disgrace of rejection from our theatres, since it
was never offered to them."[81] The *Dictionary*, by contrast, was probably, after
the *Woman of Pleasure*, Cleland's most commercially successful text, reprinted
and adapted numerous times over the following several decades by booksellers not only in London but Edinburgh and Philadelphia as well.[82] It seems to
have crossed over the gulf of what Cleland calls "the difference of language
and idiom" more successfully than *Tombo-Chiqui*, whose French original had
been "received in France with the highest applause," but whose English version sank without a trace.[83] The reason for their contrasting fortunes has less
to do with any difference in quality of the translations, both of which are spirited and clear, than with the different approaches Cleland took to the problem
not of linguistic but of cultural difference: how to cross that other gulf of "the
Difference of Manners betwixt his own Nation and that of the *French*; a Difference which must naturally render some Passages less interesting, less susceptible of Application than a thorough Conformity would have admitted."[84] The
reason for *Tombo-Chiqui*'s failure to repeat *Arlequin sauvage*'s success may be
Cleland's fidelity to the original, whose mixture of commedia dell'arte foolery
and proto-enlightenment philosophizing was alien to the tastes of English audiences and actors.[85] With the *Dictionary*, on the other hand, Cleland was freer in
his approach, cutting extensively, rewriting dialogues, adding significant new
entries of his own, thus recognizing, in tackling a work whose subject is the
unreliability of language and the difficulties of interpretation, that "too servile
and stiff an Attachment to the Letter of the Original" risked betraying its "just
Sense" and "utility" to an English readership, and so making it less marketable
a commodity.

The premise of the *Dictionary of Love* is that love itself is a language, whose
terms require translation into a more transparent idiom. On one level, as Cle-

land writes in his preface, this means that love, "having lost its plain unsophisticate nature, and being now reduced into an art, has, like other arts, had recourse to particular words and expressions" (v); like "physic" or heraldry, love has its own "hard technical nomenclature . . . of which it no more behooves lovers to be ignorant, than for seamen to be unacquainted with the terms of navigation" (iv–v). Nature is no longer a valid guide and indeed has been transmuted into a mere simulacrum of itself: "All the tribute that is now paid to Nature," Cleland writes, "is only a preservation of the appearances of it, to hinder Art from defeating its Ends by being too transparent" (vi). But as this last point suggests, the problem Cleland confronts in creating a dictionary of love is not primarily lexical—not a matter of defining unfamiliar terms, as it might be in heraldry or medicine—but forensic: the challenge of unmasking the essentially criminal aims underlying the cant of professed lovers, whom he equates with counterfeiters. The counterfeit language of love is not only false but malicious, meant to entrap. The dictionary's target audience—"young people, and especially of the fair sex, whose mistakes are the most dangerous" (x–xi)—will be "taught to distinguish the Birmingham-trash, so often palmed upon them, for the true lawful coin of the kingdom of Love, in which nothing is commoner than false coiners" (xi).[86] At least this last sentence holds open the possibility that there *is* a "true lawful coin" of love, a transparent language whose words correspond to things, and in which there is no difference between real and "apparent signification" (ix). But if that true coin exists somewhere, there is no sign of it in the *Dictionary*, whose entries are concerned rather to expose truths that the language of everyday social life obscures. Here, for example, is the entry for *slave*—not translated from the French, but original:

> SLAVE. *I am your slave; you use your slave too cruelly*; signifies, "The more power I can make you believe you have over me, the more I shall gain over you."[87]

Many of the entries have a similar structure: the word is followed by a definition, or an example of common or hackneyed usage, and then a translation laying bare the real meaning of the clichéd phrase, usually the inverse of its apparent sense.

In other entries, the translation or unmasking is more fully elaborated, creating a miniature narrative of amorous intrigue or deceit. In "To Love," for example, based on the original's "Aimer," Cleland offers three tiny stories to illustrate the broad claim that "most of the present Love is what our blunt ancestors called by another very coarse name [most likely 'whoredom'], or what is infinitely coarser yet, though unblushingly pronounced, Sordid Interest." The third of these stories, radically revamped from the French, runs as follows:

> When young Sharply says to old liquorish Lady Wishfort, *I love you*, the true English
> of this is, "I am a younger born [i.e., the younger of two sons], unfortunately born
> under a star that gave me the soul of a prince, and the fortune of a beggar. No man
> had ever a stronger passion for pleasures and expence than I have: but I am ruined
> at play; I am over head and ears in debt. As you have then a fortune that may stop
> all my leaks, and set me on float, let us supply one another's wants." And 'tis ten
> to one but he carries his point with the fond dotard, who never considers that she
> is making a bubble's bargain, for one of those few things which money can never
> purchase.

Turning love into "true English," Cleland gives us the germ of a narrative of sexual and economic predation, one of those "terrible *quid-pro-quos*" of which "modern gallantry" (x) consists: Lady Wishfort's wealth for young Sharply's sexual favors. Even though their relationship at this stage is mutually exploitative, in the longer term it is she, not he, who is making "a bubble's bargain," as once he has (by marriage) his hands on her money, he will have no more need to "supply [her] wants" or repeat the delusive phrase "I love you." Cleland adapts one of his favorite metaphors, of life as a ship's voyage, and "new-casts" it, so that the gambling debts of the profligate younger son of a rich father are rendered as "leaks" in the ship of self, which Lady Wishfort's (liquid) wealth, like pitch, will "stop." He adapts the same metaphor in his entry on *rakes*—not translated from French—writing that a "reformed Rake . . . is a being worn out, and unfit to proceed on so great a voyage as that of matrimony" and continuing, "a woman who ventures upon him is like one who would choose to put to sea in a shattered, leaky, worm-eaten vessel, that is sure to founder before half the voyage is over." The metaphor, again, is anything but original, but the adjectives "shattered, leaky, worm-eaten" evoke the ravages of venereal disease, another instance of new-casting old materials and so confounding the distinction between originality and imitation.

Cleland soft-pedals his debt to the *Dictionnaire* in his own *Dictionary*'s preface, writing that "the following work then owes its existence to an idea taken from one of their [French] authors" but not pointing out that much of it is merely translated. Yet some of the most interesting entries in his text are not taken from Dreux du Radier, among them a group of entries addressing errant or failed forms of masculinity: *beau, coxcomb, fop, fribble,* and *rake*.[88] Of these, the most striking for its resonances with Cleland's other work is the entry on *fribble*, an unfamiliar term today. Here, too, Cleland is working with "materials not [his] own," for his entry is prompted by one of David Garrick's comic roles, the simpering, effeminate fop Mr. Fribble, from his 1747 comedy *Miss in Her Teens*. According to the play's heroine, Biddy, "he speaks like a Lady for all the World, and never swears . . . but wears nice white Gloves, and tells me what Ribbons become my Complexion."[89] In the *Dictionary*, the fribble is a species, not only an individual, and while Cleland's fribbles share Garrick's Fribble's "unmanly" interest in fashion and sewing, they act out much more explicitly the potential sodomitical implications of such effeminacy. When Mrs. Cole, in *Memoirs of a Woman of Pleasure*, "explained" sodomy to Fanny, she portrayed the sodomites as

> stript of all the manly virtues of their own sex, and fill'd up with only the very worst vices and follies of ours . . . they were scarce less execrable than ridiculous in their monstrous inconsistency, of loathing and contemning women, and all at the same time, apeing their manners, airs, lisp, skuttle, and, in general, all their little modes of affectation, which become them at least better, than they do these unsex'd male misses. (159–160)

The definition of *fribble* in the *Dictionary* repeats much of Mrs. Cole's harangue:

> FRIBBLE. This word signifies one of those ambiguous animals, who are neither male nor female; disclaimed by his own sex, and the scorn of both . . . Without any of the good qualities of their own sex, they affect all the bad ones, all the impertinencies and follies of the other; whilst what is no more than ridiculous, and sometimes even a grace in the women, is nauseous and shocking in them . . . One would think, in short, that these equivocall animals imitated the women, out of complaisance to them, that they might have the higher opinion of their own sex, from seeing that there were men who endeavoured to come as near it as possible. But so far are they from succeeding, that they disfigure the graces, caricature the faults, and have none of the virtues of that amiable sex.

In another passage from this entry, Cleland imports the "plague-spots" that in Mrs. Cole's account are "visibly imprinted on all that are tainted" with the "infamous passion" (159). But in the *Dictionary* these are not only not bodily marks, they are signs of the absence of any such marks: "the muff, the ermin-facing, a cluster-ring, the stone-buckle, and now and then a patch, that on them does not always suppose a pimple, are the plague-spots, in which the folly of these less than butterflies breaks out." The plague spot is just a bauble that can be put on or taken off on a whim; no more than in *Catherine Vizzani* is the body a map or legible index of desire. Cleland thus discredits the very antisodomite posture he assumes, and insinuates that gender identity—here that of the fribble, but potentially any such identity—is not "imprinted" by nature, but is an effect of imitative performance. The fribbles' imitation of women is like Garrick's imitation of them: a caricature, a comic turn. Borrowing Garrick's "ridiculous" character and plagiarizing his own Mrs. Cole's antisodomite diatribe, Cleland reworks their material to construct a campier and more "ambiguous animal," whose visible traits are only very "equivocall" signs of his or her nature. *Fribble* can thus figurally stand for all the terms in the *Dictionary of Love*, whose "apparent signification" never corresponds to their "just value" (viii).

Tombo-Chiqui, too, is concerned with the gap between apparent and real meanings, words and things.[90] Cleland shifts the action of Delisle's *Arlequin sauvage* from Marseille to London and renames the characters so as to move them away from their commedia dell'arte sources: Scapin (It. *Scapino*), the hero's servant, becomes Tom; the rich merchant Pantalon (It. *Pantalone*), father of the hero's inamorata, becomes Golding; and, most notably, Arlequin (It. *Arlecchino*), the cunning fool, becomes Tombo-chiqui. Cleland may, as Thomas Altherr has suggested, have drawn this last name from the historical Tomochichi, a Creek headman whose friendship with the British general James Oglethorpe led him to visit England, meeting George II among others, in 1734, or he may just have chosen it for its play on "cheeky."[91] Cleland notes in the prefatory "Advertisement" that *Arlequin sauvage* had been adapted into English before, by "a very ingenious gentleman of our nation, in a play called *Art and Nature*," but this 1738 play by James Miller was not so well received as Delisle's play in France because Miller had combined it "with a very indifferent piece of [Jean-Baptiste] Rousseau's, entitled *Le Flateur*."[92] By contrast, Cleland sticks closely to Delisle's text, and despite the weight he gives the Native American origins of the play's central character by subtitling it *The American Savage*, he does not expand on the original's generic Arcadia, as in Tombo-chiqui's reply to the question, "of what country are you":

> *Tombo-chiqui.* Me? I came out of a vast great wood, where there grow none but such ignorant creatures as myself, who do not know a tittle of the laws, and yet are naturally honest. Hah, hah, hah, we want no lessons, not we, to know our duty. We are so innocent, that our reason alone is sufficient for us. (14)

"America" functions as a place-name given to the philosophical abstraction "nature," in a kind of thought experiment going back at least as far as Montaigne's essay "Of Cannibals" from about 1570: what happens if, instead of judging the "savage" or "natural" from the perspective of the "civilized," we reverse the positions of observer and observed? As Tombo-chiqui's patron or friend Clerimont puts it in the play's opening scene:

> 'twas to procure myself the pleasure of this surprize of his, that I took care he should not be instructed in our manners: the quickness of his perception, and the native shreudness of his answers, gave me the first idea of bringing him to Europe in all his ignorance. I had a notion it would divert me to observe pure simple nature working in him, in comparison with the laws, arts, and sciences amongst us. The contrast will doubtless be singular. (6)

Of course, the positions of observer and observed are not really reversed here—Tombo-chiqui's naïve or natural reactions to what he sees are themselves the object of Clerimont's amused, if also admiring, observation. But at one moment of crisis, when Clerimont and his friend Mirabel are on the verge of a duel, Tombo-chiqui's quick perception and natural reason do prevail over the rivals' rash violence, and it is he who engineers the play's happy resolution, so earning the right to pronounce its moral lesson:

> **Hence-forward let Nature and Reason be your Pilot-stars: they are surer lights than all your laws put together**. The most these [laws] can do for you, is to supply imperfectly your want of natural Reason, with an artificial or a forced one. In short, you are Men in nothing, but so far as you resemble us, **whom you call savages**. (55; phrases in boldface added by JC)

This speech is one of the very few Cleland has enlarged, the additions making Tombo-chiqui more clearly the author's mouthpiece (as a sign of which he sneaks in the metaphor of life as a voyage, with nature and reason the sailor-self's "Pilot-stars"). The final phrase also underlines one of the work's key themes: uses and misuses of language, or the problem of what to call things.

This theme is articulated around a number of antitheses: ignorance and sense, law (or art) and nature, reason and folly, riches and poverty, slavery and freedom, sanity and madness, civilized and savage. In the single day the action occupies, Tombo-chiqui has a number of chance encounters: first, with a group comprising a young woman (Sylvia), her father (Golding), and her maid (Violetta), with the last of whom Tombo-chiqui falls immediately in love; second, with a "Jew Pedlar," whose intentions Tombo-chiqui misconstrues, not having any notion of buying and selling or of money; third, with a "Stranger" in distress who mistakes him for a highwayman. These scenes alternate with others in which Clerimont "explains" civilized institutions and customs to his friend—among them laws, compliments, private property, and money—these lessons invariably ending with Tombo-chiqui more convinced than before of the folly of the civilized. As with his lessons, so with his observations of the Londoners he meets: all lead Tombo-chiqui to reverse the terms of the play's organizing antitheses, expressed by way of a paradox. For example, told there is a place called Bedlam, "where they put mad people, and those who are out of their senses," he replies, "I will be sworn that I have not been out of Bedlam since I landed" (49–50). When Clerimont tells him that "the poor work only to get the necessaries of life, but the rich labor to obtain superfluities, which with them have no bounds," Tombo-chiqui replies, "But if this be so, the rich are poorer than the poor, since their wants are more numerous." In sum, as he tells Clerimont, "I think you are fools, who believe yourselves wise; ignorant, who believe yourselves knowing, poor, who believe yourselves rich, and slaves, who believe yourselves free" (31). It may be that such paradoxes have come to seem trite; perhaps they seemed so even in 1758. But cumulatively, they unsettle the taken-for-granted meanings of ideologically encrusted keywords and expose civilized language itself as complicit with the corruptions of the social order.

At Tombo-chiqui's lowest point, when he has been arrested and threatened with hanging following his run-in with the Jewish peddler, Clerimont tells him that money "is more worth than all the words in the world," to which he replies, "Your words then are not worth much; and I do not wonder now you have told me so many lies" (29). In contrast to Clerimont, whom he insults in this scene as "a man of words, and nothing more," Tombo-chiqui offers his own "outlandishness" or estrangement from civilized customs as a mark of integrity: "I am a man of sense, though a very ignorant one: I pass here for an ass, a brute, a savage, that does not know the laws; in other respects, I am a very honest man; a man of merit" (13–14). Golding, hearing this, laughs at the evident contradictions: "A man of sense, though ignorant, an ass, a brute, and yet a man of merit. Hah, hah, hah!" (14). But the contradictions are only apparent, and when using such a duplicitous language, the only way to truth is by paradox and metaphor, for they don't pretend to transparency. While conventional uses of language aim to mask the truth behind "apparent significations," mystifications of the real, as Cleland suggests in both *Tombo-Chiqui* and the *Dictionary of Love*, paradox and metaphor draw attention to their own eccentricity or artifice and thus, perhaps, allow a reader to work out the truth that everyday language lulls us into taking for granted. In a similar way, translation, the "forced and unnatural transplantation" of foreign idioms and outlandish manners into "true English," might decenter familiar language and customs just enough to give the translator/ author a critical purchase on the everyday, on home, London, the English, and the words everyone uses without thinking. Of course, this is all only hackwork: as Young put it, "a sort of *Manufacture* wrought up by those *Mechanics, Art,* and *Labour,* out of pre-existent materials not their own." But as Bertolt Brecht, who had good reason to know, wrote a couple of centuries later, "Anyone can be creative, it's re-writing other people that's a challenge."[93] Brecht's paradox can serve as the epigraph to Cleland's career: all writing is rewriting.

CHAPTER SIX

The Man of Feeling
(1752–1768)

O f all the works he produced in the 1750s, the one whose failure stung Cleland the most was his translation of Pietro Metastasio's libretto for *La Clemenza di Tito* (1734). First set to music by Antonio Caldara, this heroic *melodramma*, best known today in Mozart's version of 1791, was transformed by Cleland into the blank verse tragedy *Titus Vespasian*, whose rejection by the actor and theatrical impresario David Garrick came as both an aesthetic and a financial blow. Although it was hard to get new work produced, especially after the 1737 Licensing Act tightened restrictions on both plays and playhouses, the theater offered writers the possibility of earnings far greater than the twenty guineas Cleland got for the copyright of the *Woman of Pleasure* or the twenty-five he would later be paid for the *Woman of Honor*. In addition to the money they could make from selling the copyright to the text itself, playwrights were paid the net takings from the play's third night (and, if they were so lucky, the sixth and even the ninth), and this "benefit," by the second half of the eighteenth century, could amount to some hundreds of pounds.[1] So it made sense for Cleland to persist in extolling to Garrick the merits of *Titus Vespasian*

even after Garrick had given it the brush-off, in the hope (vain, as it turned out) of changing his mind.

Cleland made his case in a letter dated 31 July 1754. Characteristically, the letter offers his distinctive blend of the crabby and the lofty, the sardonic and the aggrieved: while soliciting Garrick's favor, Cleland also accuses him, at least obliquely, of poor judgment and worse taste. His rhetorical strategy throughout is wholeheartedly to endorse Garrick's views on tragedy but then insinuate that Garrick fails to live up to them, having caught "that infection from a false taste, of which I can scarce name that dramatic author who has not died his theatrical death for these fifty years past."[2] He writes, for example, "The 'calm admirable' is, as you most justly indeed observe, unconstitutional to tragedy, which delights in storms," but berates Garrick for missing the essential point: "these storms must be the work of Nature, letting them loose on a subject great and worthy of their fury,—the deep, in short; not like those paltry blasts of art employed in raising storms in a tea-cup, such as tragedizing trivial or even ludicrous situations, as for example, the Adventures of a London-Prentice, or the whine of a true [girl] like Demetrius, in the Brothers" (57). Cleland's examples of the "trivial" and "ludicrous" are aimed straight at Garrick himself, who as manager of the Theatre Royal Drury Lane had kept George Lillo's *The London Merchant* (the play to which Cleland's "Adventures of a London-Prentice" refers) in repertory, and who had acted the leading role of Demetrius in Edward Young's *The Brothers* (1753) just the year before. Cleland's mocking "whine of a true [girl]" attacks Garrick's performance as much as the play itself, a neoclassical tragedy Garrick had the poor taste to choose over *Titus Vespasian*.

Cleland follows this taunt with an apparent endorsement of Garrick's theory of tragedy: "As to the Striking! the Pathetic! the Terrible! the blending of which you likewise recommend, as the very *sine qua non* of Tragedy, I subscribe without reserve to your sentiment" (58). Fair enough, but he goes on to suggest that Garrick doesn't know what these terms really mean. Of the "striking," for example, he asks, "Are rants to be called so? or those sonorous expressions which fill the ear, and leave the head empty? And yet, do not these compose the blow-bladder style of most of our modern tragedians, whose pieces have not been unjustly damned, if but for containing so many of those horrid sins against Nature, which true wit never commits" (58). Nature is as usual Cleland's touchstone of aesthetic value: his aim in *Titus* was to avoid "the abuse" of the striking, the pathetic, and the terrible, to "temper the dose of them just sufficient for [*Titus's*] health and vivacity, so as to exhibit the colouring of Nature, which I have vainly, it seems, preferred to the more striking ornaments of modern tragedies, which appear for the most part tauder'd out, like some pale hags of quality, with paint, patches, and false-brilliants of french paste" (58). Setting himself against such patched and painted hags, Cleland implicitly casts Garrick as one of their admirers, or even a hag himself, "tauder'd out" in his stage makeup and costumes. Although celebrated for his "natural" style of acting and turn away from the declamatory, Garrick's rejection of *Titus* betrays his actual fondness for the artificial.

Cleland writes to convince Garrick that *Titus* fulfills Garrick's own definition of tragedy better than other plays he preferred to it and that it would succeed on stage: the "contexture" of Metastasio's opera, he writes, "exclude[s] all declamation, all florish of sentiment, but what rise naturally out of the situations, which are numerous, and some of them appeared to me, at least, singularly theatrical" (56). In particular, "the situation in the fifth act," when Titus forgives the friends who have betrayed him and plotted his death, "was never scenefied before. It is absolutely new and original, and the effect of it . . . was such as to draw tears from eyes not much used to the melting mood" (57) when Cleland gave a private reading. In claiming that *Titus* has the power to "draw tears" from its audience, Cleland moves away from his propensity elsewhere to blame readers for the degeneracy of modern taste. Indeed he aligns himself with a popular current of taste in the later eighteenth century: an appeal to sentiment and the body—such as here, the tears that are drawn (involuntarily, irresistibly) "from eyes not much used to the melting mood."[3] Instead of blaming the "vitiated palate" of the public for the debasement of literature, he turns the tables, though still casting himself as the lone champion of literary virtue. It is not readers but authors and showmen—and no one embodied the blending of those two roles more successfully than Garrick—who are guilty of polluting the cultural waters, an act Cleland equates to bestiality and murder, as in the final paragraph of his defense of *Titus*:

> I shall leave to happier authors the by me unenvied task of elevating, surprizing, and frothing up that wonderfull sublime which is it seems so necessary to secure the acceptance, if not to make the fortune, of a new play. Let who will for me, supply with their drugs the poison-shops of taste: for should it even be true that the Public was so eat up with that green-sicness, that craving for trash which is imputed to it and which I never observed; for to me, it ever seemed rather to good-naturedly endure, than to palate, it, for want of better fare set before it; but still those authors who against their better Judgement, and taste, would nurse the distemper, for the sake of their gain by it, can with no better grace excuse themselves than the Florentine, who

being condemned to death for coupling with a She-goat, pleaded that it was not for the sin-sake he had committed the fact, but in the hopes of its producing a monster for him to get an honest livelyhood by making a Show of it. (58–59)

No wonder Garrick didn't change his mind about *Titus Vespasian*. Cleland portrays him to his face as a worse-than-sodomite, who would make a show of his own "horrid sins against Nature, which true wit never commits." Insinuating that he is a showman exhibiting monsters of his own perverse making, a murderer turning theaters into "poison-shops of taste" and forcing a "craving for trash" onto an otherwise healthy, good-natured public, Cleland could not have been more caustic in his representation to Garrick of Garrick's own crimes. It is as if he has been carried away by both the intensity of his feelings and the extravagance of his figurative imagination, so that what spills out on the page runs counter to his professed and practical aims.

If tragedy "delights in storms," Cleland's most impassioned tragic outbursts are to be found not in *Titus Vespasian* but in his private letters, such as this to Garrick.[4] The middle to late 1750s in particular—the years of *Titus, Tombo-Chiqui*, and the satirical verse epistle *The Times!*—seem to have been the most distressing and maddening of Cleland's life. The combination of financial insecurity, bordering on penury, and family antagonisms, bordering on hatred, led him to write a series of letters in which his emotions are laid barer than in any other of his writings. They are also self-consciously writerly performances, aiming to project a persona of himself as unjustly injured gentleman and maliciously disinherited son, "sick and languishing," as he puts it in one letter, "dying of every death at once," as he writes in another.[5] All letters are performances, but if Cleland's at times have the air of the theatrical "rants" he deplores in the letter to Garrick, there is no reason to doubt the genuineness of the anger, pain, and frustration he pours out in them. In a set of thirteen letters dating from November 1752 to September 1762, one to his mother, Lucy, and the others to her lawyer Edward Dickinson, Cleland rails against what he represents as her cruel treatment of him in freezing him out of the administration of his father's and her estates and tightly restricting the payment of his modest annuity (£30 per year).[6] Insofar as this is just a dispute over his allowance, his epistolary ragings might seem like the "storms in a tea-cup, such as tragedizing trivial or even ludicrous situations," that Cleland mocked to Garrick. But the letters are compelling not only for what they reveal of the severely dysfunctional state of the Clelands' family life but for the violence, excess, and extravagance of the writer-son's authorial voice. Seemingly out of control, his language in these letters—which presumably survive only because Dickinson retained them with his other business papers—captures Cleland's emotional volatility while also registering the impact of the value placed on *feeling* in the mid- to late eighteenth century.

With Cleland, the feelings in question are seldom those of tenderness, sympathy, or pity, which burst in the form of tears from the eponymous hero of Henry Mackenzie's novel *The Man of Feeling* (1771); they are more often those of fury, outrage, and scorn. Or such at least is the case in his letters from the 1750s, which are closer in spirit and rhetoric to the violent tumult of Sturm und Drang than to the sighs of sentimental novels. In his fiction of the 1760s, however, Cleland did turn to sentimental romance of a more conventional kind, even if his aim was in part to interrogate those conventions, as he had in the *Coxcomb* and *Woman of Pleasure*. Although he was still estranged from his mother—in a letter of September 1762 he wrote that he had heard from a third party "that *Mrs Cleland, did not know whether I was alive or no*"—his life after 1760 was in less of an uproar, and by later in the decade he appears to be in pretty comfortable circumstances, even going on holiday now and again in Somerset and Buckinghamshire.[7] Lucy Cleland's death in May 1763 brought him a legacy of £100 and an annuity of £60 per year, and the four comic-sentimental novellas collected in *The Surprises of Love* (1760–1764) were his first real success since the 1753 *Dictionary of Love*, so he was no longer so financially and emotionally wracked as he had been the decade before. Not that Cleland ever mellowed, exactly: in a journal entry from 1772, Boswell, who seems to have found him intriguing, describes Cleland as "a fine sly malcontent," and in a letter to Garrick the same year, eighteen years after *Titus*'s rejection, Cleland is still complaining about it.[8] But one should keep sight of the "fine sly[ness]" Boswell observed: when Cleland, near the end of this last letter to Garrick, writes, "Your having, however, been the death of my vain hopes, gives me, at least, some title to your forgiveness of the tremendous length of this address," he is needling, even baiting him, but no longer lamenting; there is some asperity in his tone, but not the anguish that shoots through the letters to and about his mother in the 1750s.

In this chapter I set Cleland's later fiction—*The Surprises of Love* and the 1768 *Woman of Honor*, a three-volume epistolary novel—against the Cleland-Dickinson-Cleland correspondence of the 1750s to explore the different registers of feeling in his private and public writing and the changing role of sentiment from his earlier to his later work. The letters seem to represent the antithesis of everything he celebrates in the later fiction: instead of delicacy and restraint, the letters seethe with violent, excessive language; instead of subordinating the passions to virtue and reason, the letters' author is overwhelmed by emotions he cannot control. "My brain is on fire," he writes in one; "I do not know what to write, or how to act."[9] Of course it is hardly surprising that the author in private life does not live up to his own prescriptions; the wonder would be if he did. But letters are not wholly private—they can be passed around, copied, read aloud— nor are they necessarily any more transparent than more obviously public writing. Cleland's letters to Dickinson may be heartfelt, but they are also intended to elicit an emotional response, to be read or sent on to Cleland's mother, to be discussed between Lucy Cleland and her sister, Lady Allen, to be pored over within his mother's circle of friends; indeed he imagines such a scene in one of them. By the historical accident of their survival as a collection, these letters present many of the same interpretive challenges as an epistolary novel: how to reconstruct a coherent story line from fragmentary materials, how to assess the motivations of the various correspondents, how much faith to place in their words. It would be facile simply to equate real and novelistic letters but no less so to separate "public" and "private" texts into mutually distinct spheres. To do so would be to ignore the fluid and plural readerships of the private texts as well as the isolation and privacy of much novel reading, and to overlook the theatricality and bombast of the letters as well as the intimacy of address of the public, published work.[10]

If too categorical a division of public and private begs the question of the different possible relationships between Cleland's texts and their real or imagined audiences, the pitting of "earlier" works against "later" poses problems of its own. When can a work be said to originate? Does the *Woman of Pleasure* date from the early 1730s or the late 1740s? Was its author (were its authors) around eighteen or closer to forty? There is no way of knowing how thoroughly Cleland "new-cast" whatever text he may have brought back with him from Bombay, so it can never be precisely placed in the author's life history. Such a history is usually plotted along the axis of publication dates, as reckoned from title pages, newspaper advertisements, and the like, but texts can circulate (or molder) in manuscript for years before seeing print. Sometimes a letter like that to Garrick can establish that a work was making the rounds for some time before it was offered for publication, or, as with the *Woman of Honor*, a bookseller's records might mark the date of a manuscript's delivery.[11] But for most eighteenth-century authors, Cleland certainly included, the biographical record is haphazard and full of gaps, leading to doubtful attributions and puzzling hiatuses. It is not always straightforward to plot a corpus of texts into a narrative of authorial development or (as tends to be said of Cleland) decline. Yet while I would guard against both the "late flowering" and the "waning powers" plotlines, *The Surprises of Love* and *The Woman of Honor* undeniably revisit and rework the romance motifs of erotic awakening and the triumph of natural love that he first explored in the two *Memoirs*. Indeed the title of his last fiction is a variation on that of his first, the *Woman of Honor* making amends for the *Woman of Pleasure*.[12] By that light, Cleland's career as a novelist might be understood as a movement from the early text's scandalous, sly assault on all forms of propriety to the late one's dreary paean to conjugal respectability, from satirical and enflaming to sentimental and chaste portrayals of love. This may be true, although the earlier work also builds to such a paean, and Fanny's language pulses with sentiment, but it ignores the defiant oddness of the *Woman of Honor*, its lumpy, intransigent structure and "loose, undigested manner," as Cleland said of another of his late works, published two years before.[13] With their "nonharmonious, nonserene tension" and their uningratiating insistence on "going *against*," to adopt Edward Said's phrase, Cleland's late works present him as out of sorts and out of step with the sensibility and values of the social world he inhabits, even as he stubbornly struggles to have his voice heard.[14] Cleland's late style is not just a function of formal awkwardness, either: the four novellas of *The Surprises of Love* are quite artfully wrought, their playfully artificial plots full of contrivances, disguises, false identities, bawdy-house abductions, and narrow escapes. Presenting themselves as "very innocent and diverting amusements," as a writer for the *Critical Review* put it, they allowed Cleland to approach issues of licit and illicit desire, and the seeming arbitrariness of romantic love, in a way that, as Said writes of Cavafy, "render[s] disenchantment and pleasure without resolving the contradiction between them."[15]

A Poor, Lone, Unsupported Being

After publishing the *Dictionary of Love* with Ralph Griffiths in November 1753, Cleland fell away from commercial authorship for most of the 1750s. He had stopped being a regular contributor to the *Monthly Review* after 1751, and *Memoirs of a Coxcomb* and the *Dictionary* were most likely the final payments on his debt to Griffiths. There is no evidence of a falling-out nor any reason to think he could not have carried on at the *Monthly* and as a "miscellaneous writer," having achieved some success over the previous five years, but he must have decided the writing trade was too wearisome, undignified, or unrewarding to abide. Judging from the letter to Garrick, he tried his luck next as a playwright, writing *Titus* in 1753–1754 and *Tombo-Chiqui* a year or so later, but even though he thanks Garrick "for the great encouragement you give me" on the comedy in progress, he writes, "The truth is, that I do not foresee to myself ease and tranquillity enough of head to finish it as it ought to be by the next season."[16] This statement may have been his last bid to gain Garrick's sympathy, and so his approval of *Titus*, but it also suggests that Cleland's circumstances and mind were in turmoil.

When Cleland moved out of his mother's house in St. James's Place, their relationship had long since deteriorated into one of bitter (on his part) and disdainful (on hers) antagonism, though he was the only one of her three children still living.[17] His 1748 imprisonment for debt was proof of what he acknowledged, in a later letter to her, as "my greatest fault, my contempt and ignorance of the value of money, but just when I feel the pinching want of it, and thence my improvidence of a child of four years of age," while her failure or refusal to secure his release was, for him, proof of "immortal hatred or what is more unnatural yet a brutal indifference to now your only child."[18] The clearest sign of her hatred and indifference, as he believed, was her will, dated 4 February 1752, of which he was pointedly not named executor and which limited his inheritance to a strictly controlled annuity, which he was forbidden to "alien sell or assign mortgage charge or otherwise incumber . . . to any person or persons whatsoever."[19] It was likely this last provision—and a similar restriction on the allowance she paid him during her lifetime—that most infuriated Cleland, for it meant he could not borrow on his future income to pay off his present, pressing debts. This was probably a smart precautionary move on Lucy's part, given his track record, but it left him at risk of being thrown a second time into debtors' prison. As he wrote in one of the earliest of his letters to Dickinson, "My persisting in a jail, and, in effect sent thither by herself would, as things appear, have been a matter of the highest indifference" to her.[20] Her "insensibleness" to his suffering, he continues, "murders me . . . it keeps me dragging my existence down in the dirt, and robs me of all the patrimony my poor father left me, and seems to justify the extremities to which it must of all necessity subject a solitary, detached, unsupported individual."

In the letters he wrote to Dickinson between 1752 and 1762, Cleland does not so much argue his case or narrate the history of their estrangement as perform a series of dramatic monologues, vivid stagings of rage and despair. But this is not to say he feigns the emotions he projects: at times he is so overcome he breaks into a kind of mad scene. He tends to write Dickinson at moments of crisis or shock, and the fact that we do not always know what precipitated the crisis only heightens the effect of a soliloquist spiraling out of control. In one letter, Cleland sets the scene by writing, "An incident perfectly new, which is like a thunder-bolt to me, occasions you this trouble."[21] The thunderbolt signifies emotional storms, but Cleland frames it in a sentence that promises to give a rational account of them. He reports that his landlady has gone to Mrs. Cleland's house to press for the rent he hasn't paid, but then he interrupts himself: "But whilst I am writing to you Mrs Kyme brings me up the enclosed. See! this poor family on the brink of destruction, only for having trusted me!" This interruption by Mrs. Kyme's entrance, threatening letter in hand, feels quite stagey, especially when Cleland figuratively gestures toward the enclosure and exhorts Dickinson to "See!" We can only guess at the enclosure's contents, but the interruption knocks the letter off course, and instead of finishing the story he began, he gives vent to the storm:

> I am raving mad to think to what scenes that woman's execrable obstinacy exposes me, and the innocent, who have depended on me. My brain is on fire. I do not know what to write, or how to act. If my going to god, or my blood will satisfy the inveteracy of my mother, I am ready to lay down my life; but, to have such innocent creatures involved, and turned out into the street upon my account, is a torture beyond that of Hell. I am in such a confusion that I can scarce subscribe myself what I really am.

Cleland's letter is a cri de coeur, the urgency of his distress conveyed by his incapacity to write. But that too is a familiar device: think of Fanny Hill dropping her pen when in the grips of a different but equally overpowering feeling. As she wrote, "Description too deserts me" (183); so Cleland. But like Fanny, Cleland is nevertheless able to convey both the feeling and the dramatic scene that brings it on: on one side, the "innocent creatures" the Kymes, threatened with "turn[ing] out into the street" by their own creditors; on the other, "that woman," Mrs. Cleland, the offstage villainess; caught between them, the hero, Cleland himself, who has, without meaning to, put "the innocent, who have depended on me" in peril, and who now offers himself as a blood sacrifice to appease the "inveteracy" of his mother. Garrick could not have asked for a scene more striking, more pathetic, more terrible.

Cleland's mother is the most vividly rendered and the most vital of his literary creations, a figure of almost demonic glamour. How closely it resembles the real Lucy Cleland is impossible to know, but Cleland's portrayal is so rhetorically extreme, his fixation on her so intense, as to make her seem less a real person than a projection of the "illness, and pain" that, as he writes at the end of one letter, "afflict me so, that I cannot longer hold the pen, on this disagreeable subject," his ill treatment at her hands.[22] Yet he returns to this subject again and again, never more histrionically than in a letter from 1758 provoked by another now-missing enclosure. It is not clear what this was, or how Cleland got hold of it, but its intent, he says, was "to insult, and grossly trifle with a gentleman under such distresses, as surely to anything of a human heart, could at least be no provocation to such a wanton piece of cruelty."[23] Whether written by Lucy Cleland or on her behalf, it was then passed around, to "the amusement of many." He breaks out in fury:

> Where is that Highwayman, that cut-throat, I could complain of, when from a mother it is I receive these stabs! Stabs, which as if of themselves not murderous enough must be poisoned too with a treacherous air of kindness to make a parade of at her wretched, comfortless fire-side, to her cronies, her little lordees and ladies . . . whilst they re-ecchoe to her *"Lord, Maam to be sure you are vast good indeed, and Mr Cleland must be mad to reject such an offer:* and this pretious stuff satisfies her tender conscience . . . But whither am I going? She is but too severely punished in being what she is, incapable of loving even herself. No! hatred is her element.

This is not the first time Cleland presented himself as a murder victim: in the first of the Bombay trials he accused Lowther of "low dishonourable Stabs," and in the note on Thomas Cannon's front door he accused Cannon of "join[ing] with his own mother to consummate the murder of an unfortunate gentleman who had saved his life, and whom, in return, he poisoned five times with common arsenic."[24] Only Cleland's mother, though, would both stab and poison him, combining the phallic violence of the highwayman and cutthroat with the stereotypically feminine, secretive violence of poisoning (not coincidentally the murder method favored by "Molly Cannon"). She, too, is one of the unsexed who haunt Cleland's writing—not unsexed by desire but by murderous impulses prompted by sordid interest. In this, she surpasses even Lady Macbeth, who only imagines the crime of filicide that Cleland's mother has committed. Lady Macbeth's terrible invocation could also be Lucy Cleland's: "Come, you spirits / That tend on mortal thoughts, unsex me here / . . . / That no compunctious visitings of nature / Shake my fell purpose."[25] Like Lady Macbeth's, Lucy Cleland's unsexing is a turning away from nature, a repudiation of the natural affections of a mother: she is, her son writes, "incapable of loving even herself" and lacks "anything of a human heart."

This strain of the inhuman runs through Cleland's epistolary portrait of his mother, always in contrast to his own ineradicable filial love (which he has a singular manner of expressing). In a letter of 1756 he writes of his mother and his aunt, Lady Allen, that "had I even deserved this implacability at their hands, if they had had a heart like mine, or but a human one, nothing could have held out against the exquisite joy of forgiving a son, a nephew, who the instant that he became so unfortunate, must cease to be at least unpardonably guilty."[26] There is something perverse and denatured in his mother's "negative persecution," her acts of refusal, estrangement, and silence.[27] She has barred him from her house and refuses to read his letters: as early as 1752 she writes a postscript to a letter to Dickinson to say that she has kept a letter from her son "to add to the large Collection I am already possessed of, of the like and worse abuse, but be assur'd 'tis the last I ever will read."[28] But if this refusal, to Cleland, is just a sign of "immortal hatred" or "brutal indifference," it cannot fail to strike us that whatever distress he may have been in, from the evidence of his letters he was relentlessly on the attack. Lucy Cleland's letters confirm this sense of the son's aggression. In one, she says she rushed to her banker's for fear that if she went later she might run into her son there, "which wou'd be mortal to me."[29] She thanks Dickinson "for all your kind attentions and indeavours, to ease me of a Load that I fear will still lye heavy on me, for his manner of accepting [his allowance] is like doing me a favour, and rather receiving an injury . . . I am very sensible I owe all my present peace to you." From these glimpses she seems weary of her son's harassment and abuse and worried that her "trouble will never cease." Around seventy years old when she wrote this, her older sister increasingly infirm, her husband and two youngest children long dead, her fortune mostly gone—her son well knows, she writes, "that his poor Father had nothing to leave me and that I have lost all I had in the world"—she might have a better title than he to call herself "a poor, lone, unsupported being."[30]

One might wonder what right Cleland thought he had to his mother's support. Dickinson raises this question in a letter to Cleland dated 18 October 1755, writing that, while he is "very sorry for your situation so it would give me great pleasure at any time to hear of its mending by your own Abilitys which you are far from wanting without dependance upon any body . . . I wish you would give your mind another turn & endeavour to work out your own happiness upon the foundation she has laid for it which would be of service to you in every one's Opinion."[31] It is not certain what Cleland wanted from her; probably it was free access to the annuity money to pay off his various debts. In one letter he writes that "when she made me a proposal, in effect, of ten times a greater sum than I desired: I might rationally entreat of her not to mock my distresses with a relief I *could not* accept in *her way*, but to procure me the assistance I wanted in *my own*, at so much less an expence, and of the fitness of which is it not for me, to spurn with the scorn it deserves, the suspicion of my not being the best Judge?"[32] The dispute is as much about control as about money: Cleland clearly felt that he had been unjustly passed over as his father's rightful heir and that his mother's conduct "robs me of all the patrimony my poor father left me." According to her, "his poor Father had nothing to leave." But whether or not he had legitimate grounds to resent the terms of her will, one might still wonder why Cleland did not "endeavour to work out [his] own happiness" more energetically at this stage of his life.

He maintained he had done everything possible, and complained of "the continuation of my distresses in spite of my most unwearied endeavors to overcome them, endeavors rendered abortive by her discountenance of me," or what in the same letter he calls "the perseverance of Mrs Cleland's open, and known disowning of me, of which my life must soon be the victim."[33] It seems to be fixed in his mind that his mother's "discountenance," her having "so cruelly set the example of deserting him," had effectively scotched his chances of being considered for one or another government post or sinecure, for which he evidently spent much of the decade waiting.[34] "Nothing is however certainer," he writes, "than that if Lady Allen and Mrs Cleland, were but to stir in the least for me; the conjunction is not unfavorable, for my procuring some employ, that might render me serviceable to my country, my employers, my family, and myself. But of this I have long totally despaired." Dickinson had already disputed this the year before, writing, "Family differences are so common that they have little or no influence upon publick affairs[.] And an employment of the importance you intimate must have depended so much upon your own Merit that your having been well or ill with her could have been of little Consequence."[35] But Cleland held fast to his belief that his success or failure depended on his mother's good or ill will; and her ill will was all he was to know.

One letter from Cleland to his mother survives. It is a small-scale de profundis, distilling all his bitterness, grief, and self-pity into one last bid to touch her, yet refusing to allow that it ever will. He wrote it after learning of the death of her sister and enclosed it with a cover to Dickinson on 6 March 1758.[36] She may never have read it. The fact that it was preserved and eventually sold with the letters from Cleland to Dickinson suggests that Dickinson never passed it on to Lucy Cleland. She could have read it and returned it to her lawyer, but she had her own "Collection" of letters from her son, it seems likely that had she read it, she would have kept it with the others, to be destroyed or lost after her death.

Although Cleland told Dickinson that his letter was "simply a compliment of condoleance, to my mother, on the death of my Aunt, which has, I assure you, greatly afflicted me," it violates the norms of the condolence letter in order to make a much more personal appeal. But as is common with Cleland, his appeal is laced with aggression. He begins by expressing his "diffidence of your even receiving this application" and immediately turns against the reader with whom he is meant to be condoling, stating in advance his "certainty of your not doing justice to the real motives of it." In this, his letter's first sentence, he has turned it into a field of combat between author and reader, so that his claim to be writing at the urging of "Nature and Gratitude" strikes a rather hollow note. Even when he offers a standard expression of condolence—"I learnt of my aunt's death with infinite concern"—he turns that, too, against his mother by stating that "it would be the height of cruelty" for her to doubt this. But in telling his would-be reader that he expects her to doubt and willfully misread what he writes, he encourages a hermeneutics of suspicion, inviting her to read warily. When he writes, for example, that his aunt's death affected him "more perhaps, than if, in a personal attendance on her, I had been prepared for it, by observing its gradual approaches," his plain statement hides a barbed reminder that it was they who forbade him to attend on her. As the epistolary monodrama unfolds, his aunt's death becomes only a pretext for a last stab at self-justification (the son, too, wields a "poinant and ready pen").[37] Every expression of tenderness or sympathy brings rage and reproach in its wake.

After observing how affected he was by the suddenness of his aunt's death, he writes that "it used to be some sort of consolation to me, amidst all the low, ignoble, scandalous misfortunes, to which you have been contented that I should be exposed for such a series of years, to think I was not utterly an unconnected being whilst you and Lady Allen should be alive." Here, the ostensible "consolation" of family ties is exposed as a cruel sham by his mother's "content[ment]" at his "low, ignoble, scandalous misfortunes"; indeed he insinuates that it was she who "exposed" him to those misfortunes in the first place. The sentences that follow exhibit a similarly disharmonious tone: "I feel more tenderly for what I am sure you must feel for this loss, than for myself. Do not then grudge me, at least, the cold consolation of joining my affliction with yours, though at the distance your unrelentingness prescribes to me." The discord of "tenderly" and "grudge" leads to the oxymoron of "cold consolation," which is no consolation at all. There may also be a wry twist to his claim to feel his mother's loss of her sister "more tenderly" than his own, for how "tenderly" could he have felt the loss of one who kept him, unrelentingly, at a distance?

If Cleland's professions of tenderness are also bitter reminders of how untender his mother has been toward him, his most profound offer of comfort is also his harshest accusation of guilt:

> My now sincerest wish is that the news of my own death may soon compensatively comfort you for that which you are now lamenting. Dirty cares, pitifull distresses, the sense of which is redoubled at once by their indignity, and by the heart-breaking circumstance of their being owing to your implacability, have long impaired my health, and made the only delivery I now expect from them, my hourly prayer. All that I complain of, is its being so slow.

He offers up his death as a comfort to his murderer. But in doing so, he makes the guilt of it all hers. This is a charge he had been making since the earliest letters to Dickinson, writing in one of his "affliction at the parricide hand that has placed and keeps me on the rack"; but even if he always intended that she should read or at least hear about what he wrote to her lawyer, the impact of reading this in a letter addressed to herself, as she was mourning her sister, must have been far greater.[38] His attempt to smuggle such an accusatory screed into his mother's house in the guise of a "compliment of condoleance" might fairly be likened to "Stabs, which as if of themselves not murderous enough must be poisoned too with a treacherous air of kindness." Yet Cleland's is a peculiar form of treachery: he wants his words to wound, and is willing to use innuendo and subterfuge, but he is not scheming to any rational end or from any secret motive. If he wanted to persuade her to change her will, for instance, he "was not such an ideot," as he notes, as to think this was the way to do it. He seems instead to want to make her feel the same distress and heartbrokenness he feels, but he masks this as an expression of "the natural affection, and tender reverence which my heart has ever born you, though sometimes over-clouded by transient fits of passion and resentment." Or perhaps this isn't a mask at all: words of "rage and pain," as Coleridge uneasily registers at the end of "Christabel," may for Cleland have been the very language of familial love.[39]

Cleland's letter to his mother has three movements. In the first and third, he thunders against her "unnatural" and "brutal" abandonment of him "to the cruelty of the world" and offers her his imminent death, which "can only give you pleasure," with this sarcastic blessing: "May the years taken from my life be added to yours!" Between these histrionic outer movements, however, he subsides into a more meditative, less tumultuous passage, in which he reflects on his own character:

I attribute then all that I have suffered by your obduracy of heart, not to you, but to a fatality not the less cruel for my not being able to account for it. You cannot, I know your excellent sense too well, be angry with me, for what I am, since what I am, I am constitutionally, and am therefore undoubtedly more to be pitied than condemned for it. My passions and errors are not more my choice than the features of my face.

Like his mother's "obduracy of heart," Cleland's "passions and errors" are constitutional, imprinted by "fatality" or nature just as his physical features were. It is intriguing that in his own case he moves away from the model of cultural imprinting or imitation by which he accounts for the "passions and errors" of Catherine Vizzani and Fanny Hill; intriguing, too, that he does not spell out what passions and errors he means—perhaps only what he goes on to call his "greatest fault, my contempt and ignorance of the value of money."[40] Yet this fault "is more nearly related to Virtue than to Vice" and should actually endear him to her, "when you consider [that fault] was exactly my father's, and has been but too faithfully transmitted with his blood to me." What he is, he is by biological, specifically paternal, inheritance. His father's character has been reproduced in him, absent one thing: "I have not, as he had, a Mrs Cleland to take care of me, and to supplement that so ruinous defect." The son's is a twofold lack, conjugal and filial, with a single name: he lacks a "Mrs Cleland" as either sexual partner or mother, and in either case as caretaker and "supplement." His estrangement is both that of an abandoned child and that of one who is, by choice or constitution, outside of the normative structures of sexual reproduction and marriage. I do not mean to read into this a "confession" of sodomitical or otherwise perverse desire, but rather to read it as acknowledging his difference or distance from the culturally encoded (and parentally reproduced) normality of the married couple and his status as an alien, a kind of changeling, within his own family.

What remains of the Cleland-Dickinson-Cleland correspondence stops in September 1762 with a letter from John Cleland entreating the lawyer "to make one effort more to heal [the] breach" between mother and son and a note from Dickinson excusing himself from the task.[41] Although there was "no one so fit, and I believe so well inclined to heal the bleeding wounds of our family," as Cleland once wrote him, Dickinson had troubles of his own. Because of what he calls "the Great Misfortune that has happened in my family," he had lately been "incapable of seeing almost any body, or attending to any thing," so he urges Cleland "to apply to some other of her acquaintance or friends" for help.[42] There is no record of whether Cleland felt the same sympathy for Dickinson's misfortune that he expected Dickinson to feel for his, nor of whether the "bleeding wounds" of the Cleland family ever healed. When Cleland wrote, his "poor mother" was in a "state of languor and decay," but characteristically, he was not thinking of her suffering so much as his own, complaining that "it would cruelly aggravate my misfortunes if Mrs Cleland should leave the world without giving me the consolation of being sure of her forgiveness and blessing. Is it in nature that she can do me so cruel an injury?"[43] As far as I know, this is his last written mention of her, and it does not hold much promise of healing. The bleeding wounds had been open too long, since well before Lucy Cleland wrote her will in 1752. In what appears to be the first of his letters to Dickinson, Cleland tells, or rather half tells, a story to show how unjustly his mother and aunt have long treated him. "About three years ago," he begins—sometime in late 1749 or early 1750—his mother and aunt offered him £50 per year to look after some properties or investments in South Carolina.[44] When he arrived there, his contact, a Mr. Fryer or Frier, had got into financial trouble and gone off to Jamaica. Having no resources of his own, Cleland followed him there, only to find Fryer dead, leaving Cleland high and dry, a colonial orphan. Accordingly, he writes,

> rather than come upon the parish at *Jamaica!* where no man was ever better treated, or with higher respect, I came home: when, I scarce dare ask you to believe it: I was welcomed, from this vile insignificant voyage, with a reproach, as for a *fault* that I had come home. Yes, for a *fault!* and punished for it, too, by a total retrenchment, of that *Bounty* which being their own voluntary subscription, constituted a kind of arrears, even equitably due: since, not the least shadow of Justice was there to accuse me of having forfeited it, by any *the least* misconduct of mine.

It is a puzzling story, all the more so as there is no mention of a voyage to Carolina anywhere else in his writings. It may be what Griffiths referred to when he testified that he asked Cleland to prepare the expurgated *Fanny Hill* as the only way to recoup his debt, "as Cleeland was going abroad"; if so, Cleland must have made his "vile insignificant voyage" between December 1749 and October 1750, when there was a lull in his writing.[45] This brief and cryptic account portrays him as a victim of maternal cruelty, first in being sent into exile, and then in being punished for the failure of a scheme he had no part in devising. Transported to the colonies by an unloving mother, he resembles both Fanny's love Charles, whose father has him kidnapped and carried off to "one of the factories in the South-Seas" (55), and the poet Richard Savage, whose equally "unnatural" mother, "not enduring me ever to approach Her, offer'd a Bribe to have had me shipp'd off in an odd Manner, to one of the Plantations."[46] From being the architect of a projected Portuguese East India company, Cleland had fallen, by his mother's will, to being "fit[ted] out, for half-a-crown, at a Wapping slop-shop with a Pea-Jacket, and Honeycomb breeches"—the kit of an indentured colonial servant. As so often in these letters, just recalling the miseries he lays to his mother's account exhausts all powers of expression: "more I would say, but my illness, and pain afflict me so, that I can no longer hold the pen, on this disagreeable subject." The author is silenced by the very excess of feeling that spurred him to write in the first place.

A Fretwork of Fluid Brilliants

Having left off his career as a "miscellaneous writer" in 1753, and thwarted in his design to make a new start as playwright with the rejection of *Titus* the next year, Cleland spent most of the 1750s in limbo, writing overwrought letters and waiting for a call that never came to offer him "some employ" worthy of a gentleman. He did publish *Titus*, with the comic entr'acte *The Ladies Subscription*, at his own expense in 1755, but judging by his letters this didn't yield any financial benefits, nor did it lead to any interest from theatrical producers. He claimed not even to have offered *Tombo-Chiqui* to the theaters, but its publication in 1758 did mark his return to the world of professional authorship, as it was offered for sale by the bookselling partnership of S. Hooper and A. Morley. As his hopes for a government post faded after 1756–1757, Cleland began to establish new working relationships with a number of booksellers, starting with Samuel Hooper, whose shop "at Gay's Head near Beaufort Buildings in the Strand" Cleland gave as his return address in a letter to Dickinson in 1758.[47] In addition to *Tombo-Chiqui*, Hooper and Morley had published Grose's *Voyage to the East Indies*, of which Cleland was likely the ghost author, in 1757, and over the next dozen years, Cleland worked with several prominent London booksellers: Israel Pottinger, who published Cleland's satirical verse epistle *The Times! An Epistle to Flavian* (1759), and a novella, *The Romance of a Day* (1760); Thomas Becket, who copublished two essays on physiology and hygiene, the *Institutes of Health* (1761, with Thomas Davies) and the *Phisiological Reveries* (with Peter DeHondt, 1765); Thomas Lowndes and William Nicoll, with whom Cleland published a collection of novellas, *The Surprises of Love* (1764), and his third novel, *The Woman of Honor* (1768); and Lockyer Davis, who issued Cleland's essays on etymology and the Celtic origins of European languages—*The Way to Things by Words, and to Words by Things* (1766), *Specimen of an Etimological Vocabulary* (1768), and *Additional Articles to the Specimen* (1769). Cleland even renewed his association with Ralph Griffiths, who published second editions of *Titus Vespasian* and *The Ladies' Subscription* in 1760.

These were all major figures in the eighteenth-century book trade. Becket and DeHondt, like Lowndes and Nicoll, were leading publishers of fiction; Samuel Hooper published Francis Grose's celebrated *Antiquities of England and Wales* (1772) and *Classical Dictionary of the Vulgar Tongue* (1785); Lockyer Davis played a key role in publishing the *Works of the English Poets* with Samuel Johnson's biographical-critical prefaces and was bookseller for the Royal Society. Israel Pottinger, trenchantly described by Robertson Davies as a "bookseller, madman, and hack," was a more shadowy character, but as publisher of the *Busy Body* and the *Weekly Magazine* (1759–1760), he played an important role in the early career of Oliver Goldsmith.[48] Pottinger worked out of the same commercial building as Griffiths, the Dunciad in Paternoster Row, and while his publishing career was checkered—his bankruptcy in January 1760 hastened the death of Goldsmith's *Weekly Magazine* the next month—the book trade was notably precarious. Indeed, of the nine booksellers who worked with Cleland between 1757 and 1769, at least five declared bankruptcy at some point in their mainly successful careers.[49] Pottinger recovered sufficiently to publish Cleland's *Romance of a Day* in September 1760, although his unstable finances or psyche may have led Cleland to publish the follow-up *Romance of a Night* with William Nicoll in 1762 and the collected *Surprises of Love* with Lowndes and Nicoll in 1764.

As checkered as his career was, then, and as bizarre as the *Phisiological Reveries* or the essays on language may seem to us (and to some of his contemporaries), Cleland was not really an outcast or pariah, and some of the most successful of eighteenth-century booksellers were willing to take a chance on even the most idiosyncratic of his writings. The chance paid off for Lowndes and Nicoll with the success of his *Surprises of Love*. Written between 1760 and 1764, these romances were Cleland's first works of fiction, and first original plots, since *Memoirs of a Coxcomb*, to which they have a certain affinity—being what Philip Dormer Stanhope, Earl of Chesterfield, called "little gallant histor[ies], which must contain a great deal of love."[50] All four of these comic-sentimental romances end happily, and while in all but the first there are real moral and physical dangers to be overcome, the prevailing approach is playful, lighthearted, deliberately superficial. Although Stanhope calls "novels" the fictions Cleland calls "romances," his definition gives the plot common to the *Surprises* and the *Coxcomb* (and the *Woman of Pleasure*): "The subject must be a love affair; the lovers are to meet with many difficulties and obstacles to oppose the accomplishment of their wishes, but at last overcome them all; and the conclusion or catastrophe must leave them happy." Cleland's two *Memoirs* expand and complicate this formula in novelistic ways, but in the *Surprises* he harks back to the approach taken by William Congreve in his 1692 masquerade-romance *Incognita*. Although Congreve had not yet written any plays, he constructed *Incognita* in imitation of "*Dramatick* Writing, namely, in the Design, Contexture and Result of the Plot."[51] In his preface to *Incognita* Congreve writes that "the Design of the Novel is obvious, after the [lovers'] first meeting . . . and the difficulty is in bringing it to pass, maugre all apparent obstacles, within the compass of two days." Cleland's design in the *Surprises* is equally obvious—to bring the fated couple together, or as Congreve puts it, "marrying [the] Couple so oddly engaged in an intricate Amour"—and he commits himself even more strictly than Congreve to the Aristotelian unities of time, place, and action. Congreve untangles his intrigue "within the compass of two days"; Cleland his within a few hours. Congreve's "Scene is continued in *Florence* from the commencement of the Amour"; Cleland's are each restricted to a neighborhood in or near London. So the first of the *Surprises* is *The Romance of a Day; or, An Adventure in Greenwich-Park Last Easter*, while the second is titled *The Romance of a Night; or, A Covent-Garden Adventure*. The third and fourth do not announce the setting in the title, but *The Romance of a Morning; or, The Chance of a Sport* takes place inside a farmhouse in Kent, while *The Romance of an Evening; or, Who Would Have Thought It?* is set in a suburban villa on the Thames in Fulham. As with Congreve, so in Cleland's romances, "every Obstacle . . . in the progress of the Story act[s] as subservient to that purpose"—the couple's marriage—"which at first it seems to oppose," a principle that in comedy, Congreve writes, is "called the Unity of the Action" and, in these romances, "Unity of Contrivance." This theatrical quality of the *Surprises* was noted by a critic in the *Monthly Review*, who wrote that the "'Romance of a Morning' . . . might be easily turned into a dramatic form and could hardly fail of succeeding on the stage"—an ironic postscript, as James Basker has noted, to Cleland's abortive career as a playwright.[52]

The *Surprises* were the most critically and commercially successful of Cleland's later works but are almost unknown today. My juxtaposition of Cleland and Congreve is meant not to claim a direct influence but to foreground the novellas' generic affinities in order to understand better how to read them. Even though he was writing seventy years after Congreve, Cleland in the *Surprises* turned his back on all the innovations in narrative fiction from the period that separates them, in particular the representational strategies we still associate with novelistic realism in its various forms, as in the work of Behn, Defoe, Haywood, Richardson, the Fieldings, Lennox, Smollett, and others. This was not his last word on the subject: with *The Woman of Honor* he adopts a version of Richardsonian epistolary realism, and is concerned to situate the narrative in a recognizable contemporary cultural and social world, which is described in some detail. Although the *Surprises* are set in locales whose names—Greenwich Park, Covent Garden, Fulham—correspond to those of real places, they are no more attached to the world outside fiction than *Incognita* was to the realities of seventeenth-century Florence. They represent, rather, a deliberate evasion of the contemporary, which is not to say that they are out of time but that they defy or stand against their own time. By returning to the mode of *Incognita*, Cleland gives the *Surprises* an anachronistic flavor—similar to what Edward Said, in his discussion of Richard Strauss's late works, calls their "strangely recapitulatory and even backward-looking and abstracted quality."[53] Said proposes that Strauss's late works "are escapist in theme, reflective and disengaged in tone, and above all written with a kind of distilled and rarefied technical mastery," and while Cleland's style is perhaps too peculiar (in both senses: individual, and odd) to qualify as "technical mastery," his overtly escapist and archaic stories, with their running commentary on their own artifice, can likewise be read as reflections on the process of making art.

I do not want to overstate their profundity: these are, after all, "pretty tale[s] . . . prettily told," as the *Monthly Review* put it.[54] Their superficiality, their interest in narrative surfaces, is precisely their point. At the start of the final tale, Cleland gives a description of the Thames that could serve as an emblem for the whole collection. The hero, Sir Lionel Heartly, idly gazes at the river, "which being barely ruffled by a gentle breeze, the undulation of its surface broke the burnish produced upon it by the beams of the setting sun into such a tremulous glitter, as presented, in full play, a dazzling fretwork of fluid brilliants."[55] The descriptive focus shifts from the watery to the luminous over the course of this sentence, from the "undulat[ing] surface" of the river "barely ruffled" by a breeze to the "broke[n] burnish" and "tremulous glitter" of reflected sunlight, culminating in the "dazzling fretwork of fluid brilliants"—the last two words turning light (as from diamonds) back into liquid. "Dazzling fretwork," too, fuses solidity, liquidity, and light into a single image, merging "fretwork" as interlacing ornament and "fret" as the action of rippling or unsettling the surface of water, producing here a light that blinds. Cleland's late style "in full play" is rococo, extravagant, as ornamental and brittle as any fretwork.

The superficiality of the *Surprises* is matched by the predictability of their happy endings, as Cleland himself repeatedly points out. At the dramatic climax of the second tale, *The Romance of a Night*, for example, when the hero, Lord Veramore, arrives at the house where the beautiful sixteen-year-old Felicia Norgrove is held captive, Cleland writes:

> And here, as nothing can be more aukward than going on with presenting to the mind what it has already pre-conceived, I might dispense myself with proceeding in this narrative. The reader is by this time somewhat relieved from his pain for innocence in danger, and will naturally have anticipated the rescue to come from Lord Veramore: But as the conclusion cannot well be told without the connexion of the intermediate particulars, a specification of them will, I hope, be forgiven in favor of that necessity. (109–110)

But if the ending is obvious, the difficulty, as Congreve wrote, lies in "bringing it to pass, maugre all apparent obstacles"—the most intractable of which is that Veramore, after falling in love with Felicia at first sight, has convinced himself she's a whore, and has come to the house (in fact a brothel) not to rescue but to "have" her at any cost and so debase her for having, as he thinks, deceived him into thinking her worthy of his love. The story turns out, that is, to hinge on the psychopathology of masculine other-sex desire. Veramore, as his name suggests, is like Sir William Delamore in the *Coxcomb*, and like Sir William's, his name is belied by his shaky grasp of the distinction between true and false love. He has fallen in love with Felicia after a single encounter in a theater, in spite of her near-complete silence; he has then leapt to the conclusion that she is a whore on equally paltry evidence. What is strange is that, disdaining her as a whore, he "conceiv[es] so fierce a desire, that he could not himself account for it" (108). Accustomed to treating women with offhand contempt—"he had, in the course of his dealings with the women, found it much easier to get them than to get rid of them" (73)—with Felicia he is split between the extremes of "love" based on only a visual impression and "desire" based on resentment and jealousy (he imagines she is the whore of another man, Sir Thomas Darkfield). Cleland so contrives events as to make Veramore realize his error, break down the door behind which Sir Thomas is about to rape Felicia, reunite her with her family, and take her as his wife. But before this "pretty tale" arrives at its inevitable end, it has exposed its hero as scarcely less "profligate" and "abandoned" (107) than its villain, making his avowed "constancy" ring a little false, especially given the extreme emotional inconstancy to which he has been prey throughout. There is a glint of the sardonic in the story's last sentence, where Cleland writes that Veramore "made it the great and pleasing care of his life, that she should have no cause to remember but with satisfaction, the storm that, in the Covent-Garden adventure of that memorable night, had so fortunately brought her into port" (150). Not only does this make it sound as if he spends his life reminding her of what must have been a terrifying ordeal, but with its verbal echo of the *Woman of Pleasure* ("Thus, at length, I got snug into port" [187]) it affiliates Felicia with Fanny, both of them "saved" from brothels by men who mistook them for whores and desired them as such.

The four romances of the *Surprises of Love*, then—as superficial, old-fashioned, escapist, and predictable as they undeniably are and aim to be—are also studies in the perverse, slyly disenchanted essays in the vagaries of romantic desire and the "pretty" contrivances of romantic fiction. Neither as outrageous and satirical as the *Woman of Pleasure* nor as unfinished in form as the *Coxcomb*, and far more decorous in their representation of eros than either, the *Surprises* nevertheless *fret* the surfaces of the romantic fantasies they retail, stirring in odd discordant notes that hint at more troubled, or capricious, undercurrents of desire. In *The Romance of a Day*, for example, the soon-to-be lovers, Frederic and Letitia, children of wealthy suburban gentlemen, each separately go in disguise to Greenwich Park—he as "a Sugar-Baker's 'prentice in the City, just out of his time" (28), she as a maid—in order to frolic with the commoners. As in Eliza Haywood's 1725 *Fantomina; or, Love in a Maze*, their slumming is not just idle or innocent play but an expression of illicit desire, a foray into underclass urban sex tourism. Cleland's Frederic mingles with the "subaltern class" of women in order to experience a degree of sexual freedom unattainable among the women of his own class:

> The half-advances and half-repulses of some, the skittish wildness, or the tractable tameness of others, the gentle glow in all of working nature, yet exalted by the conspiring heat of the weather and exercise, opportune trips and provoking falls on the green, on purpose to be taken up again by so pretty a fellow as Frederic; all this scene, in short, of low, if what is natural can be called low, merriment, had not even unsensually affected him. (9)

Cleland's perspective on the relation between sexuality and social class is not easy to pin down: if he celebrates the "subaltern class" as "natural" (exuding "the gentle glow . . . of working nature") and so not properly speaking "low" at all but rather sensually "affect[ing]," in Frederic and Letitia he links sexual desirability to social privilege. "A pair so extremely handsome and so well matched," Cleland writes, "struck all present . . . In short, there was a general murmur of extorted applause, for almost all were displeased, since the men, as the old song says, all wished to be in his place, and all the women in hers" (21). Both Frederic and Letitia, however, like Fantomina, "hav[e] the same design, that of conceal-ing their real condition of life from one another" (34), and if their sexual allure corresponds to their social rank, they need to conceal the latter to give free rein to the desires unleashed by the former. We learn at the end of the tale that their fathers are neighbors on Blackheath and have made plans for them to marry. This being so, the absurd implausibility of their never having met before their "adventure" in Greenwich Park might actually suggest a counternarrative: that, like Fantomina and Beauplaisir, they *have* met, in the suburban drawing rooms they were brought up to inhabit, but that only by assuming an identity beneath "their real condition," and escaping to "such a place of vulgar and not always decent mirth" (15) as the park can they respond to one another in a "natural," not necessarily "decent," manner. For these high-born suburbanites, erotic de-sire is fueled by the fiction that the other is a low-born stranger.

Like the other three stories in *The Surprises of Love, The Romance of a Day* moves to its happy ending by way of earnest reflections on the superiority of vir-tuous love to "debauchery" in all its beguiling but ultimately delusive forms. It is in these passages that Cleland might most plausibly be called a "sentimental" author, taking "sentimental" to mean expressing moral sentiments or precepts. It would be hard to make a case for his fiction as "sentimental" in the sense of aiming to touch the reader's heart or elicit tears; there is nothing here of the "true pathos" for which one writer in the *Sentimental Magazine* praised the scene of Le Fever's death in Sterne's *Tristram Shandy*, and which other readers sought in the novels of Richardson and Mackenzie.[56] Instead, we are treated to passages such as this, near the end of *The Romance of a Night*, after Veramore has rescued Felicia and given up his plan to pay for sex with her:

> He could not dissemble to himself, that all the joys he had hitherto experienced, in giving way to the temptations of gallantry, or of merely sensual appetite, never deserved, even in the light of voluptuousness, to enter into ballance against the exquisite sensations that were now opening a new world of pleasure to him in his heart: A pleasure, which, not excluding desires, nor setting them above virtue, like that, resided in a just medium, between the coarseness of a brutal appetite, and the chimerical pretensions of Platonism; defended from either extreme, by the senti-ments of honor and of nature. (138–139)

Such "tail-pieces of morality" are a constant in Cleland's work, and this is un-doubtedly a sentiment he meant the reader to take seriously; but he also under-cuts it by conveying it in the discourse of some very unreliable moral teachers. Veramore, although changeable and internally divided, is not a fully developed novelistic character like Fanny Hill, and it might be misguided to read his sud-den moral sententiousness too skeptically; we might agree instead with the critic in the *Monthly Review* who found the story's "moral unexceptionable."⁵⁷ Yet the pattern of allusions to Cleland's earlier fiction, with its "smack of dis-sipated manners," and to other stories within the *Surprises*, makes it difficult to take such a passage at face value.⁵⁸ The echo of Delamore in Veramore, for instance, hints at an ironic inflection to the name, while the echo of Fanny in Felicia's being brought snug "into port" reinforces her affinity to the woman of pleasure Veramore has angrily, excitedly taken her to be. If Veramore is a genuine convert to virtue, it is curious that the villain of the next story, *The Romance of a Morning*, is explicitly likened to him. Driven by resentment and jealousy, "Mr. Grubling" is determined to have the heroine, Isabella, for him-self, and as Cleland writes, "He would have yielded just in the moment's fit of sensuality, and with not a jot more delicacy, than under the like provocations of disappointed desire, and piqued vanity, he would have taken a wife out of a C—— g—— Bagnio" (182). But this is exactly what Veramore has done, driven by the same impulses, in the same place. Such parallels do not invalidate the sentiment Veramore expresses, but they insinuate that he may not merit the moral authority he assumes.

So it goes in the other romances: in each, the protagonist's moral reflections are playfully subverted by an authorial aside or narrative incongruity, leading us to question the sentiments so earnestly expressed. In *The Romance of a Day*, Frederic, ennobled by his new love for Letitia (although he thinks her a serving maid), muses at length, as they walk through the park, on the superiority of true taste to debauched appetite, the sentiments of the heart to mere "possession," only for Cleland to cut in with this comment: "It is not however probable, that Frederic made, at that instant, all these reflexions; it was enough that he acted as if he had made them" (45).The moral self-consciousness of the characters in didactic romance is pure contrivance, Cleland steps out of the tale to tell us, inciting us to wonder what Frederic might more "probabl[y]" have been think-ing, or what it could mean to act "as if he had made" the reflections ascribed to him. In *The Romance of a Morning*, the hero, Mr. Vincent, has fallen in love with a disinherited sixteen-year-old orphan, Isabella, now serving as a lady's paid companion, and this has thrown him into a quandary, on which he, too, reflects at length. Of Isabella, he suggests that "there is nothing throws more beauty into the face and person, than the goodness of the heart. Sentiments are your best cosmetic" (170). As is typical in romance, inner (goodness) and outer (beauty) are in seeming harmony, even if the word "cosmetic" adds an incongruous whiff of artifice, as if sentiments were a kind of makeup or mask. This ambiguity only increases as Vincent worries over the ethical and social implications of loving a virtuous but penniless girl. "The ridicule of falling in love with a Pamela," he begins, invoking the story's most familiar literary precursor, "would, it is true, have nearly appeared as much a ridicule to him as to any one; But such is the nature of the Passions, while they trample on Reason, to keep, however, all the measures they can with her. It is on their knees to her that they depose her" (178). This passage, half inside and half outside the character's consciousness, is a little tour de force of equivocation. It offers the usual antithesis of passion and reason, in this case love versus social decorum or prudence, and Vincent seems to be heading to the usual judgment: that passion needs to submit to reason. But from the outset, he hedges, as when he allows that falling in love with a Pamela *"would . . . have nearly appeared* as much a ridicule to him as to any one." Clearly it does not appear so to him, and in the second half of this sentence Cleland shifts away from Vincent's voice to anatomize his motives and the larger struggle between two warring forces. It is "the nature of the Passions" to "trample on Reason," but these personified passions are cunning enough to "keep . . . all the measures they can with her," as if to hide from the subject what he is really doing. Reason is Queen, and the Passions get "on their knees to her," but only to trample and "depose her." They needn't even "pay a real homage to her," Cleland writes, for "the shadow of it serves their turn." The Passions are Machiavellian, ruthless in turning the dumb show of submission to Reason (getting "on their knees to her") to their own ends. Vincent justifies his desire for this Pamela as a way of setting right "the outrages of fortune to her" (179): she should have been an heiress, not a servant. "But all this time," Cleland observes, "he took special care not to tell himself that, but for the power of her exquisite beauty, such a thought would have probably never entered into his head. In short, even our virtues are often more interested than we imagine." All Vincent's reflections on the proper relations between reason and passion are a cosmetic discourse—useful in the short term to conceal his real motives, but only from himself.

The final story, *The Romance of an Evening*, is the most complex in plot and edges closest to tragedy. It starts with the hero, Sir Lionel Heartly, saving the heroine, Melicent, from drowning, after the boat in which she is traveling overturns—a mishap that causes the death by drowning of another passenger, an old woman, and later the death of a third from the effects of cold. Our sense of the near approach of calamity only increases when we learn that the boat was the vehicle of a conspiracy to kidnap Melicent by the brutal, drunken Squire Bullurst, who meant to rape her, and the old woman who drowned, the wicked faux-religious hypocrite Mrs. Crape, who planned to keep her imprisoned as a whore in a London brothel. In this "pretty tale," the good are easily duped (Melicent and the woman she thinks is her mother believe the old bawd Mrs. Crape to be "a character of sanctity and devotion" [234]), while evil is undone only by accident. By the end, of course, virtue and true love triumph, but there is some danger that even the virtuous Sir Lionel could be driven to crime by illicit desire. Having saved the unconscious Melicent, he lays her on the riverbank, and as Cleland writes, "Nay, even the pity itself, so essentially due to the condition which she was in, was absorbed by a passion which was but the more violent for its being the first time of his life that he had felt it" (219). Here, too, Cleland echoes a scene from the *Woman of Pleasure*: the story that Fanny's fellow whore Harriet tells of her deflowering by a young man who found her unconscious on a riverbank and, trying to revive her but unable to "govern his passion" (104), raped her instead. The possibility that Sir Lionel's "passion" might also be too "violent" to govern has been raised in an earlier passage, in which Cleland tells us that, as Sir Lionel has never yet been attracted to a woman, "the first object that should raise the passion of love in him, would carry him beyond any bounds of reason" (213). Carried "beyond any bounds of reason" by "violent" passion, even Sir Lionel could act the part of Squire Bullurst or Harriet's ravisher; that he does not may be due less to virtue or reason than to circumstance (there are other people nearby). Melicent revives, but the threat of the illicit does not disappear, for no sooner have they fallen in love than they discover they are brother and sister. No "bound of reason" is more inviolable than the incest taboo, yet we know "the passion of love" can carry Sir Lionel "beyond any bounds." His character, then, makes such a transgression possible, while romance conventions, and the tale's suavity of tone, rule it out. This tension between two possible plotlines, one criminal, one chaste, generates the story's passage of greatest emotional intensity, when Sir Lionel, rather than expressing relief that he didn't learn the truth too late, bewails his misfortune, his violent passion unchecked. It is at this point that his mother turns the tragic story on its head: "As mournful, as pathetic as was the tone with which he pronounced this conclusion, and as much as Lady Heartly was herself penetrated with the worthiness of his sentiments, she could not help bursting out into a loud laugh" (260). Even if we read this as just a vivid way of confirming what other eighteenth-century stories of incest averted, like *Joseph Andrews* or *Tom Jones*, may have led us to expect—that Lionel and Melicent are not in fact brother and sister—Lady Heartly's reaction is jarring. Instead of the tender smile or comforting embrace her name seems to promise, she *"burst[s] out into a loud* laugh," both verb and adjective out of keeping with the story's genteel setting and her son's "mournful," "pathetic" lament. Her loud laugh disrupts the pathos of the scene and seems to mock "the worthiness of his sentiments": as in all the *Surprises*, worthy sentiment is undermined by the intrusion of irony or laughter.

Cleland takes pains in the last lines of *The Romance of an Evening* to reaffirm the triumph of virtue, writing that "the enjoyments of virtuous love, spiritualized by sentiment, partake of the immortality of their parent, the soul" (273–274) and concluding that "Vice may, indeed, sometimes give what is falsely called pleasure; but it is only for Virtue to give what is truly called Happiness." It would be perverse to deny that this is the author's real sentiment, but equally so to overlook all the ironies and doubts that encircle it. In these stories, happiness depends less on virtue than accident: fortuitous meetings, timely discoveries, the lucky deaths that ensure a hero will inherit a fortune. It is only in a literal sense that the *Surprises* can be labeled "chaste," as they were in the *Monthly Review*, for while no Sadean "Crimes of Love" are committed between its covers, such crimes play at the margins of the text, threatening the safety and virtue of male and female characters alike.[59] At the same time, the melodramatic and tragic are kept at bay by the "low merriment" (9) and "loud laughs" (9) that punctuate the stories, and the "dazzling fretwork" of Cleland's rococo style.

The Cure of Love

Following the success of *The Surprises of Love*, the collection's publishers, Lowndes and Nicoll, contracted with Cleland to produce a three-volume novel.[60] He was paid a first advance of ten guineas in March 1765, three months after the *Surprises* appeared, although it was to take him nearly three years to deliver the completed text of *The Woman of Honor*, which finally came out in early 1768. As things turned out, *The Woman of Honor* was a critical and commercial failure, and more or less marked the end of Cleland's authorial career: only the two supplements to *The Way to Things by Words* and a stream of pseudonymous political letters to the *Public Advertiser* in the 1770s and 1780s were to follow. The writer for the *Critical Review* deplored Cleland's reliance on the clichés of sentimental romance: "The same dull round again, of perfect, and therefore insipid and uninteresting, characters . . . the same jarring affections,—in short, the same hotch-potch of sentiment, adventure, and intrigue."[61] The critic for the *Monthly Review* interestingly suggested that the plot had "been woven together merely to serve as a vehicle of conveyance between the author and reader," not specifying what Cleland was conveying. But the author seems never to have found his reader: the only other critic to write on *The Woman of Honor* since 1768 is William Epstein, in his 1974 biography; perhaps no one else has read it. Epstein seconds the early reviews, writing that "numerous digressions inter-rupt and at times overshadow the chief narrative line, creating a haphazard and even whimsical structure," and that the novel's characters "are all stereotypes, acting out their roles like mechanical puppets."[62] My goal is not to challenge these claims but to reframe them, to make a case for *The Woman of Honor* as a text whose formal strangeness, wavering plot, and near-lifeless characters show Cleland pushing against the boundaries of the novel-romance form in a deliberately awkward, alienating way, as if to shake readers free from their absorption in what one of its multiple narrators calls "the imaginary spaces of fiction and chimæra."[63]

Like the *Woman of Pleasure* and *Coxcomb*, Cleland's third novel has for its protagonist an orphan, Clara Maynwaring, who travels from the provinces to London, comes into contact with a range of vicious and virtuous characters, and achieves conjugal felicity with an exemplary other-sex partner. Unlike the two *Memoirs*, it is epistolary in form, its thirty-nine letters divided among ten character-authors and written over an indeterminate period of time—several months to a year, perhaps. This temporal indeterminacy represents a move-ment away from Cleland's precise accounting of time in his first novel, and from the Richardsonian model of epistolary realism, which in other respects *The Woman of Honor* seems to follow. Especially in its first volume, *The Woman of Honor* imitates Richardson's *Clarissa* in the cropped names of its heroine and her rakish pursuer—Clara from Clarissa, Lovell a truncated Lovelace—and in its plot of sexual entrapment, disclosed in letters from Lovell to his fellow rake Golding. Clara, Lovell, and Golding are rather down-market copies of Clarissa, Lovelace, and Belford. Clara is beautiful, virtuous, and accomplished but has only a small legacy from an uncle who died bankrupt. Lovell is an aristocratic seducer but is derided by Clara's guardian as "a most consummate coxcomb" (1:81), "afraid of the ridicule of idiots for not resembling them" (1:151); even his sexual conquests, including "the stale battered Countess of Flauntantribus, of whom half the town had been sick these ten years" (1:161), are distinctly unimpressive. His sidekick Golding is an ignoramus and toady, "vulgar and illiterate to the last degree" (1:178). Lovell and Golding embody the theory of fiction Cleland articulated in his early critical writings—that the novelist should "[paint] the corruptions of mankind, and the world, *not as it should be, but as it really exists*"—whereas Clara exemplifies Johnson's argument that fiction should provide the reader with virtuous models for imitation.[64] In that light, *The Woman of Honor* could be viewed as an attempt to reconcile two competing strains of novelistic realism. Yet in other ways, as with the novel's vagueness as to time, Cleland breaks with the norms of realist fiction: the characters lack psychological verisimilitude or depth; the plot is discontinuous, and our expectation of development or suspense is repeatedly thwarted; many of the letters are discursive rather than narrative and have nothing to do with the story; the romantic hero is not introduced until halfway through the final volume. The letters in *The Woman of Honor* breach the conventions of literary realism in ways that make for a discomfiting reading experience.[65]

This is nowhere clearer than in the representation of Clara, the woman of honor herself. She—or as Joel Weinsheimer wittily calls Austen's Emma Woodhouse, "it"—embodies Epstein's claim that Cleland "failed to explain his characters' inner motivations in intimate detail, to invest their thoughts and actions with a credible psychological reality."[66] I basically agree, but would substitute *refused* or *declined* for "failed," as Cleland rejects Richardson's principal strategy for creating the illusion of access to his characters' supposed interiority: bringing the reader up close to the first-person "presence" of the character in the act of writing. As an early admirer of Richardson (perhaps with Richardson's help) wrote in a preface to *Pamela*, "The Letters being written under the immediate Impression of every Circumstance which occasioned them . . . the several Passions of the Mind must, of course, be more affectingly described . . . than can possibly be found in a Detail of Actions long past."[67] In *Pamela* and *Clarissa*—for all the complexity, in the latter, of Richardson's orchestration of multiple voices and narratives—by far the dominant voice is the heroine's, and by far her chief concern is the analysis of her own motives and actions. In *The Woman of Honor*, by contrast, Cleland adopts Richardson's epistolary format but does away with any first-person account of "the several Passions of the [heroine's] Mind." Clara's letters are perfunctory and unreflective, and she is immune to self-analysis or self-description. In the final volume there is only one note from Clara, an addendum to two very long letters in which her brother-in-law, Edward Mellefont, tells her London guardian, Mrs. Buckley, that Clara has fallen in love with a Lancashire neighbor's son, Leonard Sumners. But Clara herself says nothing of her "Passions" and not a word of Leonard Sumners, only offering the worthy sentiment that "love is never so strong, so invincible, as when it is a virtue" (3:187). For the last hundred pages, Clara writes nothing. This may be a daring experiment, or a bad miscalculation, but it is not an oversight: Cleland rigorously excludes any opportunity for the characters, especially Clara, to give voice to an inner life of feeling.

Adopting the form of a dialogical collection of letters but evacuating it of what Richardson thought to be its heart—the illusion of unmediated access to the interior life of characters produced by writing to the moment—Cleland keeps his protagonist at a disconcerting narrative and emotional distance. The effect is twofold: first, Clara is displaced as the center of narrative interest; second, she becomes an emblematic figure of *passionlessness*, the absence or repression of feeling, which emerges early as one of the novel's key motifs. Even though Mrs. Buckley writes on first meeting her that "with all the charms of innocence and sweetness, you see her heart breathing in every gesture, every motion, every word" (74)—an epidermal transparency that establishes Clara's fitness to be a heroine of sentimental romance—Clara utterly rejects the claims of love. When her friend Lady Harriet Lovell (the rake's sister) excitedly tells her she is engaged to marry the aptly named Marquess of Soberton, Clara writes of her own indifference to love and her inability to share Harriet's enthusiasm (letter 4). At this point, we might suspect this is a way of alerting the reader to anticipate Clara's eventual, inevitable fall into love, and in part, it is. But for the first two and a half volumes of this three-volume novel, she registers no feeling, even antipathy, to any of the men lining up to court her. The sheer repetitiveness of her refusals, in line with Cleland's refusal to give any access to the character's presumed inner life or thoughts, means she has no story of her own: no secrets, no doubts, no desires, no unconscious. Instead, she embodies what the novel presents as a rejection of, or incapacity to feel, love; and while this is portrayed at first as a sort of damage that needs to be repaired, it later offers itself as the solution to the problem of love itself, which comes to be associated with the delusive promises of fiction.

In the same early letter in which Clara declares her indifference to love, she writes that Mrs. Buckley, when shown some letters from Soberton to Harriet, found in them "not the shadow of sentiment, nor a spark of love" (91). If Clara's indifference can be read as a form of conventionally feminine modesty, Soberton's "spark"-lessness is both unromantic and unmasculine. His failure of love or desire—Harriet, too, expresses regret that he's not a more ardent lover (letter 19)—poses a threat to the prospect of a happy marriage, and it is telling that this failure is initially juxtaposed to Clara's indifference, for it suggests that neither of them is capable of "natural" feelings or desires. Whether either will experience some form of erotic or romantic awakening, and with or for whom, are key questions the plot is designed to answer; but well into the second volume, *The Woman of Honor* is less a sentimental romance than a novel of insensibility, a story of sexual dispassion.

With Clara seemingly immune to desire, the narrative interest of the first volume rests with the cut-rate rake Lovell, who in his first letter to Golding is already hatching plots to entrap her. If this story line is taken from *Clarissa*, so is the tension between rakish insouciance and glimmers of genuine feeling, as when he describes himself as "planet-struck" (117) by his first sight of Clara. This avowal belies Mrs. Buckley's claim that he is unable to love. "Beauty may give Lord Lovell desires, because he has eyes," she writes, "but never love, because he has no heart; he may possibly know the gross pleasures of sensation; but never the voluptuous raptures of sentiment" (166). This is a variation on the motif of passionlessness, but if, like Soberton and Clara, Lovell is deficient in love, at least he's stirred by desires. More important, he has space in the text to articulate those desires. Soberton and Clara are cordoned off from the reader— no letter from Soberton appears till near the end of the second volume, not even the letters scrutinized by Mrs. Buckley for "shadow[s] of sentiment"—but Lovell puts his feelings on paper, even hints he's revealing more of himself than he'd like, as when he writes of Clara, "I have been trying to establish my point with this strange, perverse, what shall I call her, Angel, for that word is at the end of my pen, and places itself on the paper, almost without my leave" (1:230). Notwithstanding Mrs. Buckley's verdict, we actually see more, and more convincing, signs of a capacity to love from Lovell in the novel's first two volumes than from either Soberton or Clara.

Nevertheless, he tries to play the rake, and it is as "a perfect Matchavell at intreagues" (1:242), as his "illiterate" friend Golding calls him, that Lovell drives the novel forward. Such, at least, is the expectation Cleland creates in the first half dozen letters. But when we see the plotter in action, any sense of danger or suspense collapses. His "Machiavellian" scheme amounts to no more than a bid to bribe Mrs. Buckley to let him kidnap Clara. A sorrier seduction plot would be hard to devise, and the likeness to Lovelace drains away as, after Clara refuses to see him, the mortified Lovell turns to drink, is injured in a tavern brawl, and falls into a dangerous, rather feminizing, fever. Cleland short-circuits the libertine seduction narrative, stripping the seducer of all his glamour and cunning and emptying his plot of any threat. Lovell's intrigues neither test nor endanger the novel's heroine, and his abrupt collapse leaves the novel foundering, as there is no other plot on offer. His fever leads to an equally abrupt reformation, and although he writes that Clara has reawakened his heart and made him "sensible of the dignity of my being" (2:166), he makes no effort to prove his love or even see her again; instead, by the novel's end he has gone abroad to repeat his grand tour. This may seem a strange way to close the novel's libertine seduction plot, but is in keeping with the theme of passionlessness and the corresponding formal strategy of distancing, as we only hear of Lovell's travel plans at third hand, in a letter from Mrs. Buckley to Mellefont. In going to the Continent, Lovell is removing himself from Clara, the object of his desire, and the proof of his reform or cure is the geographical, affective, and narrative distance that marks the suppression of all unruly or disruptive feeling. In effect, he has become another Soberton, earlier praised by Mrs. Buckley for having conducted himself properly on *his* grand tour, in particular for having avoided the "stupid circle of pandars, buona-robas, opera-singers, the canaglia virtuosa, mumping *Cicerones*, [and] silly cicisbeos" (2:85–86). At least four of the terms on this list refer to illicit sexuality—*pandars, buona-robas* (fancy-dress prostitutes), *opera singers* (either castrati, viewed as sexually available, or female singers, often affiliated, like actresses, with whores), and *cicisbeos* (gigolos or kept boys). Soberton's propriety, and now Lovell's, is tied to sexual self-regulation. But such self-regulation, for him, is inseparable from an inability to love, an absence of passion. It is as if the only cure for sexual excess is the extirpation of all desire.

This cheerless prescription is repeated in the novel's next movement when, after Lovell has been dismissed from the text, a new suitor for Clara's love appears: none other than Soberton himself. Clara seems to have awakened feelings in him that Harriet could not, for with *his* first letter, to his friend Launcelot Greville, he encloses a note in which he declares his love to Clara and proposes to break off his engagement to Harriet. Now that he wants Clara, Soberton replaces Lovell as the novel's center of attention, for in fiction, at least, desire is the motive force, the focus of all interest. This plot turn potentially puts the text's two paragons of virtue in compromising positions: they seem ideally suited to one another, yet they both have obligations to Harriet, who has encouraged their intimacy. But once again, Cleland short-circuits his own plot, enclosing Clara's refusal of Soberton in the same letter in which we learn of his proposal to her. Of course, Clara's written refusal could mask some degree of interior conflict on her part and could prove to be just one in a series of moves through which this new intrigue is played out. As before, however, Cleland denies the reader any other access to Clara's thoughts than her short letter of refusal, and when Soberton is told she has returned to Lancashire, he simply, instantly ceases to love her. He resolves to marry Harriet immediately and asserts that he really loves her, not Clara after all. Yet his putative love for Harriet seems more like a regression to his original state of passionlessness than a mature recognition of true feeling. Giving up any claim on Clara, he writes Greville that "I sin against all the laws of romance"; but "leaving that pleasant statute of the Love-code to its proper authority in the imaginary spaces of fiction and chimæra, I am not in the least afraid of submitting this recovery of my false step, to the decisions of Reason and even of Love" (3:72). That last phrase is perplexing: while it seems to hold open the possibility of love affiliated with reason, the overall burden of the sentence is to relegate love, and the "pleasant statute of the Love-code," to "the imaginary spaces of fiction and chimæra." Love, Soberton seems to claim, or hope, has no reality apart from the delusive conventions of literary romance.

Cured of his destabilizing passion, Soberton, like Lovell, is dismissed from the text: he writes no more letters, and no more is said of his love for Clara, Harriet, or anyone else. The last movement of the novel introduces Clara's third suitor: Leonard, a beautiful, wounded youth, newly orphaned, whom Clara nurses back to health. Even more than Fanny Hill's Charles, Leonard is Cleland's fantasy-ideal of the masculine hero. His father taught him so well that he is "a perfect master" of all "parts of learning, in all objects of the human inquiry" (3:169). Moreover, having grown up in Canada, where his father was stationed, he is so athletic that as a boy he surpassed

> the savages themselves in all the points of bodily agility, dexterity, and valor, which they esteem so essential a part of personal merit. He was barely fourteen when he could outstrip the fleetest of them at running, or defy them to out-swim him in the roughest lakes, or cross the stream at a tremendously small distance [above the falls] at the stream of Niagara . . . He was not superior to them only in the chace of the fox, the moose, or the elk, but would attack with more open intrepidity the bear and the panther. (3:139–140)

Cleland's hero combines intellectual and physical prowess, savage and civilized arts, European and (Native) American cultural values. He is both courageous— at fifteen years old, he fought alongside his father at the 1759 battle of Quebec— and humane: after the battle, he tended the British and the French alike, even saving a wounded French soldier from the violence of a brutal British one. He is also, needless to say, physically perfect: "In harmony with his face is the whole of his form, cast in the most exquisite model for shape, stature, and proportion" (3:165). But in keeping with the approach Cleland has taken throughout the novel, all of this is reported at third hand, in two very long letters from Mellefont to Mrs. Buckley, while Clara writes nothing. All Cleland gives us is Mellefont's observation that when she is with Leonard, Clara displays "a certain melancholic tenderness, such as I had never remarked in [her looks] before" (3:167–168). Seen only through its visible external symptoms or signs, Clara's awakening to love is not allowed to touch or engage the reader but is kept mute, held back.

The one moment in which feeling threatens to break through restraint comes in the novel's last letter, from Leonard to his friend Charles, in which he recounts in detail the scene of his declaration of love to Clara. Love, as he tells it, is instantaneous: "surely the most consummately ill-bred clown could hardly have exhibited a broader stare of surprize and wonder, at any object, than I did, just then, at the first sight of this miracle of beauty . . . It was a blaze that overpowered me: a rapture that kept my eyes motionless, and fixt on the divinest face that in my life I ever beheld" (3:251–252). This is love according to what Soberton contemptuously dismissed as "the laws of romance," and it blots out language, motion, even sentience. In short order, he proposes marriage. "But when I expected her answer," he writes, "she gave me no other than that of bursting out into tears and deep sighs" (3:260). It is the only time Clara loses control, the sole moment in which passion "burst[s] out," in the inarticulate form of tears and sighs, and it is soon over. That single outburst attests both to the rawness of feeling and to the severity of its repression elsewhere in the novel. Clara's love looks very much like anguish—she has earlier called it a "dangerous passion" (3:184)—and Leonard, too, warns that "lovers believe everything like children, or break through every thing like madmen" (3:257). The dangers of childish credulity and destructive madness, Clara writes in her only letter in the novel's last volume, are especially threatening to women, "so commonly doomed to the fatal alternative of being sacrificed or betraid!" (3:185), and her outburst of sighs and tears reflects that pained recognition. While the novel swiftly moves on from this moment of emotional surfeit to a happy ending with the couple married "under the united auspices of Love and Honor" (3:272), it can do so only because Clara reins in passion—never expressing it in writing, in fact never writing again.

When Mellefont tells Mrs. Buckley that Clara and Leonard have fallen in love, he playfully cites a literary precursor: "Our Angelica has, I fancy, found her Medoro" (3:182). Angelica is the "pagan" object of the Christian knight Orlando's unrequited love in Ariosto's sixteenth-century epic *Orlando Furioso*. When she elopes with a wounded Saracen knight, Medoro, whom she has nursed back to health, Orlando goes mad (*furioso*). This story, which Cleland may also have known in Handel's operatic version (*Orlando*, 1733), parallels that of Clara nursing and falling in love with Leonard, although neither Soberton nor Lovell follows Orlando into madness. But an apprehension that all love is a kind of madness or loss of self—as Ariosto wrote, "che non è in somma amor, se non insania" (what is love, after all, if not madness)—lingers at the margins of Cleland's novel.[68] While Clara asserts that "love is never so strong, so invincible, as when it is a virtue," Cleland makes no effort to convey a sense of an interior emotional life to which we have access, and offers no evidence through Clara's writing or reported speech that would enable us to judge whether she is able to reconcile eros and reason, passion and virtue. Instead, we have only Mellefont's note to Mrs. Buckley that he has officiated at the wedding of "the thoroughly recovered Mr. Sumners to Clara Maynwaring" (3:272)—and the word "recovered," while obviously referring to his restoration to health after his injury, also echoes an earlier passage, when we were told that Soberton, after his brief detour into passion for Clara, had "recovered, without any danger of a relapse" (3:79). Eros is a kind of illness or insanity, a loss of mastery over the self, as Soberton was warned by both Clara and his friend Greville, and just as his "recovery" entailed his retreat into passionlessness, so may Clara's and Leonard's entail the damping down of feelings that threaten to burst out as "tears and deep sighs" or as "a blaze that overpowered me."

Or might it be that it is only in fiction that one can be paralyzed by rapture or driven mad by love? No literary text is more extravagantly fictional than *Orlando Furioso*, with its hippogriffs and journey to the moon, so Cleland's citation of it as a precursor to *The Woman of Honor* invites us to reflect on the playful artificiality of his own romantic fiction. Within the novel, several characters comment on the gap between literary romance and real life, as if they're trying to work out what kind of text they inhabit. In his last letter, Leonard dismisses the romantic cliché that a person can die of joy: "I now do not believe a sillable of its possibility, or I could never have survived the rapture into which this her acceptance of my suit now threw me" (3:262). But as with Sir William Delamore, his attempt to distance the "truth" of his own experience from the hackneyed conventions of popular fiction only draws attention to how closely he, too, adheres to the codes of romance, with its overpowering blazes and swoons of "rapture." Earlier in the novel, Soberton's friend Greville argues that passion, despite what "the modern Tragedy-writers, and Novelists" pretend, is not beyond control:

"the cure of Love, conquered by virtue, is not so extremely rare, as Poets, Novelists, and Romance-writers would persuade us, in their records of fancy and fiction" (3:57). Soberton, having undergone "the cure of Love" himself, agrees, as we have seen, that "the Love-code" has "its proper authority" only "in the imaginary spaces of fiction and chimæra" (3:72). But what other spaces can the fictional Marquess of Soberton inhabit? What code, if not "the Love-code," has authority in *The Woman of Honor*? The novel is nowhere more artificial than when its characters speak out against fictional artifice, as if by doing so they could make us forget they are fictions themselves.

In fact the romance strand is only part of the text, and at times it seems as if Cleland would be happy to leave it, and the love code it enacts, behind. The critic for the *Monthly Review* sensed that the romance plot was "woven together merely to serve as a vehicle of conveyance between the author and reader," and the profusion of essayistic digressions on topics utterly unrelated to the story—horse racing, pensions, mineral waters, boxing, the ancient British constitution, and so on—suggests that Cleland was bridling at, or bored with, the restrictions of the novel form. In the letter that opens the third volume, Soberton's friend Greville acknowledges that he is "unconscionably exceeding all the common limits of a letter" and has written, instead, "an epistolar pamphlet" (3:2). Cleland, too, has written a text that messily exceeds the common limits of epistolary romance, and not accidentally. Repeatedly drifting off course from the line of its own plot, *The Woman of Honor* is both a hackneyed romance and an aggressively misshapen antiromance, a set of scattershot attacks on the corruptions of upper-class life and a wry commentary on the consoling fictions of domestic felicity—a disenchanted farewell to fiction in the guise of a novel.

CHAPTER SEVEN

A Briton
(1757–1787)

I n one of *The Woman of Honor*'s deviations from the ready-made plotlines of romance, Mellefont launches into an attack on the practice of imprisonment for debt, whose chief misery, as Cleland knew well, is "corrosive grief for the coolness or desertion of tired-out friends" (3:117). The practice, Mellefont asserts, was unknown in ancient Britain, "to which the great bulwarks of liberty, the Trials by Juries, and other privileges of the common law, can be traced" (3:128), but was introduced by the invaders of imperial Rome. Caesar and his armies extinguished the liberties of ancient Britain and so ushered in, as Cleland writes in a text on which he worked in tandem with *The Woman of Honor*, "an universal darkness . . . which lasted till the Saxon Alfred, and other our Kings, sensible of the excellence of the Druidical plan, restored it, as far as it could be adapted to a feudal government." In this second text, *The Way to Things by Words, and to Words by Things*—published in 1766, two years before *The Woman of Honor* appeared but more than a year after it was contracted—Cleland made public the first sketchy results of his "attempt at the retrieval of the antient Celtic or primitive Language of Europe," a hugely ambitious task on which he worked until at least the end of the 1760s.[1] If Cleland's "curious tracts on the Celtic language," as his obituarist calls the three etymological studies he eventually published, seem far removed from the world of his fictions, both strands of Cleland's writing construct a fantasy-ideal of an original, physically vigorous, politically independent self: an ideal he grounds in the half-historical, half-mythic ancient Britain against which he measures the corruptions and debilities, both bodily and political, of the present day.[2]

Cleland's own imprisonment for debt—the originary moment of his authorial career—thus takes its place in a history of oppression going back to the Roman "extirpation of the Druids and their laws" (*Way*, 70). In *The Woman of Honor* it is Mellefont's friend Sumners who is unjustly confined for debt, while Sumners's son Leonard is raised in the wilds of America, in something like the still uncontaminated state of pre-Roman Britain. In Leonard, physical vigor—"all the points of bodily agility, dexterity, and valor" (3:139)—is joined to intellectual acuity and contempt for the degraded political and commercial values of what he calls "the WORLD" (3:248). The symbolic heart of that world is London's Exchange Alley, where unrestricted financial speculation has produced "an overflow of fictitious wealth . . . not the least of [whose] mischiefs" is "that of raising, on so crazy a bottom, the prices of all the necessaries of life, to the manifest injury of the community" (3:231–232).[3] That the fortune Leonard inherits from his granduncle Mr. Arnold is founded in just such financial speculation is an irony not lost on him, and this adds to the tonal dissonance of *The Woman of Honor* as a whole, in which the clichés of romance—here, the orphaned hero's sudden accession to wealth, which makes him a kind of prince to Clara's Cinderella—are interspersed with astringent essays on political economy and the degeneracy of modern manners. If *The Woman of Honor*'s loose plot and discursive waywardness signal its author's impatience with the codes of commercial fiction, they infuse that fiction with the urgency and inconclusiveness of political debate, centering on what Cleland saw as the "crazy" or broken state of contemporary Britain.

Cleland's later authorial career marks a turn away from the profession of novelist—even in his novels. In fact, he turns away from professionalism altogether: in contrast to his earlier self-presentation as a jobbing writer for bread, he adopts in his later work the persona of a man of letters or distracted gentleman-amateur. His energies in this period were focused on three main areas of enquiry: politics, physiology, and language. He addressed these in a variety of genres, from his baggy monster of a last novel to guidebooks on diet and exercise, from political letters in newspapers to collections of philological essays. Disavowing all interest in praise or fame, Cleland published this work in a deliberately rough state: "rather crude beginnings of ideas, or even *reveries*," as he put it in the aptly titled *Phisiological Reveries* (1765), "than proposed as clear and authenticated conceptions."[4] Similarly, he opens the first of his etymological texts, *The Way to Things by Words*, by acknowledging "the abruptness of the beginning of the first of the following Essays, the confusedness of the Sketch, the inaccuracies and repetitions in it, the incoherence of the whole" (i). "Why then," he imagines a disgruntled reader asking, "obtrude on the public so confessedly a crudity?" It was only, he answers, "to sound the opinion of competent judges, on the probability of my ideas upon the subject, that I threw them together in the loose undigested manner in which they now appear." Unable, because of "an incident, immaterial to specify here," to carry on his research in a more methodical manner, he was persuaded by "some gentlemen, to whom I had communicated the manuscript," and who "seemed to see in it some useful discoveries of literary lights, or at least the seeds of such discoveries," to publish it, "even at the point it stood" (i–ii). He publishes not to please himself or make money, but at the bidding of "gentlemen."

This echoes Cleland's account in the letter to Stanhope of his reasons for publishing the *Woman of Pleasure*, conceived "on an occasion immaterial to mention here" and sent to the press at the urgings of "some whose opinion I unfortunately preferred to my own."[5] In both cases, he shifts blame for the published text onto unnamed others and alludes to undisclosed "incidents" and "occasions" that are only the more intriguing for being dismissed as "immaterial" to specify or mention. But Cleland's apologies for his later work omit the appeal to the pressures of material distress that led him to publish the *Memoirs*. Instead, he portrays himself acting from disinterested motives, for the public good. So, in the introduction to his first physiological work, the 1761 *Institutes of Health*, he writes that he originally drew up his guidelines for better maintenance of bodily well-being "purely in the spirit of communicativeness to a few friends, whose attention to it was rather my wish for their own sake, in my firm belief of the efficacy of them, than my hope, so unsupported as they stand by any valid authority."[6] Imagining the wider potential benefit of his "rules" to the reading public, he writes that "I should have held myself inexcusable, if I had not offered them, at the risque of whatever treatment [readers] may choose to give them" (xxiv). Though he disclaims professional "authority" in medicine, just as he acknowledges the likely errors and incoherence of his etymological work, he asserts that his medical advice is founded on the just observation of

"Nature, that supreme standard of truth" (iv), unaffected by the "authority of names, however celebrated, however great" or by the "mere theory destitute of practice" (iii–iv) that vitiates his predecessors' work.

The "apologies" Cleland prefixes to his late writing, then, the disclaimers of professional expertise, are characteristically double sided. Although, as an amateur, he lacks the authority that membership in the medical profession would confer, as an outsider he regards such authority with suspicion. Indeed "the eminent writers of that profession" (vi) are "lamentably deficient" (viii): "they contradict not only one another but themselves, in so many of the most essential points that they increase that medical scepticism of which themselves so justly complain, and bewilder instead of fixing the judgment" (x). The expertise of the professional is the mirror image of the prejudice of the ignorant: both are in thrall to received wisdom, whether that conferred by "the authority of names" or the groundless prejudices of the unlearned. The most "eminent writers" on medicine, moreover, "have the strange weakness of distrusting the plainer and more obvious methods of treatment, such as are the instinctive suggestions of nature . . . only because they are plain and obvious: nor will any reasonings on the cause of their disorders, satisfy them so much as those that are the most abstruse and unintelligible" (85–86). This perverse emphasis on abstruseness for its own sake, on "mere theory destitute of practice," is a kind of professional *vanitas* that stands in the way of truth, and not only in the field of medicine. As Cleland writes in the second of his essays on language, *Specimen of an Etimological Vocabulary*, "It is, in short, with etimologists as it is with physicians, who cannot well be pronounced able and trust-worthy, till they are arrived at knowing all the fallacy and uncertainty of their art."[7] Taking up the same theme in his third etymological study, *Additional Articles to the Specimen of an Etimological Vocabulary*, he writes that the truths he discovered "were so contrary to generally received notions, that with so little authority as I . . . have any right to claim, I could not expect so much as the honors of examination."[8] But Cleland's contrariness to received wisdom is a function not of strangeness or difficulty but rather of simplicity: his "solutions appeared so plain, so obvious, that they could not be genuine" (xvii), his critics have objected. Yet "it was precisely that elementary simplicity," he writes, "that tempted me to hope I was in the right career."

As with physiology and language, so with politics: the later Cleland represents himself as an artist of disenchantment, a lone voice aiming to "undeceive" those in the grips of prejudices, whether of ignorance or of professional subservience to political party. He has no great hope of success: as he writes in a letter to the *Public Advertiser*, "If, Sir, there is a Piece of Quixotism more than ordinarily desperate and vain, it is surely that of aspiring to the Honor of exercising that most unthankfull, most unpleasing Office of an Undeceiver of a Populace possessed by a violent Prejudice, of which it is but too often the more tenacious the less Foundation there is for it."[9] But the overarching project that links all his late writing, including the fiction, is that of chipping away at the "wretched enslavement" (*Articles*, xvi) of received wisdom, even if the readers he aims to free regard him as "harping on a String so discordant and so grating."[10] Just as the self-contradictions of the most eminent medical texts "bewilder instead of fixing the judgment," so "the present Glut of Party-Polemics," as he writes in the *Public Advertiser* for 26 September 1765, "is fitter to nauseate and bewilder the Reader than to give him just Ideas of the real State of Things." Cleland, by contrast, avows "Scorn and Contempt for all Party-spirit whatever, either on the side of those who are in Power, or of those who are out of it" (*Pub. Adv.*, 19 Aug. 1765) and argues that "at a Time when there never was a more indispensable Necessity, for fixing clear Ideas of Things, it is humanly speaking impossible to attain to that Clearness without tracing Effects to their primary Causes" (*Pub. Adv.*, 12 Dec. 1765). This is the aim of all Cleland's late work: to "fix clear Ideas of Things" by "tracing Effects to their primary Causes," to scrape away the accretions of prejudice and habit in order to locate the foundations of bodily health, national identity, and the true meanings of words. His assault on the degeneracy of his own times takes the form of a search for lost origins.

"The Consummation of Our Own Ruin"

In a letter to his mother's lawyer, Edward Dickinson, in February 1757, Cleland writes, "I am sick even to death of Politics," and expresses his "real affliction" for "the wretched condition" of Britain in a period of ministerial oppression and of shifting, opportunistic alliances and wars. "No englishman who deserves to live," he continues, "would wish to live longer in this infamous and abandoned period."[11] Notwithstanding his sickness unto death, over the next thirty years he would write extensively on political topics, even if the custom of pseudonymous authorship of political essays makes it impossible to know for certain what and how much he wrote. In a journal entry for 31 March 1772, James Boswell writes that he ran into Cleland when visiting David Garrick, and observes that Cleland is "now the grave and prolix *Parliamentarian* in the newspapers."[12] From this passing remark, William Epstein infers that the political essays in the form of letters to the *Public Advertiser* signed "Parliamentarian" between August 1770 and February 1772 must be Cleland's. Epstein draws a similar conclusion from John Nichols's claim in his Cleland obituary that "Mr. C. . . . was the author of the *long* letters given in the public prints, from time to time, signed A BRITON, MODESTUS, &c. &c." But Nichols is not quite so reliable a source as Boswell, and "Modestus," as Epstein notes, "was a traditional political pseudonym, affected by a variety of writers," so it is less certain that the letters so signed in the *Public Advertiser* are Cleland's.[13] And uncertainty extends in the other direction, too: Boswell's plural "newspapers" and Nichols's "public prints" suggest that Cleland's political essays may have appeared in multiple journals, not just the *Public Advertiser*. Similarly, Nichols's "&c. &c." may point to other, now untraceable, pseudonyms. All of which means it is to some degree a matter of conjecture or hunch what Cleland actually wrote for the papers, and it seems likely that much remains to be identified.[14]

Beyond questions of attribution is the murkier question of whether Cleland's "political pen," as Epstein puts it, "was available for a price."[15] After Josiah Beckwith visited Cleland in 1781 to discuss his work on the ancient Celtic, he wrote, "The Author some Time since enjoyed a Place or Pension under Government of 200 £ a year," which might suggest he was expected to write in support of the government on a more or less regular basis.[16] But what does he mean by "some Time since"? And what are we to make of Beckwith's claim that Cleland's pension "was taken from him on Account of his Publications"? Which publications? Apparently, the works that lost Cleland his living were not those considered obscene or overtly political but rather the Celtic tracts, which, "treating Monarchical Government in so sarcastical a Manner," Beckwith speculates, "lost [the author] his Place or Pension."

If Beckwith is right, Cleland should have lost his pension in the later 1760s, after the Celtic tracts came out, but the vast majority of the letters signed "Parliamentarian," "Modestus," and "A Briton" in the *Public Advertiser* were written after 1770.[17] If anything, this supports Cleland's oft-repeated denial that he was in the pay of one or another ministry, or that he was induced to write by mercenary or partisan interests. Of course he may have been lying, or just fudging the truth of his position as a political hack. But the letters, far from selling the policies or merits of any particular ministry, are almost relentlessly negative, chronicling a political march of folly toward "the consummation of our own ruin, already too far advanced," as he puts it in what may have been the last of his published works, a letter signed "A Briton" that appeared in the *Public Advertiser* on 21 July 1787. In that letter, still bristling over the outcome of the American War of Independence, which saw Britain "abandoning her own loyal subjects, to the haggard intractability of the mock zealots for liberty in our perverted Colonies," Cleland laments the state of the commonwealth, "debased and reduced as she is, through her own follies, nearly to insignificance and nullity." Ending in "insignificance and nullity," Cleland's thirty-year public commentary on contemporary politics is less an exercise in partisan spin-doctoring than an ongoing jeremiad, in which the ideal of a robust political constitution is set against the ruinous practices of the governing classes of his own day, and of every party.

Notwithstanding his critique of all political factions, it is of course possible that Cleland was at one time (or at different times) writing for hire at the behest of one or more political masters. Epstein maintains that in 1762–1763 Cleland worked for the then–prime minister Lord Bute, writing pamphlets in support of Bute's "north British" administration for reasons of "profit, not principle."[18] And while the documentary evidence for this seems to be nil, there is a curious passage in Boswell's journal for 26 April 1778 in which, calling on Cleland six years after meeting him at Garrick's, he writes that Cleland "talked of Lord Bute having by the medium of Lord Melcombe proposed to have him as a *Cabinet* of himself to suggest for Government, and that he should have £1,200 a year."[19] It is hard to know what to make of this story, and Boswell says "I thought he raved" when Cleland told it to him. Why Bute, appointed prime minister in May 1762, or his ally George Bubb Dodington, created first Baron Melcombe by George III in 1761, would have approached Cleland with such a proposal—given his literary notoriety, professional obscurity, and political insignificance—is difficult to say, and since Cleland makes no mention of the offer anywhere else, it remains a wild and unlikely claim. Perhaps Bute or Melcombe made some vague, extravagant promises in order to coax Cleland to write, like his colleague Smollett, in support of the government. But by the next year Melcombe was dead, and Bute, who lasted less than a year as prime minister, had "shamefully disappointed [Cleland's] hopes," Boswell writes. It may be this disappointment that led to Cleland's scathing treatment of Bute ever after: in a letter to the *Public Advertiser* on 8 August 1765, Cleland as "A Briton" rails at Bute's "portentously stupid Inconsistence," which is "aggravated by a supercilious Gloom, and a kind of mean, low, frigid Cunning, the Triumph of which constantly was to deceive himself, and such as had been unfortunately led to trust him." If the last phrase may allude to a private sense of injury, however, the general tenor of Cleland's remarks is not far from what he wrote in his letters to Dickinson the decade before, of another government and another king: "The present men of power seem to the full as self-centered as their predecessors, only with more arrogance and bravado," he writes in one; in another, he says that the government is "without principles, without rules, without theory, and, above all, without the least spirit of dignity."[20] All in all, while the letters signed "Modestus" that Epstein attributes to Cleland do smack of writing for hire—in their defense of the king and his government against the "invectives" of such critics as the fiercely polemical "Junius"—they are quite unlike the work Cleland produced in his other political voices, especially in the authorial persona of "A Briton," whose pugnacious, impassioned, even overwrought responses to contemporary events is closest to the voice of Cleland's private letters and fiction.[21]

Unlike "Modestus" (9 letters from 1769 and 1770) and "A Parliamentarian" (33 letters from 1770 to 1772), "A Briton" published more than 150 letters in the *Public Advertiser* over a thirty-year period, writing on a vast range of topics. Nothing is so "ephemerical," to adopt Cleland's own word, as political commentary on current affairs, in which "the Impression of one Essay" is "instantly cancelled by that of another, beget[ting], at length," sheer "Indifference" (*Pub. Adv.*, 26 Sept. 1765). Yet while it would likely "nauseate and bewilder the Reader" to rehash Cleland's views on all the issues of the day, and while his sometimes "grave and prolix" style, as Boswell puts it, can be heavy going, Nichols's assessment—that when Cleland "touched politics, he touched it like a torpedo, he was cold, benumbing, and soporific"—is unduly dismissive. The *torpedo*, otherwise known as a crampfish or electric ray, stuns its enemies or prey into immobility with an electric shock, but Cleland's political writing is neither benumbing nor cold. Rather, it alternates between two registers: one feisty, scrappy, and cutting; the other ardent, idealizing, and lofty.

The first is reserved for the meanness of the present, as when he condemns Bute for his "private Ambition, in his hurry to grasp the ministerial Scepter, with a Lust for Power, surely not less ridiculous and vain in him, than the Rage of Eunuchs for the Fair Sex, without the least Ability to enjoy or do Justice to it" (*Pub. Adv.*, 8 Aug. 1765). In this passage the fairly conventional tactic of accusing a political enemy of unmanliness is given an extra twist, so that Bute's "Lust" for power is equated with the sexually impotent and so ridiculous "Rage of Eunuchs," the figuratively castrated Bute unable to "enjoy" the rewards of the phallic "Scepter" he uselessly "grasps"—a neat inversion of the mock-political rhetoric of "that peculiar scepter-member, which commands us all" (183) in the *Woman of Pleasure*. The second, more high-flown register in the letters of "A Briton" signals the declaration of his political ideals, which properly belong not to the present but to a conditional realm: a possible, if unlikely, future or a projected, if unreal, past. So, in the letter just quoted, after he has made a mockery of Bute, Cleland shifts into panegyric, extolling "the tutelary Authority of that great national Council . . . a free, uncorrupt Parliament," as a counterweight to the "private Ambition" of unmanly ministers. Only Parliament, "properly put into Motion," can "restore Lustre to the Crown, Confidence to our natural Allies, Tranquillity to this Country, Vigor to the Laws, and Stability to the Public-Good." Such a free and uncorrupt Parliament will not be found, however, in the Westminster of 1765, and never was to be found there. Nor, for all the rhetoric of restoration, was there ever a historical time when the crown was perfectly lustrous or the country perfectly tranquil. The time of luster, tranquility, and vigor is just beyond the horizon of historical time, in that ancient Britain Cleland sought to reconstruct through his etymological recuperation of the lost original Celtic.

Despite the sometimes exhortatory language of his political letters, Cleland as "A Briton" does not write as an advocate but as a kind of prophet, radically alienated from the political culture of his time, and articulating his political ideal in the face of its irreversible demise. So, for example, when he writes in February 1766 on the recent "Disturbances in America"—the rebellious reaction of the Sons of Liberty and others to the Stamp Act of 1765—he refers to the colonists as "American Britons" and offers this ideal vision of the Commonwealth:

> All the British Dominions however divided, by Situation, form nevertheless one great and indivisible political Body, of which what Hippocrates says of the human Body holds strictly true, that it has neither Beginning nor End, every Part being a Center to the rest and no Part an Extremity . . . Britons will be Britons in whatever Part of the Globe Chance may have decided their Birth; they will still be free, and consequently generous and grateful. (*Pub. Adv.*, 10 Feb. 1766)

Yet Cleland knew well that this "political Body" was divided by irreconcilable interests, that the government had been ungenerous and the colonists ungrateful, and that British North America had not only a determinate historical "Beginning" but a likely historical "End": the discourse of bodily indivisibility and integrity, or of what we might call "Briton-ness," is itself a product of the very "Disturbances" against which it offers itself as a bulwark. Similarly, when Cleland writes, in a letter from July 1764, "It is now more than half a Century, since the divided Names of English and Scots have justly given Place to the more glorious Appellation of *Britons*" (*Pub. Adv.*, 13 July 1764), he does so precisely because "the more glorious Appellation" has *not* prevailed, and because the English continue to disparage Scots, Scottish laws, and Scottish representation in Parliament.[22] The ideals of *Britain* and *Britons* are ideal insofar as they have never existed in reality, and all the more ideal as they recede ever further from reach.

One of the more striking features of Cleland's political orientation is that it never really changes, despite his ongoing, often heated investment in issues and events as they unfold. The time is always out of joint for him. The last lines of the last letter of "A Briton" look forward, prophetically, to "the consummation of our own ruin," and the letter's final words condemn the nation, as we have seen, to "insignificance and nullity." But thirty years earlier he had made the same point: "No englishman who deserves to live, would wish to live longer in this infamous and abandoned period." In that letter he wrote of his horror at the impending execution of Admiral Byng—victim, as Cleland believed, of a political show trial: "I almost envy poor Byng's state, if he is to be murthered as they say he is, and as I firmly believe from an infallible rule with me of predicting what is to be, from what ought *not* to be."[23] Reflecting on his critical-prophetic role—"predicting what is to be, from what ought *not* to be"—he writes, "Nor am I in the least comforted by my vanity at having seen the purport of *all* I repeat it *all* of my predictions verified by time and events, for my real affliction at the wretched condition of that country at whose expense they have been verified." There is no comfort in being right when all he foresees is the ruin of an abandoned political ideal, that of the British constitution. In another commentary on the disturbances in America—this one from 13 July 1776, after the onset of war—Cleland urges his own countrymen to "RESTORE, RESTORE the *Constitution* FIRST here; and then think of extending its benignant Influence to America!" (*Pub. Adv.*, 13 July 1776). But as the fervor and the rather histrionic typesetting of the passage suggest, it was already too late—not just too late to avert war, but too late to restore the constitution to a Britain that had long since lost the use of it.

A sense of too-lateness pervades Cleland's political writing, and in this respect, too, his work exhibits the spirit of Edward Said's "late style," indeed underlines an idea Said got from Adorno, that late style is "socially resistant."[24] Boswell's "old Cleland"—raving, grumbling, "a fine sly malcontent," who "keep[s] harping on a String so discordant and so grating," to the manifest displeasure of his audience—might be characterized, as Said characterizes Adorno, as "a figure of lateness itself, an untimely, scandalous, even catastrophic commentator on the present" (14).[25] Especially in the persona of "A Briton," Cleland prefigures Said's reading of Adorno as "very much a late figure because so much of what he does militated ferociously against his own time . . . It is the *Zeitgeist* that Adorno really loathed and that all his writing struggles mightily to insult" (22–23).For all the important and obvious differences between the two writers, they are alike to the degree that their common irascibility expresses not just a loathing of the spirit (or dispiritedness) of the times they lived in but a rigorous relegation of their own cultural ideal to an irrecoverable, heavily nostalgic but not really historical past: a kind of phantom nineteenth century for Adorno, pre-Roman Britain for Cleland. In a way, Cleland's lost world, though further removed in time, is actually less remote than Adorno's, since even the debased language of the present still carries some of its original poetic force, conveying a cultural ideal that, if not fully attainable *in* the present, expresses an imaginable alternative *to* it.

The Original Sense of Words

The intimations of catastrophe that Said locates in late style loom over Cleland's writing on language as much as they do his political screeds. He ends the "Advertisement" to the last of his linguistic studies by anticipating its likely failure in the face of "the amazing general futility of these wretched times; in which this nation, once the sanctuary of reason, and the head-seat of philosophy, appears on the eve of sinking into all the horrors of barbarism, of ignorance, and consequently of anarchy and confusion" (*Articles*, xv). Yet if he represents himself as lacking the power to "check the general impulse to perdition, or towards stopping or retarding this impetuous spirit of our downfall," he does at least intermittently express the hope that "the retrieval of the antient Celtic or primitive language of Europe" might lead in turn to the revival of "the primitive spirit of our British ancestors in the earliest ages," when those ancestors lived "under the most admirable of all human governments" (*Specimen*, 12, 33). The stakes of Cleland's etymological researches or speculations are not narrowly linguistic but emphatically political: the retrieval of the original language of Britain "would shew us in the remotest ages the foundations of our present constitution and laws" and "would throw a light on the establishment of our Juries, our Parliaments, and the legal limitations of the power and office of Kings" (*Way*, 66). In part, then, his work is an expression of "national spirit," not only as it sheds light on the origins of British institutions and cultural identity, but also as it places Britain in the vanguard of scholarly inquiry. Having observed "that some French writers"—in particular one Le Brigant—"were going round and round the truth" of linguistic origins, "and so near it, that, humanly speaking, they can hardly fail, at the long run, of striking into it," Cleland writes, "this has made me wish to leave this humble monument, this inkling of a Briton having got the start of them" (*Way*, 23–24). Yet if he rather chauvinistically offers his texts as a contribution to a kind of ongoing knowledge race with the French, it is a double-edged gesture, for Cleland's recovery of "the primitive spirit of our British ancestors" only throws into sharper relief the barbarism, ignorance, and confusion of the present, just as his account of the "most admirable of all human governments" stands as a none-too-subtle indictment of the one currently in power.

As Carolyn D. Williams has shown, Cleland was not unique in his eagerness to discover the origins of language, or in his "Celtomania." From the self-taught etymologist Eugene Aram (1704–1759), who left behind a "manuscript specimen for a Celtic Dictionary" when he was hanged for a long-secret murder, to such scholars or "speculators" as Rowland Jones, L. D. Nelme, and James Parsons, who traced the origins of ancient Celtic back to Gomer and Magog, the sons of Japhet son of Noah, numerous amateur linguists of the period were searching for the "primitive language of Europe," as Cleland called it; and for British speculators, the desire to identify this with the origins of the British nation was almost irresistible.[26] Cleland's French rival Le Brigant also made the "Japhetic" argument in the projected work he advertised in the *Journal des Sçavans* in 1767–1768. Using the words "Celts," "Gomerites," and "Britons" interchangeably, Le Brigant promised that his two-volume work would fully recount the history of "the primitive language . . . given to Adam; by him transmitted to Noah, through one only intermediary man; from Noah to Gomer his grandson, and by him to the Gomerites or Britons, who still preserve it with the name of him from whom they are descended."[27] But if Cleland is affiliated with these other philologists in claiming that the ancient Celtic was the original or "universal elementary language of Europe" (*Way*, ii), he breaks from them in eliminating every trace of biblical ancestry or authority for this language he sought to retrieve. Gomer, Magog, and Japhet have no place in his reconstruction of linguistic origins; nor does Noah, or Adam, or God. His Celtic is a purely human language.

Accordingly, while Cleland states in the first sentence of *The Way to Things by Words* that "the Language which I flatter myself with the idea of having in a great measure recovered, is precisely that language alluded to by Homer, which he calls the language of the *Gods*" (1), he soon clarifies that "*Gods*" is just another way of writing *Goths* (9). Indeed, Homer turns out to be a bit of a fiction himself: "The name of *Homer*," Cleland writes, "is not a proper name, but a general one, for Bard or MAN of SONG" (22), and the *Iliad* and *Odyssey* are not truly Greek poems at all but translations of "Celto-Etruscan" originals (20–22, 71). Not only does Greek not merit the cultural primacy it has come to assume, but the whole Greek pantheon on which "Homer" drew is nothing but an "abuse" (10) or "corruption" (118) of originally Celtic or Druidic fictions: allegorical embodiments of natural and moral truths that the Greeks took literally and thus "prophan[ed]" by "erecting those impersonations into objects of religious worship" (10).[28] There are no such gods. "The whole of the Greek and Roman mythology," Cleland later wrote in the *Specimen of an Etimological Vocabulary*, is "a chaos of nonsense," because those later peoples lost sight of the purpose of the Druids' "stile of metaphor and allegory," which was to give, "in favor of the memory, to very solid truths and precepts the passport of instructive amusement" (152). It is no accident that Cleland here uses the same words with which he had defended the genre of the novel twenty years earlier, in his review of *Peregrine Pickle*—"calculated to convey instruction, under the passport of amusement"—for the contemporary novelist is the Druids' worthy successor. The ancient Britons invented literature, but the Greeks and Romans "prophaned" it by turning its metaphors into gods.

In his Celtic studies, Cleland uncouples his reconstructed ancient Britain from religion—both the "pagan" mythology of the Egyptians, Greeks, and Romans and the Adamic-Japhetic mythology of his contemporaries, who sought to identify the Druidic culture of ancient Britain with "Patriarchal Christianity," as in the texts of the antiquary and archeologist William Stukeley. Stukeley's pioneering studies of the stone circles of Stonehenge and Avebury, *Stonehenge: A Temple Restor'd to the British Druids* (1740) and *Abury: A Temple of the British Druids* (1743) were published as the first two parts of the projected four-volume *Patriarchal Christianity; or, A chronological history of the origin and progress of true religion, and of idolatry*, whose title announces its author's aim of reconciling Druidism and Christian orthodoxy.[29] Druidism, far from being a heathen embarrassment, was, according to one of Stukeley's acolytes, William Cooke, "the true Patriarchal Religion," and Cooke's linguistic and iconographic research aimed to complement Stukeley's archeological work to establish that "the Principles of the PATRIARCHS and DRUIDS are laid open and shewn to correspond entirely with *each other*, and BOTH with the Doctrines of *Christianity*."[30] For Cleland, by contrast, despite his occasional nod of "veneration for religion, and of reverence for its ministers" (*Articles*, xii), Christianity arrived in Britain as an opportunistic latecomer whose success is owing to its canny syncretism— that is, its appropriation and redeployment of originally Druidic practices. After the Roman conquest, Druidism, "being under every disgrace and persecution

imaginable, was, if not annulled, so greatly weakened, that it gave a fair opening for *Christianity* to enter at the breach . . . It was *here* then, that, without too
much violence to *externals* at least, Christianity got footing . . . The Cross took
place of the *May-pole* or *Holy-rood*, in the fairs and market-places, with very little
alteration of form" (*Way*, 14). Scrabbling for a footing, entering at the breach,
wrenching sacred symbols to new uses, the Christians who came to Britain in
the Romans' wake were no less invasive than the imperial armies; and if they
conveyed "a saving and superior light," Cleland places far more emphasis on
their persecution of those who "adher[ed] to the antient system of worship"
(*Way*, 116), likening this to the "judicial murder" of "innocent persons" at the
Salem witch trials.[31]

No wonder, then, that Cleland's reimagining of ancient Britain and the Druids met with hostility from some clergymen, if we are to believe a story he later
told Beckwith about "a Right Reverend Prelate now living, with whom he had
formerly been well acquainted, who was or pretended to be so disgusted at his
Account of the Celtic Origin of the Word Pentecost . . . that on Publication of it
he accused the Author of Atheism [or] Deism, and shunned his Acquaintance
ever after."[32] Cleland never argues outright against Christian faith, but he gives
it a secondary role as a posthumous or parasitic successor to the Druidism
of ancient Britain, "the primitive Christians having, in a great measure, and
surely with the best intentions imaginable, adopted and sanctified the Druidical
discipline and practices . . . No wonder that we find in the Christian church so
many vestiges of their conformity with our so ancient customs, that Christianity itself is comparatively but a matter of yesterday" (*Specimen*, 108). Christianity is neither original nor outside of history but contingent and imitative, and
Cleland tellingly keeps it at a grammatical arm's length, distinguishing "*their*
conformity" from "*our* so ancient customs," and so aligning "us" with the Druids persecuted by Romans and Christians alike.

The word *Druid* itself Cleland "derives . . . from D-Er-eud, the *Man of God*, or
what we now currently understand by the appellation of *a Divine*" (*Way*, 44–45).
In this respect he adopts the same sense the invading Caesar gave the word,
when he wrote (in Golding's English), "The Druides are occupied about holy
things: they haue the doing of publicke and priuate sacrifices, and do interpret
and discusse matters of Religion."[33] Yet terms such as *religion, holy*, and *priest*
take on unfamiliar meanings in Cleland's reconstruction of the Druidic origins
of Britain. "The words *Ecclesiastical, Diocese, Dean, Cardinal, Bishop, Priest*, and
even *Religion* itself," he writes, "do not originally mean any thing purely spiri-
tual: being, in fact, in their origin, all terms of judiciary import" (*Specimen*, vii).

While he goes on to state that "in those times . . . the law of the country was also its religion," his etymology for "religion" derives it from "*Ray*, which was the circle drawn round persons arrested or arraigned in the name of Justice . . . Out of this *ray* or *circle* it was the highest of all crimes to escape, or to transgress it till delivered by justice. This was called, *Ray-ligio*. The being *bound* by the *Ray*" (*Way*, 6). The word *holy*, too, originates in a political or legal context: "*holy*, that is to say, the general sense of the *whole* people, collectively and conclusively taken, reported, and ordered to be passed into a Law" (*Articles*, 20). Similarly, the word "*Priest*, or *Prêtre*, did not so much as mean any divine office" but derived from *par* (judge), *reich* (region), and *est* (agent or administrator), yielding *pareichest* and thence priest (*Specimen*, 14, 6–9). These etymologies may not win any adherents today, and even when they were published, Cleland's Celtic essays provoked some skeptical responses, as when the writer for the *Critical Review* ventured that they "adopt a language which actually does not exist except in imagination."[34] It may be true, as Carolyn Williams wryly puts it, that "Cleland reconstructed ancient European languages and customs with the aid of a wide acquaintance with living languages, a smattering of historical knowledge, a flair for free association, and unbounded agility at leaping to conclusions."[35] Still, his work had its advocates: Beckwith went to visit him specifically to discuss some of the details of his Celtic texts, of which he gave "very copious, and to me Satisfactory Explanations," and the clergyman-schoolmaster George William Lemon, author of the 1783 *English Etymology; or, a Derivative Dictionary of the English Language*, wrote that Cleland was "one of the greatest etymologists on our language, and a gentleman very well known in the literary world for his *Vocabulary on the Celtic tongue*; who has discovered in that work a great depth of knowledge in British antiquity; and of which work he has been pleased to grant me full permission, which I have accordingly made great use of."[36] Cleland himself, who usually took the part of the critically vilified renegade, wrote in the "Advertisement" to the *Additional Articles* that "the reception of the specimens has been, in general, favorable to me greatly beyond my expectation" (iv), referring in particular to the approval of the Society of Antiquaries (viii–ix). But whatever the critical fortunes of Cleland's "curious tracts," they are less notable for their role in the development of comparative historical linguistics than for the imaginative latitude with which Cleland explores the relations among language, the nation, his own authorship, and the body.

Bodies are brought to the fore in one apparently digressive passage in the *Specimen*, in which Cleland, investigating the origins of the word "god-father," notes a surprising Celtic law, "one of the ancientest . . . which imposed a fine on those whose corpulence should exceed the statutable standard" (182). Using this law "to show how much those exercises were held a duty, which gave agility to the limbs, and vigor to the body," Cleland writes that "it is hard to say, whether it was the most conducive to the good of a country in preserving the powers of the subject to serve it, or to the subject himself, in defending him against his own idleness, and keeping him from burying himself alive in his own fat." The vigor of the subject's physical body is directly tied to the good of the body politic, and as Cleland pursues this idea, he makes a "favorable comparison" between "the state of this island in those ages" and "the actual present one" on the basis of "the simplicity of life in those early ages" (182–183). We have reached a higher "pitch of refinement," but have passed "that point of improvement, at which it would be salutary for [nations] to stop, before that art, abusing its advantages, ceases to be subordinate to nature, and commences false refinement. The amiable simplicity and youthful vigor of taste is then degenerated into the lothsome affectation and silly dotage of a luxury verging to its own death in that of the state itself, which it will have brought on under a thousand diseases" (183). The focus of Cleland's denunciation slips between the body and the nation as he envisions the simultaneous "verging to death" of the once amiable, youthful body, wallowing in luxury, and of "the state itself," ravaged by "a thousand diseases" brought on by its subjects' "false refinement" and "lothsome affectation."[37] By a more circuitous route, Cleland arrives at the same prognosis in his etymological work that he "harp[ed] on" in his political essays: Britain is dying.

The linkage Cleland insists on here, between cultural decline and loss of bodily vigor, is also put forward by Fanny Hill in her description of Mr. H——, the most obviously "manly" of her lovers. Having observed, "while he was stripping," his "brawny structure, strong made limbs, and rough shaggy breast" (63), Fanny goes on to enumerate

> the virtues of his firm texture of limbs, his square shoulders, broad chest, compact hard muscles, in short a system of manliness, that might pass for no bad image of our antient sturdy barons, when they weilded the battle-ax, whose race is now so thoroughly refin'd and fritter'd away into the more delicate modern-built frame of our pap-nerv'd softlings, who are as pale, as pretty, and almost as masculine as their sisters. (64)

The *Specimen's* "false refinement," "lothsome affectation," and "silly dotage" are just variations on Fanny's "thoroughly refin'd and fritter'd away" race of "pap-nerv'd softlings," undone by excess of luxury. In Fanny's *Memoirs*, of course, bodily vigor is explicitly sexualized in a way it is not in the Celtic essays: vigor is virility, and the loss through overrefinement of ancient manliness yields a generation of effeminate and by implication "unsex'd male-misses."[38] But the connection between physical vigor and phallic authority is still a significant theme in the Celtic works, if in sometimes surprising ways. Carolyn Williams has argued that Cleland's idealized Druidic realm is itself "a system of manliness" underpinned by "the potent patriarchal forces" most visibly embodied in a symbol he returns to again and again: the maypole, or "*standing May* of Justice" (*Way*, 33).[39] It is true that the maypole was for Cleland "eminently the great sign of Druidism, as the Cross was of Christianity" (*Way*, 121)—indeed the latter was just an adaptation of the former—and he had made a joke of the maypole's obvious phallic associations in Fanny's account of her first view of Will undressed: "I saw with wonder and surprize, what? not the play-thing of a boy, not the weapon of a man, but a may-pole of so enormous a standard, that had proportions been observ'd, it must have belong'd to a young giant" (72). Further, as Williams has noted, such symbols of political or judicial authority as the scepter, bough, or mace are derived in Cleland's Druidical system from the phallic "*standing May.*" As he writes in the *Specimen*, "the *bough* or *wand* of the Judge . . . was figuratively taken from the great standard of Justice, the *column of the May*, which it represents, under various forms, as the staff of authority, both in the civil and in the military. It was the *rod* (radt) of Justice, or of Council. It was the *truncheon* of the Field officers" (43). The brawny Mr. H——, then, with his "stiff staring truncheon, red-topt" (63), embodies, in Williams's words, "the manly splendours of ancient Britain."[40]

Yet as Cleland writes elsewhere in the *Specimen*, the Druids' "lawful authorit[ies]" were by preference often female: "nothing is, in history, more clearly attested than this employ and capacity in the Celtic women for judiciary offices" (82). We have tended to forget this because "as Christianity prevailed, there was nothing against which it set its face more strenuously than this, among other relicks of the Druidical system" (83). But in pre-Christian Britain "a Druidess, in virtue of her wand, or staff of Office, might execute an arrest. In Gaul," Cleland adds, "that sex was pre-eminently chosen for this office" (82). Wielding the staff, wand, or "*rod* . . . of Justice," the Druidess is emphatically a phallic woman: a figure that undoes sexual difference, and another of Cleland's unsexed bodies. This malleability, or instability, of sex is also integral to the Celtic allegories from which all later literature and religion derive. As he puts it in *The Way to Things*, the Druids "appropriated no distinction of sex to their spirits, or allegorical impersonations . . . thus they made of *Pallas*, just as it suited their purpose of fiction, a male or a female Deity" (62). To assign "no distinction of sex" is to undo sex itself as a system of distinction or differentiation, whether between spirits, bodies, or words. Cleland's ancient Celtic contradicts Samuel Johnson's claim that there is "a sex in words"; rather, it unfixes words from a single sexual identity. Even the hypermanly Mr. H——, "no bad image of our antient sturdy barons," becomes a more ambiguous figure in light of Cleland's etymological retracing of "baron" to the original Celtic "*Bar*, in the sense of Judge or Judgment" (*Specimen*, 28), with the suffix *-on* meaning principal or head. Rather than defining him as the heir to an exclusively male, patrilineal title, the word *baron* affiliates Mr. H—— to the Druidical female justices, wielding their own "truncheons" or other phallic insignia of office.

"The manly splendours of ancient Britain," then, are less monolithically patriarchal than at first appears. Even Will's phallic "maypole" is curiously indeterminate, neither "the play-thing of a boy" nor "the weapon of a man"—so not properly, or narrowly, masculine at all. Indeed, as I noted in chapter 3, Fanny writes, of the skin of Will's maypole, that its "smooth polish, and velvet-softness, might vye with that of the most delicate of our sex" (72). Searching for a figure to do it justice, Fanny declares that "it must have belong'd to a young giant," which is like nothing so much as one of those "spirits, or allegorical impersonations" without "distinction of sex" that populate the Druid imaginary: a metaphorical embodiment of the phallic sublime.[41] Not only that: Will's maypole belongs not to him but to Fanny herself, who calls Will "as pretty a piece of woman's meat as you should see" (80). It is she who "wields" his "wand, or staff of Office," "taking pleasure," as she puts it, "by its right handle." If Fanny, like Cleland's Druids, unsettles a strictly masculinist sense of phallic power, she also anticipates the critique of inherited political authority or rank Cleland makes in the Celtic tracts. "The talent of pleasing, with which nature has endow'd a handsome person," she writes with regard to Will, "form'd to me the greatest of all merits; compared to which the vulgar prejudices in favour of titles, dignities, honours, and the like, held a very low rank indeed!" (80). Nature trumps rank, or constitutes a superior form of rank. So it was, too, in pre-Roman Britain, when there were no hereditary titles or honors, but kings and barons alike were subject to the will of the commons.

Cleland's speculative retrieval of the political system of the ancient Britons is most fully set out in the *Specimen of an Etimological Vocabulary*, which was rightly the most controversial of his linguistic studies.[42] In it, Cleland argues that "the most admirable of all human governments" (33), native to preinvasion Britain, was democratic, antimilitarist, radically antimonarchical. The Druids, of course, had special powers, and "the Druidical Judiciary class was superior to the *Laity*" (12)—which at first glance seems not democratic but oligarchic. Yet "though the Barons," as Cleland calls them, "were invested with the supremacy, in their respective Jurisdictions, or Baronies, they were nevertheless subordinate to the *Par-ley-mots*, or general assemblies of the People . . . It was in those Par-ley-mots, the Sovereign authority inviolably resided" (31–32). These assemblies, held in March and May "in the *Mallum* or field consecrated to that purpose" (36), entailed "the personal assembling of the whole body of the people." Just as Druidesses were often chosen for judicial office, so there was no restriction of sex at the Par-ley-mot. Judges or barons were elected and served at the people's will: "In these *Ey-commons* [law-meetings] or *Fields of May*, the People, if they saw cause, deposed or punished their Popes, their Bishops, their Barons, and their Kings" (37). "Bishop" and "Pope" are in Cleland's etymology synonyms for "Baron" or head justice, but "King" named a lesser office, that of military strongman or warlord, appointed only in cases of urgent and temporary need. Cleland insists that such "kings" were always subject to the commons, and he rails against "the falsest of all conclusions, that Britain was antiently under kingly government, or legislation." Instead, "it was purely democratical, with the support of barons or judges, and never under kings, whose service was only occasional, and always subordinate; that is to say, accountable to the people, and to the civil power" (148–149).

It is this devaluation of the office and name of "King" that, according to Beckwith, led to the outcry against Cleland and his "oppression" at the hands of "some Men in Power." His sarcastic treatment of monarchical government lost him his "Place or Pension," led to the public "Censure of being a Sodomite," and meant that, in consequence, "his valuable MSS. are condemn'd to be buried in Oblivion."[43] It is difficult to reconcile Cleland's scathing history of the demise of the democratic or populist constitution of his idealized ancient Britain with his usual characterization as "a conservative thinker in Bolingbroke's mold" or a social reactionary "obviously imbued with a Tory distrust of the 'mob.' "[44] Not that these assessments of Cleland's political views are wrong: they are well supported by many passages in his work, from his 1749 review of Bolingbroke's *Letters on the Spirit of Patriotism* to his essays for the *Public Advertiser*.[45] But in the Celtic tracts, where he gave freest rein to his political imagination, he is vitriolic in his attacks on the very principle of monarchism. After the Romans' expulsion of the Druids and their abolition of popular sovereignty, the military strongmen or kings, once subordinate to the commons, seized power. "Having the forces in their hand," Cleland writes, they "sought, with the usual selfishness of mankind, to render the Generalship hereditary in their families; and consequently, together with the title of *King*, which antiently meant *General* or leader and nothing more, and which they left to their children, they must necessarily leave withal the territorial acquisitions that were to support that dignity" (*Articles*, 5, 7). To the crime of territorial expropriation these kings joined the folly of hereditary transmission, producing "the hazard of a post requiring great talents, activity, and personal merit, descending to a tyrant, an ideot, or a minor," and indeed "the law of Chances, authenticated by historical experience, furnishes, at least, ten bad Kings for one good, or but tolerable one." Every monarchic state is a kleptocracy, founded on theft and ruled by violence. And once kings came to power, even the office of baron was corrupted:

> The Peers or Barons, instead of the having been publickly examined by Judges, and elected by the voice of a free people . . . [now] came into possession of Baronies by fraud, by violence, or by the private favor of some ignorant general, under the once inferior name of king. The procedure of these new kind of Barons was worthy of this new kind of title. The causes of Justice were decided by combats, by duels, and by force of arms. The Barons theirselves . . . turned absolutely highwaymen, having built castles and strong holds to secure their plunder, and their power of plundering. This was the pure reign of the sword, in the true spirit of the lawless military.
>
> (*Specimen*, 34–35)

Finally, to put the seal on their degradation, the Barons "fell at last so low as to be the implicit followers of a king, the supports of arbitrary power, and the tools of a Court" (40). Such is the fallen political order we have inherited in "this infamous and abandoned period."

Cleland's account of the losses of democratic sovereignty and of native British justice, as embodied in the changing meanings of words, thus leads back to the "insignificance and nullity" of the present. In that respect, the aims of his philological essays are congruent with those of his letters on the latest political news: his uncovering, as he thought, of "the foundations of our present constitution and laws," the ancient root of "our Juries, our Parliaments, and the legal limitations of the power and office of Kings" (*Way*, 66) gives historical weight to his call for "that great national Council . . . a free, uncorrupt Parliament" to be "properly put into Motion" and so "restore . . . Vigor to the Laws" (*Pub. Adv.*, 8 Aug. 1765). Pessimism of the intellect, however, outweighs optimism of the will in Cleland's work, and his idealizing retrieval of "the most admirable of all human governments" (*Specimen*, 33) serves mainly as a desolate reminder of "the amazing general futility of these wretched times" (*Articles*, xv). Yet despite his rage against the present and his prophetic vision of Britain "sinking into all the horrors of barbarism," there is nothing dolorous in Cleland's late writing—not just because rage lifts his spirits, but because language, retraced to its origins, has a restorative power.

In the preface to the last of his Celtic tracts, Cleland writes that "not a few of my readers" have told him of their surprise that, "anticipating nothing but dry, grammatical discussions, they had found an entertainment, the more pleasing for its being so little expected" (*Articles*, vi–vii).[46] This attests not only to his authorial skill but to the nature of the inquiry itself: the effect of etymology is "to give a soul to every word" and to "substitute the spirit of picturesc definition to the dead letter of acceptance by rote" (vii–viii). Unlike the *Dictionary of Love*, in which he exposed the gap between the "just value" (viii) and "apparent significa-tion" (ix) of words in the denatured milieu of "modern gallantry" (x), Cleland's goal in the etymological essays is to see past the apparent arbitrariness or con-ventionality of words as signifiers and so reclaim their "souls"—which are not supernatural but poetic. In *The Way to Things by Words* he writes that "the words we at present make use of, and understand only by common agreement, assume a new air and life in the understanding, when you trace them to their radicals, where you find every word strongly stamped with nature; full of energy, mean-ing, character, painting, and Poetry" (23). Cleland's theory of language runs counter to the axiom that language is a system of difference (between signifier and signified, between one signifier and another); it is, rather, a system of like-nesses: words lead to things, things to words. "Where the derivation is known," he asserts, "a word strikes immediately the imagination: otherwise it needs for its apprehension the remembrance of the public agreement to understand it in a certain sense" (*Articles*, viii). The social agreement to understand words in a conventional or habitual sense blinds us to their inherent plenitude of "en-ergy, meaning, character, painting, and Poetry"—qualities "stamped" in them by nature. Words, he writes in another version of this theoretical claim, "are not merely arbitrary signs, but are, in their original formation, big with meaning, emphatic and picturesque" (*Way*, 24). To return to this "original formation," or what he calls elsewhere the "primordial signification" of words (*Articles*, 40), is to unveil the thing *in* the word, in the very shape of the word: there is not, he asserts, "a single word in any language on the globe, that is purely arbitrary; no, nor so much as a single letter, or form of a letter" (*Way*, 87). This is why the word retraced to its origins "strikes immediately the imagination" and why, amid the squalor of late eighteenth-century Britain, words are the only source of hope left: however tarnished by misuse and the corruption of manners, they still preserve some trace of their lost original "energy [and] meaning."

The three Celtic studies Cleland eventually published were only "sketches" or "specimens" of the magnum opus he originally envisioned. Both the *Specimen* and the *Additional Articles* end with a sales pitch for their readers to subscribe to that work in progress and thus support its completion. It was the only subscription scheme Cleland ever undertook, and it was unsuccessful—or at any rate "The Celtic Retrieved, by the Analitic Method, or Reduction to Radicals" was never published. That work—to be "printed in two volumes quarto, on a very good paper and type, at the price of two guineas" (*Specimen*, 231)—would have comprised

> *First.* A Vocabulary of the Celtic radicals, on the analytic and synthetic plan of the Bramins *Sanscort*; authenticating every word, by a competent number of examples drawn from various languages.
>
> *Second.* A Grammar, containing general rules of the synthetic method, explaining the manner of formation or growth of various languages, antient and modern, out of these roots; the whole mechanism of language, and especially of our own.
>
> *Third.* An etymological Glossary of such words and proper names in the Greek, Latin, and other languages, particularly the English, as may . . . lead to some interesting discovery, or corroborate some doubtful point. (*Way*, 88–89)

As the three works Cleland did publish, amounting to some four hundred pages, were only fragments of the imagined whole, the project was heroically or madly ambitious. In addition to mapping, in the first and second parts, "the whole mechanism of language" in all its evolutionary profusion, he aimed in the third (of which the specimens he did publish would have formed but part) to provide "curious explanations of certain obscure points of mythology, of history, of geography, with the genuine reason of names of countries, of men, of things, so as to extirpate a multitude of popular mistakes, and substitute truth to false opinion" (*Specimen*, 230). The effect of these discoveries would be to set our understanding of our own history, culture, and political institutions on a new footing. To know what "the legal limitations of the power and office of Kings" once were, or how the "Sovereign authority" of the commons was embodied "purely democratical[ly]" in the ancient Par-ley-mots, is a step toward the possibility of radically—from the roots—remaking the present social order. This is the prophetic burden of "A Briton."

Yet even though he was soliciting subscriptions to "The Celtic Retrieved" as

late as 1769, Cleland had been signaling for some time that he knew he would
never complete it. The advertisement to *The Way to Things* begins by acknowledging that he has "interrupted my application to this study, with little or no
probability of my ever resuming it" (i–ii), and ends with the figure of a dying
tree, in which he condenses both his own failing health and the "general neglect
and state of languor" of literature in his day. It will not have been "quite a labor
in vain," he writes, "this attempt to procure a useful produce from a hitherto-
barren part of a tree, the whole of which, root and branch, is itself perishing
with the cold of the season," if "the few in whom a love of literature" persists
"do justice to my intention" (vi–vii). His health was not so failing that he didn't
live twenty-three more years, and the relative success of *The Way to Things* encouraged him to ready two further volumes for publication, including the dense
and substantial *Specimen*. But he was well aware of the likelihood, verging on
certainty, that he would never reach the end of his project.

A sense of Cleland's own mortality runs through *The Way to Things by Words*,
most strikingly in passages where he likens his authorial project to a journey. In
one he writes, "Nor is it without some regret that I see myself cruelly compelled,
instead of the torch I proposed to carry usefully into the darkest depths of the
remotest antiquity, to offer only this poor rush-light, whose feeble glimpses
serve less to remove the obscurity than to make it remarkable" (24). Here the
journey is subterranean, a kind of spelunking, and while he falls short of his
ambitious end of taking away the darkness, the "feeble glimpses" of his "poor
rush-light" attest to not only his frailty but his bravery in facing the historical
abyss. He is an explorer, a pioneer pointing the way for others to follow—a
conceit he returns to at the end of the work. There, he compares his progress to
that of a solitary walker searching for secure "footing on this perfidious ground
that was at every step sinking under me" (88). "A few truths," he writes,

> encouraged me to believe I was got on the right road; the satisfaction at which,
> made me some amends for the frequency of my falls; and thus I stumbled on, till
> I got upon what I have imagined safer ground, though still far, far short . . . of the
> end I had proposed to myself . . . I offer here a summary view, in order to point
> out, according to the best of my conception, the way in which I was stopped short,
> so that in this indication I merely make the figure of a finger-post, sticking where
> I am set fast, and pointing out the road, in which I have no more the power to stir
> a step. (88)

The figural shift in this passage from stumbling, struggling pioneer to mute
fingerpost is jarring, even comic, turning him from a heroic figure into a thing

that mocks the human form. Powerless to carry on, fated to point to the promised land he can never reach, he is like Moses on Pisgah, to whom the last words his god speaks are "I have caused thee to see *it* with thine eyes, but thou shalt not go over thither"—whereupon Moses dies.[47] This tragic intimation haunts the essay's final image, which adopts Fanny Hill's pet metaphor, of life as a ship's voyage. But whereas Fanny is herself the ship, and by the end is happily, even smugly "snug into port" (187), Cleland is a solitary mariner, "out of sight of a looked-out for land" (90). Of *his* "port of destination," he writes that "were I even as near to it as I presume I am, I never now expect to reach [it]; but leaving these lights, in the good faith of their not being false ones, I sincerely wish a better voyage to more fortunate adventurers." His only consolation, in keeping with his Mosaic unfulfillment, is also prophetic, reckoning his own failure as the condition of another adventurer's success. But even this is uncertain, for those who come after him will also be "embark[ing] on a sea, so infamous for innumerable wrecks" (*Articles*, viii).

In Cleland's late work, the "wretched condition" of Britain is figurally associated with the weariness and fragility of his own body: both are hurtling toward "the consummation of our own ruin, already too far advanced" (*Pub. Adv.*, 21 July 1787). Similarly, both his own authorial career and literature in general are in a "state of languor . . . perishing with the cold of the season" (*Way*, vi–vii). The most he can show for his life's efforts are the feeble glimpses of a "poor rush-light," which only make the surrounding darkness more visible. It is telling that in his last major works Cleland returns to the figural landscape of Fanny Hill's *Memoirs*, with their phallic maypoles and "antient sturdy barons," and their governing metaphor of the perilous voyage: it is as if his authorial career has come full circle, returned to its point of origin. Not Moses, then, but the sailor Odysseus. Cleland himself had of course reached the "port[s] of destination" of his actual voyages, to Bombay, Lisbon, Carolina, but had returned from each of them disillusioned, having to start again from zero. So while he deploys the figure of the voyage, he also, in other passages, calls the efficacy of voyages, literal and metaphorical, into question. At the end of the *Specimen*, for example, he writes, "if it be true, that, to know things rightly and solidly, they must be traced to their origin, we have, surely, hitherto, not taken the best road, in seeking that origin, every where but where it was to be found, precisely at home, in Britain itself" (219). Hence his adoption of "A Briton" as his own authorial name and his identification of the British Druids as the inventors of law, literature, language. The Druids have died out, but something of their original spirit survives, especially here, "at home, in Britain"; and as "A Briton," Cleland lays claim to it. In that light, it's intriguing that on the *Specimen*'s last page he writes, apropos of nothing, "It is not even impossible, that a long-destroyed Abby (I mean in the Druidical manner of abbies) might, in remote ages, have stood where the *Savoy* now stands, which may be a corruption of *S'Abby* or *Z'Abby*, the habitation of a Druid *Soph* or *Head*" (218). As it happens, Cleland himself had lived in the Savoy for years, and was almost certainly living there when he wrote those words.[48] There he waits, the last scion of the Druids. The search for origins has led him to this room where he begins to write his discoveries down.

Afterlife

John Cleland died on 23 January 1789, aged seventy-eight. His death was reported the next day in a notice in the *Public Advertiser*: "Yesterday died at his house in Petty France, Westminster, John Cleland, Esq." (*Pub. Adv.*, 24 Jan. 1789).[1] Cleland had lived in Petty France, a few hundred yards from his childhood home in St. James's Place, since 1782, and it was there he had written his last letter to the same *Public Advertiser*, ending with its prophetic vision of Britain "debased and reduced . . . nearly to insignificance and nullity" (*Pub. Adv.*, 21 July 1787). In keeping with his long-running identification of his own "perishing" health with that of the nation—"A Briton" as a miniature and mirror of "Britain"—Cleland intimates in this last letter that "insignificance and nullity," death's oblivion, awaited him too. So they did; but that's not where the story ends, for insignificance is trumped by textuality, nullity by recuperative acts of reading.

When John Nichols, in the obituary he wrote for the *Gentleman's Magazine*, stated that *Fanny Hill* "brought a stigma on [Cleland's] name, which time has not obliterated," he pointed to one way, the most obvious, by which an author can overcome, or at least outlast, his own death: by continuing to be tied to a text that continues to be read. Cleland himself, so he said, wished the book in question to be "buried and forgot," but as Boswell wrote of its author, it "resolutely persisted"—or in Nichols's words, "its poisonous contents" remained "in circulation."[2] And this circulation, sustained by the interest of readers like Boswell, is the necessary condition of authorial afterlife. In Cleland's case, the afterlife may have been scandalous—shadowed by a stigma "consigned to his memory" as long as the book survived—but weighed against the "nullity" of being "buried and forgot," that may not have been a bad bargain.

Fanny Hill's notoriety, or the ill effects of it, may in any case have been overstressed. Not that there has not been much moralistic denunciation over the years, and a short-lived threat of legal prosecution of Cleland himself, albeit never followed through on, but the novel's literary qualities were also openly praised, and it never stood in the way of Cleland getting other work published. In 1762, William Rider included Cleland in his catalog of the significant "living authors of Great Britain," writing that the *Woman of Pleasure*, "tho' justly censured by Men of rigid Morals, must be allowed to be the best executed and the most picturesque of any Work of the Kind, not excepting that of *Petronius*, and the celebrated Dialogues of *Meursius*."[3] Further, Rider's concession that the work was "justly censured by Men of rigid Morals" is tepid at best: "rigid Morals" hardly has a positive ring, and could even be read as a mocking double entendre.

Some passages in Nichols's obituary suggest that he knew Cleland, even that he had visited him at home, as when he writes that a portrait of William Cleland "hung up in the son's library till his death, which indicates all the manners and *d'abord* of a fashionable town-rake in the beginning of this century." The impression of familiarity is reinforced when Nichols writes that Cleland "lived within the income of his pension for many years, in a retired situation in Petty France, surrounded by a good library, and the occasional visits of some literary friends, to whom he was a very agreeable companion." But even the firsthand accounts of those who visited Cleland at home have a certain elusiveness. When Boswell visited him in April 1779, Cleland told him that a French visitor said he "had not only the finest situation of a house in London, but in Europe. It was fine, romantic, and pleasant."[4] Could this "fine, romantic, and pleasant" spot be the same "old house in the Savoy" where Boswell had found Cleland twelve months before, served by a crone, in a "room, filled with books in confusion and dust"? Perhaps Cleland had moved in the meanwhile, although we know from Beckwith that he was still in the Savoy two years later, in 1781, but could any house in the Savoy ever have been described as "romantic," or as having "the finest situation" in Europe?

Similar questions emerge from the accounts witnesses offer of Cleland's mysterious pension. The most famous, and unlikeliest, version comes from Nichols. Amid the furor aroused by the *Woman of Pleasure*, he writes, Cleland "was called before the privy council; and the circumstance of his distress being known, as well as his being a man of some parts, John Earl Granville, the then president, nobly rescued him from the like temptation, by getting him a pension of 100 l. per year, which he enjoyed to his death." Is it really possible that Granville would have got Cleland a lifelong pension just on the condition that he *not* write any further obscene books? News of such a reward would surely have made the rounds of Grub Street, tempting other gentleman-authors in distress to repeat the experiment. Nichols's story, implausible on its face, is also at odds with what Cleland told Beckwith: that he had "enjoyed a Place or Pension under Government of 200£ a year, which was taken from him on Account of his Publications." Boswell's Cleland, meanwhile, evidently claimed that Lord Bute, when prime minister, had offered him £1,200 a year to serve as a kind of one-man cabinet: a story so far-fetched that Boswell "thought he raved." All three of these stories, true or false (or neither or both), must have been started by Cleland himself, but each gives rise to a different reading of the shape of his authorial career and of the political contexts within which it unfolded. Likewise, the contrasting glimpses we have of his domestic circumstances—a room "with books in confusion and dust" versus "surrounded by a good library"; enjoying "the occasional visits of some literary friends, to whom he was a very agreeable companion" versus passing "under the Censure of being a Sodomite, as he now does, and in Consequence thereof Persons of Character decline visiting him"— lead to widely discrepant understandings of his social and cultural position, and of his character and habits. It might just be possible to reconcile these seeming contradictions among Nichols's, Beckwith's, and Boswell's sketches of Cleland, but each appears to belong to the life of a different author.

The crux of any such life is the corpus of writings to which the author's name is attached. To attribute a text is to begin constructing a narrative of authorship, but this is tricky and frustrating in periods like the eighteenth century, when anonymous or pseudonymous publication was the norm. In his catalog of living authors, Rider attributed just two specific works to Cleland, the *Woman of Pleasure* and the *Coxcomb*, but Nichols, in his obituary, made a stab at something like a comprehensive or at least representative list. Although he passes over its name in silence, the *Woman of Pleasure* overshadows Nichols's list, so that every other text is subsidiary to it, whether, like *Memoirs of a Coxcomb*, it exhibits the same "smack of dissipated manners" or, like *The Man of Honour*, it was written as "an *amende honourable* for his former exceptionable book." But not so fast: what is this *Man of Honour*? It looks like a simple mistake, a misprint for *The Woman of Honor*, which Nichols does not mention, and it was long assumed not to exist. But in 1987, James Basker showed that a three-volume novel by that title *was* published three years after the *Woman of Honor* and so reopened the question of Cleland's authorship.[5] If it were found and shown to be his, what rethinking of the trajectory of his career might it compel?

As it turns out, more information has since come to light, and *The Man of Honour; or The History of Harry Waters* can be pretty confidently ascribed to another jobbing writer, John Huddlestone Wynne.[6] But the general problem, and the shimmer of uncertainty, remain. In an intriguing comment near the end of his obituary, Nichols writes that Cleland "shewed himself best in novels, song-writing, and the lighter species of authorship." But there is no trace of any songs by Cleland—does that mean Nichols was wrong, or might there be a cache of lost songs somewhere awaiting discovery? Nichols includes little from the 1750s, when Cleland largely worked as a writer for hire, but looks mainly to his last two decades of writing: to the political letters and the "curious tracts on the Celtic language." That could be because this was the period when Nichols knew him best, or because this is what Cleland wished to have remembered. Either way, Nichols gives less weight than I to Cleland as translator, polemicist, reviewer, and experimenter with literary form, and he plays down what I have stressed: the perversity and strangeness of much of his output. The details, emphases, and omissions in Nichols's account, as in mine, combine to produce a version of Cleland's history in keeping with a particular view or interpretive stance, a way of reading the material remains; and in making this version public, getting his life into print, he offers his subject another way of outlasting his own death: as the protagonist of another author's biography or "Life."

In Nichols's biography, Cleland is first and last his father's heir. "He was the son," Nichols begins, "of Col. Cleland, that celebrated fictitious member of the Spectator's Club, whom Steele describes under the name of Will Honeycombe. A portrait of him hung up in the son's library till his death." While I share Epstein's skepticism as to the often-repeated claim that William Cleland was the model for Steele's character, I find it a suggestive starting point for this account of the son's life, for it makes him the offspring of an already "fictitious" figure and blurs the distinction between the actual person and his representation in print. Or in paint: the image of the father as a young "fashionable town-rake in the beginning of this century" hangs over the son's library to the day of his death, a sign of affiliation leading to the statement that Cleland inherited "the scatterings of his father's fortune, and some share of his dissipations." Those "dissipations" pervade the work that "tarnished his reputation," but had been exacerbated, as Nichols tells it, by a journey abroad that Cleland made between leaving school and shipping off to Bombay. At some point between the ages of thirteen and seventeen, he suggests, Cleland "went as consul to Smyrna, where, perhaps, he first imbibed those loose principles" that later would bear "poisonous" fruit in his fiction. Only "on his return from Smyrna" did Cleland set sail for India and the career I set out in the first chapter of this book.

Where did this story, unsupported by even a shred of documentary evidence, come from? I can only infer that it came from Cleland himself, who might be read as the ghost author of his own obituary. Since it is not a story that anyone else recorded, and since Nichols writes as a familiar, it seems most likely that he had it from Cleland firsthand—although it is certainly possible that, as with the *Woman* turned *Man of Honour*, he did not quite get it right. Cleland was never consul for the Levant Company in Smyrna, nor is it likely he lived there before setting out as a foot soldier to Bombay.[7] He could conceivably have gone there at some later period, but Nichols's chronology is quite clear, and I don't think he is just garbling an anecdote he misheard or misremembered (as one might misremember a book's name). Like the story of Cleland before the Privy Council, the story of Cleland the boy consul of Smyrna, imbibing the "loose principles" of oriental decadence, does not read as if it could have originated with anyone but the subject himself. Who else would bother to invent such a tale? It takes its place with a handful of other puzzling or fantastic stories that crop up now and again in the Cleland archive. Some of these, such as Cowan's 1733 accusation that Cleland "not many years since deserted his King, Country & even the Colour Nature design'd him," come to us secondhand, but most were told by Cleland himself: the story of his mother and aunt packing him off on a "vile insignificant voyage" to Carolina and Jamaica, for instance, or the allegation that Thomas Cannon and *his* mother joined forces "to consummate the murder of an unfortunate gentleman who had saved his life, and whom, in return, he poisoned five times with common arsenic."[8] It is impossible to know from these one-off claims if there's any truth to them. Surely he would not just have made up the voyage to Carolina in a letter to his mother's lawyer, but what of the Cannons' poison plot, or the pension for *not* writing, or the posting to

Smyrna? Yet if the evidence is missing that would allow us to judge the truth of these strange claims, we can guess how Nichols came by the two he included in his obituary: "in conversation," he writes, of Cleland entertaining his "literary friends," "he was very pleasant and anecdotical." Even after his death, the stories he authored of his own life—true, half true, or false; self-deceiving or knowingly counterfeit—might stay in circulation, and generate new stories in turn.

One of the effects of the "stigma" that shadowed Cleland's name from the start of his writing career was a tendency for other writers and critics to accuse him of involvement in a variety of literary forgeries and fakes or to identify him as the author of some disreputable work. Sometimes the motives are obviously mercenary, as when the publisher of the 1766 *Memoirs of Maria Brown* (whose subtitle promises "the life of a courtezan in the most fashionable scenes of dissipation") declared it on the title page to be "Published by the Author of a W** of P***"; or when, in 1969, the proprietors of Sphere Books not only credited the reissued *Memoirs of an Oxford Scholar* (1756) to Cleland (the original was published anonymously) but thoughtfully inserted some new, sexually explicit parts to make good on the link to *Fanny Hill*.[9] More often, the scandal associated with his first book was taken as sufficient reason for assuming he was available for any scheme of literary piracy or fraud that came his way. So, nearly twenty years after his death, rumors began to circulate in print that Cleland was involved in the machinations that led to the illicit publication of Lady Mary Wortley Montagu's *Letters* in 1763—including, in one version of the story, the claim that he was one of "two English gentlemen" who pilfered the manuscripts from a clergyman to whom Lady Mary had entrusted them and smuggled copies to the publisher Thomas Becket, who issued them against the will of Lady Mary's heirs.[10] As far as I have been able to find, this rumor first aired in 1803, forty years after the *Letters*' publication and fifteen after Cleland's death. I know of no evidence to support it from Cleland, Becket, or any of their contemporaries, although their professional ties during this period (Becket published the *Institutes of Health* and *Phisiological Reveries*) make it at least possible. Fifty years later, Robert Carruthers, in his biography of Pope, used Nichols's Smyrna story to bolster the charge that not only had Cleland been involved in pirating the genuine Lady Mary letters, he had also written the fake ones published by Becket four years later. Cleland, he writes, "was an adept at literary fraud, and disreputably connected with the original publication of Lady Mary's correspondence"; and the fake letters "are evidently from the same mint, which, as Cleland had resided in Turkey, and travelled widely, and was besides a man of talent and imagination, [he] was capable of producing a base coinage little inferior to the genuine metal."[11]

The charge Carruthers repeats here, like the story of Cleland as teenage consul at Smyrna, is, as to evidence, utterly baseless. Even Cleland's supposed animosity against Lady Mary, which is often adduced as a likely motive for his participation in these piracies and counterfeits, is doubtful, and is belied by his comments in print.[12] I have no wish to clear him of any role in this literary conspiracy; I would actually like to think he was one of the mysterious gentlemen-thieves, and that he did author the spurious letters (one of them alluding to the "preposterous loves" of Hadrian and Antinous).[13] It may be that the rumors of Cleland's part in this and other forgeries are true, and it is likely that more works will be attributed to him as other evidence is found. The Cleland canon, first put on a scholarly footing by Epstein in 1974, has almost doubled in size since then, thanks to the detective work of James Basker and especially of Roger Lonsdale, who added eight significant works to the corpus of a dozen or so identified in Epstein's biography.[14] Some of these more recent attributions, including the Penlez and Vizzani pamphlets, Pinot-Duclos's *Memoirs*, and *The Dictionary of Love*, are integral to my reconstruction of Cleland's writing life, for the life, as I have written it, is an outgrowth of my readings of the texts, not the other way round. Only the texts are real; the life is a phantasm. In that sense, at least, the life is unfinished as long as the work is read, reread, salvaged by readers from insignificance and nullity.

Cleland's *Mémoire* to King João V of Portugal
(1742)

The author of this memorandum, having resided for the span of many years in the East Indies, has long been in a position to learn a great deal about the situation and interests of the Portuguese nation in India, from the many dealings and conversations he has had on this matter with the most respectable persons of that nation, both ecclesiastic and lay, as well as by his endeavors to acquire all the knowledge necessary to maintain trade in the Orient, whether between India and Europe or within the Indies. And the knowledge he has acquired provides the basis on which he states that it would be at least as practicable as it is desirable, for the benefit of the Portuguese nation, to set its colonial settlements—which it has long allowed to run at a loss—on a profitable basis, so long as His Majesty is willing to lend the weight of His authority to encourage the enterprise and support its realization, by means of which, beyond the general good that would result to the State, He would restore the fortunes of a number of families whom the war with the Marathas has reduced to the most painful extremities. [This is] a war one might henceforth describe as advantageous and useful to the entire Portuguese nation if it has provided solid proof of the value and even necessity of restoring its Indian trading colonies and drawing from them all the profit and benefit which the cultivation of commerce cannot fail to produce. And to achieve this, there is no question here of a vaguely defined project but rather of a simple system which can easily be put into effect, His Majesty's favor permitting, since even after the loss of many previously conquered properties and territories, there remain enough favorably situated settlements and valuable resources to form a plan of trade in the Orient which once begun, supported, and perfected to the degree of which it is capable, will more than make up for past losses. Beyond the situation of the Kingdom of Portugal—its colonial settlements well positioned along the East Indian trading routes—the Portuguese language, diffused throughout the East, and many other evident advantages seem to invite this Nation to regard this trade as a matter of highest priority for the state, and so to dedicate to it all its genius and power.

Translated from the original French, as enclosed in a letter from Sebastião José de Carvalho e Melo to Cardinal da Mota, 19 February 1742 (in Carvalho e Melo, *Escritos Económicos*, 158–161).

The author of this memorandum does not presume to impose any scheme for the establishment of a Portuguese Company or for the regulation and supervision of trade under His Majesty's auspices within the Kingdom itself; he is not competent to decide such questions. He leaves it to the wisdom of His Majesty and his Council to establish this Company or Service and to determine under what conditions, modifications, or limits and by what means they will establish and regulate this trade, whose object is to increase His Majesty's revenue, to strengthen His Kingdom's Navy, to cause His colonies in the East Indies (and indirectly and as a result those of Brazil) to flourish, and to obtain for His Majesty's subjects the benefits of their location in the East, on the example of other nations which have well known how to profit from this, and whose systems of administration can be instructive as examples to adopt what is useful and reject everything that on examination appears defective, improper, or incompatible with the good of the State and the constitution of the Kingdom.

The aim of this memorandum's author is simply to offer to contribute his knowledge, his information, and all the service in his power toward the formation and establishment, in the Indies themselves, of that system of trade which will prove most practicable and most suited to the aims and the good of the interested parties, as it is undeniable that a commerce established under a new system or conducted on other premises and principles than in the past undoubtedly requires the advice of some person or persons of sufficient experience, particularly in Indian affairs and the practice of trade there, in order to guide and steady its first steps, which otherwise could not help but be wavering and uncertain. He offers in particular to provide, to those persons His Majesty chooses to nominate for this purpose, the most accurate information on all the procedures used for the ordering and regulation of trade which many years' experience have demonstrated to be worthy of imitation, especially in the following areas:

- The responsibilities and powers of a Council of Trade in the Indies themselves, answerable and subject to such authority as it pleases the King to determine, according to the particular form of the administration and regulations established for the general conduct of trade in the Indies.
- The allocation of officers and secretarial, revenue, and accounting offices.
- The sale of consignments, the provision of goods in return, the acquisition of bulk fabrics and chintzes from Surat and the purchase of pepper, coffee, and other goods for import.
- The establishment of a commercial center and of a method for subordinating all the other forts, stations, trading posts, or settlements in that degree of dependency that will be found most effective for maintaining and improving trade in general.
- The surest and most suitable means for drawing merchants under the protection of His Majesty in the Indies and for increasing the number of useful subjects.

The author therefore willingly offers to travel to Portugal in order to communicate, in person and in detail, all the necessary records, written instructions, and other information, in whatever manner or form required, without setting any conditions in advance and seeking no reward other than as it pleases His Majesty and in proportion to the actual, useful service he finds himself in a position to provide.

NOTES

INTRODUCTION. "OLD CLELAND"

1. Boswell, *In Extremes*, 316.

2. Boswell, *In Search of a Wife*, 336.

3. Boswell and Johnson had visited the "old Lady Eglinton," then in her eighties, on their tour of Scotland in 1773.

4. Ramsay's portrait of Rousseau is now in the National Gallery of Scotland. Boswell's reference to Rousseau's cap could suggest that Cleland was also wearing a dressing gown something like the "Armenian" coat Rousseau wears in the portrait. Rousseau, too, was described by one contemporary as having "sharp black eyes," and Boswell may have been influenced by Ramsay's painting in drawing his sketch of Cleland. See Warburton, "Art and Allusion."

5. Boswell, *For the Defence*, 81.

6. Cleland to Lovel Stanhope, also quoted in Foxon, *Libertine Literature*, 54.

7. Nichols, Obituary of John Cleland.

8. See, for example, Christensen, *Practicing Enlightenment*; Kernan, *Printing Technology*; Deutsch, *Resemblance and Disgrace* and *Loving Doctor Johnson*. See also Donoghue, *Fame Machine*, which includes case studies of Sterne, Smollett, and Goldsmith and brings together the biographical and critical-theoretical strands of literary scholarship in novel ways.

9. Johnson, *Adventurer* no. 115, Tuesday, 11 December 1753, in Johnson, *"Idler" and "Adventurer,"* 457. Subsequent references will be cited parenthetically.

10. Cleland to Stanhope.

11. Campbell [attrib.], *The Sale of Authors*, 139.

12. Barthes, *Pleasure of the Text*, 27, and "The Death of the Author," in *Image, Music, Text*, 142–148. Subsequent references will be cited parenthetically.

13. Burke, *Death and Return*, esp. 20–61; Bennett, *The Author*, esp. 9–28. See also "The Author" in Bennett and Royle, *Introduction to Literature*, 18–26.

14. Bennett and Royle, *Introduction to Literature*, 22.

15. Epstein, *Images of a Life*, 112.

16. For critical reflections on the problems and possibilities of literary biography

after "the death of the author," see Epstein, *Recognizing Biography*, and *Contesting the Subject*; and Donoghue, *Fame Machine*.

17. Cleland, review of Smollett's *Peregrine Pickle*, in *Monthly Review* (March 1751), reprinted in Cleland, *Memoirs of a Coxcomb*, 228, 226.

18. Josiah Beckwith, manuscript note in copy of Cleland's Celtic tracts (Cambridge University Library, class mark Aa-18-6), quoted in Merritt, "Biographical Note," 305–306.

19. Foxon untangled the *Memoirs'* early publishing history in *Libertine Literature*, 52–63. I discuss Drybutter and his possible connections with Cleland in chapter 3.

20. Smollett, review of Cleland's *Memoirs of a Coxcomb*, reprinted in Cleland, *Memoirs of a Coxcomb*, 223–224.

21. Rider, *Lives and Writings of the Living Authors*, 16.

22. Cleland to Stanhope; Boswell, *Laird*, 76.

23. Boswell, *Laird*, 76–77.

24. Catherine Gallagher offers a historicist account of the author as ghost in *Nobody's Story*. In print culture, she argues, "the disembodiment of the writer . . . was the condition of her appearance as an *author*" (62). As she writes of Aphra Behn, "the sale of the manuscript and the inconceivability of any property in the text were indeed forms of alienation from the work, but they were also the conditions of what Behn seemed to imagine as her ghostly endurance in the text" (64). On authors and ghosts, see also Bennett and Royle, *Introduction to Literature*, 18–26 and 133–141.

25. Cleland to Stanhope.

26. Boswell, *Laird*, 77.

27. In "From Work to Text," written after "The Death of the Author," Barthes allows for the "Author" to " 'come back' in the Text, but he then does so as a 'guest' . . . His life is no longer the origin of his fictions but a fiction contributing to his work" (*Image, Music, Text*, 161).

28. Said, *On Late Style*, 7.

29. Review of *The Surprises of Love*, in *Monthly Review* 23 (October 1760), 327, quoted in Basker, "Wages," 189.

CHAPTER 1. FANNY HILL IN BOMBAY (1728–1740)

1. Cleland to Stanhope.

2. Foxon, *Libertine Literature*, 7.

3. Cleland to Stanhope.

4. Stevenson, "Note on the Scotsman," 40.

5. Boswell, *Laird*, 76–77. The editors note that their reconstruction of the sentence peppered with braces and square brackets is "highly conjectural," owing to defects in the manuscript. Words within braces represent the editors' conjectures as to illegible words while those within brackets supply words omitted by Boswell.

6. On John Carmichael, see Boswell, *Laird*, 77n7; Stevenson, "Note on the Scotsman," 40.

7. India Office Collection (IOC), Miscellaneous Letters Received 27, E/1/27, item 133 (letter from William Henry Draper, dated Bombay 28 October 1736, folio j).

8. On Cleland's family background and education, see Epstein, *Images of a Life*, 3–31.

9. IOC, Miscellaneous Letters Received 22, E/1/22 [1731], f. 36. Also quoted in Epstein, *Images of a Life*, 35.

10. Epstein, *Images of a Life*, 36.

11. Stevenson, "Note on the Scotsman," 40–41; Boswell, *Laird*, 77n7.

12. IOC, List of Bombay Civil Servants, 1712–1752, O/6/37. His name is always spelled Carmichaell in the primary sources I've located.

13. IOC, Secretary's List of Deceas'd Persons at Bombay & Factorys Subordinate, Anno 1733, in N/3/1, f. 149; and IOC, An Account of the Births, Christnings, Weddings, & Burials at Bombay, Anno 1733, N/3/1, f. 154. I have not yet found a record of Carmichael's date of birth, but 1712 seems plausible.

14. On the Cleland family's social and political connections, see Epstein, *Images of a Life*, 12–22.

15. The English text is printed in Mudge, *When Flesh Becomes Word*, 1–57. Mudge notes that apparently only one copy survives of the 1680 edition, in the Bayerischer Staatsbibliothek in Munich. See also Wagner, *Eros Revived*, 227; Foxon, *Libertine Literature*, 30–37. Another translation was published by Daniel Lynch and John Stevens in 1744 (Mudge, xvi). On *L'École des filles* more generally, see Turner, *Schooling Sex*, 106–164.

16. Samuel Pepys, diary entries for 8 and 9 February 1668, quoted in Foxon, *Libertine Literature*, 5–6.

17. IOC, List of Bombay Civil Servants, 1712–1752, O/6/37; Epstein, *Images of a Life*, 36–52.

18. Attorney to the Mayor's Court: IOC, Register of Proceedings of the Mayor's Court, P/416/103, f. 210. Secretary for Portuguese Affairs: IOC, Bombay Public Consultations, P/341/9, f. 159. Secretary to the Bombay Council: Bombay Public Consultations, P/341/10, ff. 17–18. These appointments and others are discussed in Epstein, *Images of a Life*, 35–39.

19. This case is discussed in detail in Epstein, *Images of a Life*, 38–48, on which I draw for my summary of events.

20. Vossontroy's name is variously spelled in the legal documents; this spelling is from IOC, Register of Proceedings of the Mayor's Court, P/416/108, f. 229.

21. IOC, Bombay Public Consultations, P/341/8, f. 19.

22. Epstein, *Images of a Life*, 44, 210n52.

23. IOC, Bombay Public Consultations, P/341/8, ff. 19, 22.

24. In another passage Cleland is equally uncompromising in his warning to the court of the likely fallout of a decision for Lowther: "But, shou'd the Justice of this Civil Government be refused to a Mogull Subject only suing for his own, on such a Plea as this, wou'd it not bring those Priviledges into a certain Danger: & if they were totally cancell'd & Destroy'd, on account of such a flagrant injustice; where wou'd the blame lie? Or to whom wou'd the first Breach of Faith & the Law of Nature & Nations be justly imputed to [*sic*]: Or with what face cou'd our Nation complain that they were not observed?" (IOC, Bombay Public Consultations, P/341/8, f. 20).

25. IOC, Bombay Public Consultations, P/341/8, ff. 10–12.

26. Ibid., f. 11.

27. The word "colour" does not necessarily refer to skin or race: it could also mean appearance more generally or might allude to the military or company colors under which Cleland served. But the charge that Cleland "deserted his King, Country & even the Colour Nature design'd him," with its rise in rhetorical pitch from king to country to "even . . . Colour," and its linkage of "Colour" to "Nature," suggests that Cleland turned against or deserted his own fundamental or innate nature, and the racializing implication of Cleland as "pinion'd slave" is strong.

28. IOC, Bombay Public Consultations, P/341/8, f. 18.

29. Ibid., ff. 20, 15.

30. Ibid., ff. 19, 15.

31. IOC, Bombay Public Consultations, P/341/8, f. 23.

32. IOC, Bombay Public Consultations, P/341/8, f. 25. See also Epstein, *Images of a Life*, 44.

33. IOC, Bombay Public Consultations, P/341/8, ff. 11, 20.

34. Epstein, *Images of a Life*, 42, 46, 210–211nn55–58.

35. IOC, Bombay Public Consultations, P/341/8, f. 19.

36. IOC, Index of Court Minutes, B/63, f. 585.

37. IOC, Bombay Public Consultations, P/341/8, f. 15. The phrase "inveteracy and Venom" is quoted by Cleland from Lowther's complaint, P/341/8, f. 6.

38. IOC, Index of Court Minutes, B/63, f. 584; Epstein, *Images of a Life*, 46–47, 211nn.57, 61.

39. IOC, Correspondence with the East, Despatch Books for 1733–1736, E/3/106, f. 660. See also Epstein, *Images of a Life*, 47.

40. IOC, Index of Court Minutes, B/63, f. 584.

41. IOC, Register of Proceedings in the Mayor's Court, P/416/109, ff. 123–144, on 123. Subsequent references to the case will be cited parenthetically.

42. For a discussion of this pattern in eighteenth-century fiction, see Brissenden, *Virtue in Distress*, esp. 84–95.

43. Date of Cleland's answer: IOC, Register of Proceedings of the Mayor's Court, P/416/108, f. 178.

44. The evidence that Marthalina prosecuted King is found in John Bradyll's testimony for the defense (that is, in support of Cleland), in which he refers to her as "a woman (who afterwards Prosecuted at the quarter sessions by the name of Marthalinah)" (f. 141).

45. Chatterjee, *Gender, Slavery and Law*, 3.

46. On "pornotopia," see Marcus, *Other Victorians*, esp. 268–281.

47. The complicated translation and publication history of *Venus in the Cloister* is best presented in Turner, *Schooling Sex*, xxviii; Foxon, *Libertine Literature*, 14, 43–45; and Baines and Rogers, *Edmund Curll*, 155–160. See also Wagner, *Eros Revived*, 72–73, 229–231.

48. Cleland, *Memoirs of a Woman of Pleasure*, 93, 88. Subsequent references will be cited parenthetically. The equation of prostitution and marriage is a commonplace of the period, whether explicit, as in *Moll Flanders* or *The Beggar's Opera*, or darkly implied,

as in *Clarissa*; Cleland merely engages with the prostitution side of the equation more graphically than his contemporaries.

49. Cleland's family moved to St. James's Place when JC was a child, probably in 1722, and his parents remained there until William Cleland's death in 1741; JC's mother, Lucy, continued to live on or just off St. James's until her death in 1763, JC living with her for much or most of the period 1741–1753 (see Epstein, *Images of a Life*, 29, 58–59, 128–129). Fanny writes that she and Charles lodged "in D—— street, St James's" (50), perhaps Duke Street, equidistant from St. James's Place and St. James's Square.

50. Cleland, *Unfortunate Penlez*, 9.

51. See Olsson, "Idealized and Realistic Portrayals." Olsson argues against critics who have faulted the *Memoirs* for its idealized or unrealistic representation of prostitution, notably Randolph Trumbach in "Modern Prostitution and Gender."

52. It was Boswell who described the *Woman of Pleasure* as "that most licentious and inflaming book." Boswell, *For the Defence*, 81–82.

53. In July 1760, Cleland wrote a letter to Herbert Mayo, "Fellow of Brazen-noze College," Oxford, in response to a request for information about a "collection of miniature-portraits of the Sovereigns of Indostan" that Cleland had acquired while living in Bombay, probably in 1735–1736 (Cleland, [copy of] letter to Herbert Mayo, IOC, Orme Manuscript Collection, vol. 147, ff. 47–50, on 47). The volume had been given by the governor of Surat, Teg beg Khaun (or Khan) to a "Mr Frazer," who later gave or sold it to Cleland, who in turn sent it to Alexander Pope, "with whom," Cleland writes, "I was then in correspondence" (f. 49). Pope, "judging it too great a curiosity for his private study" (f. 49), presented it to the Bodleian Library in 1737. The letter offers some interesting glimpses of Mughal politics as well as protoethnographic observations on the "tartarian origin" (f. 48) of both Mughal religious toleration and the facial features of Tamerlane and his successors. In the portrait of Tamerlane, Cleland writes, "you may very clearly remark . . . the distinctive tartar lineaments, a broad flattish face with small Eyes. These in his Son & Successor are somewhat less conspicuous, & as the line of Descent proceeds, they melt by degrees into the softness of the indian features" (f. 49). See also Epstein, *Images of a Life*, 50–52 and 212–213nn79–80.

54. Douglas, *Glimpses*, 255. A *Voyage* was published in one-volume form in 1757 and in two-volume editions in 1766 and 1772; it is unclear what Douglas's dates of 1750–64 refer to.

55. Schürer, "Impartial Spectator of Sati," 25.

56. Grose, *Voyage aux Indes Orientales*, n.p. Translation mine.

57. Cleland to Dickinson, 18 Feb. 1757, BL MS RP 4335[g] (see chapter 6, n. 5, for more on the letters in RP 4335).

58. Grose, *Voyage to the East Indies*, 407, 184. Subsequent references will be cited parenthetically. On seraglios and dancing girls, see pp. 218–231.

59. See Farrant, "Grose, John Henry (*b.* 1732, *d.* in or after 1774)," *ODNB*.

60. The story can be dated 1734–1736 because John Horne, referred to as the governor of Bombay, only assumed this position in 1734, and William Boag died on 28 May 1736.

CHAPTER 2. DOWN AND OUT IN LISBON AND LONDON (1741–1748)

1. Douglas, *Glimpses*, 254. Cleland features in a chapter oxymoronically titled "People Whom India Has Forgotten."

2. Ibid., 255.

3. The outlines of Charlotte Louisa's life in Bombay are drawn from a number of documents in the India Office Collection. She first appears on the List of Free Merchants Seafaring Men & c for 25 October 1736, under the heading "Maids," as Charlotte Louisa Cleland (IOC, European Inhabitants of Bombay, 1719–1792, O/5/31, vol. 1, f. 38). On the List of Births, Christenings, Weddings, & Burials on Bombay for 1737, the entry for 24 June records the wedding of "Mr. George Sadler, & Miss Charlotte Lucy Cleland" (N/3/1, f. 189, dated "from the 1st of Jan. 1736/7 to the 22d of Dec.br 1737"). The same list for 1739 registers the birth of "John the Son of Mr. George and Mrs. Charlotte Sadleir" on 3 October, his christening on 26 October, and his burial on 4 December (N/3/1 for 31 Dec. 1738 to 10 Jan. 1739/40, f. 222). The List of Deceased Persons of Bombay in the same volume, which is in Cleland's hand and signed by him, records his nephew's death: "Bombay—John Sadleir an Infant—Dec. 4—of Flux"(N/3/1, f.213).

4. IOC, Bombay Public Consultations, P/341/11, for 5 Sept. 1740, n.p.

5. Charlotte's name is included on the lists of European inhabitants of Bombay through 20 September 1740 but is absent thereafter, not reappearing until October 1743, while her husband continues to be recorded as present—which almost certainly means she sailed with her brother and stayed in London for two years. See IOC, European Inhabitants of Bombay, 1719–1792, O/5/31, ff. 38, 40, 42, 44, 46, 48, 52, 54, 65v, 67v, 72v, 73v (for Charlotte), and List of Bombay Civil Servants, 1712–1752, O/6/37 (for George). On William Cleland's poor state of health—he suffered among other things from "the Gravell," or kidney stones—and his insecure position as civil servant, see Epstein, *Images of a Life*, 54–57.

6. As Epstein notes, Henry Cleland is recorded as having been appointed "collector" in Montserrat in the West Indies on 12 November 1745 (*Images of a Life*, 215). Pope described him as the "Favorite Son" in a letter dated 3 November 1730, when Henry was a student at Christ Church College, Oxford. Favorite he may have been, but his father was uneasy; as Pope writes, "He apprehends he may fall into mean company, unless some experienced worthy Man would countenance, & have an eye over him, or recommend him to proper Companions" (*Correspondence*, 3:144). On 1 January 1742, Pope wrote nostalgically to Hugh Bethel of William Cleland "having a few weeks before his death received at one post three Letters, from each of his children, from different Ends almost of the Earth, with the News that two of them were upon the way to see him . . . as extraordinary an Event as ever I heard of. He accordingly lived to receive his Eldest Son with great Satisfaction, & so be pretty easy as to the other two" (*Correspondence*, 4:378). Epstein conjectures that Henry was already in the West Indies—a "different End" of the Earth from his brother—and I agree that this is likely. I reckon the likely period of Henry's death from the fact that he is not mentioned in Lucy Cleland's will of 1752, and from a letter of John's of 23 October 1755, in which he refers to himself as his mother's "only, and unfortunate son" (BL MS RP 4335[e]; see chapter 6, n. 5, for more on the letters in RP 4335).

7. See Epstein, *Images of a Life*, 36–37.

8. See ibid., 52 and 213n83.

9. In his biography, Epstein rightly called these Cleland's "lost years," while recognizing that it was a "crucial period" (*Images of a Life*, 60) in his formation as an author.

10. Johnson, *Life of Savage*, 12. Savage was also linked, coincidentally, to Cleland's father, William: both were allies of Pope in the paper war that raged after the publication of *The Dunciad Variorum* in 1728. As Pope's friend Fenton wrote in a letter, "The war is carried on against him furiously in pictures and libels; and I heard of nobody but Savage and Cleland who have yet drawn their pens in his defence" (Pope, *Correspondence*, 3:37).

11. Cleland's involvement in the Portuguese scheme was evidently first revealed by J. Lúcio de Azevedo in *O Marquês de Pombal e a Sua Época* (Rio de Janeiro, 1922) but only fully explained some sixty years later with the research undertaken by José Barreto, published in his edition of *Escritos Económicos de Londres (1741–1742)* by Sebastião José de Carvalho e Melo, later Marquês de Pombal. Epstein, in his entry on Cleland for the *Dictionary of Literary Biography*, was the first to refer to this scheme in English but did not go into detail (104). In what follows I draw from Barreto's edition of Pombal, which includes the original French text of Cleland's *mémoire* addressed to the Portuguese king, never before translated. See also Maxwell, *Pombal*, 6–8.

12. See Stevenson, *The Beggar's Benison*, esp. 23–29 and 37–43; Stevenson, "Note on the Scotsman"; and Epstein, *Images of a Life*, 69–71. Although Stevenson holds that the Beggar's Benison minute "is the only known reference to Cleland's text circulating before it was printed" ("Note on the Scotsman," 39), the evidence is too insecure to rely on. Neither Cleland's nor Carmichael's Scottish connections link them to Anstruther, nor can this "Fanny Hill" be securely identified with Cleland's, however suggestive the coincidence. The only real extratextual evidence for the *Memoirs'* origins in the early 1730s is the consistency of Cleland's account, from the letter to Stanhope to his statement to Boswell, when he had no more motive for prevarication.

13. Quoted in Maxwell, *Pombal*, 4–6 (translation Maxwell's). My précis of British diplomatic relations with Portugal in the period 1739–1743 is taken from Maxwell and from Rodrigues and Craig, "English Mercantilist Influences."

14. Rodrigues and Craig, "English Mercantilist Influences," 334–337.

15. Barreto, introduction to *Escritos Económicos*, liii, lxxii–lxxiiin140; and Carvalho e Melo to Cardinal da Mota, 19 February 1742, in *Escritos Económicos*, 134–135. See also Rodrigues and Craig, "English Mercantilist Influences," 338.

16. This summary of William Cleland's career is based on Epstein, *Images of a Life*, 10–16 and 54–56.

17. Cleland to the Duke of Newcastle, 22 May 1741. See also Epstein, *Images of a Life*, 55–56.

18. Cleland to the Duke of Newcastle, 22 May 1741.

19. Ibid.

20. Carvalho e Melo to Cardinal da Mota, 19 Feb. 1742, in *Escritos Económicos*, 134 (translation mine). Cardinal da Mota was chief minister of the Portuguese king João V.

21. Carvalho e Melo, *Escritos Económicos*, 135 (translation mine).

22. Ibid., 134 (translation mine).

23. See Barreto, introduction to *Escritos Económicos*, xii–xiii and liii; and Maxwell, *Pombal*, 7.

24. Maxwell, *Pombal*, 7 (translation Maxwell's) and Barreto, introduction to *Escritos Económicos*, xiii. Barreto argues that his brother's death was among the key reasons for Carvalho's interest in the Portuguese East India company plan.

25. Quoted in Rodrigues and Craig, "English Mercantilist Influences," 338 (translation theirs). The original text of the *Relação dos Gravames* is in Carvalho e Melo, *Escritos Económicos*, 33–95; the passage quoted is on 94.

26. Printed (in French) in Carvalho e Melo, *Escritos Económicos*, 158–161. See appendix to the present volume for an English translation of the full text.

27. Carvalho e Melo, *Escritos Económicos*, 134. On Carvalho e Melo's enemies and rivals, see Maxwell, *Pombal*, 8; and Barreto, introduction to *Escritos Económicos*, lv.

28. See Barreto, introduction to *Escritos Económicos*, xii–xiii, where he writes that not only did the company keep the government from providing military support to the Portuguese in the wake of the Marathas' seizure of the Portuguese-controlled island of Salsete (just north of Bombay) and their attack on Goa, but it provided the Marathas with arms.

29. Carvalho e Melo, *Escritos Económicos*, 158, quoted in Rodrigues and Craig, "English Mercantilist Influences," 336 (translation theirs).

30. The scheme's demise is most fully discussed in Barreto, introduction to *Escritos Económicos*, lv–lvi. See also Maxwell, *Pombal*, 8; and Rodrigues and Craig, "English Mercantilist Influences," 338–339.

31. Quoted in Barreto, introduction to *Escritos Económicos*, lv. The passage is from Carvalho's 1748 letter to Coutinho (translation mine).

32. Charlotte died in Surat—a subordinate company station north of Bombay—on 11 October 1747 and was probably buried there (she is not listed in the records of Bombay burials); see IOC, Secretary's List of Deceas'd Persons, N/3/1, ff. 281 and 285. Her husband, George Sadleir, evidently died on his way back to England from India in 1752; there were no surviving children. See Stoney, *Life and Times of Sir Ralph Sadleir*, 251.

33. My summary of the legal case is based on Epstein, *Images of a Life*, 61–62. Cannon himself, in the affidavit discussed below (NA KB 1/10/1) says that he had "recovered a Verdict" for £800 plus £16 damages. Epstein speculates that Cannon's and Lane's charges may have been false, but the evidence is inconclusive.

34. Annual rent of the house on Cleveland Court West, St. James's Place, where Lucy Cleland lived from late 1741, was £30 (Epstein, *Images of a Life*, 58).

35. See Warner, "Cannon, Robert (1663–1722)," *ODNB*.

36. Cleland to Stanhope, quoted in Foxon, *Libertine Literature*, 54.

37. Whiston, *Memoirs of the Life and Writings of Mr William Whiston* (1749), 110, quoted in Warner, "Cannon, Robert."

38. Petition of Elizabeth Cannon to Thomas Pelham-Holles, Duke of Newcastle, n.d. [ca. 1754–1755], NA T1/338, f. 66.

39. I conjecture that when Cleland first knew him, Thomas lived with his mother at her house in Delahay Street, Westminster, on the basis of some of the details in the

affidavit discussed below (NA KB 1/10/1)—in particular, the claim that the mother and son were acting in concert to fatally poison Cleland.

40. Pope, *Correspondence*, 4:378.

41. On William's and Lucy's wills, see Epstein, *Images of a Life*, 57 and 127–128; on Cleland's railing, see below and chapter 6.

42. Cleland to Dickinson, 23 Nov. 1752, BL Ms. RP 4335[b].

43. William Henry Draper, letter from Bombay, 28 Oct. 1736, in IOC, E/1/27, no. 133, folio j.

44. Affidavits for Hilary Term 22nd George II [i.e., 1749], 5 Feb. 1748/49, NA KB 1/10/1.

45. A catamite is a kept boy, Latin *catamitus* from Greek *Ganymedes* or Ganymede; "molly," as is now well known, was a standard slang term for what might generally be called a male homosexual, although the term's precise meanings and nuances have been much debated in recent scholarship. See, among others, Bray, *Homosexuality in Renaissance England*, esp. 81–114; Norton, *Mother Clap's Molly House*; Trumbach, "London's Sodomites"; McFarlane, *The Sodomite*.

46. Apart from Cleland's and Cannon's texts, discussed below and in the following chapter, a small number of other published works in English contain sodomitical episodes or discussions of same-sex desire, notably *Roderick Random* (1748) and *Peregrine Pickle* (1751) by Cleland's occasional colleague Tobias Smollett—both of which are more straightforwardly antisodomite than either Cleland's or Cannon's works. Another short book, the *Love Letters Between a certain late Nobleman and the famous Mr. Wilson* (1723), offers an extended if extremely elliptical treatment of a sodomitical relationship. For discussions of other eighteenth-century works in English, see Rousseau, "Pursuit of Homosexuality"; McFarlane, *The Sodomite*; and Norton, *Mother Clap's Molly House*.

47. Foxon, *Libertine Literature*, 52; Gladfelder, "In Search," 22.

48. Cleland to Stanhope.

49. On Ralph Griffiths (ca. 1720–1803), see Forster, "Griffiths, Ralph (1720?–1803)," *ODNB*; Knapp, "Ralph Griffiths"; and Foxon, *Libertine Literature*, 52–63. Doubts have been raised about the very existence of Fenton Griffiths, but his existence is confirmed by a group of letters written to Ralph Griffiths by Fenton between 1785 and his death on 15 August 1791, now held in the Bodleian (MS Add C.89, ff. 5–51 and 132–137, cited in Epstein, *Images of a Life*, 219n36), in which he details his poor state of health, his 1785 marriage to "the Widow Cudlipp," and their difficulties raising her children from an earlier marriage.

50. Quoted in Foxon, *Libertine Literature*, 53, original document in National Archives, SP 36/111, f. 159.

51. Epstein, *Images of a Life*, 72 and 219n36.

52. Examination of Ralph Griffiths before Lovel Stanhope, NA SP 36/112, f. 145. The story that Cleland was paid twenty guineas for the copyright to the *Woman of Pleasure* seems to have originated in the Nichols obituary; see also Nichols, *Literary Anecdotes of the Eighteenth Century* (London, 1812), 2:456–458.

53. Cleland to Stanhope.

54. Quoted in Watt, *The Rise of the Novel*, 53–54.

55. On Savage and Iscariot Hackney, see my article "The Hard Work of Doing Nothing." Kate Levin, in "The Meanness of Writing for a Bookseller," argues that "at a time when authorship was shifting from a system of patronage to a commercial relationship between author and publisher, Cleland used Fanny as a mouthpiece to challenge his own exploitation by the literary market" (330–331). I question Levin's conclusion that Cleland, in a novel written before he had become a professional author, used Fanny as a figural embodiment of his own condition, but her article is suggestive in its reading of the *Woman of Pleasure*.

56. Affidavit of John Purser, Affidavits for Hilary Term 24th George II (1751), 9 Feb. 1750/51, NA KB1/10/4. By unlucky coincidence, the affidavits of Purser and his associate Hugh Morgan were given before the same W. Foster of Serjeants Inn who had taken Cannon's affidavit against Cleland a year earlier: it can't have helped Cannon that Foster knew he'd recently been labeled "an execrable white-faced, rotten catamite." Purser had been prosecuted at least seven times over the preceding twenty years for seditious libel: see Prosecutions in the Crown Office for Seditious Libels in the Reign of George II, NA KB 15/54, ff. 154–157; see also Chapman, "Purser, John (*fl.* 1728–1747)," *ODNB*.

57. Affidavit of John Purser, NA KB 1/10/4.

58. Affidavit of Hugh Morgan, Affidavits for Trinity Term 24–25 George II (1751), 6 May 1751, NA KB 1/10/5.

59. Thomas Pelham-Holles, Duke of Newcastle [then secretary of state], to the Attorney General, Dudley Ryder 20 Jan. 1749/50, NA SP 44/134, f. 9.

60. Cleland to Stanhope.

61. Newcastle to Ryder, 20 Jan. 1749/50, NA SP 44/134, f. 9.

CHAPTER 3. SODOMITES (1748–1749)

1. Quoted in Merritt, "Biographical Note," 305–306.

2. Quoted in Foxon, *Libertine Literature*, 15.

3. Cannon, quoted in Gladfelder, "Indictment of John Purser," 40. Further references both to Cannon's text and to Ryder's indictment are from this source and will be cited in the text.

4. It was Boswell who called the *Woman of Pleasure* "inflaming." Boswell, *For the Defence*, 81.

5. See Sabor, "From Sexual Liberation to Gender Trouble," for an overview of critical discussions of Cleland's novel. Of the essays he discusses, those by Nancy K. Miller and David Weed exemplify the tendency to read the novel as complicit with hegemonic structures of masculine or heteronormative authority. See Miller, "I's in Drag"; and Weed, "Fitting Fanny"; as well as Fowler, "This Tail-Piece of Morality"; and Markley, "Language, Power, and Sexuality."

6. Petition of Elizabeth Cannon to Thomas Pelham-Holles, Duke of Newcastle, n.d. [ca. 1754–1755], NA T1/338, f. 66.

7. *The Tryal and Condemnation of Mervin, Lord Audley*, A3r.

8. Norton, "Reformation Necessary to Prevent Our Ruin, 1727," in *Homosexuality in Eighteenth-Century England*.

9. *Reasons for the Growth of Sodomy*, 51.

10. Ibid., 51, 52, 54.

11. Quoted in Norton, *Mother Clap's Molly House*, 159.

12. *The Trial of Richard Branson*, 24–25.

13. Jody Greene reaches similar conclusions from different cases in "Public Secrets: Sodomy and the Pillory in the Eighteenth Century and Beyond": "So dangerous, so potentially seductive is the appeal of non-normative sexuality that its very name cannot be spoken for fear of provoking an epidemic, a conflagration of buggery sweeping across the land" (225).

14. Petition of Elizabeth Cannon. For more detail on the legal proceedings, see Gladfelder, "In Search," 26–28, and "Indictment of John Purser," 58–59n1.

15. Foxon, *Libertine Literature*, 61.

16. Gladfelder, "In Search," 28 and 37n19.

17. Heywood, *Pleasant Dialogues and Drammas*, 96.

18. For a lucid and nuanced discussion of the classical Athenian model of pederasty, see Halperin, *One Hundred Years of Homosexuality*, in particular chapters 1 and 2 and the addendum.

19. The malleability of bodies and desires in Cannon's text affiliates it to a seventeenth-century work by the Italian priest and professor of rhetoric Antonio Rocco, whose *Alcibiade fanciullo a scuola* is explored at length by James Grantham Turner in *Schooling Sex*. "Ambiguous beauty," Turner writes, "places Alcibiade between active and passive, powerful and weak, heaven and earth, male and female" (94). Despite these similarities, especially to the breakdown of categorical distinctions in the Hyacinth-Amorio narrative discussed later, there is no evidence Cannon borrowed directly from Rocco.

20. A passage I quoted earlier from the Eumolpus narrative represents sexual climax in similar language: "grasping Love's Bolt, [I] spurt myself away, plunging in a Gulph of unutterable Delight" (45). In context, it's unclear whose "Bolt" Eumolpus is grasping, which only augments the sense of loss of self. Several other passages represent pleasure in terms of water or fluidity: Hyacinth exclaims "in what a Gulph of Pleasure have I been plung'd" (50), while pseudo-Lucian's Theomnestes asks, "What; are we perpetually to converse with Youths of a Fairness, which only does not overflow the Eyes; and, when we can lay our Lips to it, and take a Draught shall we be such foolish *Tantalus's* to suffer Thirst?" (51). The same speaker concludes with this summary of "my way of Loving": "master'd by desire, [I] enter a narrow passage, which carries to the Ocean of absorbing Rapture" (51).

21. In *How to Do the History of Homosexuality*. Halperin identifies four "pre-homosexual categories of male sex and gender deviance": "(1) effeminacy, (2) paederasty or 'active' sodomy, (3) friendship or male love, and (4) passivity or inversion" (109). Amorio and Hyacinth embody all these categories at once, so that Hyacinth, for example, while manifestly feminine, is simultaneously "active" and "invert" and lives happily in "the world of male friendship and love which can claim an equally ancient discursive tradition" (117).

22. The allusion here is to Mitchell and Leavitt, *Pages Passed from Hand to Hand*, and their positing of a sexual outsider/outlaw culture defined at least in part by the clandestine circulation of certain highly coded (if not explicitly "homosexual") texts.

23. My use of the term "sodomitical practice" differs from McFarlane's "sodomitical practices" in *The Sodomite in Fiction and Satire*. McFarlane uses the phrase to refer to the "representational practices" by which "sodomy" and "the sodomite" were discursively constructed (largely by others) in the period (see esp. 20–21 and 25–68); I use it to refer to the behaviors or acts in which sodomites engaged or were said (by themselves or others) to engage.

24. See Kopelson, "Seeing Sodomy"; and Edelman, "Seeing Things: Representation, the Scene of Surveillance, and the Spectacle of Gay Male Sex," in *Homographesis*, 173–191, esp. 183–188.

25. See McFarlane, *The Sodomite*, 172. McFarlane's reading is the strongest of the many critical discussions of this scene over the last twenty years. For an overview of these up to the late 1990s, see Sabor's important review essay, "From Sexual Liberation to Gender Trouble." For discussion of some more recent work, and a provocative analysis in its own right, see Robinson, *Closeted Writing*, esp. 37–51 and 77–80. In addition to these and the essays by Kopelson and Edelman cited above, I have been most influenced by Mengay, "The Sodomitical Muse."

26. Mengay, "The Sodomitical Muse," 188.

27. See also ibid., 194–195.

28. See, for example, the illustrative 1709 and 1711 quotations from Steele in the *OED* definitions of "romp" and "romping": "This careless Jade was eternally romping with the Footman" (*Tatler* 15, p. 2); "The Air she gave herself was that of a Romping Girl" (*Spectator* 187, p. 3).

29. See, for example, Ellis, *Sexual Inversion*. See also Bristow, "Symonds's History, Ellis's Heredity." For a fuller discussion of Ellis and Symonds in relation to earlier theories of sodomy and Cleland's challenge to these, see my essay "Plague Spots."

30. Norton, "The Trial of Richard Manning and John Davis, 1745," at *Homosexuality in Eighteenth-Century England*, 25 Jan. 2001, updated 1 Mar. 2003, http://rictornorton.co.uk/eighteen/1745mann.htm, accessed 15 Apr. 2009. This trial is also discussed in relation to Cleland's text by Robinson in *Closeted Writing*, 51–53. For an extended analysis of this and the Dicks trial in relation to the sodomitical scene in Cleland, see Haggerty, "Keyhole Testimony."

31. Norton, "The Trial of John Dicks, 1722," at *Homosexuality in Eighteenth-Century England*, updated 1 Dec. 1999, http://rictornorton.co.uk/eighteen/1722dick.htm, accessed 7 Sept. 2004.

32. Ibid.

33. Campbell [attrib.], *The Sale of Authors*, 139.

34. As the novel's editor, Peter Sabor, notes, citing the *OED*, a "carpet-road" is "smooth, sheltered water 'near the shore, where vessels may lie at anchor in safety'" (201n). Fanny here echoes the nautical metaphors of the sailor episode and Mrs. Cole's pronouncement about pleasure as "the universal port of destination" (144), thus "normalizing" this moment. Cleland's phrase "the streights of entrance" echoes Cannon's description of Amorio, "piloted into a Streight whose potent Cling draws all the Man in clammy streams away" (50).

35. See also Mengay, "The Sodomitical Muse," 193–194; and Kubek, "Man Machine," 186.

36. For other examples of disproportion as a vital constituent of desire, see Fanny's description of Polly and the Genoese merchant with his "grand movement . . . of a size to frighten me, by sympathy, for the small tender part, which was the object of its fury" (30); her first intercourse with Charles, when "the largeness of his machine (for few men could dispute size with him) made all the difficulty" (40); her whipping session with Mr. Barvile who, stimulated by her lashings, presents Fanny with a "machine . . . grown not only to a prodigious stiffness of erection, but to a size that frighted even me: a non-pareil thickness indeed!" (147); or, most vividly, the encounter of Louisa with Good-Natur'd Dick, whose "standard of distinction . . . was positively of so tremendous a size, that prepar'd as we were to see something extraordinary, it still, out of measure surpass'd our expectation" (162).

37. The alternative to "immense disproportion" in Fanny's narrative is not "natural" or proportionate desire, but no desire—as when she describes Mr. Norbert's "machine" as "one of those sizes that slip in and out without being minded" (133), leaving her "unappeas'd" (140). When Fanny first tells Phoebe of her "doubts and apprehensions" (27) regarding the threat posed by the "terrible weapon," Phoebe laughingly dismisses Fanny's "fears from that imaginary disproportion" (28). "Disproportion" is "imaginary"— that is, a figure for desire itself. So, at a later tryst with Will, with whom she has already had sex repeatedly, Fanny once again touches his "enormous machine," writing that "its dimensions, mocking either grasp or span, almost renew'd my terrors. I could not conceive how, or by what means, I could take, or put such a bulk out of sight" (81–82). This is an imaginary inconceivability: an arousal of desire by a fiction of impossibility.

38. It may be useful for North American readers to note that in Britain "fanny" does not refer to the backside but rather to the female genitals, so that fanny hill = mount-pleasant = mons veneris (mount or hill of Venus). The first references to "fanny" in either sense listed in the *OED* are from the late nineteenth century, but "Fanny Hill" itself suggests that the usage is much older.

39. See n. 9 above.

40. See also the discussion of this passage in Edelman, *Homographesis*, 184; and Robinson, *Closeted Writing*, 46–49.

41. See also Mengay, "The Sodomitical Muse," 191, for a discussion of Fanny herself as a phallic figure. Felicity Nussbaum argues that "Cleland . . . radically implies that Fanny Hill's body is both male and female" and that the novel "tolerates a sexual ambiguity not entertained or represented in eighteenth-century science" (*Torrid Zones*, 104–105). Nussbaum also discusses the gender ambiguity of Will's body and the similar ambiguities and doublings in the sodomitical and "nipple of love" passages, though the conclusions she draws from these are very different from mine: see *Torrid Zones*, 103–113.

42. On the Dulwich schoolboys, see n. 12 above. Lisa L. Moore, in *Dangerous Intimacies*, reads Cleland's discussion of "plague spots" in the *Memoirs* in the context of works like *Satan's Harvest Home* that represent sodomy as a foreign import. See also Greene, "Arbitrary Tastes," esp. 250–253. Greene notes "the gap between the depiction of the homosexual characters and the theory of homosexuality the otherwise reliable Mrs. Cole articulates" (252n13) but leaves this as an "inexplicable" problem. My own view is that

this "gap" is precisely Cleland's point: Mrs. Cole's comments are patently baseless, as is also indicated by her retreat from her own claim that *all* are tainted: "among *numbers* of that stamp whom she had known, *or at least were universally under the scandalous suspicion of it*, she could not name an exception *hardly of one of them*" and so on (159, emphasis added).

43. In his 1753 *Dictionary of Love*, Cleland introduces another possible meaning of "plague spot" in his article on "Fribble," defined as "one of those ambiguous animals, who are neither male nor female; disclaimed by his own sex, and the scorn of both"—a definition inspired by Garrick's foppish William Fribble from *Miss in Her Teens; or, The Medley of Lovers* (1747). Noting the fribbles' habit of giving women advice on how to dress, Cleland writes: "Nor is their own dress neglected: the muff, the ermin-facing, a cluster-ring, the stone-buckle, and now and then a patch, that on them does not always suppose a pimple, are the plague-spots, in which the folly of these less than butterflies breaks out." Here, the plague spot is explicitly not a bodily mark. Instead, it's an accessory or signal to others in the coterie, a badge of subcultural identification, not an imprint of nature. (Quoted in Cleland, *Memoirs of a Coxcomb*, 255.)

44. Mengay writes that virtually "all of the male characters are Ganymedes of sorts, patterned after Zeus' catamite" ("Sodomitical Muse," 190); certainly the more her male partners conform to this type, the more she desires them.

45. As work in the history of sexuality and gender over the past twenty-five years has established, notions and categories of masculinity in the eighteenth century were complex, contradictory, and in constant flux. Effeminate foppishness, as described here by Mrs. Cole, sometimes carried associations of same-sex desire, as in Smollett's Captain Whiffle in *Roderick Random* (1748), and sometimes (perhaps more often) did not. See, among many other discussions, Haggerty, *Men in Love*, 44–80; Staves, "A Few Kind Words for the Fop"; McFarlane, *The Sodomite*, 42–49; and Trumbach, "Erotic Fantasy and Male Libertinism."

46. Affidavit of John Ibbutt, 19 June 1750, Affidavits for Trinity term 24–25 George II, NA KB 1/10/3. This was the second of three affidavits sworn by Ibbutt, all to the same effect. The others are dated 26 May 1750 (Easter term 23 George II) and 27 June 1750 (Trinity term 24–25 George II).

47. Petition of Elizabeth Cannon.

48. Cannon's "Retraction" was first cited by Faramerz Dabhoiwala, to whom I owe the discovery, in his 2010 article "Lust and Liberty," 167. Cannon does not refer to *Ancient and Modern Pederasty* by name in the retraction but "bitterly deplores" (8) his earlier writing, whose effect was "to subvert Religion, and introduce the utmost Profligacy of Manners" (4). In its later pages, the retraction, written when Cannon was still under threat of prosecution, offers a poignant glimpse of the misery to which he had been reduced: "no Happiness can arrive to me in this World: my Nerves are so broke, as to render any Enjoyment, without a Miracle, impracticable, and to give me an *immense* Desire of the Grave" (9). Copies of the "Retraction" and the *Treatise on Charity* are held by the Lambeth Palace Library, the Huntington Library, and the University of Toronto Library.

49. Prosecutions in the Crown Office for Seditious Libels, NA KB 15/54, p. 157. In her petition, Elizabeth Cannon claims that Purser "underwent one part of the Sentence

inflicted upon him by the Law, but, as your Petitioners are informed, was pardoned the infamous part of it," which suggests that he might not have had to stand in the pillory.

50. Petition of Elizabeth Cannon. One letter by Thomas Cannon survives, dated "Toulouse, Aug: 21, 1751," two years before he published his "Retraction." Writing to the lord chancellor, Philip Yorke, Cannon asks that his recognizance be "suspended"— that is, that he be allowed to return to England but not be prosecuted except in case of further "misbehavior." "I had not fled from justice," Cannon writes, "but at the entreaty of an unhappy, aged mother, who could not see me carried to prison and removed for further punishment in a languishing state of health, for I have laboured under a severe hysteric disorder above 11 years. Since my flight," he continues, "perpetually afflicted with a nervous headache and my inveterate lowness of spirits, become more terrible by the uncertainty of subsistence, I have suffered a continuance of agony experience alone could shew man can live in." From Yorke, *Life and Correspondence*, 2:545. Thanks to Randolph Trumbach for pointing me to this source, as cited in his article "London's Sodomites," 14.

51. Thomas Pelham-Holles, Duke of Newcastle, to Dudley Ryder, Attorney General, 12 Apr. 1750, NA SP 44/134, f. 28. See also Newcastle's Letter to the Attorney General of 27 Nov. 1750, NA SP 44/134, f. 32. These documents are further discussed in Foxon, *Libertine Literature*, 57–58; and Epstein, *Images of a Life*, 78–82.

52. Nichols, Obituary of John Cleland.

53. Even in this primly dismissive sentence, of course, there are the usual double entendres and ambiguities: "went to such lengths" and "soon satisfied me" hint both at what she sees and at her own sexual gratification.

54. Cleland, *Memoirs of Fanny Hill*, 320, 311, 315. For a discussion of the differences between the abridged and unabridged texts, including a few passages where the lack of detail actually makes the action more perversely ambiguous, see Sabor, "Censor Censured."

55. Quoted in Foxon, *Libertine Literature*, 61; and in Sabor, "From Sexual Liberation to Gender Trouble," 571.

56. Norton, *Mother Clap's Molly House*, 174–184. See also Norton, "The Macaroni Club: Homosexual Scandals in 1772," at *Homosexuality in Eighteenth-Century England*, http://rictornorton.co.uk/eighteen/macaroni.htm, accessed 18 Apr. 2009. Norton's information is valuable, although there is no evidence to support the claim that Drybutter wrote the sodomitical material in the *Woman of Pleasure*, which Foxon convincingly established was written by Cleland for the novel's first edition (*Libertine Literature*, 61–62).

57. Sabor, "Censor Censured," 194, 199.

58. Campbell [attrib.], *The Sale of Authors*, 141, 140. Subsequent references will be cited parenthetically.

59. John Harris was the putative author of *Harris's List of Covent Garden Ladies or Man of Pleasure's Kalendar*, which began appearing in 1758. According to Hallie Rubenhold, the real author was Samuel Derrick, who bought rights to the name from Harris (a.k.a. John Harrison), the self-styled Pimp General. See Rubenhold, *Covent-Garden Ladies*.

60. See also Haggerty, *Men in Love*, which suggests that the greatest threat posed by the men whose molly-house behavior was described in antisodomite texts may have

been love: "For bourgeois culture there is no love outside of marriage and the heteronormative relations leading to marriage . . . The mollies appropriate love for other purposes, and this is when they pose the greatest threat" (59).

61. Holcroft, *The Life of Thomas Holcroft*, 208. Subsequent references will be cited parenthetically. Piozzi, *Anecdotes of the Late Samuel Johnson*, 218n1. I owe the reference to Holcroft to McCalman, *Radical Underworld*, 211 and 288n22. McCalman speculates that Thomas Cannon, whom he calls a "radical freethinker," may have been related to the dissenting minister and pornographer George Cannon, active in London in the 1810s and 1820s. See also McCalman, "Unrespectable Radicalism."

62. Beert C. Verstraete has written that Tibullus wrote "a homoerotic love poetry that was dramatically more intricate and psychologically more complex and nuanced than that of his predecessors in extant Greek and Roman literature." See his "Originality of Tibullus's Marathus Elegies," 311. Cannon described his aim to produce "spirited" English versions in *Ancient and Modern Pederasty*, 41.

CHAPTER 4. THREE MEMOIRS (1748–1752)

1. Peter Sabor writes that in the expurgated version of the *Woman of Pleasure*, the 1750 *Memoirs of Fanny Hill*, "there is little attempt at epistolary verisimilitude" ("Censor Censured," 195), and the same is true of the unexpurgated text. On epistolary form and the complexities of Richardson's handling of it, see Keymer, *Richardson's "Clarissa."* See also Bray, *The Epistolary Novel*.

2. Richardson, preface to *Sir Charles Grandison* [1753–1754], 4. On temporal open-endedness—"the spontaneity of the inconclusive present"—see Bakhtin, "Epic and Novel," in *Dialogic Imagination*, 27.

3. In this respect, Cleland's text is affiliated to Henry Fielding's anti-Richardsonian *Shamela*, whose *Pamela*-loving Parson Tickletext undermines his own moral asseverations by the bawdy double entendres that reveal his true licentious spirit.

4. The translation of Pinot-Duclos's *Mémoires* was first attributed to Cleland by Lonsdale ("New Attributions," 280–284), who discusses the importance of Cleland's translator's preface.

5. Cleland, translator's preface to Pinot-Duclos's *Memoirs* (1752), in *Memoirs of a Coxcomb*, 232–241, on 232. Subsequent references will be cited parenthetically. Pinot-Duclos, *Mémoires*, 7.

6. Basker established from advertisements in the *London Evening Post* that *Memoirs of a Coxcomb* was published in September 1751 ("Wages," 180). Volume editor Henri Coulet writes that Pinot-Duclos's *Mémoires* appeared "dans les derniers mois de 1751" (in the last months of 1751) (Pinot-Duclos, *Mémoires*, 1). On this basis it seems unlikely that either imitated or plagiarized the other.

7. Lonsdale, "New Attributions," 281.

8. See Cusset, "Suspended Ending." A longer version of this essay appears in Cusset, *No Tomorrow*, 65–88. Crébillon, *The Wayward Head and Heart*. Subsequent references will be cited parenthetically.

9. Nichols, Obituary of John Cleland. Peter Wagner discusses Cleland's relationship

to the French libertine tradition in his introduction to the *Woman of Pleasure*, 23–29 and 33–34.

10. Nancy K. Miller addresses Cleland's authorial impersonation of a female narrative voice in "'I's' in Drag." Madeleine Kahn explores similar issues in *Narrative Transvestism* but concludes that "Cleland's use of a female narrator . . . does not meet the criteria of the structural device I have called narrative transvestism" (154). For an incisive discussion of issues raised by critical invocations of "drag" in relation to Cleland's novel, see Moore, *Dangerous Intimacies*, esp. 56–59.

11. In addition to Miller, Kahn, and Moore, see Julia Epstein, "Fanny's Fanny"; Graham, "The Prostitute in the Garden"; Nussbaum, *Torrid Zones*, esp. 97–113; and Robinson, *Closeted Writing*, esp. 37–51 and 77–83.

12. Nussbaum, *Torrid Zones*, 105. See also Simmons, "John Cleland's *Memoirs of a Woman of Pleasure.*" Although Simmons concludes, unlike me, that Cleland's novel "ultimately reaffirm[s] the primacy of chastity, heterosexuality, and patriarchal authority" (47), I agree with him that "we should see the 'female reader' and the 'male reader' not as static entities but as zones of conflict" (48).

13. We know that something like eighteen years have passed because their son is old enough that Charles has introduced him to "the most noted bawdy-houses in town" (188)—an "experiment" in aversion therapy to which I return later in this chapter. The fact that Fanny takes up her pen years after her marriage belies Nussbaum's claim that their sexual reunion represents "the climactic relinquishing of her power to write" (*Torrid Zones*, 111) or that in "the prison of domesticity . . . her pen is silenced" (113).

14. Defoe, preface to *Moll Flanders*, 2.

15. Sabor, introduction to *Fanny Hill*, xxii. See also Keymer and Sabor, *"Pamela" in the Marketplace*, esp. 104–105.

16. Protesting against her confinement, Pamela writes Mr. B: "Were my Life in question, instead of my Honesty, I would not wish to involve you, or any body, in the least Difficulty for so worthless a poor Creature. But, O Sir! My Soul is of equal Importance with the Soul of a Princess; though my Quality is inferior to that of the meanest Slave" (Richardson, *Pamela*, 158). "Honesty" signifies both chastity and integrity; indeed, the first is an effect or instance of the second, rather than an "original" or "innocent" state of the body.

17. See Life, "Charteris, Francis (c. 1665–1732)," *ODNB*.

18. See Rosenthal, *Infamous Commerce*, esp. 97–120; Richetti, *Popular Fiction before Richardson*, 35–41; and Wagner, *Eros Revived*, 133–143, 220–225. On Cleland's novel and prostitution in midcentury London, see Trumbach, "Modern Prostitution and Gender"; and Olsson, "Idealized and Realistic Portrayals."

19. Fielding, *Enquiry into the Causes*, 144.

20. Cleland, *Unfortunate Penlez*, 9. Subsequent references will be cited parenthetically. Excerpts from this work can also be found in Cleland, *Memoirs of a Coxcomb*, 276–282.

21. Even though she refers to her relationship with Phoebe as an instance of that "acquaintance and communication with the bad of our own sex" that is "fatal to innocence" (12–13), Fanny never characterizes their sexual relations as unnatural, but rather as ex-

pressions or enactments of nature, as when she writes that "the first sparks of kindling nature, the first ideas of pollution, were caught by me that night." Later, she writes, of this first sexual experience, that "nature . . . had been too warmly stir'd, and fermented to subside without allaying by some means or other" (13).

22. See Moore, *Dangerous Intimacies*, 58–67; and Beynon, "Traffic."

23. Miller contends that "the erotics erected by female impersonation is a mirroring not of female desire but of a phallic pride of place, a wish-fulfillment that ultimately translates into structures of masculine dominance and authority" ("I's in Drag," 54). Carol Houlihan Flynn, by contrast, emphasizes the parodic or ridiculous qualities of Fanny's phallic descriptions, contending that the essence of the novel's sexual "fantasy is not phallocentric power but the fear rendered ironic through hyperbole that the phallus lacks the power to be felt" ("What Fanny Felt," 292).

24. In the *Woman of Pleasure* I have identified six "cruces," points where a narrative crossroads is reached. (1) Fanny, alone in London, takes up Mrs. Brown's invitation to live at her house, not knowing it to be a brothel; (2) Fanny elopes with Charles and so escapes Mrs. Brown's; (3) Charles disappears, forcing Fanny, because of her debts, to become Mr. H——'s mistress; (4) Mr. H—— discovers Fanny's affair with his footman Will and sends her away, leading her to accept an offer to work at Mrs. Cole's brothel; (5) Mrs. Cole retires, and Fanny takes up with an old bachelor, the "rational pleasurist"; (6) Fanny, heiress to a vast fortune upon the pleasurist's death, is accidentally reunited with Charles and marries him. I use the term "romance" in keeping with Cleland's own practice: "Romances, Novels, and Novel-Memoirs" all belong to the same "Branch of Writing" (translator's preface to Pinot-Duclos's *Memoirs*, 236), but within that branch he distinguishes the formulaic, "unnatural" plots of romance from the work of "Authors who naturalized Fiction" (238). Yet Cleland's novelistic practice plays at the boundaries of novel and romance, natural and unnatural—delighting in amatory fiction while also dismantling it.

25. On the relationship between pain and pleasure in the novel's representation of female sexuality, see Anderson, "Gendered Pleasure, Gendered Plot." In her analysis of a specifically female "erotics of plot" (113), Anderson writes that "the repetitive sequence of deflorative moments that surround the ['real'] defloration suspends linearity" and so disrupts the "male plot" of initiation and education (120). See also Miller, *The Heroine's Text*, in which she compares Fanny's defloration to that of Sade's *Justine* (56–58).

26. Nussbaum, *Torrid Zones*, 106–107, 111, 113; see also Fowler, Weed, Miller, Kahn, and Julia Epstein for similar arguments.

27. Nussbaum, *Torrid Zones*, 104; Mengay, "The Sodomitical Muse," 191–194.

28. See Jagose, "Critical Extasy," esp. 475–478, for an interrogation of "the tendency to assume heterosexuality as the explanatory key to the novel's design" (475). See also Roussel, *Conversation of the Sexes*, 37–66; and Moore, *Dangerous Intimacies*, 60–61, on the ambiguity of Phoebe's sex.

29. Beynon, "Traffic," 20–21; Nussbaum, *Torrid Zones*, 137.

30. Moore, *Dangerous Intimacies*, 66.

31. See Moore, who argues that "the text produces and represents male and female homosexual desires and subjectivities, in characters and implied readers" (*Dangerous*

Intimacies, 57); and Nussbaum, who writes that it "makes available to its heroine, author, and readers heterosexual, homosexual, bisexual, autosexual, and omnisexual erotic responses" (*Torrid Zones*, 105), although she concludes that in the end the novel validates only heterosexual monogamy.

32. Fanny mourns Charles's absence in the immediate wake of his departure, but once she is resigned to living with Mr. H——, she doesn't mention Charles again until twelve pages from the end of the novel.

33. On the "accountable" and "unaccountable" in Fanny's writing, see Beynon, "Traffic," 8–12 and 16–17.

34. See Gautier, "Fanny's Fantasies," esp. 137–139.

35. Markley, "Language, Power, and Sexuality," 345.

36. Beynon, "Traffic," 6–7. Beynon's argument echoes Steven Marcus's claim in *The Other Victorians* that the pornographic text "really has no ending, since one of its cardinal principles of existence is repetition . . . The ideal pornographic novel, as everyone knows, would go on forever . . . If it has no ending in the sense of completion or gratification, then it can have no form" (195).

37. Jagose, "Critical Extasy," 459, 463.

38. Anderson, "Gendered Pleasure, Gendered Plot," 112, 110, 117.

39. Markley, "Language, Power, and Sexuality," 343.

40. Marcus, *Other Victorians*, 279.

41. Markley, "Language, Power, and Sexuality," 350.

42. Cleland, review of *Amelia*, in *Monthly Review* (Dec. 1751), reprinted in *Memoirs of a Coxcomb*, 230.

43. Ibid.

44. Ibid., 231.

45. Cleland, *Memoirs of a Coxcomb*, 39. Subsequent references will be cited parenthetically.

46. Cleland, review of *Peregrine Pickle*, in *Monthly Review* (Mar. 1751), in *Memoirs of a Coxcomb*, 227–228.

47. Johnson, *Rambler* 4 (31 March 1750), in *Essays from the "Rambler," "Adventurer," and "Idler,"* 11.

48. Ibid., 14.

49. Cleland, review of *Amelia*, in *Memoirs of a Coxcomb*, 231.

50. Cleland, review of *Peregrine Pickle*, in *Memoirs of a Coxcomb*, 226.

51. Smollett, review of *Memoirs of a Coxcomb*, 223.

52. Basker, "Wages," 181.

53. Smollett, review of *Coxcomb*, in Cleland, *Memoirs of a Coxcomb*, 224; Basker, "Wages," 181.

54. Basker cites a 1759 article from Smollett's *Critical Review* on another novel, *The Intriguing Coxcomb*, of which Smollett writes, "This is a miserable plagiarism, partly from a French novel, and partly from a performance of the same nature in English, called the *Memoirs of a Coxcomb*, which was published some years ago, but not finished" ("Wages," 181). Smollett and Cleland, as Basker has established, knew each other well, and it is possible that Smollett was passing on what Cleland had told him and that the

Coxcomb was intended to run to further volumes. But I argue later in this chapter that while Cleland probably did alter his original plan, he did not intend any sequel to the three-part novel as published. See also Basker, *Tobias Smollett*, 251.

55. John Locke, *Some Thoughts Concerning Education*, 86.

56. Ibid., 103.

57. Todd C. Parker contends that William's narrative "portrays heterosexual attraction as the self-evident meaning of a bodily sexuality that erupts into the world of the social" (*Sexing the Text*, 142). I agree that this is how William accounts for other-sex desire but disagree with Parker's argument that Cleland wishes to "shore up" (175) such a model of "heterosexuality" as socially unmediated or natural. See Parker, *Sexing the Text*, 28–29 and 135–175.

58. The first Statira was the wife of the Persian king Darius III, whom Alexander the Great defeated in 334 BCE; after that defeat, Statira became Alexander's lover until her death in childbirth. The second Statira was the daughter of the first and Darius; originally named Barsine, she took the name of her mother when she in turn married Alexander in 324 BCE.

59. Cleland, translator's preface to Pinot-Duclos's *Memoirs*, 236.

60. Fielding, *Shamela*, 311.

61. Grundy, *Lady Mary Wortley Montagu*, 519. Grundy writes that "dread and disgust well up in this climactic scene, where comedy of manners gives way to a kind of proto-gothic."

62. Boswell, *Laird*, 77.

63. Halsband, *The Life of Lady Mary Wortley Montagu*, 250–251; Grundy, *Lady Mary Wortley Montagu*, 519. The Buralt-Fribourg resemblance, which strikes me as the strongest evidence that Cleland based Lady Travers on Lady Mary, is not addressed as such in either Halsband or Grundy, but see Halsband, 260, 278; and Grundy, 464, 481, 509.

64. Grundy, *Lady Mary Wortley Montagu*, 519.

65. Cleland, *Institutes of Health*, 98–99n.

66. Near the end of the novel, William accompanies his aunt back to Warwickshire so that she can attend to "certain indispensable affairs" (196), but he evidently has no such business to attend to on his estates.

67. Smollett, review of *Coxcomb*, in Cleland, *Memoirs of a Coxcomb*, 223.

68. Basker, "Wages," 181.

69. Ibid.

70. Fanny holds open another door of possible continuation when she remarks, of the "rational pleasurist," that "I propose to devote a letter entirely to the pleasure of retracing to you all the particulars of my acquaintance with this ever, to me, memorable friend" (174). Eighteenth-century authors often floated such trial balloons to see what interest there might be in a sequel; the absence of anything of the kind in the *Coxcomb* is in keeping with Cleland's shutting down of possible new plotlines in the text's final pages.

71. Crébillon, *Wayward Head and Heart*, 769–770.

72. Cusset, "Suspended Ending," 754.

73. Ibid., 762–763.

74. Cusset writes that Crébillon's suspended ending "is both a narrative strategy that

frustrates readers from the end they had a right to expect, and a psychological device that teaches them not to trust their idealistic, moral, and sentimental impulse" ("Suspended Ending," 764).

75. Flynn, "What Fanny Felt," 293; Levin, "Meanness of Writing," 338–339; Gautier, "Fanny's Fantasies," 141–142. See also Julia Epstein, "Fanny's Fanny," 149.

76. On the marriage proposal, see Gautier, "Fanny's Fantasies," 139; and Levin, "Meanness of Writing," 338–339.

77. Boswell, *Laird*, 76–77.

78. Yeazell, *Fictions of Modesty*, 119–120.

79. Boswell, *Laird*, 76.

80. Samuel Richardson, in a letter to Mark Hildesley, bishop of Sodor and Man, condemned Sterne's "execrable" novel in terms that mirror both Cleland's critique and Sterne's vindication: "One extenuating circumstance attends his works, that they are too gross to be inflaming." Richardson to Hildesley, n.d. [early 1761], in Richardson, *Selected Letters*, 341.

81. Boswell, *For the Defence*, 81.

CHAPTER 5. THE HACK (1749–1759)

1. Cleland to Stanhope.

2. Examination of Ralph Griffiths, 26 Mar. 1749 [i.e., 1750], NA SP 36/112, f. 145.

3. Nichols, Obituary of John Cleland.

4. Cleland to Andrew Stone, 10 Nov. 1749, NA SP 36/111, ff. 152, 151; also quoted in Epstein, *Images of a Life*, 76, 67.

5. Cleland to Stanhope.

6. Ibid.

7. Ibid. In the letter to Stone, he makes a similar plea: "As to myself, sir, I am perfectly resigned up to the worst of my fate, but it gives me great pain to see others torn from their families, and business, upon an occasion in which they are entirely innocent" (NA SP 36/111, f. 152, also quoted in Epstein, *Images of a Life*, 75).

8. Epstein, *Images of a Life*, 75.

9. See Forster, "Griffiths, Ralph." On Smollett's antipathy to Griffiths, see Donoghue, *Fame Machine*, 29–31; Basker, *Tobias Smollett*, esp. 36–38, 42–43, and 58–59; and Knapp, *Tobias Smollett*, esp. 134–136, 170–172, and 188–190.

10. Forster, "Griffiths, Ralph." Biographical information on Griffiths is taken from this source unless otherwise noted.

11. Griffiths to Newcastle, 25 Aug. 1746, quoted in Knapp, "Ralph Griffiths," 198.

12. Raven, *Judging New Wealth*, 59. But see also Gallagher, *Nobody's Story*, which contains a remark concerning *Evelina* supposedly made by the bookseller Mr. Bowen to Hesther Thrale: "O, ma'am, what a Book thrown away was that!—all the Trade cry shame on Lowndes" (227). Whatever outcry there may have been against Lowndes was most likely prompted by the jealousy of other booksellers over his success with Burney's novel. In another study cited by Gallagher, Raven writes that in the 1780s "the leading novel publisher, William Lane, was paying his authors £10–20 for outright purchase of

the manuscript" but that "a payment of half-a-guinea per volume was the final offer to many an untried novelist" (quoted in Gallagher, *Nobody's Story*, 154).

13. Epstein, *Images of a Life*, 155.

14. That Griffiths knew there was risk in publishing the *Woman of Pleasure* is evident from the use of the pseudonym "G. Fenton" for the book's publisher on the title page as well as his statement to Stanhope on 13 November 1749, in which he says that "some time last Winter his brother Fenton Griffith came to him & asked his advice whether it would be safe for him to publish the said Book" (NA SP 36/111, f. 159, quoted in Foxon, *Libertine Literature*, 53). Fenton Griffiths's involvement in publishing Cleland's novel was secondary at best, given his lack of any other publications and Ralph's subsequent involvement in Cleland's career.

15. The figure of £20,000 is given in Nichols, *Literary Anecdotes*, 8:412; see also Epstein, *Images of a Life*, 219n38.

16. See Basker, "Wages," 179; Foxon, *Libertine Literature*, 60; and Sabor, "Censor Censured," 194.

17. Raven, *Judging New Wealth*, 60, 69.

18. Gallagher, *Nobody's Story*, xx. Although Gallagher focuses on women writers, whose "femaleness" affected the specific forms of their "disembodiment" and "dispossession," she contends that women writers are "representatives of the condition of the author" (xv) in general: "Authors in general . . . were in the 'feminized' position of perpetuating themselves only by renouncing their property" (196).

19. Gallagher, *Nobody's Story*, 152.

20. Ibid., 152n23. Ralph went so far as to write that "there is no Difference between the Writer in his Garret, and the Slave in the Mines; but that the former has his Situation in the Air, and the latter in the Bowels of the Earth" (*Case of Authors*, 22).

21. Examination of Ralph Griffiths.

22. Sabor, "Censor Censured," 198; on the ways in which Cleland's style is "impoverished" by expurgation, see 197–199.

23. Cleland to Stanhope.

24. Sabor, "Censor Censured," 198.

25. On Cleland's letters to Griffiths, see Epstein, *Images of a Life*, 97–98 and 140–141.

26. For a complete list of Cleland's articles in the *Monthly Review*, see Epstein, *Images of a Life*, 189–190.

27. Cleland's burlesque is a parody of Robert Dodsley's *Œconomy of Human Life* (1750), formerly attributed to Philip Dormer Stanhope, fourth Earl of Chesterfield, and purporting to be a translation from an ancient Brahmanic (Hindu) text. Dodsley was an ex-footman turned prominent London poet, playwright, and bookseller; among the authors whose work he published were Pope, Johnson, Sterne, and, in 1752, Cleland: the translation of Pinot-Duclos's *Memoirs*.

28. Lonsdale suggests that "T. Clement" is a false imprint, as "no such bookseller is listed in Plomer's *Dictionary of Booksellers and Printers* or in David Foxon's exhaustive index of imprints in his *English Verse 1700–1750*" ("New Attributions," 272).

29. Norman Edwin Oakes, "Ralph Griffiths and *The Monthly Review*" (PhD diss., Columbia University, 1961), cited in Epstein, *Images of a Life*, 112–113.

30. See Gallagher, *Nobody's Story*, 152–154. As Raven notes, all such estimates of numbers need to be used with caution, both because bibliographical information is incomplete and because what gets counted as a "novel" is open to debate; see Raven, *Judging New Wealth*, 31–41. By 1750–1752 the fiction craze of ten years earlier had died down, making booksellers more reluctant to take on new titles, especially by untried authors.

31. Greene, introduction to *Major Works*, by Samuel Johnson, xi–xxvii. In one of his letters to the *Public Advertiser*, Cleland referred to the journalistic practice of freely inventing parliamentary speeches, in this case to disparage the oratorical talents of William Pitt, first Earl of Chatham. Of one speech attributed to him, Cleland wrote that it was "penned in a white-limed Garret, in Exeter-street in the Strand, by one whom the Compiler of a Magazine employed to frame Speeches for the Members, rather in their respective *Characters* than in the *Words* actually spoke by them . . . The undoubted Truth however is, that Mr. P——t was never in his Life capable of writing, and less yet surely of speaking such a Speech as that of which he had the Honor" ([Cleland], writing as A Briton, letter to the *Public Advertiser*, 29 Nov. 1770). The term "miscellaneous writer" carries a disparaging connotation, as when Robert Carruthers refers to "John Cleland, the unfortunate and worthless man of letters, author of an infamous novel, and an extensive miscellaneous writer" (*Life of Alexander Pope*, 262).

32. [Cleland], writing as A Briton, letter to the *Public Advertiser*, 23 Sept. 1765. The two words in brackets are conjectural.

33. [Cleland], writing as A Briton, letter to the *Public Advertiser*, 21 July 1787.

34. Kernan, *Printing Technology*, 78.

35. Cleland, *Economy of a Winter's Day: A New Edition*, 25–26. This second edition of the 1750 *Œconomy of a Winter's Day* was published, according to Basker, "sometime between 1772 and 1789, the years when the bookseller 'P[eter] Brett' traded in the Strand under that name" ("Wages," 180)—Basker's source being Ian Maxted, *The London Book Trades, 1775–1800: A Preliminary Checklist of Members* (Folkestone: Dawson, 1977), 28. The passage I've cited was one of those added to the revised edition.

36. Carruthers, in his *Life of Alexander Pope*, calls Cleland "an adept in literary fraud" (148) for his alleged part in pirating the letters of Lady Mary Wortley Montagu published in 1763 and forging a further group of four letters that appeared in *An Additional Volume to the Letters of the Right Honourable Lady M——y W——y M——e* in 1767. The charge of forgery was first made in the *Gentleman's Magazine* in 1803 (p. 1043), fourteen years after Cleland's death.

37. For a chronological list of Cleland's contributions to the *Monthly Review*, based on Benjamin Nangle's bibliographical research, see Epstein, *Images of a Life*, 189–190.

38. Young, *Conjectures on Original Composition* (1759), 54, 12.

39. Cleland to Stanhope.

40. There is no way of knowing whether Fielding read Cleland's pamphlet before writing his or if Cleland had some advance information as to what Fielding was to write when he was working on the *Unfortunate Penlez*. See Zirker, "General Introduction," xxxiv and xlii–xliii. He concludes that Fielding's pamphlet was composed and printed in October, which would mean neither had seen the other's work. I think it's just possible, on the basis of the evidence proffered by Zirker and by Fredson Bowers in his "Textual

Introduction" to the same edition (cxvii–cxviii), that the last part of Fielding's text, including the protest against other authors' "light and ludicrous Colours," was written or revised after Fielding had read Cleland's pamphlet. In an ironic coda to his involvement in the Penlez controversy, Cleland reviewed both his own and Fielding's pamphlets in the same issue of the *Monthly Review* (Nov. 1749), 61–65, assuming an appearance of neutrality that highlights the fieriness of his initial polemical stance.

41. Cleland, trans. and ed., *Catherine Vizzani*, 34. Subsequent references will be cited parenthetically.

42. Cleland, review of *Peregrine Pickle*, in *Memoirs of a Coxcomb*, 226.

43. Ibid. Three of the four texts on which I focus in this chapter (all but *Tombo-Chiqui*) were attributed to Cleland by Lonsdale in "New Attributions," based on Ralph Griffiths's manuscript notes in his own set of the *Monthly Review*.

44. Cleland, *Unfortunate Penlez*, 2nd ed., 17. Subsequent references will be cited parenthetically. As Basker states, this is probably not a true second edition but a reissue of the first with a new title page, altering the date from 1749 to 1750 and adding the phrase "By a Gentleman Not Concern'd," which had first been used in newspaper advertisements to distinguish this from Fielding's pamphlet ("Wages," 179–180).

45. Linebaugh, "Tyburn Riot," esp. 89–102; Zirker, "General Introduction," xxxiii–lii. Linebaugh has two sailors, Zirker (citing the *Gentleman's Magazine*) three; Linebaugh two moidores, Zirker four. Both of these scholarly accounts are excellent, but the contemporary evidence is extremely inconsistent. I have discussed Fielding's account, *A True State of the Case*, in *Criminality and Narrative*, 181–186. See also Rogers, "Penlez, Bosavern (1726–1749)," *ODNB*. I have drawn on all these sources but have not commented on differences of detail except where significant.

46. *Gentleman's Magazine*, "Historical Chronicle" for July 1749, cited in Zirker, "General Introduction," xxxiv.

47. Zirker, "General Introduction," xl; see also, more generally, Zirker, "General Introduction," xxxviii–li; and Linebaugh, "Tyburn Riot," 93–98.

48. Linebaugh, "Tyburn Riot," 98.

49. Linebaugh's reading of the logic of the government's actions—that an extreme degree of severity in punishing Penlez was necessary in order to "prove" that the representatives of the law had been justified in the first place in calling out the military to suppress what they mistakenly characterized as seditious riots—offers a suggestive inversion of Fielding's statement "that the Outrages actually committed by the Mob . . . were such as no Government could justify passing over without some Censure and Example" (*True State*, 57). But while I agree with Linebaugh that the execution of Penlez was an egregious miscarriage of justice, I'm skeptical of this reading of Fielding's or the government's motives, because as far as I'm aware there were no demands for them to justify having called out the troops and no groundswell of criticism for their having done so, until *after* Penlez's conviction and after the jury's plea for mercy was turned down. That is, it was the perceived injustice of the government's scapegoating of "the unfortunate" Penlez that had to be justified, not the recourse to military force—especially as all the soldiers had done was to beat their drums to disperse the crowd.

50. Fielding, *True State*, 60. As Fielding points out, Penlez had been indicted by the

grand jury for burglary as well as for riot, but since he had been convicted of the latter, "there was no Occasion of trying him again" (*True State*, 60).

51. I accept Zirker's view that Fielding believed Penlez to be guilty of theft as well as of riot, and Penlez's garbled and conflicting accounts of how he came by the linens, as recorded in the watchmen's testimony in the *True State*, may arouse suspicion that he did indeed steal them from Peter Wood's house. No evidence in Fielding's text, however, places Penlez at the scene of the crime, and in any case, as Zirker writes, "It is not at all clear that a jury would ever have convicted him of a capital offense for his theft. Eighteenth-century juries commonly spared a thief's life either by finding him guilty of a lesser offence . . . or by undervaluing the goods he had stolen . . . Such 'pious perjury,' as Blackstone called it, was especially common when the culprit was a first offender of good reputation" ("General Introduction," l–li). Fielding's claim that the evidence of theft was such "as I think every impartial Man must allow would have convicted him (had he been tried) of Felony at least" (*True State*, 60) is thus doubtful.

52. The testimony is quoted from the *Old Bailey Sessions Papers* for 6–14 Sept. 1749, 134.

53. Cleland uses the phrase "Raw-head and Bloody-bones" to mock claims that the bawdy-house actions were in any way alarming or threatening (20). At the beginning of his own account of the trial, Cleland refers his readers to "the Account of the Trial publish'd in the Sessions-Paper, and to the actual Dying-Speech of *Penlez*, and the intended one of *John Wilson*" (25) and writes that "the Reader may then compare the Depositions of the Man [i.e., Wood] who hang'd one, and was near hanging more, upon this Occasion, with the dying Declarations of two Men of unblemish'd Characters, and from thence collect the Measure of the Veracity and Credibility on both Sides" (26)—an invitation to adopt a forensic manner of reading, as well as a gesture affirming the truth of his own account of events.

54. Fielding, *True State*, 60.

55. For other uses of "Frolic," "Mirth," "Joke," and "Fun" to characterize the disorders, see, for example, Cleland, *Unfortunate Penlez*, 5, 23, 33, 37, 39, 41, in addition to the passages cited below.

56. The notion of a "moral economy" was formulated by E. P. Thompson in "The Moral Economy of the English Crowd" (1971). While Thompson's focus is on the economic relations among different parts of the community, especially during times of dearth, I use the term in his more general sense of the crowd's "consistent traditional view of social norms and obligations" (188).

57. In a later passage, Cleland writes that Penlez was drawn into the disorders "by seeing such Numbers at work, with great Mirth and Jollity, in so open and bare-fac'd a Manner, as if they had thought that the Guards, if they came, would sooner defend *them* than the *Bawdy-Houses*, or at least wink at their Escape" (39; see also 33n).

58. The use of "impress" in a sexual sense can be found at least as far back as Gay's *Beggar's Opera* (1728), in which Mrs. Peachum's air "A Maid Is like the Golden Ore" equates the passage from maidenhood to sexual commodification with that from ore to coin, "*tried* and *impressed* in the mint." See Gay, *Beggar's Opera* [I, v (Air 5)], 14.

59. See Sutherland, "Where Does Fanny Hill Keep Her Contraceptives?" 11–18. Fan-

ny never mentions a contraceptive use of the sponges, but I think Sutherland's conjecture is plausible. The relevant passage in the *Woman of Pleasure* is on 135–136.

60. Cleland, *Catherine Vizzani*, title page. Under a new title, *The True History and Adventures of Catherine Vizzani*, the text was reissued (using, according to Lonsdale, "unsold sheets of the first edition" [280] and adding a new title page and frontispiece) by W. Reeve and C. Sympson in 1755.

61. Bianchi, *Breve storia della vita di Catterina Vizzani*. My thanks to Corrinne Harol for providing me with a copy of Bianchi's text. Information on the publishing history and background of Bianchi's text is taken from Donato, "Public and Private Negotiations of Gender." Donato suggests that Bianchi's text reached Cleland by way of Horace Walpole and Horace Mann, both of whom were friendly with Doctor Antonio Cocchi, a colleague of Bianchi's. Cleland or his publishers may have become interested in Vizzani following the modest commercial success of Henry Fielding's 1746 pamphlet *The Female Husband*, the half-moralistic, half-screwball story of another real-life cross-dressing female seducer of other women. Apart from that premise, the two works have little in common, but it is interesting to compare Fielding's squeamish hints that Mary Hamilton deceived her wives by means of a dildo—"means which decency forbids me even to mention" (371), "something of too vile, wicked and scandalous a nature, which was found in the Doctor's trunk" (379)—to Cleland's more complex treatment, as discussed below.

62. Lanser, "Sapphic Picaresque," 256.

63. Bianchi, *Breve storia della vita di Catterina Vizzani*, 4. All quotations in this paragraph are from pp. 3–4 in Bianchi and pp. 2–4 in Cleland's *Catherine Vizzani*.

64. Bianchi, *Breve storia della vita di Catterina Vizzani*, 9.

65. In his introductory paragraph, Bianchi writes that Catterina is "una Fanciulla, che ne a Saffo, ne all'altre Donzelle di Lesbo nell'amare solamente quelle del medesimo sesso ha ceduto, ma che da gran lunga le ha trapassate" (3), which Cleland translates pretty literally as "a Girl, who, so far from being inferior to *Sappho*, or any of the *Lesbian* Nymphs, in an Attachment for those of her own Sex, has greatly surpassed them" (2). While "Lesbian" clearly means "from Lesbos," Cleland's use of the term moves it some distance toward referring to a category of sexual identity.

66. Another example of the ways in which Cleland expands on Bianchi's text: at one point Giovanni's master has to keep him away from Montepulciano because of some scrapes he's got into by his womanizing. Bianchi writes, "Ivi ancora molto le donne vagheggiava, e per una d'esse colà un altra volta in un grande intrico si trovò" (There too he really went after the women, and for love of one of them he got himself into another mess there) (11). Cleland translates, "*Giovanni's* amorous Pursuits . . . were not in any wise abated; **whether Nature were actually uncontrolable, or Gratitude had not its proper Weight, or she was hardened against Pain, Infamy, or any other Consequence.** She some Time after, at that Place, was brought into a dangerous Plunge by her intriguing Effrontery" (18). Cleland's added asides, here in boldface, raise the question of whether Catherine's behavior is best understood as an "uncontrolable" effect of "Nature," or if its causes need to be looked for elsewhere. Bianchi then notes that Giovanni "never made the least Difficulty to lie in the same Bed with other Men," as Cleland literally translates it, but when Bianchi adds "ne mai con alcuno di esser femmina confidè" (nor ever told

any of them that she was female), Cleland writes that she "also forbore making any Advances to her Bedfellow, though he were an *Adonis*" (18–19), making the erotic charge of the situation more vivid.

67. Bianchi, *Breve storia della vita di Catterina Vizzani*, 8. It should be noted, when comparing this passage with the translation that follows, that the subject pronoun is usually omitted in Italian, so that Bianchi does not need to choose between "he" and "she" in most cases. In this passage, the one time he uses the pronoun, he opts for "egli," he.

68. See Donato, "Public and Private Negotiations of Gender," esp. 183–185; and Donoghue, *Passions*, 80–86.

69. Cleland, review of *Peregrine Pickle*, in *Memoirs of a Coxcomb*, 226.

70. My reading of Vizzani's "leathern Contrivance" is indebted to Traub, *Renaissance of Lesbianism*, esp. 195–197. As she argues, "Early modern women's prosthetic supplementation of their bodies is . . . both additive and substitutive: as a material addition to the woman's body and as a replacement of the man's body *by* the woman's, prosthesis not only displaces male prerogatives, but exposes 'man' as a simulacrum, and gender as a construction built on the faulty ground of mutually exclusive binaries" (196). Many commentators have been struck by the symbolic suggestiveness of Catherine Vizzani's worthless, emptied-out phallus: see, for example, McCormick, *Secret Sexualities*, 176; and Donoghue, *Passions*, 83. It can also be read in light of Thomas Laqueur's claim that in the early modern period (which runs to "sometime in the eighteenth century" [*Making Sex*, 149]), "biological sex, which we generally take to serve as the basis of gender, was just as much in the domain of culture and meaning as was gender. A penis was thus a status symbol rather than a sign of some other deeply rooted ontological essence: *real* sex. It could be construed as a certificate of sorts, like the diploma of a doctor or lawyer today, which entitled the bearer to certain rights and privileges" (*Making Sex*, 134–135).

71. Some confusion on this point has arisen because of the subtitle of the second (1755) edition of *The Case*, where Catherine is upgraded to "A Young Gentlewoman a Native of Rome." But in the text of the second edition Catherine/Giovanni is still unambiguously the daughter of a carpenter and a servant all her life.

72. It may seem obvious that the purpose of what Donoghue calls Catherine's "strap-on dildo" is sexual, and Donoghue writes that "apparently it deceives, and profoundly pleases, all the women she has sex with" (*Passions*, 82). But as she goes on to observe, "It is difficult to know how to read this part of the biography. Could so many sexually experienced women have been fooled by a dildo in the dark, when many female husbands seem to have been found out, even by timid and naïve wives, within a few weeks? It seems much more likely that at least some of her lovers knew her to be a woman and that her fame was based on coded recommendations." Possibly so, but there's no evidence one way or the other in Bianchi's or Cleland's texts—not even of the "she used this leathern machine to commit acts too shocking to tell" sort. Instead, Catherine owes her fame as a ladies' man to the stratagems I've referred to: buying remedies for venereal diseases she only pretends to have, furtively half-exposing her phallus to her companions, telling the village laundress how "liberal" nature has been. I have no wish to desexualize Vizzani, but we should not take it for granted that sexual desire is necessarily acted out genitally or that, for Vizzani, erotic pleasure was necessarily dependent on what we might call sex;

it seems to be at least as much linked to the excitement of elopements, midnight visits, and the circulation of admiring rumors about her masculinity, on "which she hugged herself with such Pride and Delight" (11).

73. Bianchi writes (in Cleland's translation) that he has "reposited" Vizzani's hymen "among those which I found in many Virgins of different Age at *Sienna* . . . for that the Hymen is no Fancy, but actually found in all Virgin Females, is not controverted among experienced Anatomists; yet, as there are not wanting in some at *Sienna*, who sneer at such a Thing, let them only take a View of my Collection of these Membranes; and, if they will not stand out against ocular Evidence, they must own the Reality thereof" (43).

74. On early modern theories of tribadism, see Traub, *Renaissance*, 45–48 and 188–228.

75. *Reasons for the Growth of Sodomy*, 51.

76. Diderot, *Le Rêve de d'Alembert* (1769), 91.

77. On Cleland's treatment of the imagination in this passage, see also Sha, *Perverse Romanticism*, 70–72, although he attributes Cleland's argument to Bianchi.

78. Donoghue, *Passions*, 85.

79. *Monthly Review* (March 1751), cited in Lonsdale, "New Attributions," 277.

80. Cleland, review of *Peregrine Pickle*, in *Memoirs of a Coxcomb*, 226.

81. Cleland, "Advertisement" to *Tombo-Chiqui*, n.p. The possibility that Cleland's translation was written with Garrick in mind is raised in Epstein, *Images of a Life*, 134, where he quotes from a letter from Cleland to Garrick referring to "the barely yet embryo of a production, *the Clown polished by Love*" and notes that the basic premise Cleland describes there "is not far removed" from that of *Tombo-Chiqui*. I agree that there is a connection, but the missing link is a comedy written by Pierre de Marivaux, also for the Théâtre-Italien, *Arlequin poli par l'amour*, which was performed along with *Arlequin sauvage* in 1730 and 1734. Cleland knew Marivaux's writing well, referring to it in his introduction to Pinot-Duclos's *Memoirs*, and the title of his "embryonic" production is a literal translation of Marivaux's. He must have decided to work on Delisle's play instead of Marivaux's, intending that Garrick would take on the Harlequin character, now under the name of Tombo-chiqui. On the performance history of Delisle's and Marivaux's plays, see Forsans, introduction to Delisle, *Arlequin sauvage*, 16–19.

82. Lonsdale records more or less faithful editions of Cleland's 1753 text in 1776 (London, Bell and Etherington), 1787 (London, Bell), and 1824 (Edinburgh, Buchanan) and modified or abridged versions in 1777 (London, J. Bew et al.), 1795 and 1806 (London, Minerva), and 1798 (Philadelphia). The British Library owns another edition (London, Morgan, n.d. [likely post-1800]) in which "John Wilmot, Earl of Rochester" is credited as author. See Lonsdale, "New Attributions," 287; and Basker, "Wages," 184.

83. The first phrase is from the preface to Cleland, *Dictionary of Love*, iv; the second from the "Advertisement" to *Tombo-Chiqui*. Subsequent references will be cited parenthetically. Cleland's statement about the success of Delisle's *Arlequin sauvage* (first performed 1721; pub. 1722) is borne out by the research of Ola Forsans: the work was both a commercial and a critical success, reprinted numerous times in the eighteenth century and later, and was a favorite with the actors as well.

84. Cleland, translator's preface to Pinot-Duclos's *Memoirs*, 240.

85. The Marquis d'Argenson praised *Arlequin sauvage* as a "pièce philosophique" (quoted in Forsans, introduction to Delisle, *Arlequin sauvage*, 18) and indeed acknowledged that some might fault it for being *too* philosophical.

86. *Birmingham*, especially in its old alternative form, *Brummagem* (whence *Brummie*, etc.), has long been a byword for sham, counterfeit, worthless goods.

87. The pages in Cleland's dictionary are not numbered, but the entries are arranged alphabetically. All the entries discussed here can also be found in Cleland, *Memoirs of a Coxcomb*, appendix C, 252–260.

88. There is an entry for "beau" in the French text, but Cleland's is not based on it.

89. Garrick, *Miss in Her Teens; or, The Medley of Lovers*; excerpts reprinted in Cleland, *Memoirs of a Coxcomb*, 242–248 (quotation on 243).

90. As Scott J. Juengel notes, Cleland's effort to establish the "just value" of words in the *Dictionary* "would become a broader philological preoccupation" in later years—a preoccupation whose most significant product was the 1766 work *The Way to Things by Words*, to whose title I allude. See Juengel, "Doing Things with Fanny Hill," 427–429.

91. See Altherr, "*Tombo-Chiqui: or, The American Savage*," 412.

92. Rousseau's *Le Flatteur* was first performed in 1696 and makes up about half of Miller's *Art and Nature*.

93. Quoted in Bentley, *The Brecht Memoir*, 30.

CHAPTER 6. THE MAN OF FEELING (1752–1768)

1. See Donkin, *Getting into the Act*. Donkin writes that later in the century a really successful play might earn its author £500–£600 from the proceeds of these benefit nights. For that reason, however, theater managers stood to earn more by staging older plays for which they did not have to pay out the take of every third performance, and if the managers, like Garrick, were also playwrights themselves, they had good reason to stage their own works instead of others' and so keep the benefits (*Getting into the Act*, 7–8). But see also Milhous and Hume, "Playwrights' Remuneration." They write that "Garrick was a skilled judge of what his company could put across to the audience"; while he "was much maligned in his lifetime for refusing scripts . . . he made a real effort to let the playwrights he did produce earn as much as possible from their work" (16).

2. Cleland to Garrick, 31 July 1754, in Garrick, *Private Correspondence*, 58. Subsequent references will be cited parenthetically. The conjectural reading of "girl" in the quotation that follows is that of the 1831 editor.

3. The critical literature on sentiment and sensibility in eighteenth-century fiction is considerable, but see especially Brissenden, *Virtue in Distress*; Barker-Benfield, *Culture of Sensibility*; Mullan, *Sentiment and Sociability*, esp. 57–113; Todd, *Sensibility: An Introduction*; and Van Sant, *Eighteenth-Century Sensibility and the Novel*.

4. *Titus Vespasian*, like *Tombo-Chiqui* and the 1755 comic afterpiece *The Ladies Subscription*, has apparently never been staged. Apart from one essay on *Tombo-Chiqui* and the noble savage myth by Thomas L. Altherr, the only critical remarks on any of the plays, as far as I know, are in Epstein's biography. Of *Titus*, Epstein contends that the interweaving "of the play's several borrowed plot lines produces a confusing and ultimately

distracting array of stage business" (129) and that the events of the plot "fail to animate the printed version" (131). But it is hard to gauge the theatrical viability of these plays in the absence of any production history, and the fact that they were not performed, in a period when there were so few venues and so many constraints (economic and censorial) on new plays, is not in itself damning. As with *Tombo-Chiqui*, Cleland's fidelity to the original work may have set him at odds with the tastes of contemporary English audiences—and certainly with Garrick's taste. Metastasio has never been very well known in Britain (except among musicians, such as Charles Burney, who published a study of his work in 1796), and Metastasian melodrama is far from Shakespearean tragedy—of which Garrick, of course, was one of the key champions. Few English-language writers in the period would have endorsed Cleland's assertion, in this same letter to Garrick, that Metastasio was "the greatest dramatic genius now living" (58); for one thing, his work wasn't translated, other than by Cleland, until 1767. And while Stendhal held that Metastasio attained a greater degree of perfection than Dante, Petrarch, or Ariosto, his work has never attracted anything like as much attention as those authors from English-speaking critics. Even Mozart's setting of *La Clemenza di Tito* was long considered dull, stilted, and dramatically dead, its characters implausible and its music incapable of bringing them to life. But just as Mozart's opera has in recent years started to be championed by such conductors as René Jacobs, so it might be time for a reappraisal—or really a first appraisal—of Cleland's blank-verse adaptation of Metastasio's text. See Jacobs, "Seven Misconceptions about *La Clemenza di Tito*."

5. Cleland to Edward Dickinson, n.d. [late 1752?], British Library manuscript photocopies BL MS RP 4335[a] and BL MS RP 3476. The manuscripts of these letters and the others to and from Edward Dickinson and Cleland's mother, Lucy, are held in the Pierpont Morgan Library in New York. The British Library holds photocopies in accordance with the law concerning manuscripts of British origin that have been sold for export abroad. Some of the letters are dated; others are not. The undated letters can sometimes be approximately dated based on internal evidence, but this is necessarily conjectural. RP 4335 contains eighteen letters in all, and to keep them distinct I've assigned each one a letter in brackets (e.g., RP 4335[a]), but they are not arranged in chronological sequence.

6. According to the terms of Lucy Cleland's will, her son was to be paid an annuity of £60 per year after her death, but in a letter dated 31 Jan. 1759 (BL MS RP 4335[j]) Cleland writes that his allowance during his mother's lifetime amounts to "a miserable 20 d" (twenty pence) per day, which is equivalent to thirty pounds per year.

7. Cleland to Dickinson, 21 Sept. 1762, BL MS RP 4335[l]. Cleland wrote a letter to the *Public Advertiser* from "Somersetshire" dated 9 September 1767 and one from Buckinghamshire on 4 July 1768; in the first of these he referred to himself, wryly, as a "Country Gentleman."

8. Boswell, *For the Defence*, 81; Cleland to Garrick, 22 May 1772, in Garrick, *Private Correspondence*, 466–468.

9. Cleland to Dickinson, n.d. [Jan. 1759?], BL MS RP 4335[d]. Cf. Brachiano in Webster's *The White Devil*, 5.3: "Oh, my brain's on fire! / The helmet is poison'd." Given the theatricality of several of these letters, it could be that the echo is a deliberate allusion.

10. On the slipperiness of the boundary between the genuine and the fictive, the heartfelt and the designing, in both real familiar letters and novelistic ones, see Keymer, *Richardson's "Clarissa,"* esp. 1–44.

11. See Epstein, *Images of a Life*, 155. Both Epstein and Basker have dug out information on Cleland's publications that allows us to date them with some precision.

12. In his obituary, John Nichols states that Cleland wrote a novel titled *The Man of Honour* "as an *amende honourable* for his former exceptionable book," the *Woman of Pleasure*. Basker has argued that Nichols's attribution was plausible ("Wages," 192–193), but in the *London Chronicle* 30 (17–19 Oct. 1771): 384, *The Man of Honour* is attributed to J[ohn] H[uddlestone] Wynne, and that attribution is now generally accepted. (A copy of the first volume, which I have not read, is held in the library of the Colonial Williamsburg Foundation.) In any case, *The Woman of Honor* seems more obvious than *The Man of Honour* as the title of a work intended to make amends for the *Woman of Pleasure*. My guess is that Nichols (who did not list *The Woman of Honor* in his obituary) simply confused the two titles, perhaps not having read either, but I think Basker is likely right that the idea of the later novel as an *amende honourable* for the earlier was told to Nichols by Cleland himself.

13. Cleland, "Advertisement" to *Way to Things*, i.

14. Said, *On Late Style*, 7.

15. Ibid., 148.

16. Cleland to Garrick, 31 July 1754, in Garrick, *Private Correspondence*, 59.

17. Epstein provides evidence from the Poor Rate and Watch Rate record books that Cleland was living with his mother in St. James's Place until around the time she moved to a different house in the same street, in late summer 1753 (*Images of a Life*, 128–29 and 228n51). However, in a letter to Dickinson dated 23 Nov. 1752, Cleland refers to money he owes some "poor wretched creditors" for a "Hired lodging" and furnishings, which strongly suggests he had been living on his own for some time before that. That letter, and others from the same period, also make it clear that he had not seen or spoken to his mother in quite a while and that their only "contact" had been by way of letters to and from Dickinson. I think it's probable that Cleland had left St. James's Place some months or years before Lucy Cleland moved house and that she continued to pay the rates on his behalf, but this is highly conjectural (Cleland to Dickinson, 23 Nov. 1752, BL MS RP 4335[b]). As noted in chapter 2, Cleland's sister Charlotte died in India in 1747, and his brother Henry (probably) in the West Indies around 1750.

18. John Cleland to Lucy Cleland, 6 Mar. 1758, BL MS RP 4335[i].

19. Lucy Cleland, Last Will and Testament, NA PROB 11/888, ff. 221v–226v. The body of the will is dated 4 February 1752, but over the subsequent years she added some twenty codicils. In a note attached to one of the last of these, dated 13 August 1761, she addresses her lawyer, Edward Dickinson, directly, expressing her "desire [that] you will think me with the utmost Gratitude and affectionate yours at this Instant I think I am Dying." See also Epstein, *Images of a Life*, 22–23, 127–128, and 228n50.

20. Cleland to Dickinson, 23 Oct. 1755, BL MS RP 4335[e].

21. Cleland to Dickinson, n.d. [Jan. 1759?], BL MS RP 4335[d].

22. Cleland to Dickinson, n.d. [late 1752?], BL MS RP 4335[a].

23. Cleland to Dickinson, 16 Feb. 1758, BL MS RP 4335[h].

24. IOC, Bombay Public Consultations, P/341/8, f. 18; Affidavits for Hilary Term 22nd George II, 5 Feb. 1748/49, NA KB 1/10/1.

25. Shakespeare, *Macbeth* 1.5.39–40, 44–45; see also 1.7.54–59.

26. Cleland to Dickinson, 9 Dec. 1756, BL MS RP 4335[f].

27. In another formulation of this idea of "negative persecution," he writes, "I have found her bare negative of countenance, her non-concurrence to my interest as fatally destructive as the most active rancor of enmity" (Cleland to Dickinson, 23 Oct. 1755, BL MS RP 4335[e]).

28. Lucy Cleland to Dickinson, n.d., BL MS RP 4335[m]. This letter certainly dates from the early 1750s, as Cleland responds to some of the points in it in a letter to Dickinson that I think based on internal evidence must be from late 1752.

29. Lucy Cleland to Dickinson, n.d., BL MS RP 4335[n]. This is a second letter, photocopied with the letter above; I think the approximate date is 1752–1755, but it could be later.

30. This last phrase is from John Cleland's letter to Dickinson dated 9 December 1756 (BL MS RP 4335[f]). The preceding phrase is from the first of Lucy Cleland's letters to Dickinson (BL MS RP 4335[m], n.d. [1752?]).

31. Dickinson to John Cleland, 18 Oct. 1755, BL MS RP 4335[r]. I have generally left spellings and the like as they appear in the original manuscript, but in this case I have spelled out words such as "which" and "would" when these are abbreviated.

32. Cleland to Dickinson, n.d. [late 1752?], BL MS RP 4335[a].

33. Cleland to Dickinson, 23 Oct. 1755, BL MS RP 4335[e].

34. Cleland to Dickinson, 9 Dec. 1756, BL MS RP 4335[f].

35. Dickinson to Cleland, 18 Oct. 1755, BL MS RP 4335[r].

36. Cleland to Dickinson, 6 Mar. 1758, BL MS RP 4335[c]; John Cleland to Lucy Cleland, 6 Mar. 1758, BL MS RP 4335[i].

37. The phrase is from a letter by W. H. Draper, Bombay, 28 Oct. 1736 (IOC, E/1/27, item 133, folio j).

38. Cleland to Dickinson, n.d. [late 1752?], BL MS RP 3476.

39. See "The Conclusion to Part II" of "Christabel," ll. 656–657, 662–665, 673, 675–677, in Coleridge, *Poetical Works*, 225–226.

40. Lucy Cleland is similarly elliptical in a letter to Dickinson, writing, "I shall not enter into the abundance of reasons He [JC] must be conscious of, why I might excuse myself from doing Him any service. They are well known to you, and the world" (BL MS RP 4335[m]). She may be referring to his financial irresponsibility, his abusive language toward her, the shame he brought on their family by writing the *Woman of Pleasure*, or other rumors and "reasons . . . well known to you, and the world" and so not necessary to be written.

41. Cleland to Dickinson, 21 Sept. 1762, BL MS RP 4335[l].

42. Cleland to Dickinson, 31 Jan. 1759, BL MS RP 4335[j]; Dickinson to Cleland, 23 Sept. 1762, BL MS RP 4335[q].

43. Cleland to Dickinson, 21 Sept. 1762, BL MS RP 4335[l].

44. Cleland to Dickinson, n.d. [late 1752?], BL MS RP 4335[a].

45. Ralph Griffiths's reference to Cleland going abroad is from his examination by Stanhope on 20 March 1750, but it refers to events of late 1749, probably after their arrests in November 1749, when it would have been reasonable for Griffiths to think of issuing an expurgated *Fanny Hill*. Although Griffiths was examined in March 1750 when Stanhope was considering prosecuting him for that very expurgated work, there is no record of Cleland being arrested or examined then, which suggests he may have been abroad. Cleland published no articles in the *Monthly Review* between November 1749 and November 1750, which also supports the hypothesis that he was away during this period. If Cleland revised the *Memoirs of Fanny Hill* between November 1749 and January 1750, Griffiths had time to prepare it for publication in March 1750. Cleland's next known publications were his review of Dodsley's *The Œconomy of Human Life* in November 1750 and the short burlesque *The Œconomy of a Winter's Day* the following month, which suggests he was back and working in London from about September or October 1750.

46. Savage, preface to *Miscellaneous Poems* (1726), in *Poetical Works*, 268. See also Nussbaum on Savage and "unnatural" mothers in *Torrid Zones*, 47–66; and Gladfelder, "Hard Work," 462–466.

47. Cleland to Dickinson, 6 Mar. 1758, BL MS RP 4335[c]. Cleland's return address, or "direction," indicates only where his mail was held, not where he was living. According to another letter to Dickinson, Cleland's lodgings between 1756 and 1762 were at "Mrs Meredith's a Staymaker in the Savoy where I have been near these six years" (Cleland to Dickinson, 21 Sept. 1762, BL MS RP 4335[l]). However, in January 1759 Cleland names his landlords as a Mr. and Mrs. Kyme, so until more information comes to light, Cleland's domicile has to remain uncertain.

48. Davies, quoted in Cope, review of *Revels History of Drama in English*, 641. On Israel Pottinger, see Norgate, "Pottinger, Israel (*fl.* 1759–1761)," rev. Michael Bevan, *ODNB*; Lonsdale, "Goldsmith and the *Weekly Magazine*"; Basker, "Wages," 187–188; and Maxted, "London Book Trades."

49. See Maxted, "British Book Trade." The bankruptcies of Cleland's publishers listed by Maxted are those of Israel Pottinger (1760), Thomas Davies (1778), Samuel Hooper (1778), Thomas Becket (1779), and William Nicoll (1789).

50. Philip Dormer Stanhope, Earl of Chesterfield, from *Letters . . . to His Son* (1774), vol. 1, letter 3, excerpted in Williams, *Novel and Romance*, 100.

51. Congreve, preface to *Incognita* (1692), in Williams, *Novel and Romance*, 27–28.

52. Review of *The Surprises of Love*, in *Monthly Review* 32 (February 1765): 156–157, quoted in Basker, "Wages," 191.

53. Said, *On Late Style*, 25.

54. Quoted in Basker, "Wages," 189. The phrase is from a review of the first of Cleland's four novellas, *The Romance of a Day*, which was first published on its own in September 1760.

55. Cleland, *The Romance of an Evening; or, Who Would Have Thought It?* in *The Surprises of Love*, 214. As Basker notes, the volume was published on 15 December 1764 but with the following year's date on the title page—a common device for extending a work's "newness." Subsequent references to *The Surprises of Love* will be cited parenthetically.

56. *Sentimental Magazine* (Jan. 1774), 6, quoted in Mullan, "Sentimental Novels," 242. On the varied uses to which such terms as "sentiment" and "sensibility" could be put in eighteenth-century writing, see also Brissenden, *Virtue in Distress,* 96–139.

57. Review of *The Romance of a Night,* in *Monthly Review* 27 (November 1762): 386–387, quoted in Basker, "Wages," 190.

58. Nichols, Obituary of John Cleland.

59. Review of *The Surprises of Love,* in *Monthly Review* 20 (1765), quoted in Basker, "Wages," 191.

60. On Lowndes and Nicoll's business dealings with Cleland, see Epstein, *Images of a Life,* 155 and 235n140. As Epstein notes, Cleland's delivery of the manuscript on 23 October 1767 was accepted by Lowndes in exchange for the twenty-five guineas Cleland had been paid in advances over the previous two and a half years.

61. Review of Cleland, *The Woman of Honor,* in *Critical Review* 25 (Apr. 1768): 284; quoted in Basker, "Wages," 191.

62. Epstein, *Images of a Life,* 157 and 159.

63. Cleland, *The Woman of Honor,* 3:72. Subsequent references will be cited parenthetically.

64. Cleland, review of *Amelia,* in *Memoirs of a Coxcomb,* 231.

65. In other words, Cleland's intrusive disruptions of the expectations readers acquired through their familiarity with other novels violate the apparent naturalness and transparency of conventional novelistic realism.

66. Weinsheimer, "Theory of Character." As he writes, "Emma Woodhouse is not a woman nor need be described as if it were" (187). Epstein, *Images of a Life,* 159.

67. "J. B. D. F." [Jean Baptiste de Freval], Prefatory Letter, in Richardson, *Pamela,* 5.

68. Ariosto, *Orlando Furioso,* 600 (canto 24, 3). On love and madness in Ariosto, see Weaver, "Interlaced Plot."

CHAPTER 7. A BRITON (1757–1787)

1. Cleland, *Way to Things,* 70, 1. Subsequent references will be cited parenthetically.

2. Nichols, Obituary of John Cleland.

3. Leonard's account of the economic and moral consequences of financial speculation could almost have been written amid the British banking and financial crisis of the early twenty-first century, after years during which "the solid advantages" of industry and "commerce, foreign and domestic" were "impolitically sacrificed to an unwholesome bloated appearance of false opulence, from a nation's being mortgaged without necessity, and posterity burthened without deserving it" (3:232). The word "crazy," as Cleland uses it in the passage cited in the text, means not (or not only) mad or insane but "broken, decrepit," as Johnson defines it in his *Dictionary.*

4. Cleland, *Phisiologial Reveries,* 3. As its title suggests, this work is a loose, sometimes dreamlike collection of three brief meditations: the first on respiration; the second on similarities between saliva (the "reparative fluid" [9]) and semen (the "generative fluid" [9]); the third on fevers as "increase[s] in the vital fire" (18) by which nature aims "to rid us of an obstruction, or of some noxious matter" (23). Although the writer for the

Critical Review declared that Cleland "should ask pardon for the whole performance" (qtd. in Lonsdale, "New Attributions," 290), the observations on fever are more or less in keeping with later medical thinking, and there are flashes of imaginative brilliance throughout. The short essay on respiration is especially striking, with its nightmarish vision of the surface of the human body "perforated like a sieve" (7) with "millions of air-mouths" (pores) engaged in "one continual vicissitude of respiration and expiration" (6), producing this image of the body as machine: "this diffusive chain-work of air-pumps spread over and through the whole body of man, gives you the idea of one great pneu-matic engine, the incessant play of which, at once, keeps up the motion of our hydraulic machinery, and fans that vital fire in virtue of which the chimical laboratory within us is perpetually at work" (7).

5. Cleland to Stanhope, quoted in Foxon, *Libertine Literature*, 54.

6. Cleland, *Institutes of Health*, iii. Subsequent references will be cited parentheti-cally.

7. Cleland, *Specimen of an Etimological Vocabulary*, xii. Subsequent references will be cited parenthetically.

8. Cleland, *Additional Articles to the Specimen*, iv. Subsequent references will be cited parenthetically.

9. [Cleland], writing as A Briton, letter to the *Public Advertiser*, 18 Oct. 1765.

10. [Cleland], writing as A Briton, letter to the *Public Advertiser*, 12 Dec. 1765.

11. Cleland to Dickinson, 18 Feb. 1757, BL MS RP 4335[g].

12. Boswell, *For the Defence*, 81.

13. Epstein, *Images of a Life*, 145. Of the fifteen letters signed Modestus in the *Public Advertiser* between June 1767 and October 1783, Epstein states that five were "probably not written by Cleland" (192), presumably on stylistic grounds.

14. For example, in a letter to Dickinson dated 26 February 1757 (BL MS RP 4335[k]), Cleland enclosed "three papers" he wrote on the subject of Admiral John Byng's court-martial for dereliction of duty at the siege of Minorca in 1756. Cleland, who took Byng's side, contending that Byng was sacrificed as a scapegoat for wider ministerial failures in the conduct of the war against France, tells Dickinson that he "gave" his three letters or papers "to the Public" sometime in the preceding week and that they had met with "approbation"—but these papers have not yet been found or identified.

15. Epstein, *Images of a Life*, 146.

16. Quoted in Merritt, "Biographical Note," 305–306.

17. See Epstein, *Images of a Life*, 191–192. Of the 197 letters Epstein attributes to Cleland, 160 were written from 1770 on.

18. Epstein, *Images of a Life*, 145–146.

19. Boswell, *In Extremes*, 316.

20. Cleland to Dickinson, 9 Dec. 1756 and 16 Feb. 1758, BL MS RP 4335[f, h].

21. Epstein attributes nine of the *Public Advertiser* "Modestus" letters to Cleland from the period November 1769–October 1770 and contends that Cleland was "employed by the administration to respond to 'Junius''s attacks" (151; see also 152, 192, and 234–235n128). He bases his attributions on the reference to "Modestus" in Nichols's obituary of Cleland and on stylistic similarities to Cleland's other writing.

22. See also letters from "A Briton" to the *Public Advertiser* on 26 Oct. 1767 and 11 July 1768.

23. Cleland to Dickinson, 18 Feb. 1757, BL MS RP 4335[g].

24. Said, *On Late Style*, 13. Subsequent references will be cited parenthetically.

25. For Cleland "raving," see above, n. 19. Boswell describes Cleland as "a fine sly malcontent" in his journal entry for 31 March 1772, in which he also writes of Cleland "grumbling": see above, n. 12. For Cleland "harping on a string," see above, n. 10.

26. Williams, *"Way to Things,"* 251; Cleland, *Way to Things*, title page. The link between the origins of Britain and the migrations of the sons of Japhet can be traced at least as far back as the ninth-century *Historia Brittonum* of Nennius—see Bernau, "'Britain': Originary Myths," esp. 631–632—but the "Celtomania" of the eighteenth century, of which the Ossian craze of the 1760s is the best-known example, was also driven by contemporary anxieties and desires related to the emergence of the modern nation-state and questions of national identity and culture. See Weinbrot, *Britannia's Issue*, 477–556, for a discussion of the Celtic revival centering on James Macpherson's Ossian poems and Scottish culture. Cleland, however, despite his family's Scottish heritage, does not link the "antient Celtic" to Scotland but rather to a common originary *British* nation.

27. Le Brigant's advertisements were translated by Cleland and placed after his "Advertisement" to the *Specimen*, xiii–xvi; the passage quoted is from xv–xvi. Cleland's "Mons. *Brigant*" was Jacques Le Brigant (1720–1804), Breton parliamentarian and co-founder (in 1804) of L'Académie Celtique (later the Société des Antiquaires de France). Le Brigant published his *Éléments succincts de la langue des Celtes-Gomérites, ou Bretons* in 1779 and the more wide-ranging *La Langue primitive conservée* in 1787. As the French title of the 1779 work suggests, Cleland's translation of Le Brigant's advertisement conceals the double meaning of "*Breton*," which means both "Briton" and "Breton"—indeed it is the latter sense that Le Brigant is mainly interested in, another instance of the nationalistic impulse underlying much of the etymological research of the period, Cleland's included.

28. Once the Druids' allegorical fictions were mistaken for real "personages," Cleland writes, "thence arose another mythology, in which the Egyptian, the Greek, and the Roman Gods manifestly sprung out of the corruption of Druidism, or rather of the worst part of Druidism" (*Way*, 118).

29. Haycock, "Stukeley, William (1687–1765)," *ODNB*.

30. Cooke, *Enquiry into the Patriarchal and Druidical Religion*, 61 and title page. Cooke's publisher, Lockyer Davis, was also the publisher of Cleland's three Celtic tracts, despite their different interpretations of Druidic religion. For a discussion of eighteenth-century theories of the supposed genealogical links between Celtic and Hebrew, see Weinbrot, *Britannia's Issue*, esp. 481–495. Against such theories, Cleland writes: "Nothing can be more demonstrably erroneous than a recourse for the origin of the Teutonic or British languages to the Phenician or Hebrew" (*Articles*, viii).

31. In another passage from *The Way to Things*, Cleland writes that "the primitive Christians, for rearing the fabric of their Church, took what suited them, of the ruins of demolished Druidism, for a scaffolding; which they struck, and put out of the way, as soon as they had finished a much nobler structure, and, as it is to be hoped, a more

permanent one" (102). The qualifying phrase "as it is to be hoped" calls the permanence of the "nobler structure" into question, and the "primitive Christians," distanced from author and reader by the use of the third-person "their," "them," and "they," are presented, again, as opportunistic scavengers concealing their structural dependence on Druid "ruins." See also *Way to Things*, 114.

32. Quoted in Merritt, "Biographical Note," 305. Cleland's etymology for *Pentecost* derives it from a Druid ordination ceremony for newly qualified members of the judiciary in which "the spirit of authority" was "conveyed by touching the head: *Pen*, head. *T'ick*, touch. *Ghast*, Spirit" (*Specimen*, 10).

33. Arthur Golding, *The Eyght Bookes of C. J. Caesar* (1565), 6:155, cited in *Oxford English Dictionary Online*, "Druid, n. (a.)."

34. Quoted in Epstein, *Images of a Life*, 164.

35. Williams, *"Way to Things,"* 258.

36. Beckwith, quoted in Merritt, "Biographical Note," 305; Lemon, *English Etymology*, xxiii. The passage on Cleland is also reprinted in Epstein, *Images of a Life*, 194. Although Lemon is a significant enough figure to be included in the *Oxford Dictionary of National Biography*, his *English Etymology* is described there as "an eccentric and useless exposition of his theory that most English words were derived from a Greek radix"— interestingly contrary to Cleland's own theory, notwithstanding Lemon's admiration. See Tancock, "Lemon, George William (1726–1797)," rev. S. J. Skedd, *ODNB*.

37. Cleland developed the contrast between "amiable simplicity and youthful vigor of taste" and the "silly dotage of a luxury verging to its own death" at much greater length in the 1761 *Institutes of Health*, which he prefaces with the example of his own case as a warning of the dangers of excess, describing himself as "too far now advanced in years, when probably my stamina have suffered irretrievable damage by the most abandoned intemperance of all sorts" (iv). It's hard to resist the invitation to speculate on that "abandoned intemperance," but the aim of the temperance he advocates as a countermeasure is not puritan self-denial but pleasure, "the permanent voluptuousness inseparable from every function of life in a firm state of health" (48). This voluptuousness consists of "sensations more exquisite, a mind more alert . . . a body more disposed for action, and more delighting in it, more sprightliness, a clearer command of the imagination to produce or augment pleasure, powers greater and more lasting" (96–97). Cleland illustrates the benefits of natural diet and exercise by contrasting a young peasant—"that ignoble freshness of his complexion, that muscular vigor, that air of health breathing in his every motion" (50)—to the "quality-paleness, that bloodless, green-sick look, one would think the birthmark of the people of fashion" (51), reminiscent of the contrast Fanny draws between Mr. H—— or her "country lad" Will (71) and "our pap-nerv'd softlings" (64). Despite his fears of his "stamina hav[ing] suffered irretrievable damage," Cleland lived a further twenty-eight evidently healthy years, testament to his sensible recommendations: fresh air, local produce, not too much salt or animal fat, daily exercise, frequent bathing.

38. "Unsex'd male-misses" is Mrs. Cole's epithet for sodomites in the *Woman of Pleasure* (160).

39. For "potent patriarchal forces," see Williams, *"Way to Things,"* 258–259.

40. Ibid., 274. Cleland's preoccupation with the ancient British "system of manliness" is also evident in the 1749 *Case of the Unfortunate Bosavern Benlez*, in which he extols the "antient Manliness" from which "the Spirit of the *English* is already too much broke, sunk, and declin'd" (46).

41. On the relationship between masculinity and the sublime in Cleland's novel, see Blackwell, "It Stood an Object of Terror and Delight."

42. That the *Specimen* was controversial I infer from the defensiveness of the advertisement Cleland prefaced to the *Additional Articles* the following year, in which he protests at length against "the suspicion of my having intended any offence to the Church" (xi) and maintains that "there was nothing of a theological import so much as thought of" (x). Declaring his "unfeigned sentiments of veneration for religion, and of reverence for its ministers," he writes, "I could not well imagine it possible for ignorance or for malice to suggest the suspicion of any design in me of offence to either" (xii). Characteristically, however, Cleland's self-justification bleeds into an attack on his attackers, as when he writes, of the clergy, that "I presumed them . . . infinitely superior to the injustice of little groundless jealousies of unimaginable attacks, and at once the best judges and the most equitable protectors of the truth" (xiii)—his phrasing clearly insinuating that this "presumption" in their favor was wrong. By the end of the advertisement, he asserts that the "Judgment" of those who "slighted or depreciated" his previous publication "is, literally speaking, not their own, but under a wretched enslavement . . . to inveterate prejudices" (xvi).

43. Merritt, "Biographical Note," 305–306.

44. Epstein, "John Cleland," 110; Basker, "Wages," 185. See also, more generally, Epstein, *Images of a Life*, 146–153.

45. Cleland reviewed Bolingbroke's *Letters*, including "On the Spirit of Patriotism" and "On the Idea of a Patriot King," in the *Monthly Review* 1 (May–June 1749): 52–64 and 147–158. But even here, Cleland's rhetorical extremism and loathing of the present is evident, as when he refers to "the little less than universal degeneracy, that like the plague, leaves scarce a door uncrossed" (60).

46. The writer for the *Critical Review*, although skeptical of some of Cleland's "bold conjectures," agreed: "Whatever the author's aim may be, the reader will find great entertainment" (qtd. in Epstein, *Images of a Life*, 164).

47. Deuteronomy 34:4 (King James Version).

48. It is not always easy to track where Cleland was living when. Epstein has established that from September 1782 on he was living in Petty France, Westminster, between St. James's Park and Tothill Fields (*Images of a Life*, 176 and 238–39n197). It's possible he had lived there before—a letter to the *Public Advertiser* for 13 July 1764 is dated from Petty France—but the bulk of the surviving evidence suggests he was living in the neighborhood of the Strand, including the Savoy, for most of the period 1756–1781. In a letter to Dickinson dated 21 September 1762, he writes that "my present apartment is at Mr[s?] Meredith's a Staymaker in the Savoy where I have been near these six years" (BL MS RP 4335[l], 21 Sept. 1762). A letter from 1758 gives his return address as care of "Mr Hooper, Bookseller at Gay's head near Beaufort Buildings in the Strand"—this is the same Hooper who published *Tombo-Chiqui* and other texts by Cleland—but this

was most likely simply the office where Cleland could retrieve his post, rather than a residence (BL MS RP 4335[c]). The same is probably true of "Mr Coles Peruke Maker in Beaufort buildings in the Strand," to whom Dickinson directed a letter for Cleland on 23 September 1762 (BL MS RP 4335[p]). In any case, the Beaufort Buildings were just a few yards from the Savoy. Epstein provides evidence that from 1770 to 1772 Cleland may have rented a house in a much more expensive area, on what is now Soho Square (*Images of a Life*, 174–175), but if so, he was back in the Strand by late 1772, when he is listed as sharing a house with John Leslie in Buckingham Street. Cleland was living in the Savoy when he wrote to the Marquis of Rockingham in 1776, when Boswell visited in 1778, and when Beckwith came to call in 1781, so while he may have moved around during this period, the Savoy and the Strand have to be considered his home for most of those twenty-five years.

EPILOGUE. AFTERLIFE

1. Quoted in Epstein, *Images of a Life*, 177.

2. Nichols, Obituary of John Cleland; Cleland to Stanhope, quoted in Foxon, *Libertine Literature*, 54; Boswell, *In Extremes*, 316.

3. Rider, *Account*, 16. "Dialogues of Meursius" was pseudonymous shorthand for Nicolas Chorier's *Satyra sotadica* (ca. 1660), known in French as *L'Académie des dames* (1680) and in English as *Dialogue between a Married Lady and a Maid* (1688, 1740); see Wagner, *Eros Revived*, 227–228. Petronius's *Satyricon*, of course, was the source for some of the key passages of Cannon's *Ancient and Modern Pederasty*.

4. Boswell, *Laird of Auchinleck*, 77.

5. Basker, "Wages," 192–193.

6. See chapter 6, n. 12. From the mocking reviews in *Critical Review* 32 (Oct. 1771): 311, and *Monthly Review* 48 (Jan. 1773): 71, it doesn't sound like Cleland's work, but I have not read it, so there remains, for me, still a sliver of doubt.

7. In his biography, Epstein reviewed the (lack of) evidence for the Smyrna claim and concluded, convincingly, that it had no plausible basis (*Images of a Life*, 213–214n85).

8. IOC, Bombay Public Consultations, P/341/8, f. 11. On Cleland's voyage to Carolina, see chapter 6, nn. 44–45. On Cannon as murderer, see chapter 2, n. 44.

9. On these two attributions, see Epstein, *Images of a Life*, 144–145 and 233nn108–109; Basker, "Wages," 183.

10. Epstein, *Images of a Life*, 142–145; Halsband, introduction to Montagu, *Complete Letters*, xiv–xviii.

11. Carruthers, *Life of Pope*, 148. Henry Bohn, that book's publisher, also appears to be the source of the claim that the *Woman of Pleasure*'s sodomitical scene was interpolated by Drybutter (see Foxon, *Libertine Literature*, 61), although he may have been drawing on rumors already current.

12. On Cleland and Lady Mary, see chapter 4, p. 126–127.

13. The reference to Hadrian and Antinous is in Montagu, *Additional Volume*, 34.

14. I have accepted Epstein's and Lonsdale's attributions, for all of which the evidence is convincing. Basker has provided further evidence for some of these, located

copies of missing works, and made two new attributions: *The Man of Honour* and one or more volumes of *The History of the Marchioness de Pompadour* (1758–1760). In my view, *The Man of Honour* is not by Cleland, but the Pompadour *History*, which Basker attributed on the basis of a remark in a review probably written by Goldsmith, might well be Cleland's work, given his connection during this period with the *History*'s publisher, Samuel Hooper, who also published *Tombo-Chiqui* and Grose's *Voyage to the East-Indies*. All three volumes of the Pompadour *History*, copies of which were only located after Basker wrote his essay, await closer critical study.

BIBLIOGRAPHY

ARCHIVAL SOURCES

Bodleian Library, Oxford

Cleland, John. Letters to Ralph Griffiths, 1749 and 1756. Letters to R. Griffiths, editor, *Monthly Review*. Bodl. MS Add. C. 89, f. 29.
Griffiths, Fenton. Letters to Ralph Griffiths, 1785–1791. Letters to R. Griffiths, editor, *Monthly Review*. Bodl. MS Add. C. 89, ff. 50–51 and 132–137.

British Library, London

India Office Collection (IOC), Asian and African Library

B/63: East India Company. Index of Court Minutes, 1732–1742.
E/1/22: Bombay. Miscellaneous Letters Received 22 [1731].
E/1/27: Bombay. Miscellaneous Letters Received 27 [1736].
E/1/28: Bombay. Miscellaneous Letters Received 28 [1737–1739].
E/3/106: General Correspondence. Correspondence with the East, Despatch Books for 1733–1736.
N/3/1: Ecclesiastical Returns of Births, Baptisms, Marriages, and Burials, Bombay, 1709–1757.
O/5/31: List of European Inhabitants of Bombay, 1719–1792.
O/6/37: List of Bombay Civil Servants, 1712–1752.
P/341/8: Bombay Public Consultations, Jan. to Dec. 1734 [i.e., 1735]–6.
P/341/9: Bombay Public Consultations, Jan. 1736/7–Dec. 1738.
P/341/10: Bombay Public Consultations, Jan.1738/9–Dec. 1739.
P/341/11: Bombay Public Consultations, Jan. 1739/40–Dec. 1740.
P/416/103: Bombay. Register of Proceedings of the Mayor's Court, 7 Jan.–23 Sept. 1730.
P/416/108: Bombay. Register of Proceedings of the Mayor's Court, Jan. 1734–Jan. 1735.
P/416/109: Bombay. Register of Proceedings of the Mayor's Court, 29 Jan.–20 Dec 1735.
P/416/110: Bombay. Register of Proceedings of the Mayor's Court, 7 Jan.–29 Dec. 1736.
P/418/66: Bombay. Mayors Court, Journals and Ledgers, 1749–1766.

P/419/167: Bombay. Journals and Ledgers—Journal for 1734–35.

P/420/1: Bombay. Journals and Ledgers—Ledger for 1734–35.

Orme Manuscript Collection, vol. 147.

Other Collections

Cleland, John. Letter to Edward Dickinson, n.d. Photocopy of letter held in the Pierpont Morgan Library, New York. BL MS RP 3476.

———. Letters (11) to Edward Dickinson, 23 Nov. 1752 to 21 Sept. 1762. Photocopies of letters held in the Pierpont Morgan Library, New York. BL MS RP 4335.

———. Letter to Lucy Cleland, 6 Mar. 1758. Photocopy of letter held in the Pierpont Morgan Library, New York. BL MS RP 4335.

Cleland, Lucy. Letters (2) to Edward Dickinson, n.d. [ca. 1752–1755]. Photocopies of letters held in the Pierpont Morgan Library, New York. BL MS RP 4335.

Cleland, William. Letter to the Duke of Newcastle, 22 May 1741. Newcastle Papers, vol. 12. BL Add. MS 32.697, f. 39.

Dickinson, Edward. Letters (5) to John Cleland, 18 Oct. 1755–23 Sept. 1762. Photocopies of letters held in the Pierpont Morgan Library, New York. BL MS RP 4335.

———. Copy of letter to Lucy Cleland, n.d. [ca. 1755–1759?]. Photocopy of letter held in the Pierpont Morgan Library, New York. BL MS RP 4335.

British National Archives (incorporating the former Public Record Office), Kew

Affidavits for Court of King's Bench. KB 1/10/1–KB 1/10/5.

Cannon, Elizabeth. Petition to Thomas Pelham-Holles, Duke of Newcastle, n.d. [ca. 1754–1755]. T1/338, f. 66.

Cannon, Thomas. Affidavit against John Cleland, 5 Feb. 1748 [i.e., 1749]. KB 1/10/1.

[———. Extracts transcribed from *Ancient and Modern Pederasty Investigated and Exemplify'd*]. In Dudley Ryder, Indictment of John Purser, Printer. KB 10/29, part 1.

Cleland, John. Letter to Andrew Stone, 10 Nov. 1749. SP 36/111, ff. 151–152.

———. Letter to Lovel Stanhope, 13 Nov. 1749. SP 36/111, ff. 157–159.

Cleland, Lucy. Last Will and Testament, 4 Feb. 1752 [proved 20 June 1763]. PROB 11/888, ff. 221v–226v.

Griffiths, Ralph. Examination of Ralph Griffiths before Lovel Stanhope, 20 Mar. 1749 [i.e., 1750]. SP 36/112, ff. 145–146.

———. Examination of Ralph Griffiths before Lovel Stanhope, 13 Nov. 1749. SP 36/111, ff. 159–160.

Indictments for Court of King's Bench, KB 10/29, parts 1–3.

Parker, Thomas. Examination of Thomas Parker before Lovel Stanhope, 13 Nov. 1749. SP 36/111, f. 158.

Pelham-Holles, Thomas, Duke of Newcastle. Letter to Dudley Ryder, Attorney General, 20 Jan. 1749/50 [i.e., 1750]. SP 44/134, f. 9.

———. Letter to Dudley Ryder, Attorney General, 12 Apr. 1750. SP 44/134, f. 28.

———. Letter to Dudley Ryder, Attorney General, 27 Nov. 1750. SP 44/134, f. 32.

Prosecutions in the Crown Office for Seditious Libels in the Reign of George the 2nd. KB 15/54, ff. 154–157.

State Papers Domestic [incl. Recognizances of John Cleland, 24 Nov. 1749, and Thomas Cannon, 10 Feb. 1749 (i.e., 1750)]. SP 44/85, ff. 161 and 166.

PUBLISHED SOURCES

Altherr, Thomas L. "*Tombo-Chiqui; or, The American Savage*: John Cleland's Noble Savage Satire." *American Indian Quarterly* 9:4 (1985): 411–420.

Anderson, Antje Schaum. "Gendered Pleasure, Gendered Plot: Defloration as Climax in *Clarissa* and *Memoirs of a Woman of Pleasure*." *Journal of Narrative Technique* 25:2 (1995): 108–138.

Ariosto, Ludovico. *Orlando Furioso* [1532]. Edited by Cesare Segre. Milan: Mondadori, 1976.

Baines, Paul, and Pat Rogers. *Edmund Curll, Bookseller*. Oxford: Clarendon, 2007.

Bakhtin, Mikhail M. *The Dialogic Imagination*. Edited by Michael Holquist, translated by Caryl Emerson and Michael Holquist. Austin: University of Texas Press, 1981.

Barker-Benfield, G. J. *The Culture of Sensibility: Sex and Society in Eighteenth-Century Britain*. Chicago: University of Chicago Press, 1992.

Barreto, José. Introduction to *Escritos Económicos de Londres (1741–1742)*, by Sebastião José Carvalho e Melo, vii–lxxiii. Edited by José Barreto. Lisbon: Biblioteca Nacional, 1986.

Barthes, Roland. *Image, Music, Text*. Edited and translated by Stephen Heath. New York: Noonday, 1988.

———. *The Pleasure of the Text*. Translated by Richard Miller. London: Cape, 1967.

Basker, James G. *Tobias Smollett: Critic and Journalist*. London: Associated University Presses, 1988.

———. "'The Wages of Sin': The Later Career of John Cleland." *Études anglaises* 40:2 (1987): 178–194.

Bennett, Andrew. *The Author*. London: Routledge, 2005.

Bennett, Andrew, and Nicholas Royle. *Introduction to Literature, Criticism and Theory*. 3rd ed. Harlow: Pearson/Longman, 2004.

Bentley, Eric. *The Brecht Memoir*. Manchester: Carcanet, 1989.

Bernau, Anke. "'Britain': Originary Myths and the Stories of Peoples." In *The Oxford Handbook of Medieval Literature in English*, edited by Elaine Treharne and Greg Walker with William Green, 629–648. Oxford: Oxford University Press, 2010.

Beynon, John C. "'Traffic in More Precious Commodities': Sapphic Erotics and Economics in *Memoirs of a Woman of Pleasure*." In *Launching Fanny Hill: Essays on the Novel and Its Influences*, edited by Patsy S. Fowler and Alan Jackson, 3–26. New York: AMS, 2003.

Bianchi, Giovanni. *Breve storia della vita di Catterina Vizzani*. Venice: Simone Occhi, 1744.

Binhammer, Katherine. "The 'Singular Propensity' of Sensibility's Extremities: Female Same-Sex Desire and the Eroticization of Pain in Late Eighteenth-Century British Culture." *GLQ* 9:4 (2003): 471–498.

Blackwell, Mark. "'It Stood an Object of Terror and Delight': Sublime Masculinity and the Aesthetics of Disproportion in John Cleland's *Memoirs of a Woman of Pleasure.*" *Eighteenth-Century Novel* 3 (2003): 39–63.

Boswell, James. *Boswell for the Defence, 1769–1774.* Edited by William K. Wimsatt Jr. and Frederick A. Pottle. New York: McGraw-Hill, 1959.

———. *Boswell in Extremes, 1776–1778.* Edited by Charles McC. Weis and Frederick A. Pottle. New York: McGraw-Hill, 1970.

———. *Boswell in Search of a Wife, 1766–1769.* Edited by Frank Brady and Frederick A. Pottle. London: William Heinemann, 1956.

———. *Boswell, Laird of Auchinleck, 1778–1782.* Edited by Joseph W. Reed and Frederick A. Pottle. New York: McGraw-Hill, 1977.

Bray, Alan. *Homosexuality in Renaissance England.* 2nd ed. London: Gay Men's Press, 1988.

Bray, Joe. *The Epistolary Novel: Representations of Consciousness.* London: Routledge, 2003.

Brissenden, R. F. *Virtue in Distress: Studies in the Novel of Sentiment from Richardson to Sade.* London: Macmillan, 1974.

Bristow, Joseph. "Symonds's History, Ellis's Heredity: *Sexual Inversion.*" In *Sexology in Culture: Labelling Bodies and Desires,* edited by Lucy Bland and Laura Doan, 79–99. Chicago: University of Chicago Press, 1998.

Burke, Seán. *The Death and Return of the Author: Criticism and Subjectivity in Barthes, Foucault and Derrida.* 2nd ed. Edinburgh: Edinburgh University Press, 1998.

Campbell, Archibald [attrib.]. *The Sale of Authors, A Dialogue, in imitation of Lucian's Sale of Philosophers.* London, 1767.

Cannon, [Thomas]. *A Treatise on Charity, By Mr. Cannon. To which is prefix'd, The Author's Retraction.* London: printed for the author, 1753.

Carruthers, Robert. *The Life of Alexander Pope.* 2nd ed. London: Henry G. Bohn, 1857.

Carvalho e Melo, Sebastião José. *Escritos Económicos de Londres (1741–1742).* Edited by José Barreto. Lisbon: Biblioteca Nacional, 1986.

Chapman, Paul. "Purser, John (*fl.* 1728–1747)." In *Oxford Dictionary of National Biography.* Oxford University Press, 2004–. www.oxforddnb.com/view/article/73720. Accessed 20 Dec. 2010.

Chatterjee, Indrani. *Gender, Slavery and Law in Colonial India.* New Delhi: Oxford University Press, 1999.

Christensen, Jerome. *Practicing Enlightenment: Hume and the Formation of a Literary Career.* Madison: University of Wisconsin Press, 1987.

Cleland, John. *Additional Articles to the Specimen of an Etimological Vocabulary.* London: Lockyer Davis, 1769.

———. *The Case of the Unfortunate Bosavern Penlez.* 2nd ed. London: T. Clement, 1750.

———. *The Dictionary of Love.* London: Ralph Griffiths, 1753.

———. *The Economy of a Winter's Day: A New Edition, with Additions and Alterations.* London: P. Brett, n.d.

———, trans. and ed. *Historical and Physical Dissertation on the Case of Catherine Vizzani.* By Giovanni Bianchi. London: W. Meyer, 1751.

———. *Institutes of Health.* London: T. Becket and P. A. De Hondt, 1761.

————, trans. *Memoirs Illustrating the Manners of the Present Age*. By Monsieur Du Clos [Charles Pinot-Duclos]. Vol. II. London: J. Whiston and B. White, R. Dodsley, J. and J. Rivington, and G. Woodfall, 1752.

————. *Memoirs of a Coxcomb* [1751]. Edited by Hal Gladfelder. Peterborough, ON: Broadview, 2005.

————. *Memoirs of a Woman of Pleasure* [1748–1749]. Edited by Peter Sabor. Oxford: Oxford University Press, 1985.

————. *Memoirs of Fanny Hill*. London: Ralph Griffiths, 1750. Facsimile ed. In *Eighteenth-Century British Erotica II*, Alexander Pettit and Patrick Spedding, general editors, vol. 4, *The Prostitute's Life: Sally Salisbury and Fanny Hill*, edited by Lena Olsson. London: Pickering and Chatto, 2004.

————. *Phisiological Reveries*. London: T. Becket and P. A. De Hondt, 1765.

————. *Specimen of an Etimological Vocabulary; or, Essay by Means of the Analitic Method, to Retrieve the Antient Celtic*. London: L. Davis and C. Reymers, 1768.

————. *The Surprises of Love*. London: T. Lowndes and W. Nicoll, 1765 [for 1764].

————. *Tombo-Chiqui; or, The American Savage*. London: S. Hooper and A. Morley, 1753.

————. *The Way to Things by Words, and to Words by Things; Being a Sketch of an Attempt at the Retrieval of the Antient Celtic, or, Primitive Language of Europe*. London: L. Davis and C. Reymers, 1766. Facsimile ed. Menston: Scolar, 1968.

————. *The Woman of Honor*. London: T. Lowndes and W. Nicoll, 1768.

Coleridge, Samuel Taylor. *Poetical Works*. Edited by Ernest Hartley Coleridge. Oxford: Oxford University Press, 1912; paperback ed. 1969.

Cooke, William. *An Enquiry into the Patriarchal and Druidical Religion*. London: Lockyer Davis, 1755.

Cope, Jackson I. Review of *The Revels History of Drama in English*, vol. 6, *1750–1880* (London: Methuen, 1975). *Eighteenth-Century Studies* 9:4 (1976): 640–643.

Crébillon fils. *The Wayward Head and Heart*. Translated by Barbara Bray. Oxford: Oxford University Press, 1963. Originally published as *Les Égarements du coeur et de l'esprit* [1738]. Citations refer to reprint in *The Libertine Reader: Eroticism and Enlightenment in Eighteenth-Century France*, edited by Michel Feher, 766–910. New York: Zone, 1997.

Cusset, Catherine. *No Tomorrow: The Ethics of Pleasure in the French Enlightenment*. Charlottesville: University Press of Virginia, 1999.

————. "The Suspended Ending or Crébillon fils's Irony." In *The Libertine Reader: Eroticism and Enlightenment in Eighteenth-Century France*, edited by Michel Feher, 750–765. New York: Zone, 1997.

Dabhoiwala, Faramerz. "Lust and Liberty." *Past & Present* 207 (2010): 89–179.

Defoe, Daniel. *Moll Flanders* [1722]. Edited by G. A. Starr. Oxford: Oxford University Press, 1971.

Delisle, Louis-François de La Drevetière. *"Arlequin sauvage"* [1721], *"Timon le misanthrope"* [1722], *"Les Caprices du coeur et de l'esprit* [1739]."* Edited by Ola Forsans. Paris: Société des Textes Français Modernes, 2000.

Deutsch, Helen. *Loving Dr. Johnson*. Chicago: University of Chicago Press, 2005.

————. *Resemblance and Disgrace: Alexander Pope and the Deformation of Culture*. Cambridge, MA: Harvard University Press, 1996.

Diderot, Denis. *Le Rêve de d'Alembert* [1769]. Published with *Entretien entre d'Alembert et Diderot.* Edited by Jacques Roger. Paris: Garnier-Flammarion, 1965.

Donato, Clorinda. "Public and Private Negotiations of Gender in Eighteenth-Century England and Italy: Lady Mary Wortley Montagu and the Case of Catherine Vizzani." *British Journal for Eighteenth-Century Studies* 29:2 (2006): 169–189.

Donkin, Ellen. *Getting into the Act: Women Playwrights in London, 1776–1829.* London: Routledge, 1995.

Donoghue, Emma. *Passions between Women: British Lesbian Culture, 1668–1801.* New York: HarperCollins, 1995.

Donoghue, Frank. *The Fame Machine: Book Reviewing and Eighteenth-Century Literary Careers.* Stanford, CA: Stanford University Press, 1996.

Douglas, James. *Glimpses of Old Bombay and Western India.* London: Sampson Low, Marston, 1900.

Easton, Fraser. "Gender's Two Bodies: Women Warriors, Female Husbands and Plebeian Life." *Past & Present* 180 (2003): 131–174.

Edelman, Lee. *Homographesis: Essays in Gay Literary and Cultural Theory.* New York: Routledge, 1994.

Ellis, Havelock. *Sexual Inversion.* 3rd ed. In *Studies in the Psychology of Sex,* vol. 1, part 4. New York: Random House, [1942].

Epstein, Julia. "Fanny's Fanny: Epistolarity, Eroticism, and the Transsexual Text." In *Writing the Female Voice: Essays on Epistolary Literature,* edited by Elizabeth C. Goldsmith, 135–153. Boston: Northeastern University Press, 1989.

Epstein, William H., ed. *Contesting the Subject: Postmodern Theory and Practice of Biography and Biographical Criticism.* West Lafayette, IN: Purdue University Press, 1991.

———. "John Cleland." In *Dictionary of Literary Biography,* vol. 39, *British Novelists 1660–1800,* edited by Martin C. Battestin, 101–112. New York: Gale, 1985.

———. *John Cleland: Images of a Life.* New York: Columbia University Press, 1974.

———. *Recognizing Biography.* Philadelphia: University of Pennsylvania Press, 1997.

Farrant, John H. "Grose, John Henry (*b.* 1732, *d.* in or after 1774)." In *Oxford Dictionary of National Biography.* Oxford University Press, 2004–. www.oxforddnb.com/view/article/11662. Accessed 11 Nov. 2009.

Fawcett, Charles. *The First Century of British Justice in India.* Oxford: Clarendon, 1934.

Fielding, Henry. *An Enquiry into the Causes of the Late Increase of Robbers* [1751] *and Related Writings.* Edited by Malvin R. Zirker. Oxford: Clarendon, 1988.

———. *The Female Husband* [1746]. In *"The Journal of a Voyage to Lisbon," "Shamela," and Occasional Writings,* edited by Martin C. Battestin with Sheridan W. Baker Jr. and Hugh Amory, 355–384. Oxford: Clarendon, 2008.

———. *Shamela* [1741]. In *Joseph Andrews and "Shamela,"* edited by Douglas Brooks-Davies, revised by Thomas Keymer. Oxford: Oxford University Press, 1999.

———. *A True State of the Case of Bosavern Penlez* [1749]. In *An Enquiry into the Causes of the Late Increase of Robbers and Related Writings,* edited by Malvin R. Zirker, 31–60. Oxford: Clarendon, 1988.

Flynn, Carol Houlihan. "What Fanny Felt: The Pains of Compliance in *Memoirs of a Woman of Pleasure.*" *Studies in the Novel* 19:3 (1987): 284–295.

Forsans, Ola. Introduction to *Arlequin sauvage, Timon le misanthrope*, and *Les Caprices du coeur et de l'esprit*, by Louis-François de La Drevetière Delisle, 7–68. Edited by Ola Forsans. Paris: Société des Textes Français Modernes, 2000.

Forster, Antonia. "Griffiths, Ralph (1720?–1803)." In *Oxford Dictionary of National Biography*. Oxford University Press, 2004–. www.oxforddnb.com/view/article/11621. Accessed 3 Mar. 2009.

Fowler, Patsy S. "'This Tail-Piece of Morality': Phallocentric Reinforcements of Patriarchy in *Memoirs of a Woman of Pleasure*." In *Launching Fanny Hill: Essays on the Novel and Its Influences*, edited by Patsy S. Fowler and Alan Jackson, 49–80. New York: AMS, 2003.

Foxon, David. *Libertine Literature in England, 1660–1745*. New Hyde Park, NY: University Books, 1965.

Gallagher, Catherine. *Nobody's Story: The Vanishing Acts of Women Writers in the Marketplace, 1670–1820*. Oxford: Clarendon, 1994.

Garrick, David. *Miss in Her Teens; or, The Medley of Lovers*. London: J. and R. Tonson, 1757.

———. *The Private Correspondence of David Garrick*. Vol. 1. London: H. Colburn and R. Bentley, 1831.

Gautier, Gary. "Fanny's Fantasies: Class, Gender and the Unreliable Narrator in Cleland's *Memoirs of a Woman of Pleasure*." *Style* 28:2 (1994): 133–145.

Gay, John. *The Beggar's Opera* [1728]. Edited by Edgar V. Roberts. Lincoln: University of Nebraska Press, 1969.

Gladfelder, Hal. *Criminality and Narrative in Eighteenth-Century England: Beyond the Law*. Baltimore: Johns Hopkins University Press, 2001.

———. "The Hard Work of Doing Nothing: Richard Savage's Parallel Lives." *Modern Language Quarterly* 64:4 (December 2003): 445–472.

———. "In Search of Lost Texts: Thomas Cannon's *Ancient and Modern Pederasty Investigated and Exemplify'd*." *Eighteenth-Century Life* 31:1 (Winter 2007): 22–38.

———, ed. "The Indictment of John Purser, Containing Thomas Cannon's *Ancient and Modern Pederasty Investigated and Exemplify'd*." *Eighteenth-Century Life* 31:1 (Winter 2007): 39–61.

———. "Plague Spots." In *Social Histories of Disability and Deformity*, edited by David M. Turner and Kevin Stagg, 56–78. London: Routledge, 2006.

Graham, Rosemary. "The Prostitute in the Garden: Walt Whitman, *Fanny Hill*, and the Fantasy of Female Pleasure." *English Literary History* 64:2 (1997): 569–597.

Greenberg, David. *The Construction of Homosexuality*. Chicago: University of Chicago Press, 1988.

Greene, Donald. Introduction to *The Major Works*, by Samuel Johnson, xi–xxvii. Edited by Donald Greene. Oxford: Oxford University Press, 2000.

Greene, Jody. "Arbitrary Tastes and Commonsense Pleasures: Accounting for Taste in Cleland, Hume, and Burke." In *Launching "Fanny Hill": Essays on the Novel and Its Influences*, edited by Patsy S. Fowler and Alan Jackson, 221–265. New York: AMS, 2003.

———. "Public Secrets: Sodomy and the Pillory in the Eighteenth Century and Beyond." *The Eighteenth Century: Theory and Interpretation* 44:2–3 (2003): 203–232.

Grose, Jean-Henri [John Henry]. *Voyage aux Indes Orientales*. Translated by [Philippe] Hernandez. London, Lille, and Paris, 1758.

———. *A Voyage to the East Indies, with Observations on Various Parts There*. London: S. Hooper and A. Morley, 1757.

Grundy, Isobel. *Lady Mary Wortley Montagu*. Oxford: Oxford University Press, 1999.

Haggerty, George E. "Keyhole Testimony: Witnessing Sodomy in the Eighteenth Century." *The Eighteenth Century: Theory and Interpretation* 44:2–3 (2003): 167–182.

———. *Men in Love: Masculinity and Sexuality in the Eighteenth Century*. New York: Columbia University Press, 1999.

Halperin, David M. *How to Do the History of Homosexuality*. Chicago: University of Chicago Press, 2002.

———. *One Hundred Years of Homosexuality and Other Essays on Greek Love*. New York: Routledge, 1990.

Halsband, Robert. *The Life of Lady Mary Wortley Montagu*. Oxford: Oxford University Press, 1956.

Haycock, David Boyd. "Stukeley, William (1687–1765)." In *Oxford Dictionary of National Biography*. Oxford University Press, 2004–. www.oxforddnb.com/view/article/26743. Accessed 30 Apr. 2010.

Heywood, Thomas. *Pleasant Dialogues and Drammas, Selected out of Lucian, Erasmus, Textor, Ovid, &c*. London: printed by R. O. for R. H., 1637.

Hitchcock, Tim. *English Sexualities, 1700–1800*. New York: St. Martin's, 1997.

Holcroft, Thomas. *The Life of Thomas Holcroft, Written by Himself*. Edited by William Hazlitt. Newly edited by Elbridge Colby. 2 vols. London: Constable, 1925.

Hughes, S. F. D. "John Cleland's Role in the History of Sanskrit Studies in Europe." *Archivum Linguisticum*, new series, 7:1 (1976): 3–12.

Jacobs, René. "Seven Misconceptions about *La Clemenza di Tito*." Published with recording of W. A. Mozart, *La Clemenza di Tito*, conducted by René Jacobs. Arles: Harmonia Mundi, 2006.

Jagose, Annamarie. " 'Critical Extasy': Orgasm and Sensibility in *Memoirs of a Woman of Pleasure*." *Signs: Journal of Women in Culture and Society* 32:2 (2007): 459–482.

Johnson, Samuel. *Essays from the "Rambler," "Adventurer," and "Idler."* Edited by W. J. Bate. New Haven, CT: Yale University Press, 1968.

———. *"The Idler" and "The Adventurer"* [1753–1760]. Edited by W. J. Bate, John M. Bullitt, and L. F. Powell. New Haven, CT: Yale University Press, 1963.

———. *Life of Savage* [1744]. Edited by Clarence Tracy. Oxford: Clarendon, 1971.

Juengel, Scott J. "Doing Things with Fanny Hill." *ELH* 76 (2009): 419–446.

Kahn, Madeleine. *Narrative Transvestism: Rhetoric and Gender in the Eighteenth-Century English Novel*. Ithaca, NY: Cornell University Press, 1991.

Kernan, Alvin. *Printing Technology, Letters, and Samuel Johnson*. Princeton, NJ: Princeton University Press, 1986.

Keymer, Thomas. *Richardson's "Clarissa" and the Eighteenth-Century Reader*. Cambridge: Cambridge University Press, 1992.

Keymer, Thomas, and Peter Sabor. *"Pamela" in the Marketplace: Literary Controversy and Print Culture in Eighteenth-Century Britain and Ireland*. Cambridge: Cambridge University Press, 2005.

Kimmel, Michael S. "From Lord and Master to Cuckold and Fop: Masculinity in Seventeenth-Century England." *University of Dayton Review* 18:2 (1986–87): 93–109.

Knapp, Lewis M. "Ralph Griffiths, Author and Publisher, 1746–1750." *The Library*, 4th series, 20:2 (Sept. 1939): 197–213.

———. *Tobias Smollett: Doctor of Men and Manners*. Princeton, NJ: Princeton University Press, 1949.

Kopelson, Kevin. "Seeing Sodomy: *Fanny Hill*'s Blinding Vision." In *Homosexuality in Renaissance and Enlightenment England: Literary Representations in Historical Context*, edited by Claude J. Summers, 173–183. New York: Harrington Park, 1992.

Kubek, Elizabeth. "The Man-Machine: Horror and the Phallus in *Memoirs of a Woman of Pleasure*." In *Launching "Fanny Hill": Essays on the Novel and Its Influences*, edited by Patsy S. Fowler and Alan Jackson, 173–197. New York: AMS, 2003.

Lanser, Susan S. "Sapphic Picaresque, Sexual Difference and the Challenges of Homo-Adventuring." *Textual Practice* 15:2 (2001): 251–268.

Laqueur, Thomas. *Making Sex: Body and Gender from the Greeks to Freud*. Cambridge, MA: Harvard University Press, 1990.

Lemon, George William. *English Etymology; or, A Derivative Dictionary of the English Language*. London: G. Robinson, 1783.

Lenhard, Danielle. "Unravelling the Curtain: Subversive Folds, Cleland's *Memoirs*, and the Sublime in Jean-Honoré Fragonard's *Le Verrou*." *Rutgers Art Review* 25 (2010): 1–20.

Levin, Kate. "'The Meanness of Writing for a Bookseller': John Cleland's *Fanny* on the Market." *Journal of Narrative Technique* 28.3 (Fall 1998): 329–349.

Life, Page. "Charteris, Francis (c. 1665–1732)." In *Oxford Dictionary of National Biography*. Oxford University Press, 2004–. www.oxforddnb.com/view/article/5175. Accessed 22 Mar. 2011.

Linebaugh, Peter. "The Tyburn Riot against the Surgeons." In *Albion's Fatal Tree: Crime and Society in Eighteenth-Century England*, edited by Douglas Hay et al., 65–117. New York: Pantheon, 1975.

Locke, John. *Some Thoughts Concerning Education* [1693]. Edited by John W. Yolton and Jean S. Yolton. Oxford: Clarendon, 1989.

Lonsdale, Roger. "Goldsmith and the *Weekly Magazine*: The Missing Numbers." *Review of English Studies*, new series, 37:146 (1986): 219–225.

———. "New Attributions to John Cleland." *Review of English Studies*, new series, 30:119 (1979): 268–290.

Love Letters between a certain late Nobleman and the famous Mr. Wilson. London: A. Moore, n.d. [1723].

Marcus, Steven. *The Other Victorians: A Study of Sexuality and Pornography in Mid-Nineteenth Century England*. London: Weidenfeld and Nicolson, 1966.

Markley, Robert. "Language, Power, and Sexuality in *Fanny Hill*." *Philological Quarterly* 63:3 (1984): 343–356.

Maxted, Ian. "The British Book Trade, 1731–1806: A Checklist of Bankrupts." Exeter Working Papers in British Book Trade History, 4. 11 Jan. 2007. www.bookhistory .blogspot.com/2007/01/bankrupts.html.

Maxted, Ian, and Victor Berch. "The London Book Trades of the Later Eighteenth Century." Exeter Working Papers in British Book Trade History, 10. 18 Jan. 2007. www .bookhistory.blogspot.com/2007/01/berch.html.

Maxwell, Kenneth. *Pombal: Paradox of the Enlightenment.* Cambridge: Cambridge University Press, 1995.

McCalman, Iain. *Radical Underworld: Prophets, Revolutionaries, and Pornographers in London, 1795–1840.* Oxford: Clarendon, 1988.

———. "Unrespectable Radicalism: Infidels and Pornography in Early Nineteenth-Century London." *Past & Present* 104 (1984): 74–110.

McCormick, Ian, ed. *Secret Sexualities: A Sourcebook of Seventeenth- and Eighteenth-Century Writing.* London: Routledge, 1997.

McFarlane, Cameron. *The Sodomite in Fiction and Satire, 1660–1750.* New York: Columbia University Press, 1997.

Mengay, Donald H. "The Sodomitical Muse: *Fanny Hill* and the Rhetoric of Crossdressing." In *Homosexuality in Renaissance and Enlightenment England,* edited by Claude J. Summers, 185–198. New York: Haworth, 1992.

Merritt, Henry. "A Biographical Note on John Cleland." *Notes and Queries* 226 (August 1981): 305–306.

Milhous, Judith, and Robert D. Hume. "Playwrights' Remuneration in Eighteenth-Century London." *Harvard Library Bulletin,* new series, 10:2–3 (1999): 3–90.

Miller, Nancy K. *The Heroine's Text: Readings in the French and English Novel, 1722–1782.* New York: Columbia University Press, 1980.

———. "I's in Drag: The Sex of Recollection." *The Eighteenth Century: Theory and Interpretation* 22 (1981): 45–57.

Mitchell, Mark, and David Leavitt, eds. *Pages Passed from Hand to Hand: The Hidden Tradition of Homosexual Literature in English from 1748 to 1914.* Boston: Houghton Mifflin, 1997.

Montagu, Lady Mary Wortley [attrib.]. *An Additional Volume to the Letters of the Right Honourable Lady M——y W——y M——e.* Dublin: P. Wilson et al., 1767.

———. *The Complete Letters of Lady Mary Wortley Montagu.* Vol. 1. Edited by Robert Halsband. Oxford: Clarendon, 1965.

Moore, Lisa L. *Dangerous Intimacies: Toward a Sapphic History of the British Novel.* Durham, NC: Duke University Press, 1997.

Mudge, Bradford K., ed. *When Flesh Becomes Word: An Anthology of Early Eighteenth-Century Libertine Literature.* Oxford: Oxford University Press, 2004.

———. *The Whore's Story: Women, Pornography, and the British Novel, 1684–1830.* Oxford: Oxford University Press, 2000.

Mullan, John. *Sentiment and Sociability: The Language of Feeling in the Eighteenth Century.* Oxford: Clarendon, 1988.

———. "Sentimental Novels." In *The Cambridge Companion to the Eighteenth-Century Novel,* edited by John Richetti, 236–254. Cambridge: Cambridge University Press, 1996.

Nichols, John. *Literary Anecdotes of the Eighteenth Century* [London, 1812–1815]. 9 vols. Facsimile ed. New York: AMS, 1966.

———. Obituary of John Cleland. *Gentleman's Magazine* 59 (February 1789): 180.

Norgate, G. le G. "Pottinger, Israel (*fl.* 1759–1761)." Revised by Michael Bevan. *Oxford Dictionary of National Biography.* Oxford University Press, 2004–. www.oxforddnb .com/view/article/22627, accessed 30 Nov. 2009.

Norton, Rictor, ed. *Homosexuality in Eighteenth-Century England: A Sourcebook.* http:// rictornorton.co.uk/eighteen/. Accessed 15 Apr. 2009.

———. *Mother Clap's Molly House: The Gay Subculture in England 1700–1830.* London: Gay Men's Press, 1992.

Nussbaum, Felicity. *Torrid Zones: Maternity, Sexuality, and Empire in Eighteenth-Century English Narratives.* Baltimore: Johns Hopkins University Press, 1995.

Olsson, Lena. "Idealized and Realistic Portrayals of Prostitution in John Cleland's *Memoirs of a Woman of Pleasure.*" In *Launching "Fanny Hill": Essays on the Novel and Its Influences,* edited by Patsy S. Fowler and Alan Jackson, 81–101. New York: AMS, 2003.

Parker, Todd C. *Sexing the Text: The Rhetoric of Sexual Difference in British Literature, 1700–1750.* Albany: State University of New York Press, 2000.

Pinot-Duclos, Charles. *Mémoires pour servir à l'histoire des moeurs du XVIIIe siècle* [1751]. Edited by Henri Coulet. Paris: Éditions Desjonquères, 1999.

Piozzi, Hester Lynch Thrale. *Anecdotes of the Late Samuel Johnson* [1786]. In *Johnsonian Miscellanies,* edited by George Birkbeck Hill, 1:141–352. London: Constable, 1897. Reprint, New York: Barnes and Noble, 1966.

Pope, Alexander. *The Correspondence of Alexander Pope.* 5 vols. Edited by George Sherburn. Oxford: Clarendon, 1956.

Ralph, James. *The Case of Authors by Profession or Trade, Stated.* London: Ralph Griffiths, 1762.

Raven, James. *Judging New Wealth: Popular Publishing and Responses to Commerce in England, 1750–1800.* Oxford: Clarendon, 1992.

Reasons for the Growth of Sodomy. Published with *Satan's Harvest Home; or, The Present State of Whorecraft, Adultery, Fornication, Procuring, Pimping, Sodomy, and the Game at Flatts* [London, 1749]. Facsimile ed. New York: Garland, 1985.

Richardson, Samuel. *Pamela; or, Virtue Rewarded* [1740]. Edited by Thomas Keymer and Alice Wakely. Oxford: Oxford University Press, 2001.

———. *Selected Letters of Samuel Richardson.* Edited by John Carroll. Oxford: Clarendon, 1964.

———. *Sir Charles Grandison* [1753–1754]. Edited by Jocelyn Harris. Oxford: Oxford University Press, 1986.

Richetti, John. *Popular Fiction before Richardson: Narrative Patterns, 1700–1739.* Oxford: Clarendon, 1969.

Rider, William. *An Historical and Critical Account of the Lives and Writings of the Living Authors of Great Britain* [1762]. Augustan Reprint Society 163. Los Angeles: William Andrews Clark Memorial Library, University of California, 1974.

Robinson, David M. *Closeted Writing and Lesbian and Gay Literature: Classical, Early Modern, Eighteenth-Century.* Aldershot, Hampshire: Ashgate, 2006.

Rodrigues, Lúcia Lima, and Russell Craig. "English Mercantilist Influences on the Foundation of the Portuguese School of Commerce in 1759." *Atlantic Economic Journal* 32:4 (2004): 329–345.

Rogers, Nicholas. "Penlez, Bosavern (1726–1749)." In *Oxford Dictionary of National Biography*. Oxford University Press, 2004–. www.oxforddnb.com/view/article/89648. Accessed 16 Sept. 2009.

Rosenthal, Laura J. *Infamous Commerce: Prostitution in Eighteenth-Century British Literature and Culture*. Ithaca, NY: Cornell University Press, 2006.

Rousseau, G. S. "The Pursuit of Homosexuality in the Eighteenth Century: 'Utterly Confused Category' and/or Rich Repository." In *'Tis Nature's Fault: Unauthorized Sexuality during the Enlightenment*, edited by Robert Purks Maccubbin, 132–168. Cambridge: Cambridge University Press, 1987.

Roussel, Roy. *The Conversation of the Sexes: Seduction and Equality in Selected Seventeenth- and Eighteenth-Century Texts*. New York: Oxford University Press, 1986.

Rubenhold, Hallie. *The Covent-Garden Ladies: Pimp General Jack and the Extraordinary Story of Harris's List*. London: Tempus, 2005.

Sabor, Peter. "The Censor Censured: Expurgating *Memoirs of a Woman of Pleasure*." In *'Tis Nature's Fault: Unauthorized Sexuality during the Enlightenment*, edited by Robert Purks Maccubbin, 192–201. Cambridge: Cambridge University Press, 1987.

———. "From Sexual Liberation to Gender Trouble: Reading *Memoirs of a Woman of Pleasure* from the 1960s to the 1990s." *Eighteenth-Century Studies* 33:4 (2000): 561–578.

———. Introduction to *Memoirs of a Woman of Pleasure*, by John Cleland, vii–xxv. Edited by Peter Sabor. Oxford: Oxford University Press, 1985.

Said, Edward W. *On Late Style: Music and Literature against the Grain*. London: Bloomsbury, 2006.

Savage, Richard. Preface to *Miscellaneous Poems* [1726]. Reprinted in *The Poetical Works of Richard Savage*, edited by Clarence Tracy. Cambridge: Cambridge University Press, 1962.

Schürer, Norbert. "The Impartial Spectator of Sati." *Eighteenth-Century Studies* 42:1 (2008): 19–44.

Select Trials for Murder, Robbery & c at the Sessions-House in the Old Bailey. 4 vols. London, 1742.

Sha, Richard C. *Perverse Romanticism: Aesthetics and Sexuality in Britain, 1750–1832*. Baltimore: Johns Hopkins University Press, 2009.

Shakespeare, William. *Macbeth* [ca. 1606]. In *The Complete Works*, edited by Stephen Orgel and A. R. Braunmuller, 1616–1650. New York: Penguin, 2002.

Simmons, Philip E. "John Cleland's *Memoirs of a Woman of Pleasure*: Literary Voyeurism and the Techniques of Novelistic Transgression." *Eighteenth-Century Fiction* 3:1 (1990): 43–63.

Staves, Susan. "A Few Kind Words for the Fop." *Studies in English Literature*, 22:3 (1982): 413–428.

Stevenson, David. *The Beggar's Benison: Sex Clubs of the Scottish Enlightenment and Their Rituals*. East Linton: Tuckwell, 2001.

———. "A Note on the Scotsman Who Inspired Fanny Hill." *Scottish Studies Review* 2:1 (2001): 39–45.

Stoney, Frances Sadleir. *A Memoir of the Life and Times of the Right Honourable Sir Ralph Sadleir*. London: Longmans, Green, 1877.

Sutherland, John. "Where Does Fanny Hill Keep Her Contraceptives?" In *Can Jane Eyre Be Happy? More Puzzles in Classic Fiction*, 11–18. Oxford: Oxford University Press, 1997.

Tancock, O. W. "Lemon, George William (1726–1797)." Revised by S. J. Skedd. In *Oxford Dictionary of National Biography*. Oxford University Press, 2004–. www.oxforddnb.com/view/article/16431. Accessed 2 May 2010.

Thompson, E. P. "The Moral Economy of the English Crowd" [1971]. In *Customs in Common: Studies in Traditional Popular Culture*, 185–258. New York: New Press, 1993.

Todd, Janet. *Sensibility: An Introduction*. London: Methuen, 1986.

Traub, Valerie. *The Renaissance of Lesbianism in Early Modern England*. Cambridge: Cambridge University Press, 2002.

The Trial of Richard Branson [London, 1760]. Facsimile ed. In *Sodomy Trials: Seven Documents*. New York: Garland, 1986.

Trumbach, Randolph. "Erotic Fantasy and Male Libertinism in Enlightenment England." In *The Invention of Pornography: Obscenity and the Origins of Modernity, 1500–1800*, edited by Lynn Hunt, 253–282 and 381–390. New York: Zone, 1993.

———. "London's Sodomites." *Journal of Social History* 11 (1977): 1–33.

———. "Modern Prostitution and Gender in *Fanny Hill*: Libertine and Domesticated Fantasy." In *Sexual Underworlds of the Enlightenment*, edited by G. S. Rousseau and Roy Porter, 69–85. Chapel Hill: University of North Carolina Press, 1988.

The Tryal and Condemnation of Mervin, Lord Audley [London, 1699]. Facsimile ed. In *Sodomy Trials: Seven Documents*. New York: Garland, 1986.

Turner, James Grantham. *Schooling Sex: Libertine Literature and Erotic Education in Italy, France, and England, 1534–1685*. Oxford: Oxford University Press, 2003.

Van Sant, Ann Jessie. *Eighteenth-Century Sensibility and the Novel: The Senses in Social Context*. Cambridge: Cambridge University Press, 1993.

Verstraete, Beert C. "The Originality of Tibullus's Marathus Elegies." *Journal of Homosexuality* 49:3–4 (2005): 299–314.

Wagner, Peter. *Eros Revived: Erotica of the Enlightenment in England and America*. London: Paladin, 1990.

———. Introduction to *Fanny Hill; or, Memoirs of a Woman of Pleasure*, by John Cleland, 7–30. Edited by Peter Wagner. Harmondsworth: Penguin, 1985.

Warburton, Nigel. "Art and Allusion." *Philosophers' Magazine* 19 (2002): 40–42. www.open.ac.uk/Arts/philosophy/docs/warburton.pdf.

Warner, Rebecca Louise. "Cannon, Robert (1663–1722)." *Oxford Dictionary of National Biography*. Oxford University Press, 2004–. www.oxforddnb.com/view/article/4560. Accessed 16 Feb. 2009.

Watt, Ian P. *The Rise of the Novel: Studies in Defoe, Richardson, and Fielding*. Berkeley: University of California Press, 1957.

Weaver, Elissa B. "A Reading of the Interlaced Plot of the *Orlando Furioso*: The Three Cases of Love Madness." In *Ariosto Today: Contemporary Perspectives*, edited by Donald Beecher, Massimo Ciavolella, and Roberto Fedi, 126–153. Toronto: University of Toronto Press, 2003.

Webster, John. *The White Devil* [ca. 1612]. In *"The Duchess of Malfi" and Other Plays*, edited by René Weis, 1–101. Oxford: Oxford University Press, 1996.

Weed, David. "Fitting Fanny: Cleland's *Memoirs* and the Politics of Male Pleasure." *Novel* 31 (1997): 7–20.

Weinbrot, Howard D. *Britannia's Issue: The Rise of British Literature from Dryden to Ossian*. Cambridge: Cambridge University Press, 1993.

Weinsheimer, Joel. "Theory of Character: *Emma*." *Poetics Today* 1:1–2 (1979): 185–211.

Whitley, Raymond K. "The Libertine Hero and Heroine in the Novels of John Cleland." *Studies in Eighteenth-Century Culture* 9 (1979): 387–404.

Williams, Carolyn D. "*The Way to Things by Words*: John Cleland, the Name of the Father, and Speculative Etymology." *Yearbook of English Studies* 28 (1998): 250–275.

Williams, Ioan, ed. *Novel and Romance*. New York: Barnes and Noble, 1970.

Yeazell, Ruth Bernard. *Fictions of Modesty: Women and Courtship in the English Novel*. Chicago: University of Chicago Press, 1991.

Yorke, Philip C. *The Life and Correspondence of Philip Yorke, Earl of Hardwick*. 3 vols. Cambridge: Cambridge University Press, 1913.

Young, Edward. *Conjectures on Original Composition* [1759]. Facsimile ed. Leeds: Scolar, 1966.

Zionkowski, Linda. "Territorial Disputes in the Republic of Letters: Canon Formation and the Literary Profession." *The Eighteenth Century: Theory and Interpretation* 31:1 (1990): 3–22.

Zirker, Malvin R. "General Introduction." In Henry Fielding, *An Enquiry into the Causes of the Late Increase of Robbers and Related Writings*, edited by Malvin R. Zirker, xvii–cxiv. Oxford: Clarendon, 1988.

INDEX

Davis, Lockyer (bookseller and publisher of JC), 193–194, 284n30

Defoe, Daniel, 89–90

De Hondt, Peter (bookseller and publisher of JC), 193–194

Delisle, Louis-François de La Drevetière (French playwright), 147, 173

Dickinson, Edward (Cleland family lawyer), 34–35, 47, 180–182, 184–193, 278n5, 279n17, 279n19

Dicks, John (tried for sodomy), 73

Dictionnaire d'amour (Dreux du Radier), 13, 146, 147, 171

Diderot, Denis, 167

Dodsley, Robert (bookseller and author), 270n27

Donato, Clorinda, 274n61

Donkin, Ellen, 277n1

Donoghue, Emma, 168, 275–276n72

Donoghue, Frank, 249–250n8, 250n16

Douglas, James, 34, 37, 39

Draper, William Henry (resident of Bombay), 16 (quoted), 189 (quoted)

Dreux du Radier, J. F., 13, 146, 147, 171

Druids and Druidism, 213–214, 224–237, 284n28; the Druidess as phallic woman, 229–230

Drybutter, Samuel (bookseller and accused sodomite), 6, 56; alleged to be author of "sodomitical" episode of the *Woman of Pleasure*, 81–82, 263n56

L'École des filles, 8, 16, 19, 32

Edelman, Lee, 67

Les Égarements du coeur et de l'esprit (Crébillon), 12, 87–88, 132–134

Epstein, Julia, 89

Epstein, William H., 5, 50, 141, 204–205, 217–219, 231 (quoted), 244, 249–250n16, 251n19, 255n11, 256n33, 276n81, 277–278n4, 279n17, 282n60, 283n13, 283n21, 286–287n48, 287n7

Fantomina (Haywood), 198–199

Fénelon, François (French romance author), 108–109

fiction: debates over aims and effects, 86–88, 107–113, 205; epistolary, 85–86, 204–206, 279n10; first-person or autobiographical, 86–87; formal experimentation and the novel, 12, 85–91, 102–107, 194–203, 204–212,

282n65; romance, 96–98, 113–115, 118–121, 129–138, 194–203, 206–212, 214, 266n24; sentimental, 181, 199–203. *See also* libertinism and libertine fiction

Fielding, Henry: *Amelia*, 106–108; *Enquiry*, 93 (quoted); *Female Husband*, 274n61; *Shamela*, 90–91, 120, 264n3; *True State of the Case of Bosavern Penlez*, 12, 147, 149–153, 271–272n40, 272–273n50, 273n51

Fielding, Sarah, 108

Le Flateur (Jean-Baptiste Rousseau), 173, 277n92

Flynn, Carol Houlihan, 134, 266n23

Foote, Samuel (playwright and actor; accused of sodomy), 81

Forsans, Ola, 276n83

Foxon, David, 6, 250n19, 263n56

Fryer (or Frier), Mr. (JC's business contact in Carolina), 192

Gallagher, Catherine, 142, 144, 250n24, 269–270n12, 270n18

Garrick, David (actor and theater manager), 169, 172–173, 177–181, 183–185, 276n81, 277n1

Gautier, Gary, 102, 135

Gay, John, 273n58

gender: as effect of imitation, 172–173; multiplicity and instability of, 158–160, 162–165. *See also* masculinity; sexual desire; sexuality and sexual difference

Gentleman's Magazine, reports on Penlez riots, 148–149

Goldsmith, Oliver, 51, 141, 194

Graham, Rosemary, 89

Granville, John Carteret, 1st Earl (president of Privy Council), 80, 240

Gray (or Grey), Samuel (messenger of the press), 15

Greek and Roman mythology as corruption of Druidic allegory, 224–225, 284n28

Greene, Jody, 259n13, 261–262n42

Griffiths, Fenton (brother of Ralph, copublisher of the *Woman of Pleasure*), 49–50, 257n49, 270n14

Griffiths, Ralph (bookseller and publisher of JC), 15, 49–51, 139–144, 183, 192, 194, 270n14, 281n45; arranges for JC's release from Fleet prison, 50, 139, 143; arrested for obscenity, 49–50; begins publishing *Monthly Review*, 51

Statira (wife/wives of Alexander the Great), 119–120, 268n58

Steele, Richard, 19, 241

Sterne, Laurence: as sentimental author, 199; condemned by Richardson, 269n80; told off by JC, 137

Stevenson, David, 16, 255n12

Stone, Andrew (under-secretary of state), 140–141

Strauss, Richard, Edward Said on, 196

Stukeley, William (antiquary and archaeologist), 225

Sutherland, John, 273–274n59

Swan, Robert (printer), buys copies of *Ancient and Modern Pederasty*, 52

Tancock, O. W., 285n36

Télémaque (Fénelon), 109

Thompson, E. P., on moral economy, 273n56

Tibullus (Latin elegist), 83, 264n62

Tomlinson, Robert, distributes *Ancient and Modern Pederasty* to pamphlet shops, 52

Tomochichi (Creek headman), 173

translation: as form of cultural imitation or contagion, 57–59, 165–169; literary, 111, 146–148, 158–162, 168–171, 175–176

Traub, Valerie, 275n70

Treatise on Charity (Cannon), 80, 262n48

Trial of Richard Branson (for sodomy), 58

Tristram Shandy (Sterne), 137, 199

True State of the Case of Bosavern Penlez (Fielding), 149–153

Trumbach, Randolph, 253n51, 263n50

Tryal and Condemnation of Mervin, Lord Audley (for sodomy), 57 (quoted)

Turner, James Grantham, 252n47, 259n19

d'Urfé, Honoré (French romance author), 109, 119

Vanini, Lucilio (executed for heresy), 53

Vénus dans le cloître, 32

Verstraete, Beert C., 264n62

Vizzani, Catterina (cross-dressing adventurer and seducer), 157–168

Vossontroy, Lollaboy Susunker Ballanauth (legal client of JC in Bombay), 20–24

Voyage to the East Indies (J. H. Grose; likely ghostwritten by JC), 34–36, 193

Wagner, Peter, 6, 56, 264–265n9

Walpole, Robert (first minister and political patron of William Cleland), 38, 40–41

Webster, John, *The White Devil*, 278n9

Weed, David, 258n5

Weinbrot, Howard D., 284n26, 284n30

Weinsheimer, Joel, 205, 282n66

Whiston, William (scientist and clergyman), 46

whore narratives, 32, 91–92, 96–98. *See also* pornography; prostitution and sexual commodification

Williams, Carolyn D., 224, 227, 229

Wilson, John (accused of riot along with Penlez), 150–152

Wood, Jane (wife of bawdy-house keeper), 151

Wood, Peter (bawdy-house keeper), 150–152, 155

Wynne, John Huddlestone (novelist), 241, 279n12

Yeazell, Ruth Bernard, 137

Yorke, Philip (attorney general), 55, 263n50

Young, Edward (poet and playwright), 13, 146–147, 176, 178

Zirker, Malvin R., 271–272n40, 272n45, 273n51